REBOUND

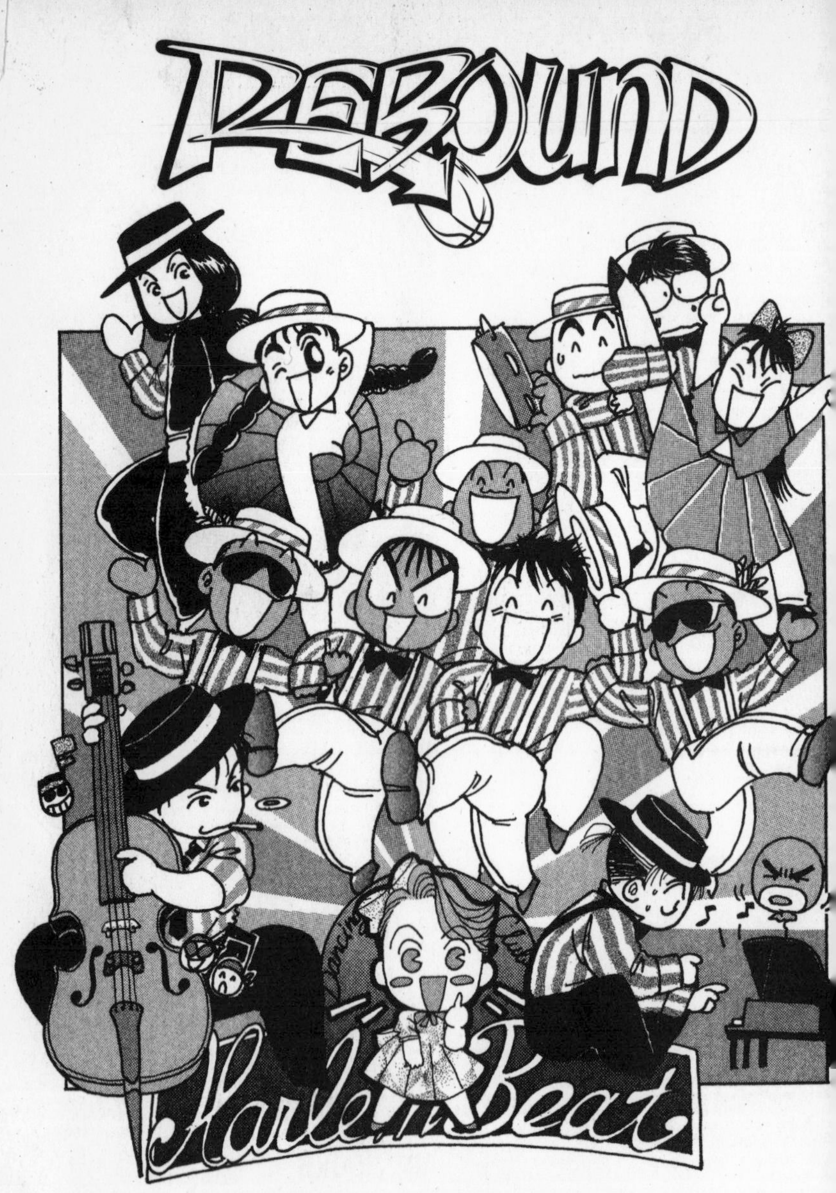
Harlem Beat

Presented by

YURIKO NISHIYAMA

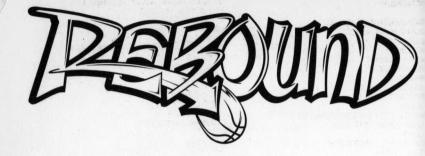

By Yuriko Nishiyama

Volume 3

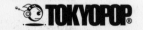

Los Angeles • Tokyo • London

Translator - Shirley Kubo
English Adaption - Jordan Capell
Retouch and Lettering - James Lee
Cover Layout - Patrick Hook

Editor - Luis Reyes
Managing Editor - Jill Freshney
Production Coordinator - Antonio DePietro
Production Manager - Jennifer Miller
Art Director - Matthew Alford
Editorial Director - Jeremy Ross
VP of Production & Manufacturing - Ron Klamert
President & C.O.O. - John Parker
Publisher & CEO - Stuart Levy

Email: editor@TOKYOPOP.com
Come visit us online at www.TOKYOPOP.com

A 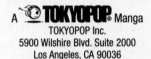 Manga
TOKYOPOP Inc.
5900 Wilshire Blvd. Suite 2000
Los Angeles, CA 90036

ISBN: 1-59182-221-1

First TOKYOPOP® printing: August 2003

10 9 8 7 6 5 4 3 2 1
Printed in the USA

4-28-03

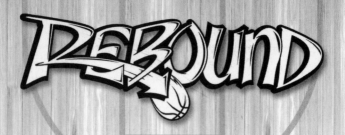

-Play by Play-
The Season So Far...

The Johnan High basketball team has
worked hard all year and has finally gotten
to the national championships in Sapporo.
However, if the team loses just one game,
they're on the first plane back to Tokyo.
Hopes are high after winning their first game
against Okinawa Kyan Marine Industry High
School. But now Johnan has to face Tsukuba
High School, the very team that knocked them
out of the finals last year. That's tomorrow,
though. Tonight is a time for celebration,
relaxation and, with any luck, inspiration.

Today on REBOUND

TRES...

REBOUND

*This is a work of fiction. Any resemblance to real-life people or works of art is purely coincidental.

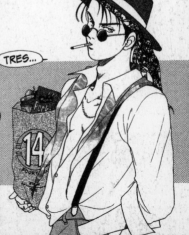

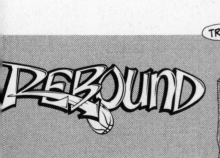

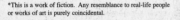

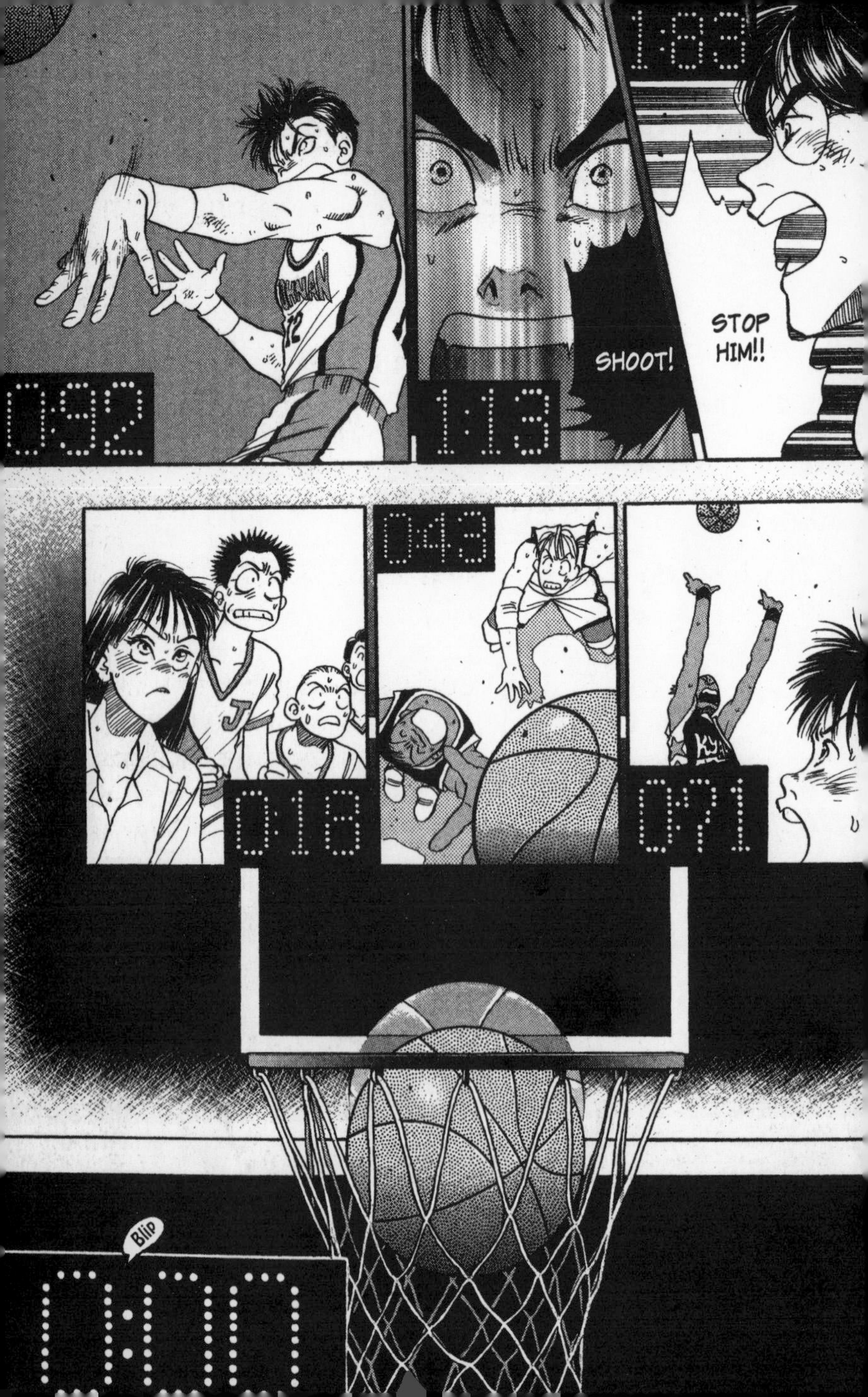
STOP HIM!!
SHOOT!
Blip

Yuriko Nishiyama's very own Rebound Popularity Vote
The results!!

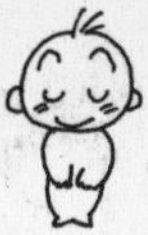
Thank you so much, everyone!!

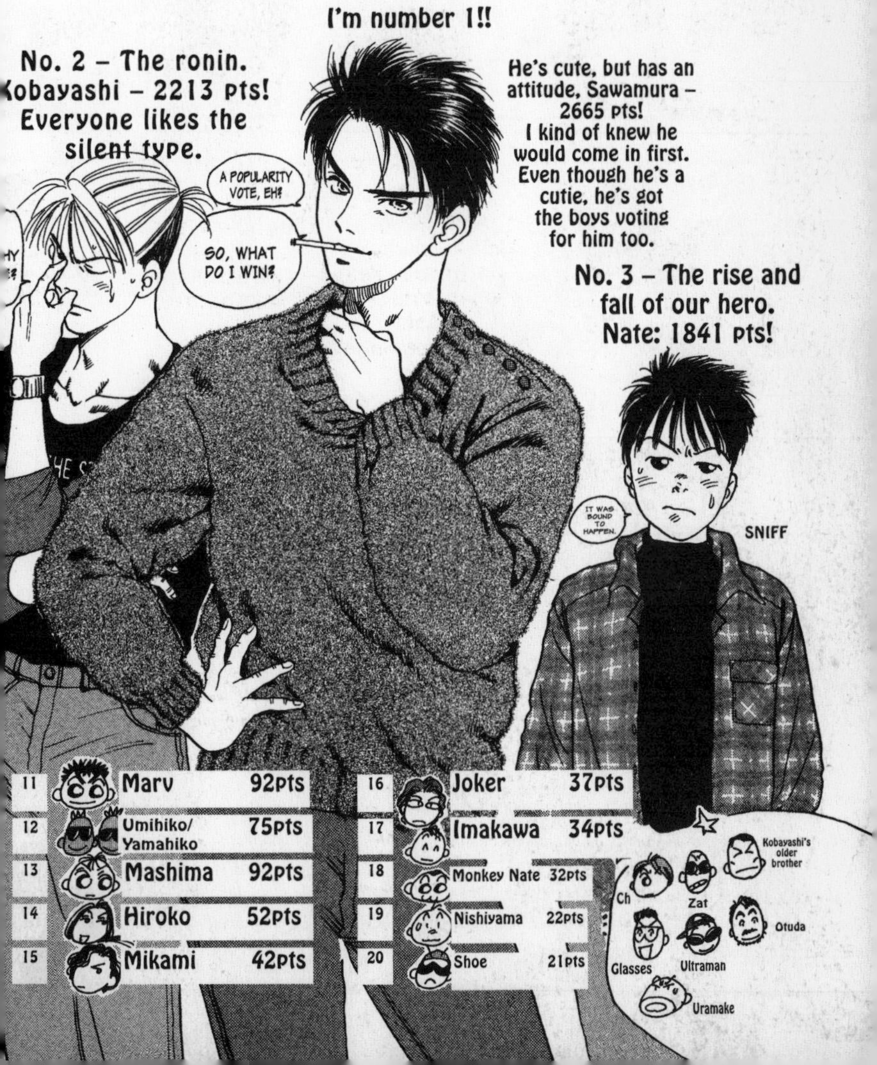
I'm number 1!!
He's cute, but has an attitude, Sawamura – 2665 pts! I kind of knew he would come in first. Even though he's a cutie, he's got the boys voting for him too.
A POPULARITY VOTE, EH?
SO, WHAT DO I WIN?
No. 2 – The ronin. Kobayashi – 2213 pts! Everyone likes the silent type.
No. 3 – The rise and fall of our hero. Nate: 1841 pts!
IT WAS BOUND TO HAPPEN.
SNIFF
11 Marv 92pts
12 Umihiko/Yamahiko 75pts
13 Mashima 92pts
14 Hiroko 52pts
15 Mikami 42pts
16 Joker 37pts
17 Imakawa 34pts
18 Monkey Nate 32pts
19 Nishiyama 22pts
20 Shoe 21pts
Kobayashi's older brother
Ch
Zat
Otuda
Glasses
Ultraman
Uramake

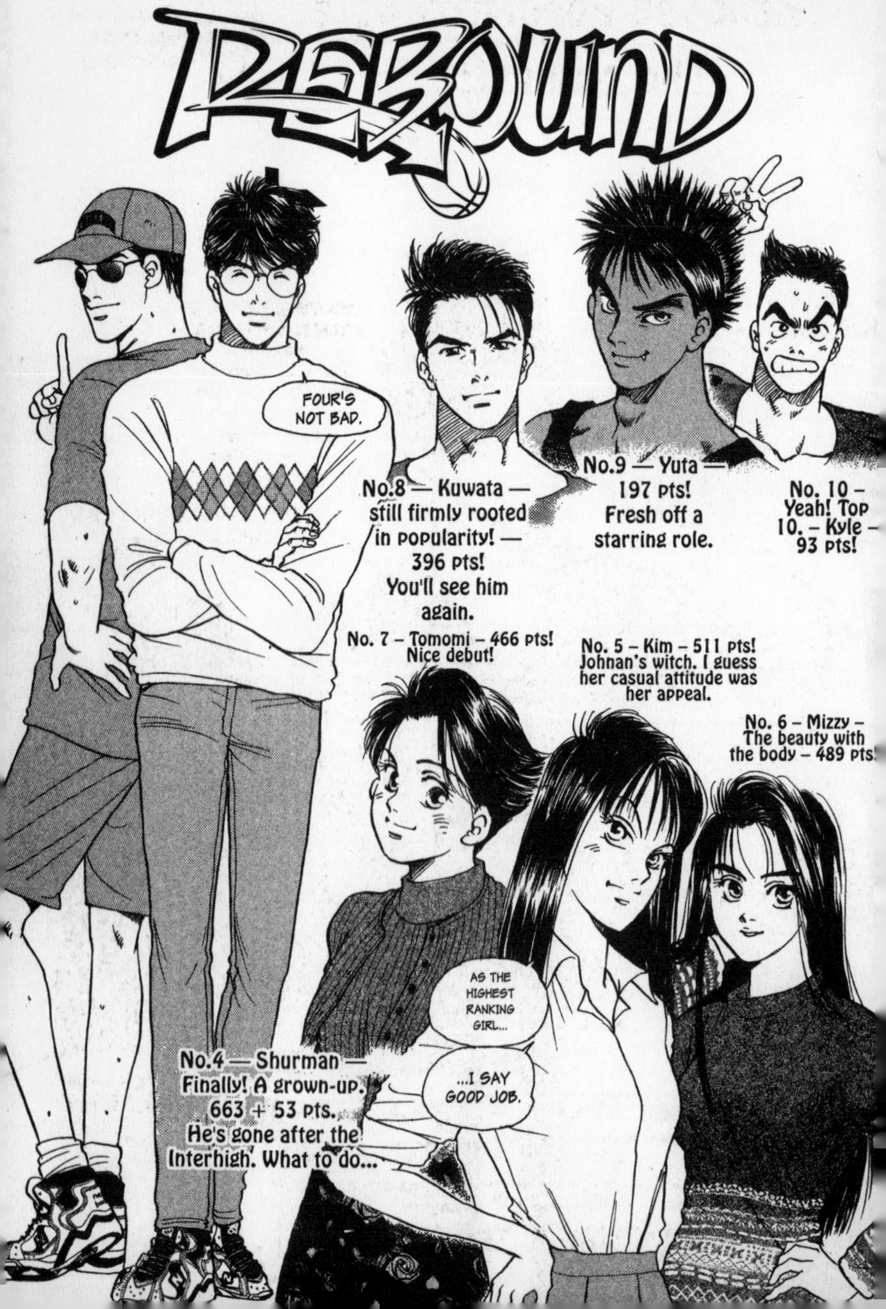
REBOUND
No.9 — Yuta — 197 pts! Fresh off a starring role.
No. 10 – Yeah! Top 10. – Kyle – 93 pts!
No.8 — Kuwata — still firmly rooted in popularity! — 396 pts! You'll see him again.
FOUR'S NOT BAD.
No. 5 – Kim – 511 pts! Johnan's witch. I guess her casual attitude was her appeal.
No. 7 – Tomomi – 466 pts! Nice debut!
No. 6 – Mizzy – The beauty with the body – 489 pts!
AS THE HIGHEST RANKING GIRL...
...I SAY GOOD JOB.
No.4 — Shurman — Finally! A grown-up. 663 + 53 pts. He's gone after the Interhigh. What to do...

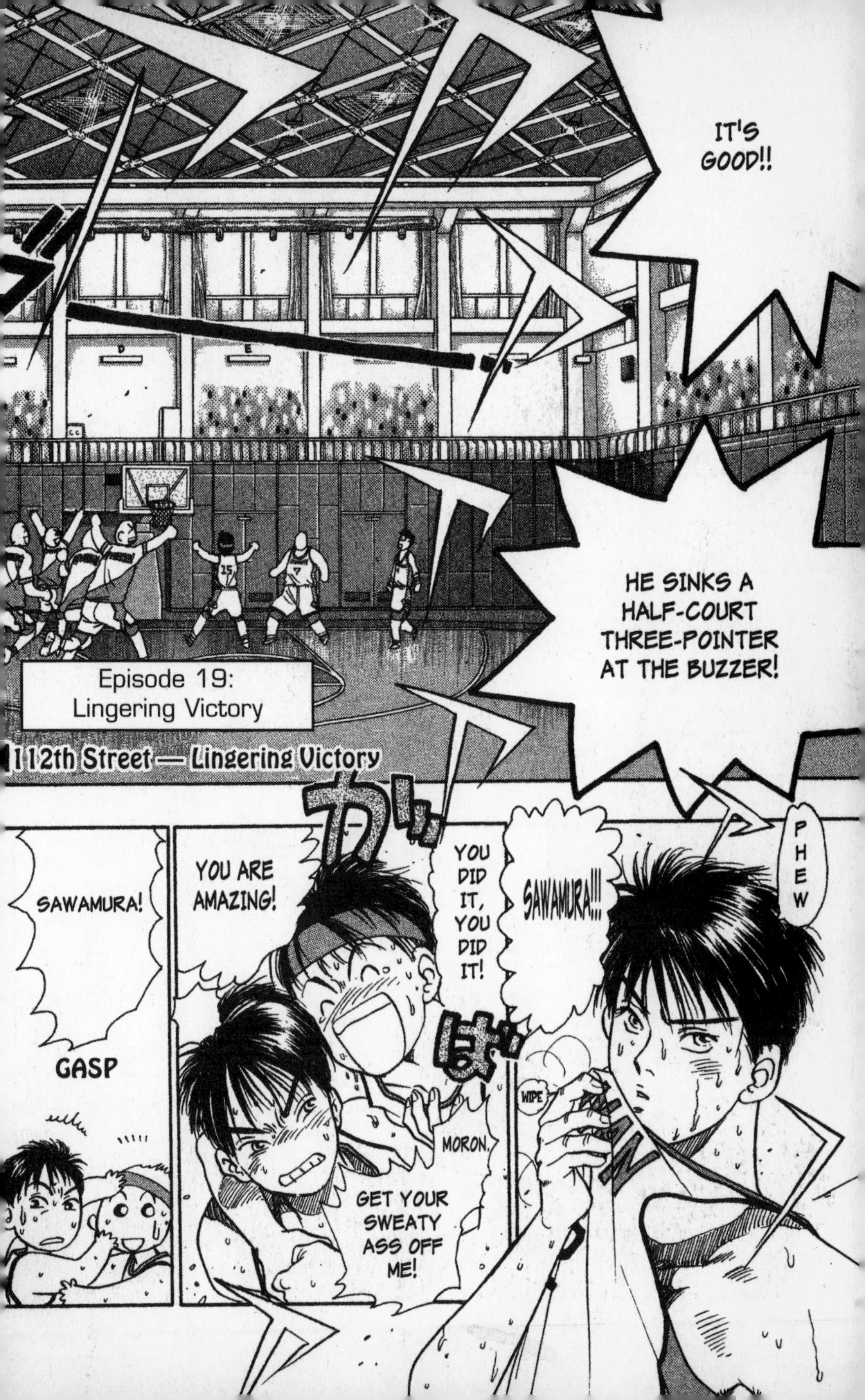
IT'S GOOD!!
HE SINKS A HALF-COURT THREE-POINTER AT THE BUZZER!
Episode 19: Lingering Victory
112th Street — Lingering Victory
PHEW
SAWAMURA!!!
WIPE
YOU DID IT, YOU DID IT!
YOU ARE AMAZING!
MORON.
GET YOUR SWEATY ASS OFF ME!
SAWAMURA!
GASP

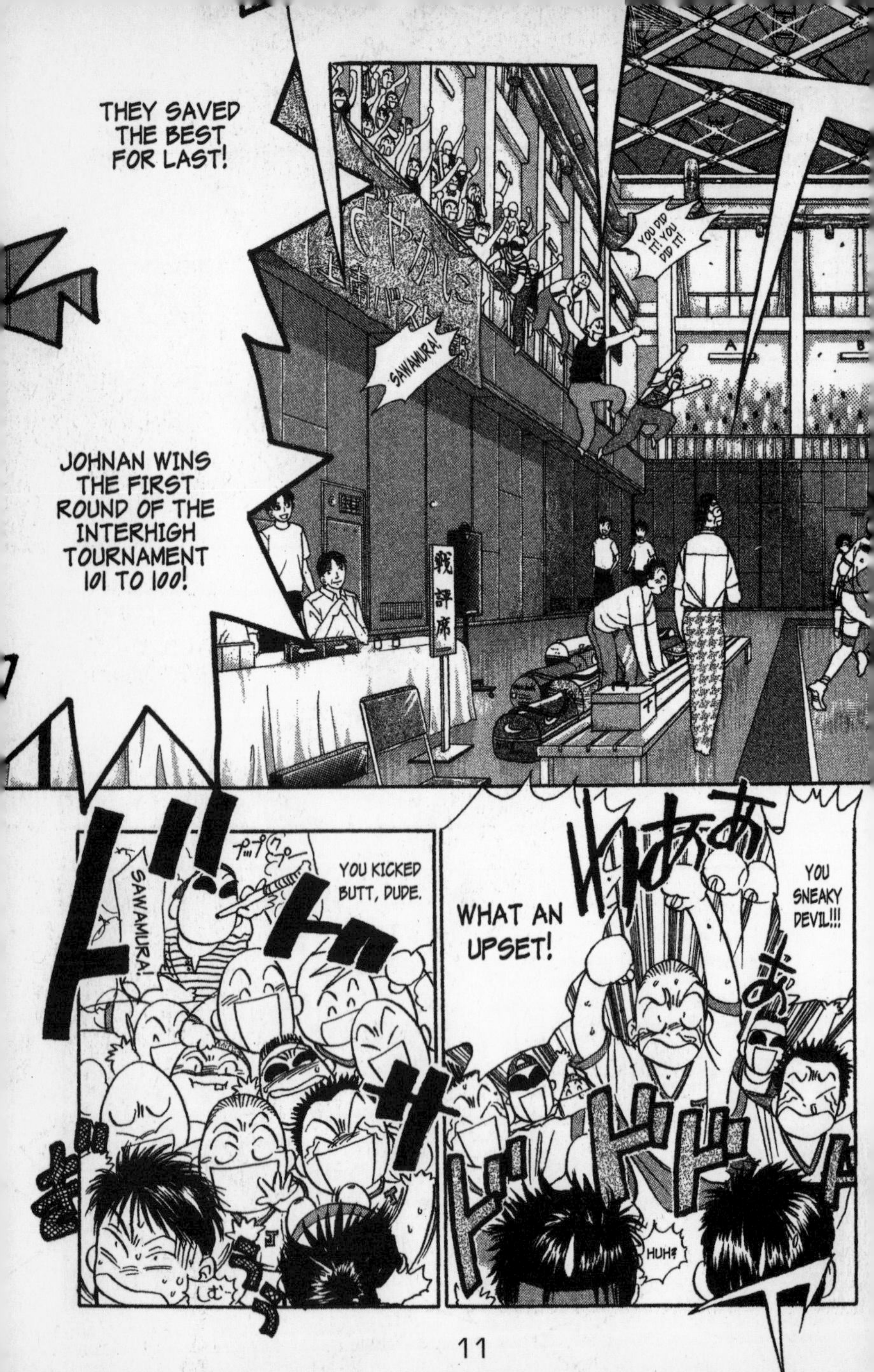
YOU DID IT! YOU DID IT!
SAWAMURA!
THEY SAVED THE BEST FOR LAST!
JOHNAN WINS THE FIRST ROUND OF THE INTERHIGH TOURNAMENT 101 TO 100!
YOU SNEAKY DEVIL!!!
WHAT AN UPSET!
HUH?
YOU KICKED BUTT, DUDE.
SAWAMURA!

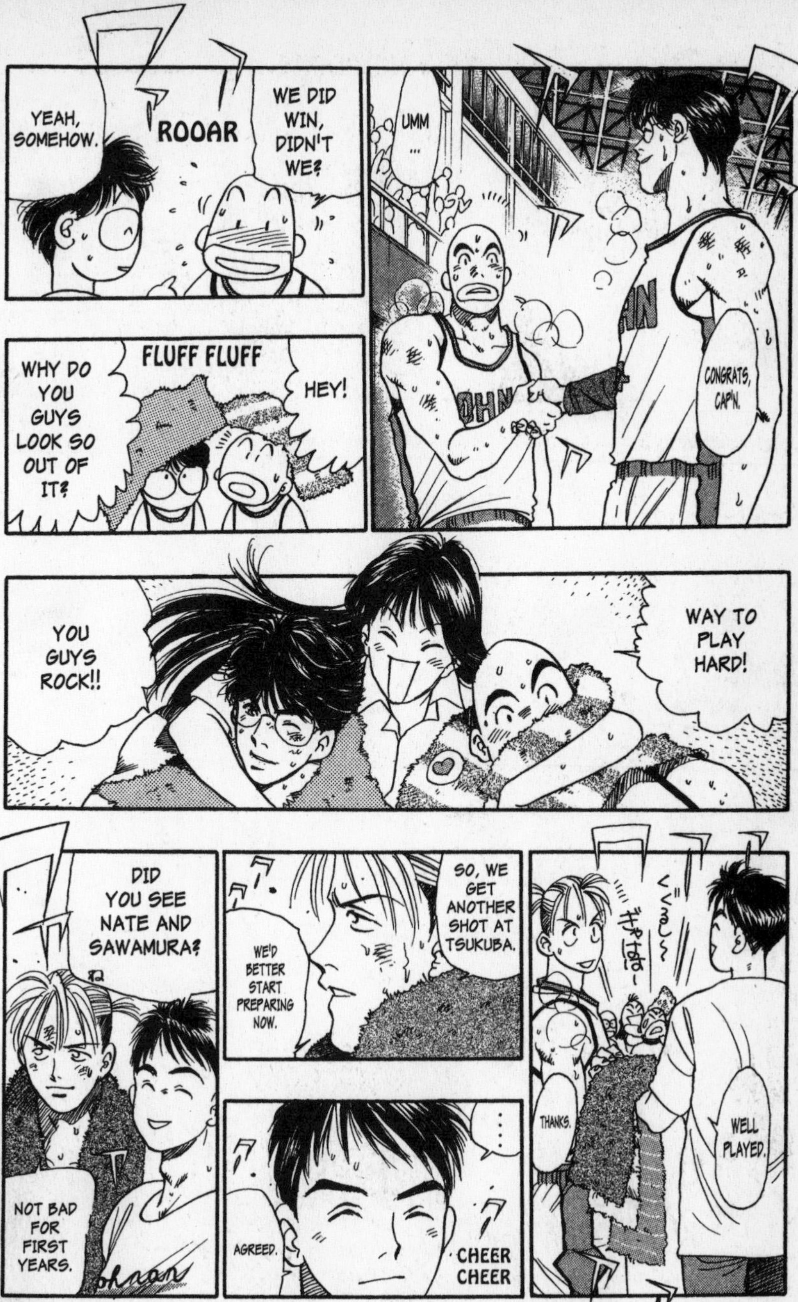
UMM ...
CONGRATS, CAP'N.
WE DID WIN, DIDN'T WE?
ROOAR
YEAH, SOMEHOW.
HEY!
FLUFF FLUFF
WHY DO YOU GUYS LOOK SO OUT OF IT?
WAY TO PLAY HARD!
YOU GUYS ROCK!!
ぎゃはー
WELL PLAYED.
THANKS.
SO, WE GET ANOTHER SHOT AT TSUKUBA.
WE'D BETTER START PREPARING NOW.
...
CHEER CHEER
AGREED.
DID YOU SEE NATE AND SAWAMURA?
NOT BAD FOR FIRST YEARS.

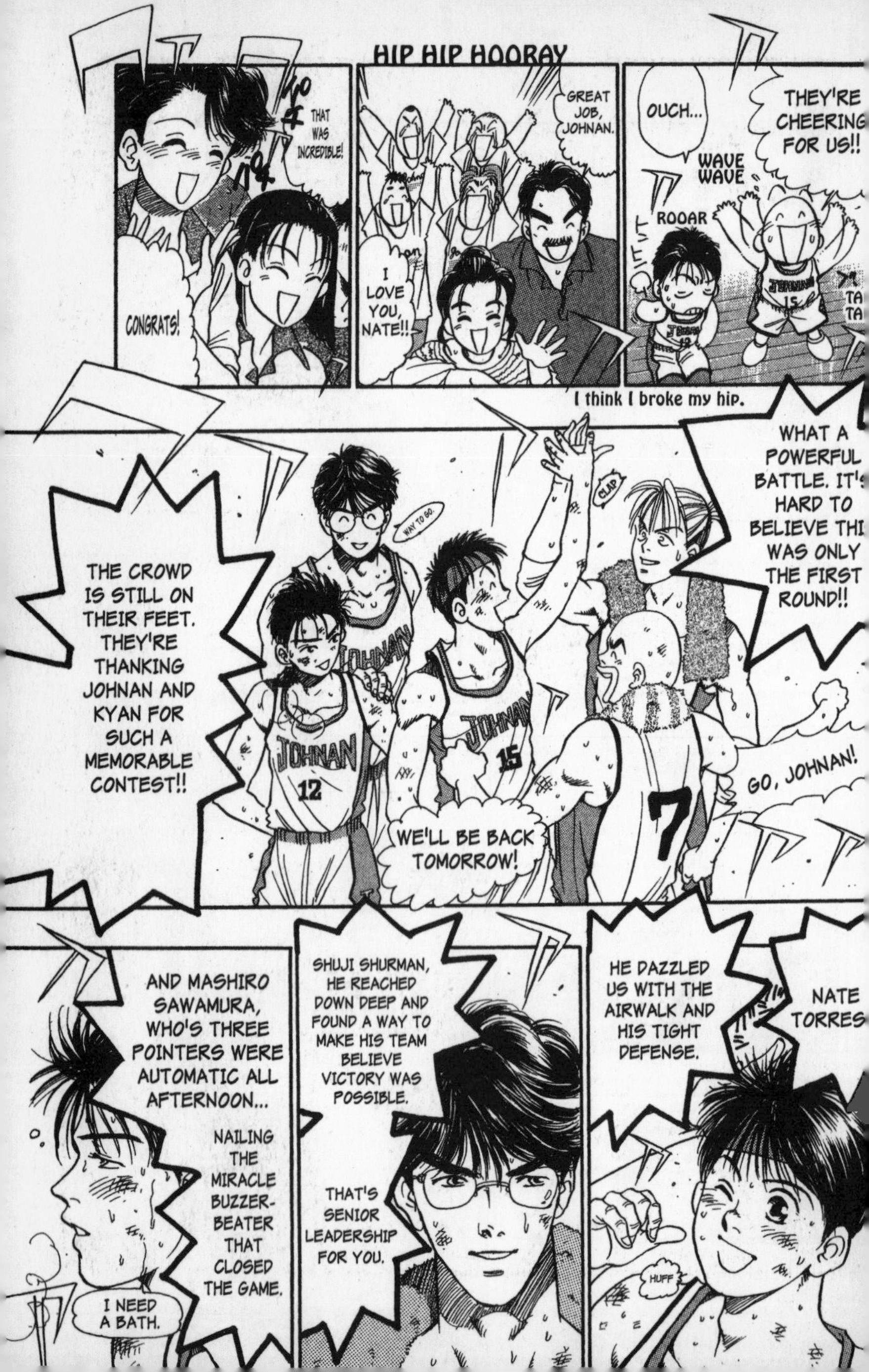
HIP HIP HOORAY
THEY'RE CHEERING FOR US!!
OUCH...
WAVE WAVE
ROOAR
I think I broke my hip.
GREAT JOB, JOHNAN.
I LOVE YOU, NATE!!
THAT WAS INCREDIBLE!
CONGRATS!
WHAT A POWERFUL BATTLE. IT's HARD TO BELIEVE THI WAS ONLY THE FIRST ROUND!!
CLAP
WAY TO GO.
THE CROWD IS STILL ON THEIR FEET. THEY'RE THANKING JOHNAN AND KYAN FOR SUCH A MEMORABLE CONTEST!!
GO, JOHNAN!
WE'LL BE BACK TOMORROW!
NATE TORRES
HE DAZZLED US WITH THE AIRWALK AND HIS TIGHT DEFENSE.
HUFF
SHUJI SHURMAN, HE REACHED DOWN DEEP AND FOUND A WAY TO MAKE HIS TEAM BELIEVE VICTORY WAS POSSIBLE.
THAT'S SENIOR LEADERSHIP FOR YOU.
AND MASHIRO SAWAMURA, WHO'S THREE POINTERS WERE AUTOMATIC ALL AFTERNOON...
NAILING THE MIRACLE BUZZER-BEATER THAT CLOSED THE GAME.
I NEED A BATH.

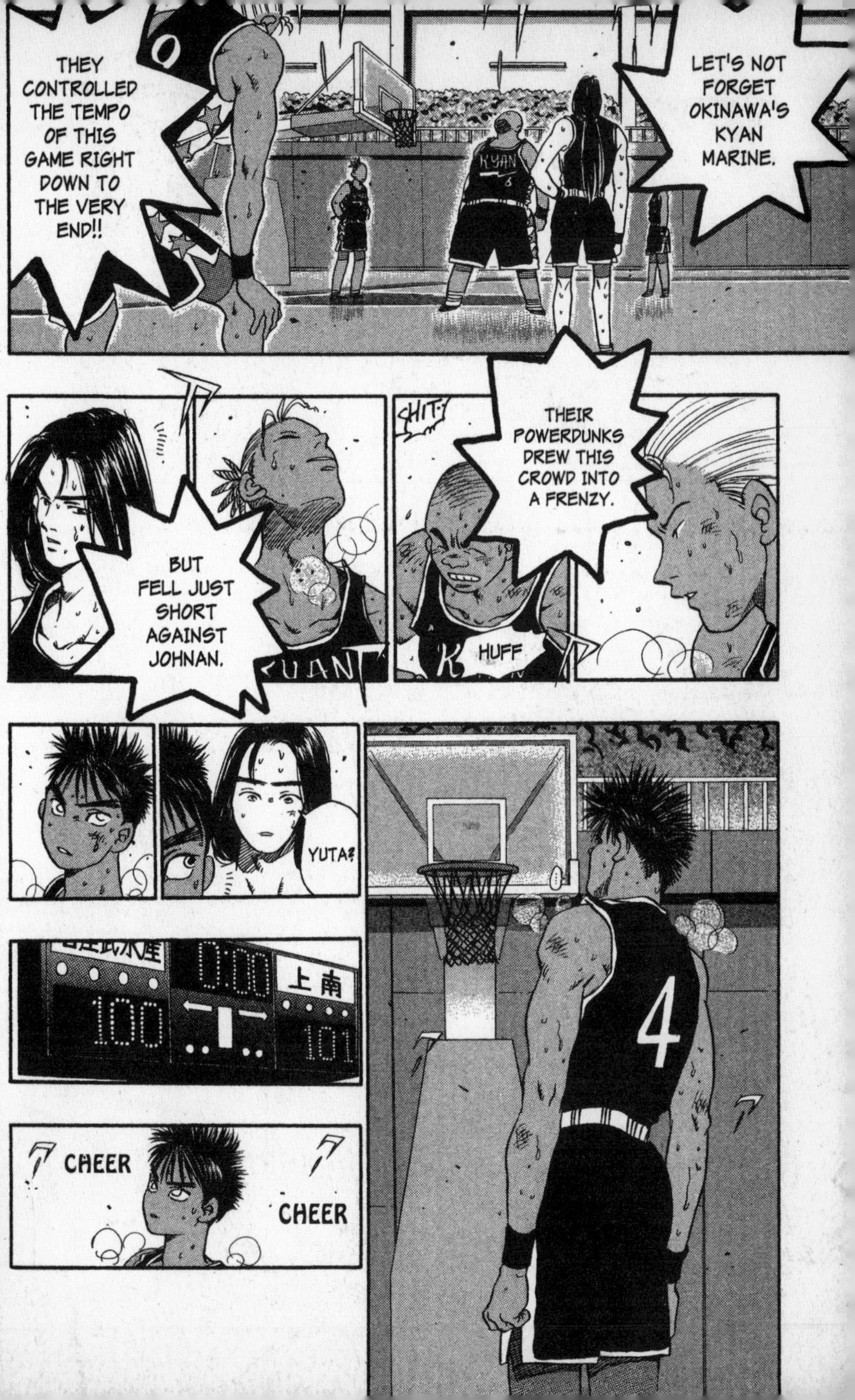
LET'S NOT FORGET OKINAWA'S KYAN MARINE.
THEY CONTROLLED THE TEMPO OF THIS GAME RIGHT DOWN TO THE VERY END!!
THEIR POWERDUNKS DREW THIS CROWD INTO A FRENZY.
SHIT
HUFF
BUT FELL JUST SHORT AGAINST JOHNAN.
YUTA?
0:00
上南
100
101
CHEER
CHEER

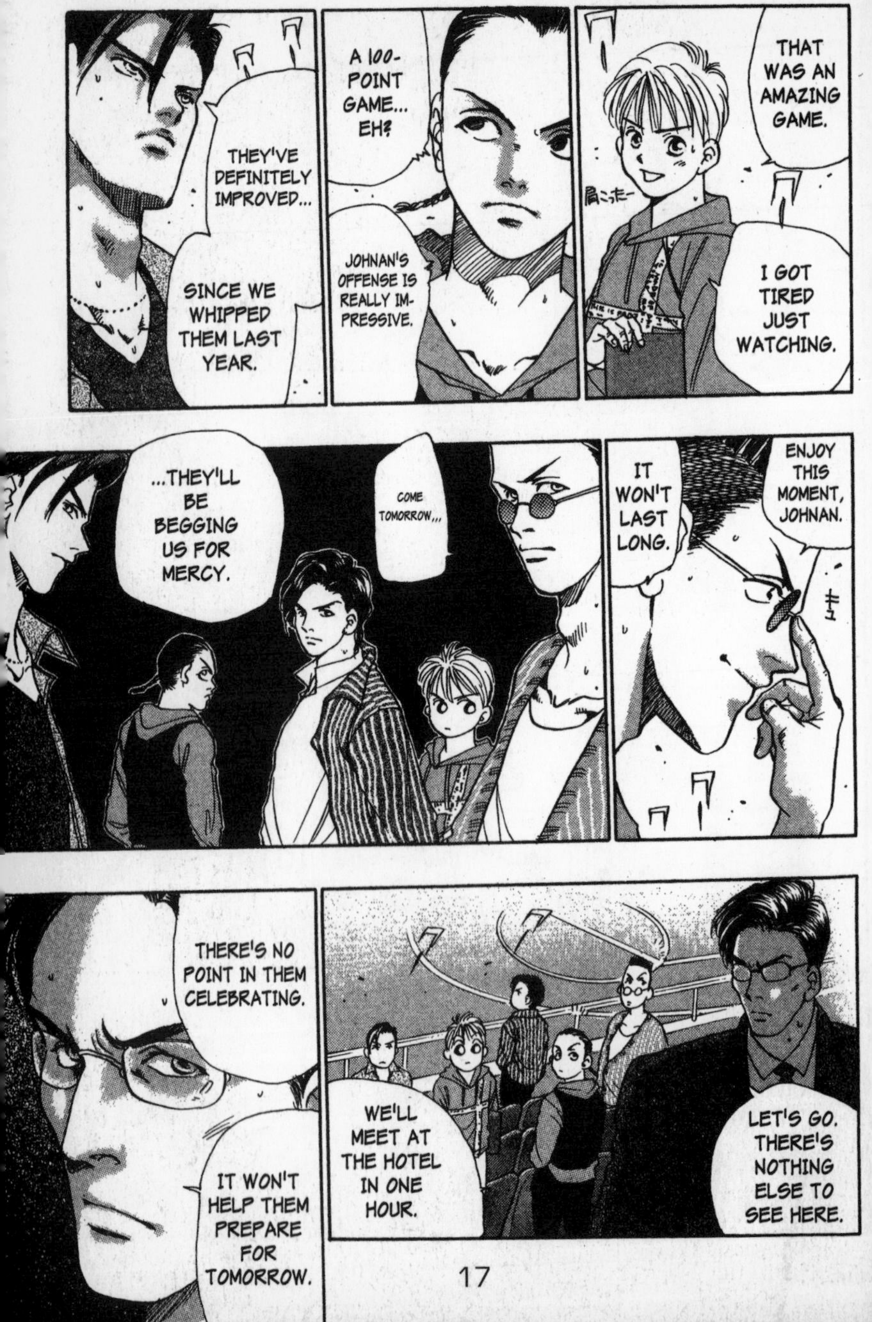
THAT WAS AN AMAZING GAME.
I GOT TIRED JUST WATCHING.
A 100-POINT GAME... EH?
JOHNAN'S OFFENSE IS REALLY IMPRESSIVE.
THEY'VE DEFINITELY IMPROVED...
SINCE WE WHIPPED THEM LAST YEAR.
ENJOY THIS MOMENT, JOHNAN.
IT WON'T LAST LONG.
COME TOMORROW,,,
...THEY'LL BE BEGGING US FOR MERCY.
LET'S GO. THERE'S NOTHING ELSE TO SEE HERE.
WE'LL MEET AT THE HOTEL IN ONE HOUR.
THERE'S NO POINT IN THEM CELEBRATING.
IT WON'T HELP THEM PREPARE FOR TOMORROW.

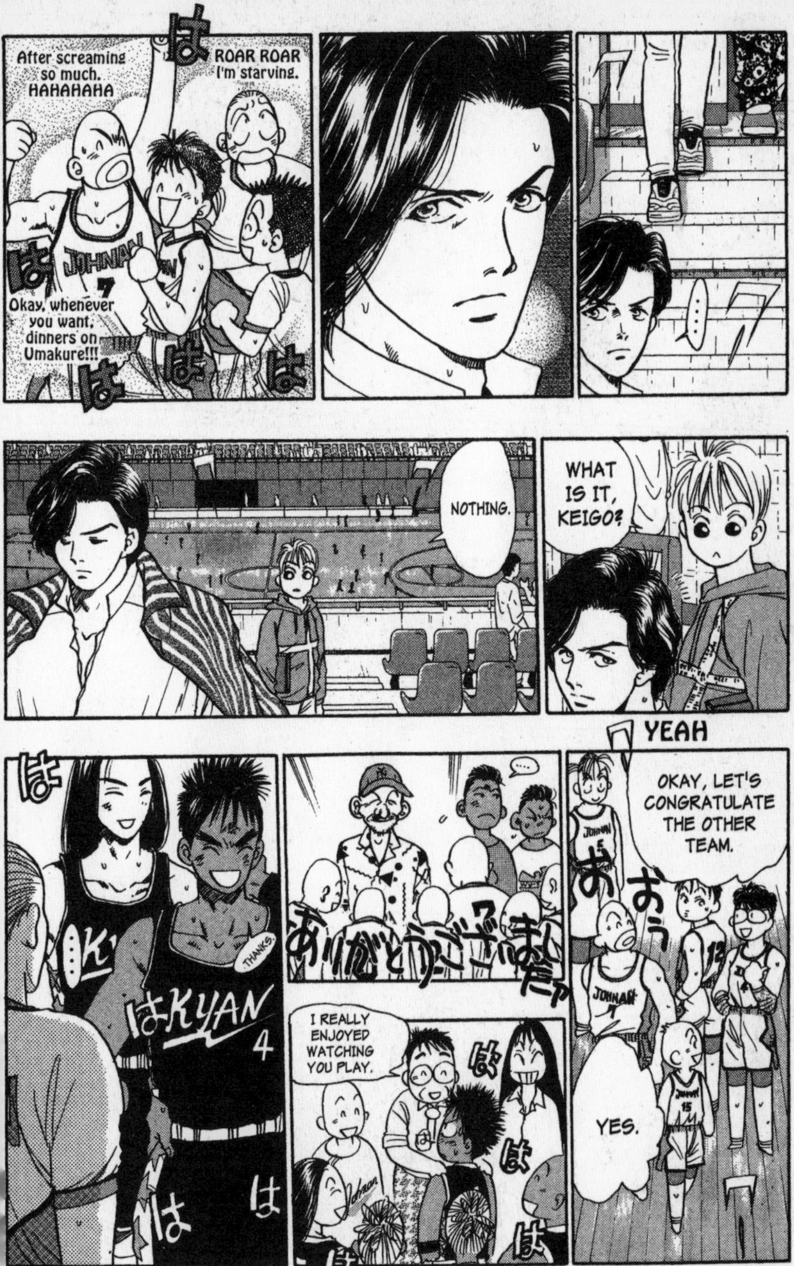
...
ROAR ROAR I'm starving.
After screaming so much. HAHAHAHA
Okay, whenever you want, dinners on Umakure!!!
WHAT IS IT, KEIGO?
NOTHING.
YEAH
OKAY, LET'S CONGRATULATE THE OTHER TEAM.
おおう
YES.
...
ありがとうございました
I REALLY ENJOYED WATCHING YOU PLAY.
THANKS.
...

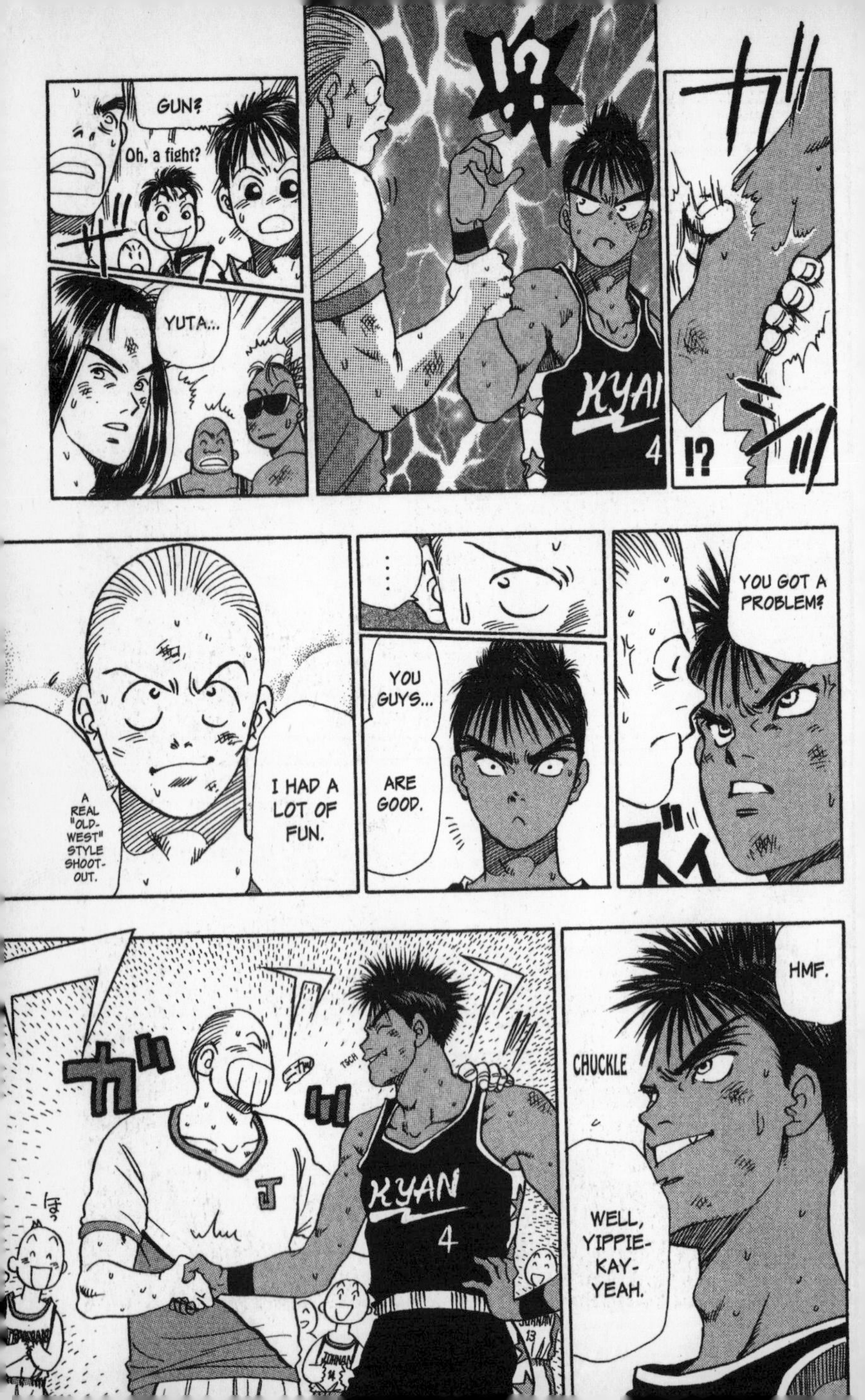
!?
!?
GUN?
Oh, a fight?
YUTA...
YOU GOT A PROBLEM?
. . . .
YOU GUYS...
ARE GOOD.
I HAD A LOT OF FUN.
A REAL "OLD-WEST" STYLE SHOOT-OUT.
HMF.
CHUCKLE
WELL, YIPPIE-KAY-YEAH.
TSCH
KYAN
4

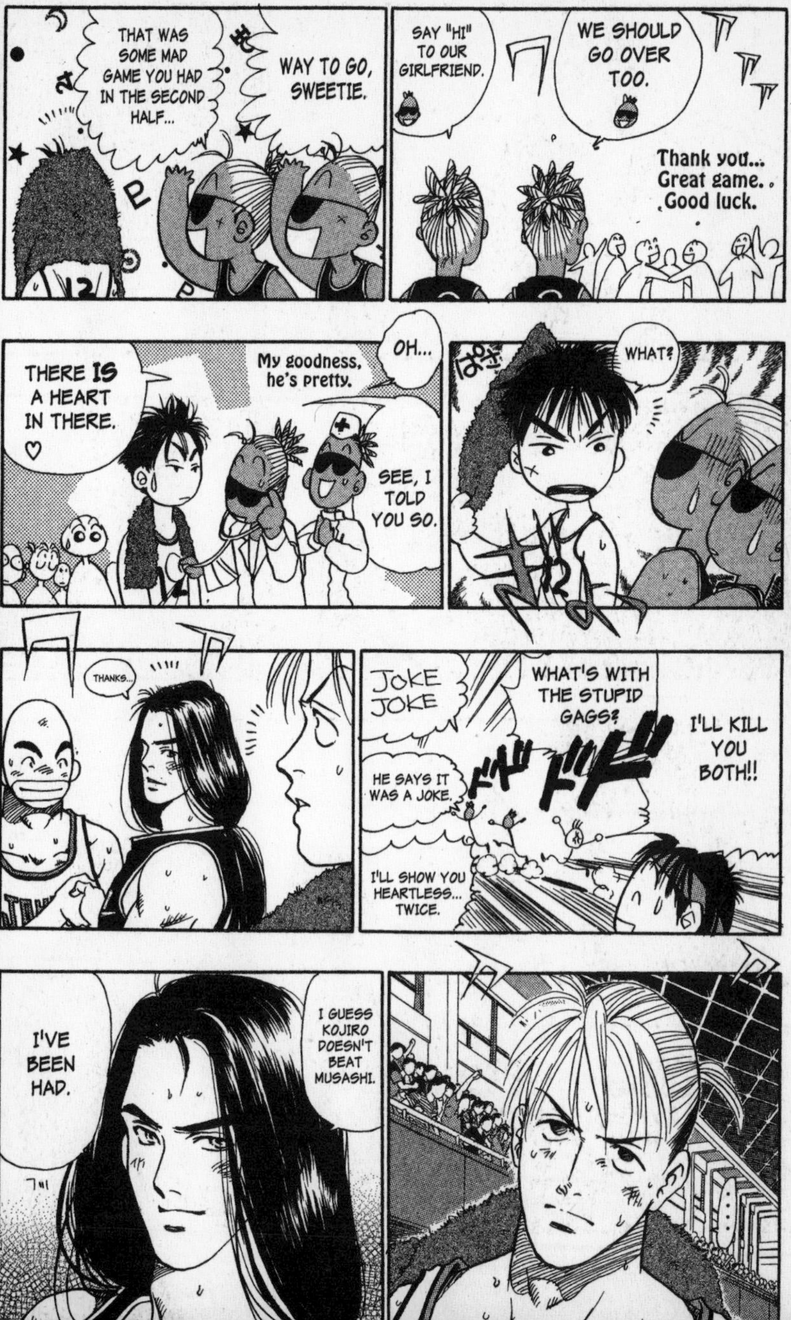
WE SHOULD GO OVER TOO.
SAY "HI" TO OUR GIRLFRIEND.
Thank you... Great game. Good luck.
WAY TO GO, SWEETIE.
THAT WAS SOME MAD GAME YOU HAD IN THE SECOND HALF...
WHAT?
OH...
My goodness, he's pretty.
THERE IS A HEART IN THERE. ♡
SEE, I TOLD YOU SO.
WHAT'S WITH THE STUPID GAGS?
I'LL KILL YOU BOTH!!
JOKE JOKE
HE SAYS IT WAS A JOKE.
I'LL SHOW YOU HEARTLESS... TWICE.
THANKS...
I GUESS KOJIRO DOESN'T BEAT MUSASHI.
I'VE BEEN HAD.

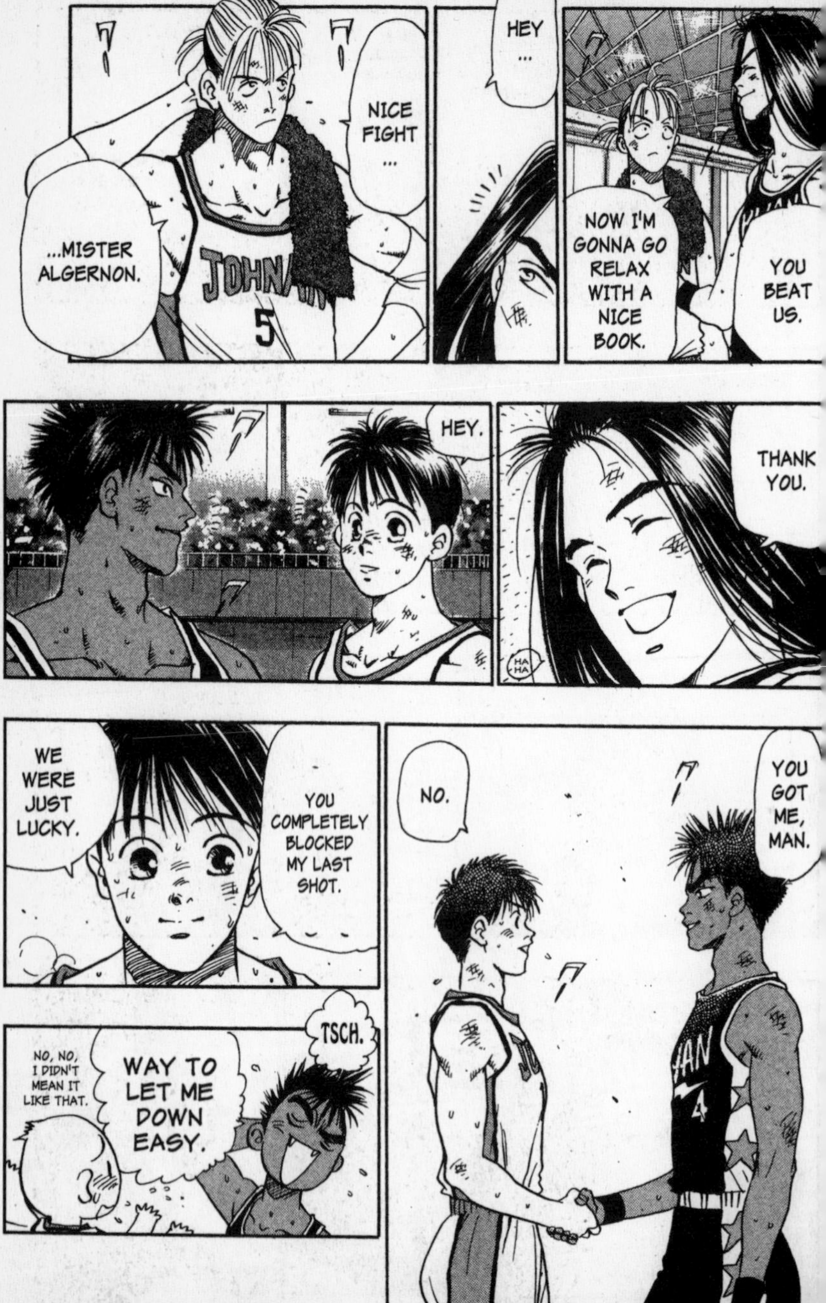
YOU BEAT US.
NOW I'M GONNA GO RELAX WITH A NICE BOOK.
HEY ...
NICE FIGHT ...
...MISTER ALGERNON.
THANK YOU.
HA HA
HEY.
YOU GOT ME, MAN.
NO.
YOU COMPLETELY BLOCKED MY LAST SHOT.
WE WERE JUST LUCKY.
TSCH.
WAY TO LET ME DOWN EASY.
NO, NO, I DIDN'T MEAN IT LIKE THAT.

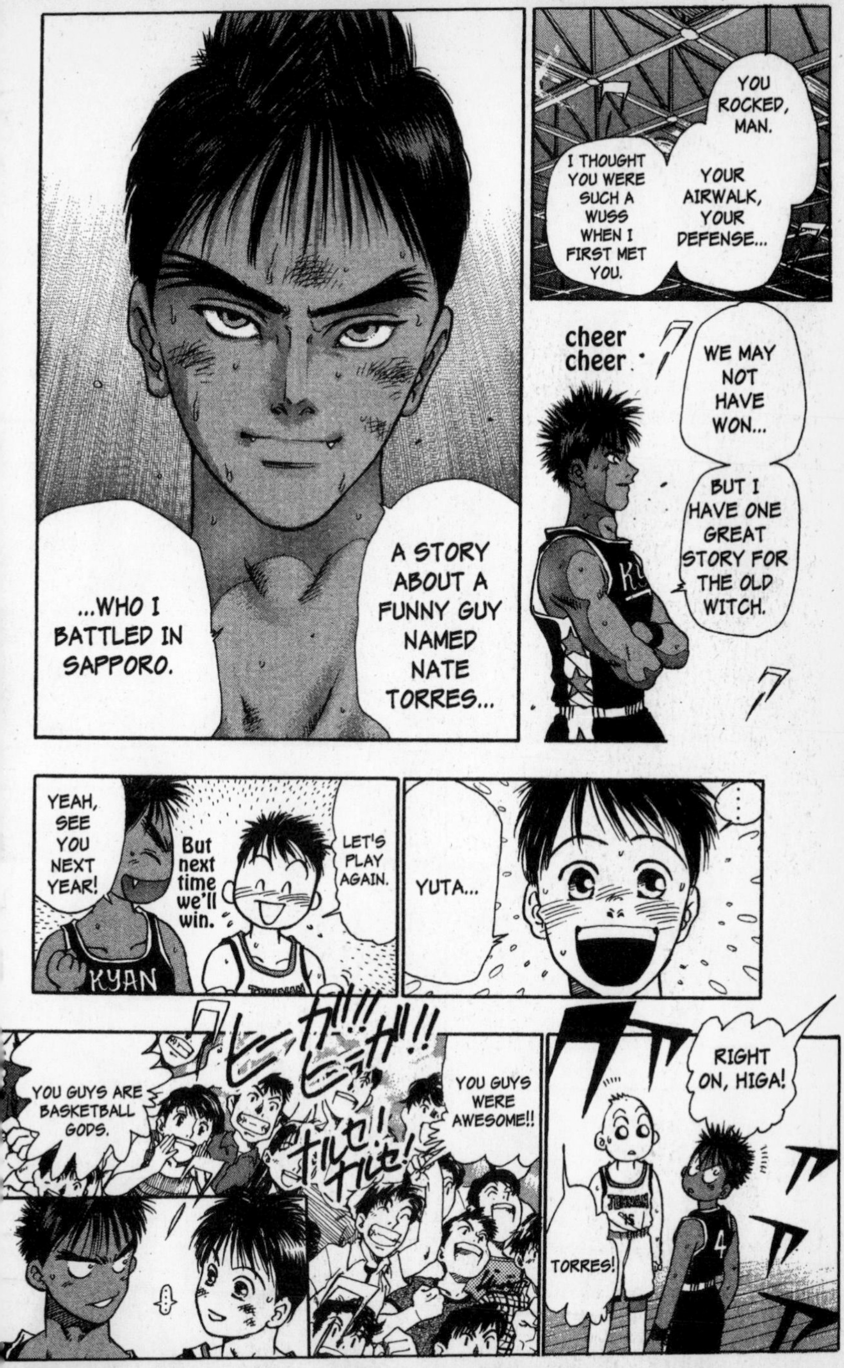
YOU ROCKED, MAN.
YOUR AIRWALK, YOUR DEFENSE...
I THOUGHT YOU WERE SUCH A WUSS WHEN I FIRST MET YOU.
WE MAY NOT HAVE WON...
BUT I HAVE ONE GREAT STORY FOR THE OLD WITCH.
cheer cheer
A STORY ABOUT A FUNNY GUY NAMED NATE TORRES...
...WHO I BATTLED IN SAPPORO.
....
YUTA...
LET'S PLAY AGAIN.
But next time we'll win.
YEAH, SEE YOU NEXT YEAR!
KYAN
RIGHT ON, HIGA!
TORRES!
ヒーガ!!! ヒーガ!!!
ナルセ! ナルセ!
YOU GUYS WERE AWESOME!!
YOU GUYS ARE BASKETBALL GODS.
...!

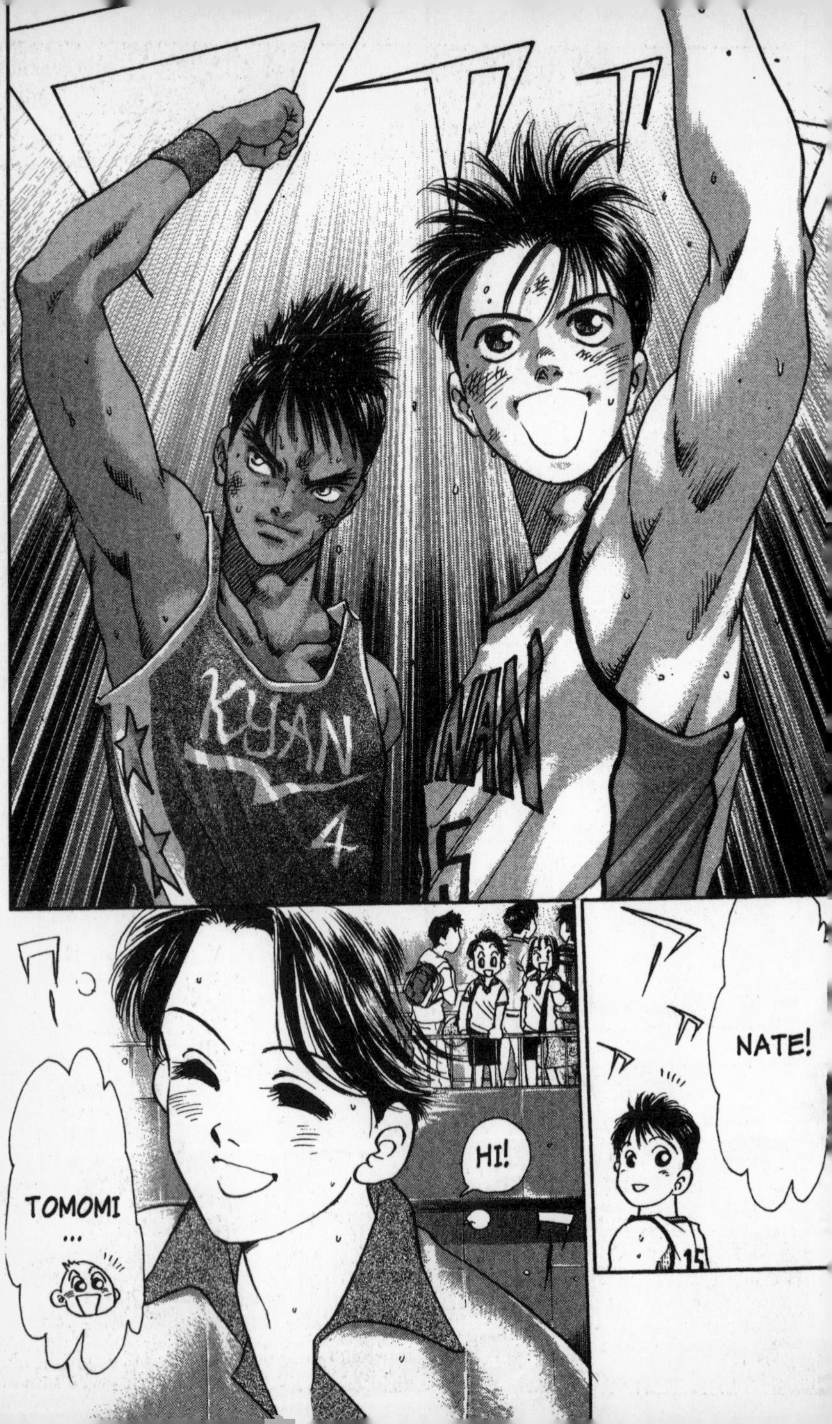

NATE!
HI!
TOMOMI
...

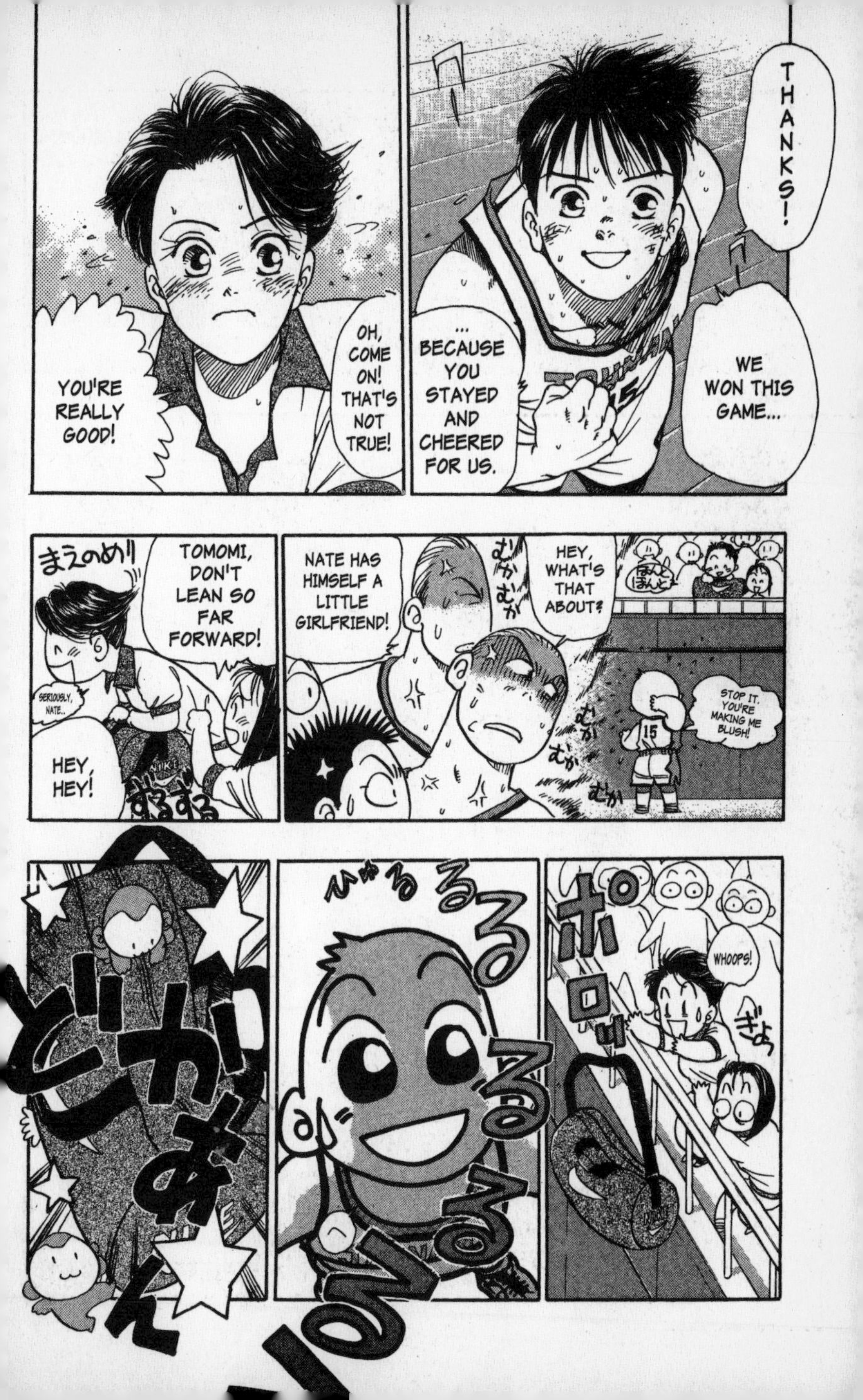
THANKS!
WE WON THIS GAME...
... BECAUSE YOU STAYED AND CHEERED FOR US.
OH, COME ON! THAT'S NOT TRUE!
YOU'RE REALLY GOOD!
HEY, WHAT'S THAT ABOUT?
ほんとほんと
むかむか
STOP IT. YOU'RE MAKING ME BLUSH!
NATE HAS HIMSELF A LITTLE GIRLFRIEND!
まえのめり
TOMOMI, DON'T LEAN SO FAR FORWARD!
SERIOUSLY, NATE...
HEY, HEY!
するする
ポロッ
WHOOPS!
ぎょっ
ひゅるるるる

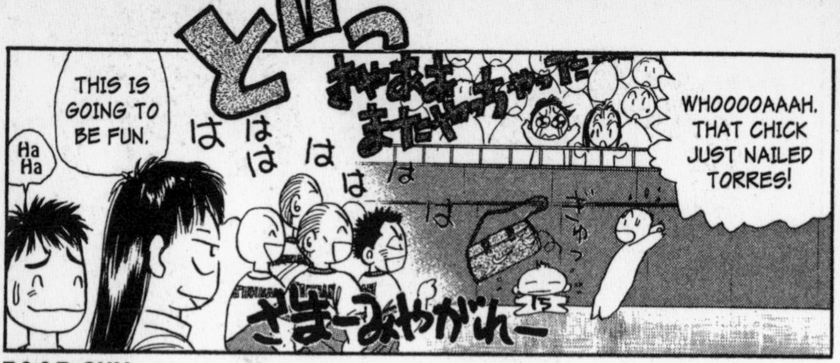
WHOOOOAAAH. THAT CHICK JUST NAILED TORRES!
THIS IS GOING TO BE FUN.
Ha Ha

POOR GUY

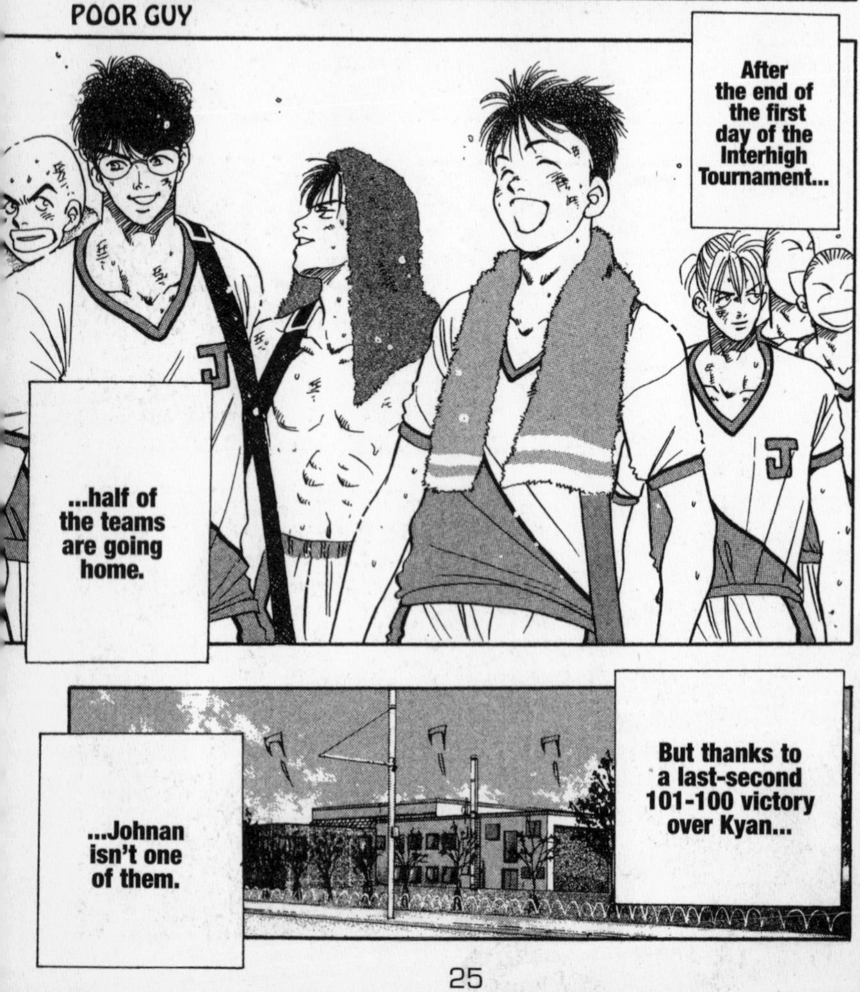
After the end of the first day of the Interhigh Tournament...
...half of the teams are going home.
But thanks to a last-second 101-100 victory over Kyan...
...Johnan isn't one of them.

REBOUND

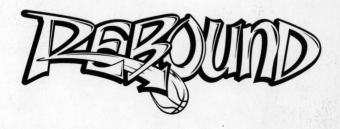

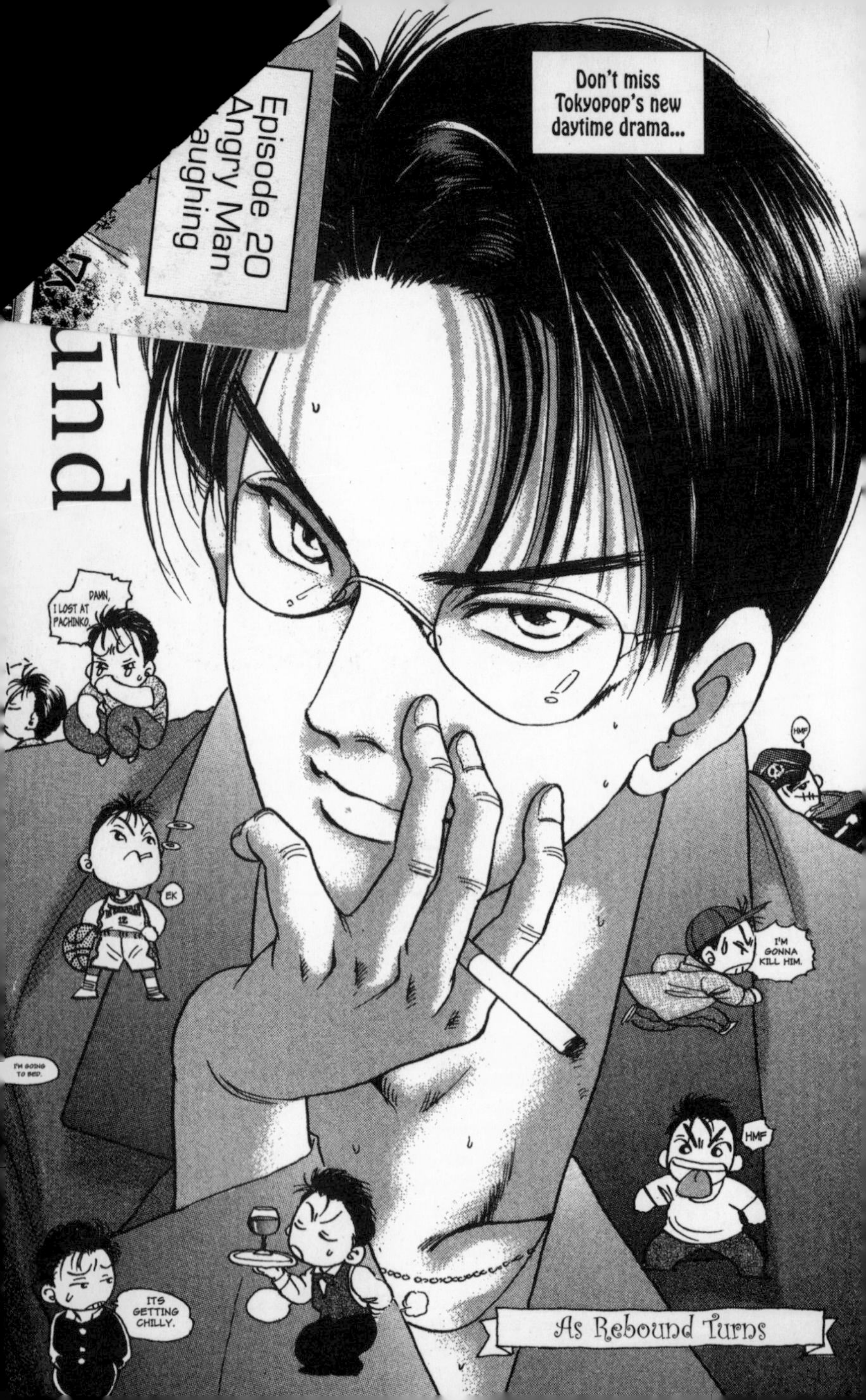

Don't miss Tokyopop's new daytime drama...
Episode 20
Angry Man
aughing
HMF
DAMN, I LOST AT PACHINKO.
I'M GONNA KILL HIM.
EK
I'M GOING TO BED.
HMF
ITS GETTING CHILLY.
As Rebound Turns

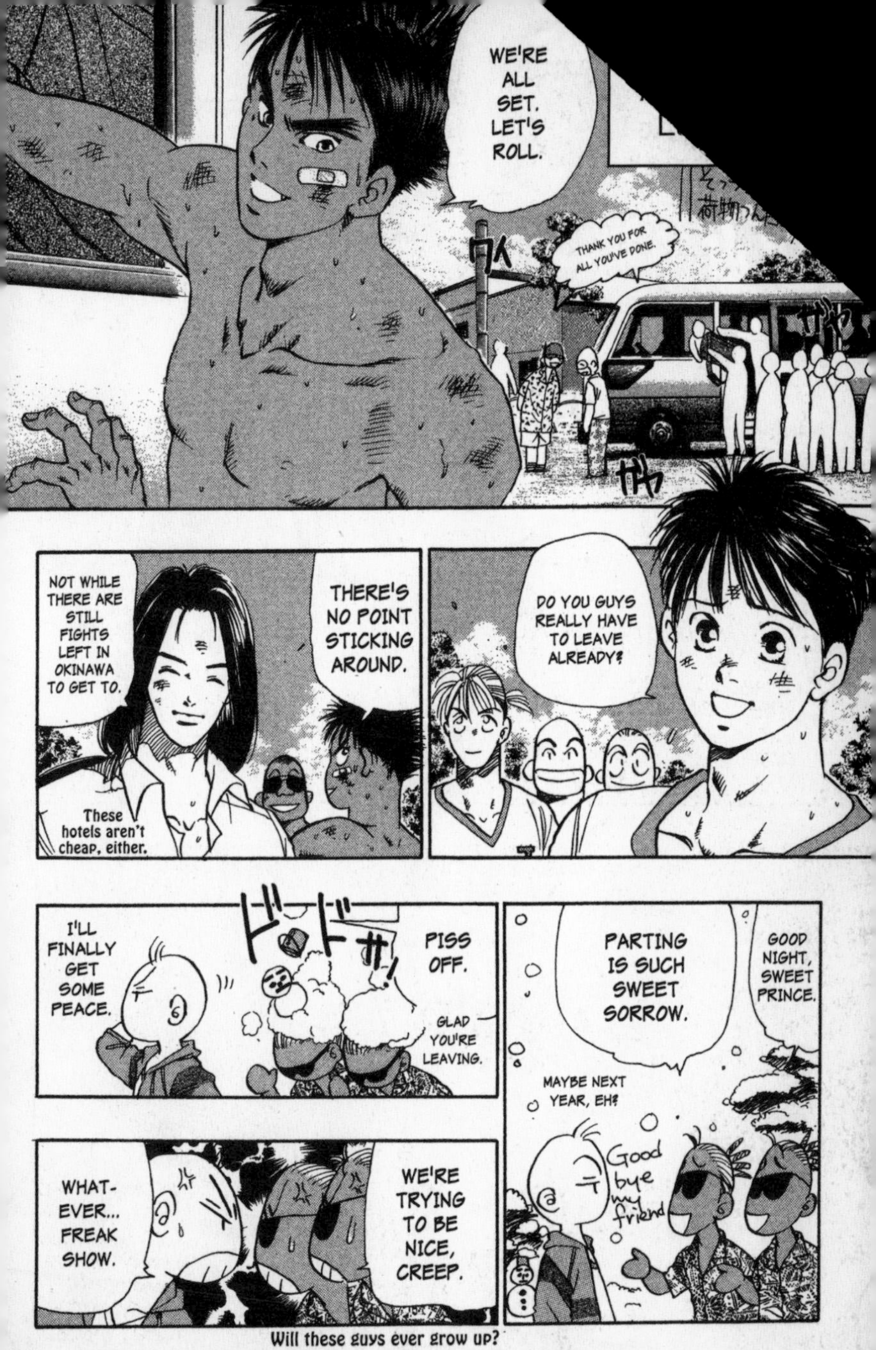
WE'RE ALL SET. LET'S ROLL.
THANK YOU FOR ALL YOU'VE DONE.
DO YOU GUYS REALLY HAVE TO LEAVE ALREADY?
THERE'S NO POINT STICKING AROUND.
NOT WHILE THERE ARE STILL FIGHTS LEFT IN OKINAWA TO GET TO.
These hotels aren't cheap, either.
GOOD NIGHT, SWEET PRINCE.
PARTING IS SUCH SWEET SORROW.
MAYBE NEXT YEAR, EH?
Good bye my friend
PISS OFF.
GLAD YOU'RE LEAVING.
I'LL FINALLY GET SOME PEACE.
WE'RE TRYING TO BE NICE, CREEP.
WHAT-EVER... FREAK SHOW.

Will these guys ever grow up?

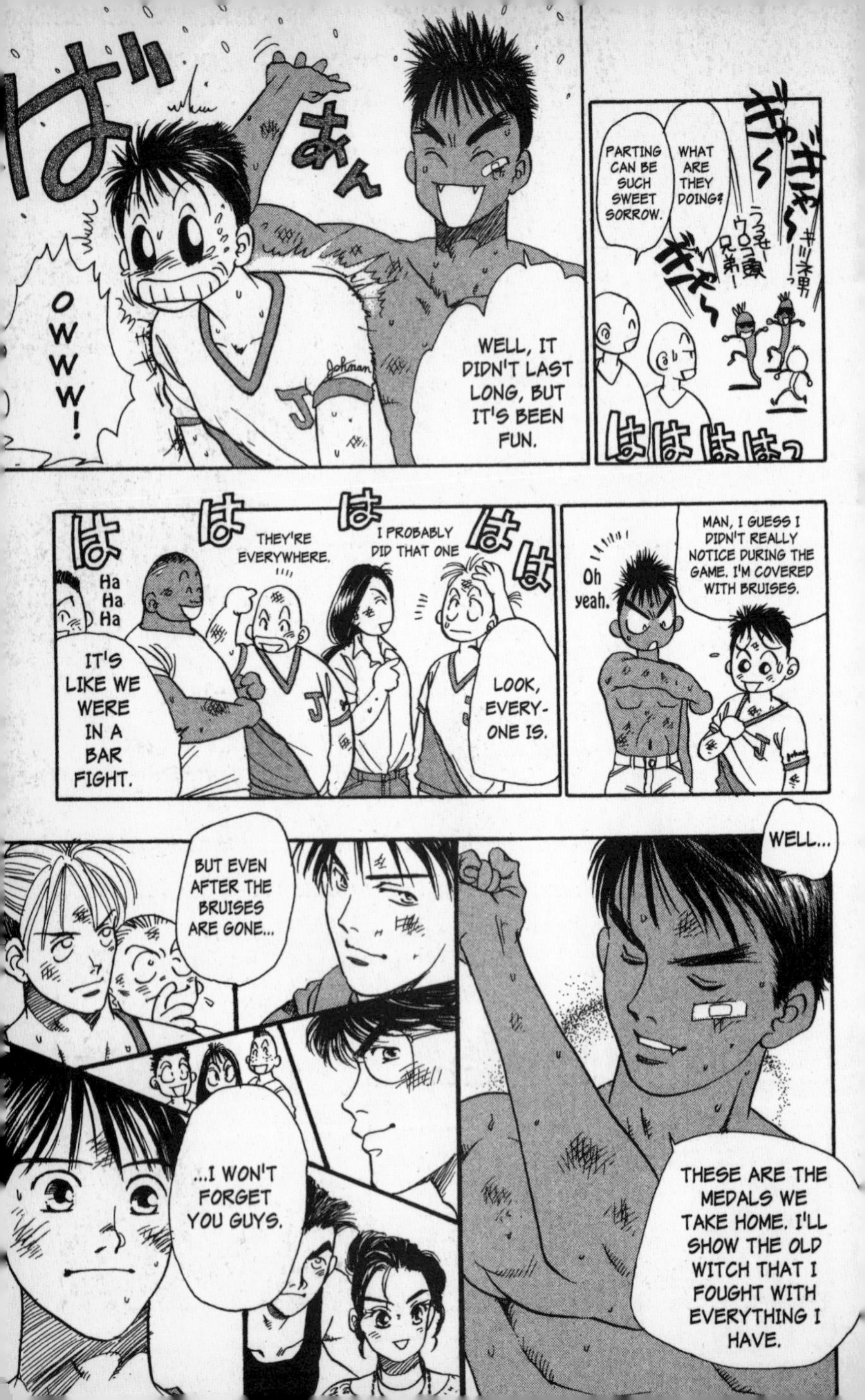

ぎゃぎゃ
WHAT ARE THEY DOING?
PARTING CAN BE SUCH SWEET SORROW.
ぎゃ〜
ははははっ
ばぁん
WELL, IT DIDN'T LAST LONG, BUT IT'S BEEN FUN.
OWWW!
MAN, I GUESS I DIDN'T REALLY NOTICE DURING THE GAME. I'M COVERED WITH BRUISES.
Oh yeah.
ははははは
I PROBABLY DID THAT ONE
THEY'RE EVERYWHERE.
LOOK, EVERY-ONE IS.
Ha Ha Ha
IT'S LIKE WE WERE IN A BAR FIGHT.
WELL...
THESE ARE THE MEDALS WE TAKE HOME. I'LL SHOW THE OLD WITCH THAT I FOUGHT WITH EVERYTHING I HAVE.
BUT EVEN AFTER THE BRUISES ARE GONE...
...I WON'T FORGET YOU GUYS.

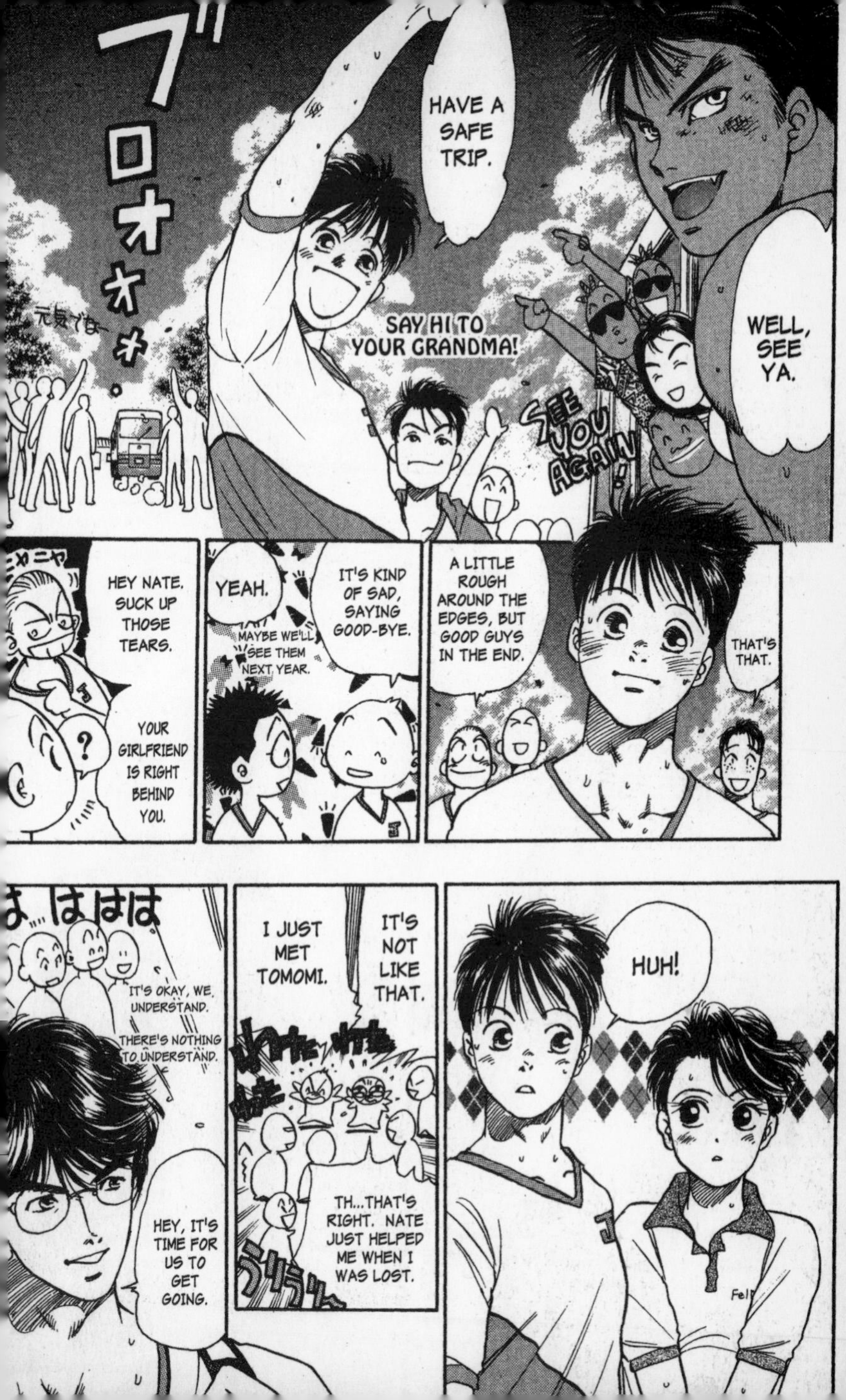

WELL, SEE YA.
HAVE A SAFE TRIP.
ブロオオオ
SAY HI TO YOUR GRANDMA!
SEE YOU AGAIN!
元気でなー
THAT'S THAT.
A LITTLE ROUGH AROUND THE EDGES, BUT GOOD GUYS IN THE END.
IT'S KIND OF SAD, SAYING GOOD-BYE.
YEAH.
MAYBE WE'LL SEE THEM NEXT YEAR.
HEY NATE. SUCK UP THOSE TEARS.
?
YOUR GIRLFRIEND IS RIGHT BEHIND YOU.
HUH!
IT'S NOT LIKE THAT.
I JUST MET TOMOMI.
TH...THAT'S RIGHT. NATE JUST HELPED ME WHEN I WAS LOST.
は...ははは
IT'S OKAY, WE UNDERSTAND.
THERE'S NOTHING TO UNDERSTAND.
HEY, IT'S TIME FOR US TO GET GOING.

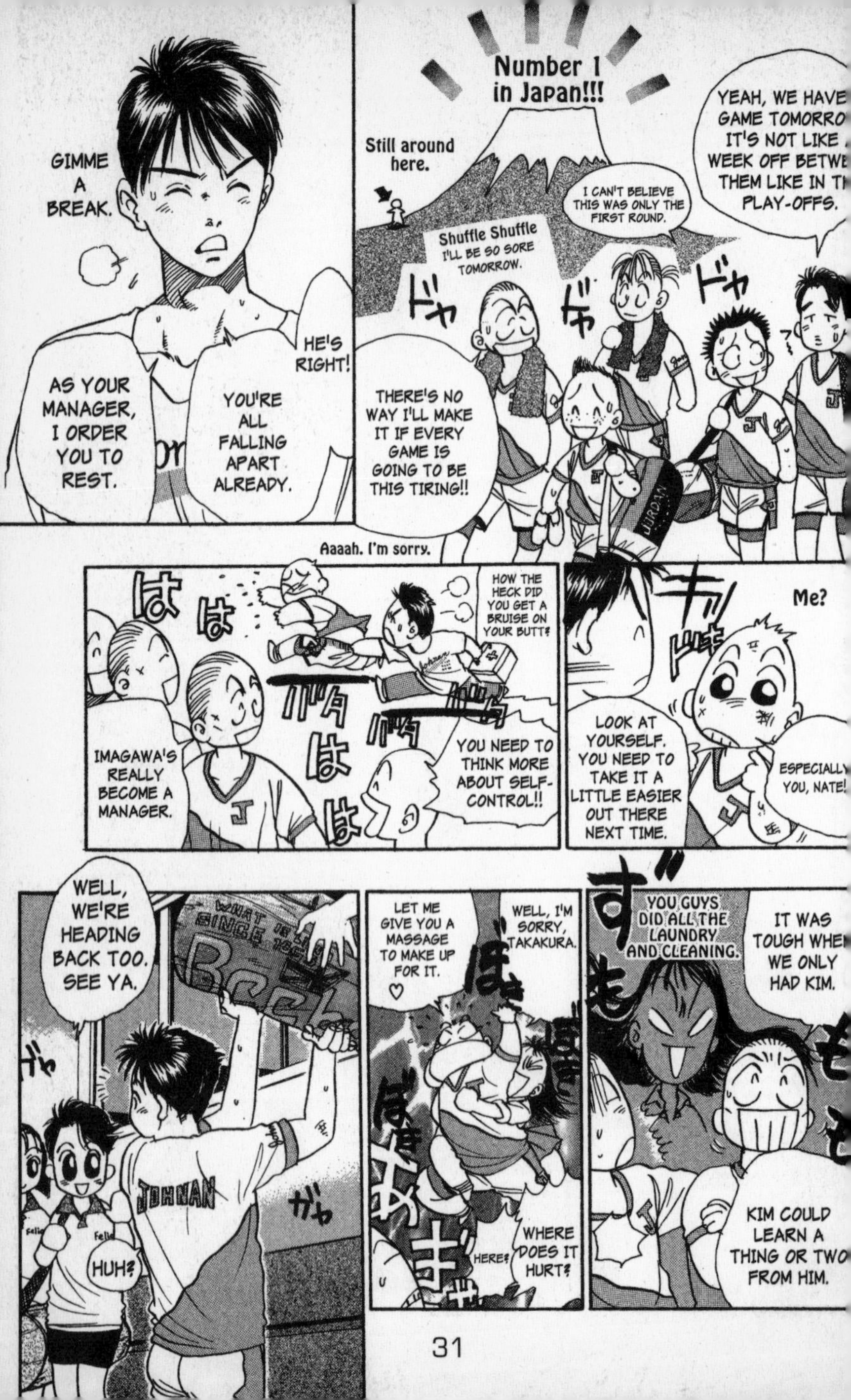
YEAH, WE HAVE GAME TOMORRO IT'S NOT LIKE WEEK OFF BETWE THEM LIKE IN T PLAY-OFFS.
Number 1 in Japan!!!
I CAN'T BELIEVE THIS WAS ONLY THE FIRST ROUND.
Still around here.
Shuffle Shuffle
I'LL BE SO SORE TOMORROW.
ドヤ
ドヤ
THERE'S NO WAY I'LL MAKE IT IF EVERY GAME IS GOING TO BE THIS TIRING!!
Aaaah. I'm sorry.
HE'S RIGHT!
YOU'RE ALL FALLING APART ALREADY.
GIMME A BREAK.
AS YOUR MANAGER, I ORDER YOU TO REST.
Me?
LOOK AT YOURSELF. YOU NEED TO TAKE IT A LITTLE EASIER OUT THERE NEXT TIME.
ESPECIALLY YOU, NATE!
HOW THE HECK DID YOU GET A BRUISE ON YOUR BUTT?
YOU NEED TO THINK MORE ABOUT SELF-CONTROL!!
はは
はは
IMAGAWA'S REALLY BECOME A MANAGER.
IT WAS TOUGH WHE WE ONLY HAD KIM.
YOU GUYS DID ALL THE LAUNDRY AND CLEANING.
KIM COULD LEARN A THING OR TWO FROM HIM.
WELL, I'M SORRY, TAKAKURA.
LET ME GIVE YOU A MASSAGE TO MAKE UP FOR IT. ♡
WHERE DOES IT HURT?
HERE?
WELL, WE'RE HEADING BACK TOO. SEE YA.
JOHNAN
HUH?

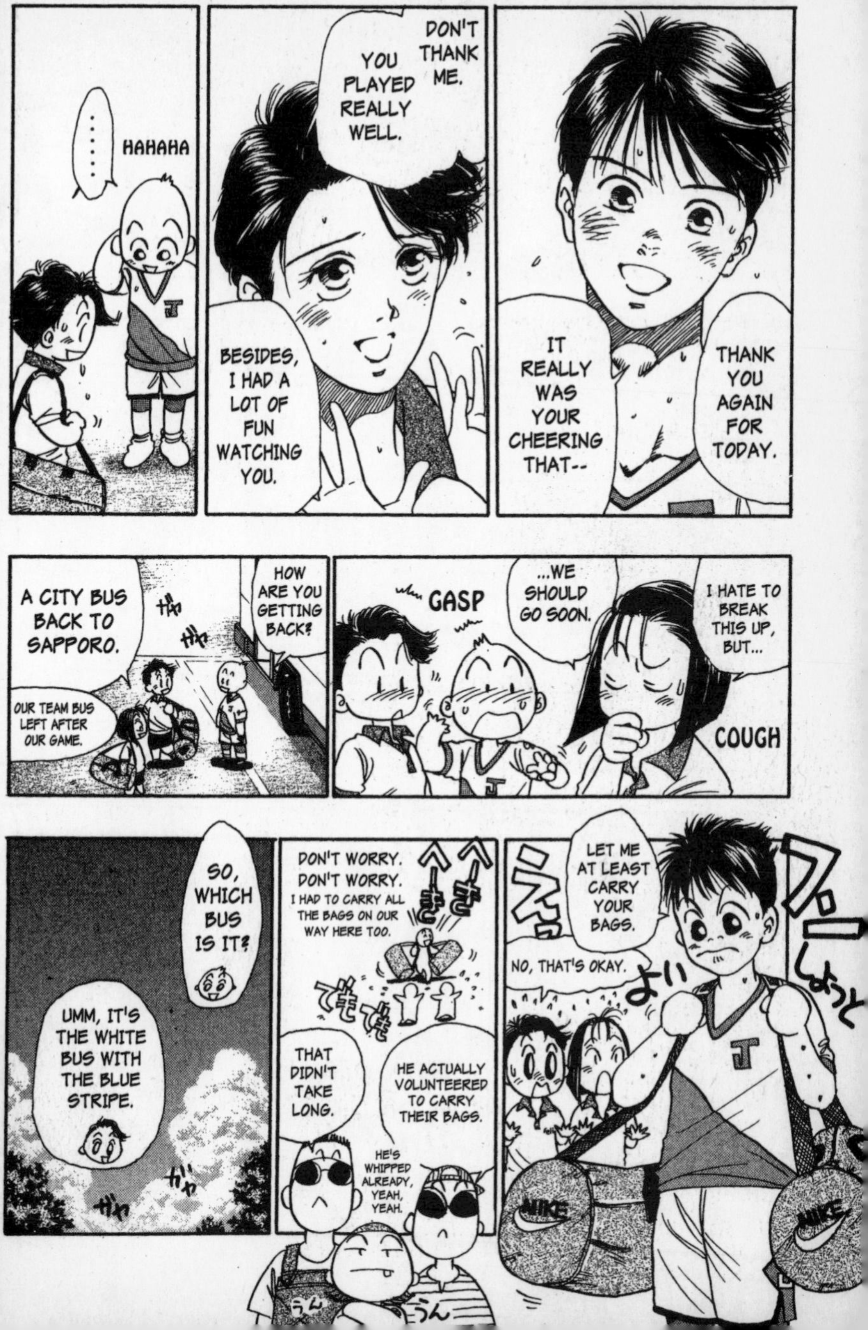
THANK YOU AGAIN FOR TODAY.
IT REALLY WAS YOUR CHEERING THAT--
DON'T THANK ME.
YOU PLAYED REALLY WELL.
BESIDES, I HAD A LOT OF FUN WATCHING YOU.
HAHAHA
......
I HATE TO BREAK THIS UP, BUT...
COUGH
...WE SHOULD GO SOON.
GASP
HOW ARE YOU GETTING BACK?
A CITY BUS BACK TO SAPPORO.
OUR TEAM BUS LEFT AFTER OUR GAME.
LET ME AT LEAST CARRY YOUR BAGS.
NO, THAT'S OKAY.
DON'T WORRY. DON'T WORRY. I HAD TO CARRY ALL THE BAGS ON OUR WAY HERE TOO.
HE ACTUALLY VOLUNTEERED TO CARRY THEIR BAGS.
THAT DIDN'T TAKE LONG.
HE'S WHIPPED ALREADY, YEAH, YEAH.
SO, WHICH BUS IS IT?
UMM, IT'S THE WHITE BUS WITH THE BLUE STRIPE.

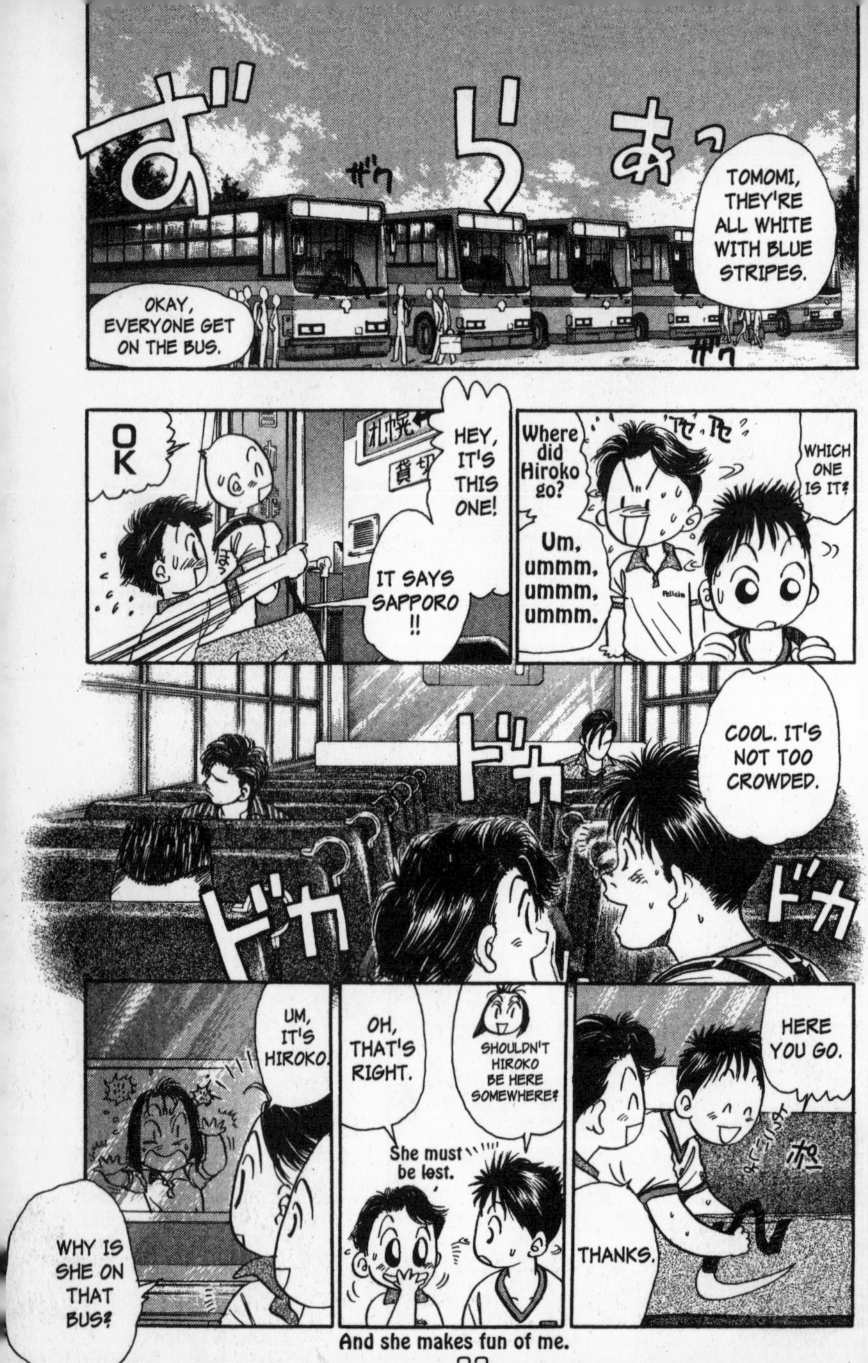
ずらあっ
TOMOMI, THEY'RE ALL WHITE WITH BLUE STRIPES.
OKAY, EVERYONE GET ON THE BUS.
WHICH ONE IS IT?
Where did Hiroko go?
Um, ummm, ummm, ummm.
HEY, IT'S THIS ONE!
IT SAYS SAPPORO !!
OK
COOL. IT'S NOT TOO CROWDED.
ドカ
ドカ
ドカ
HERE YOU GO.
THANKS.
SHOULDN'T HIROKO BE HERE SOMEWHERE?
OH, THAT'S RIGHT.
She must be lost.
UM, IT'S HIROKO.
WHY IS SHE ON THAT BUS?

And she makes fun of me.

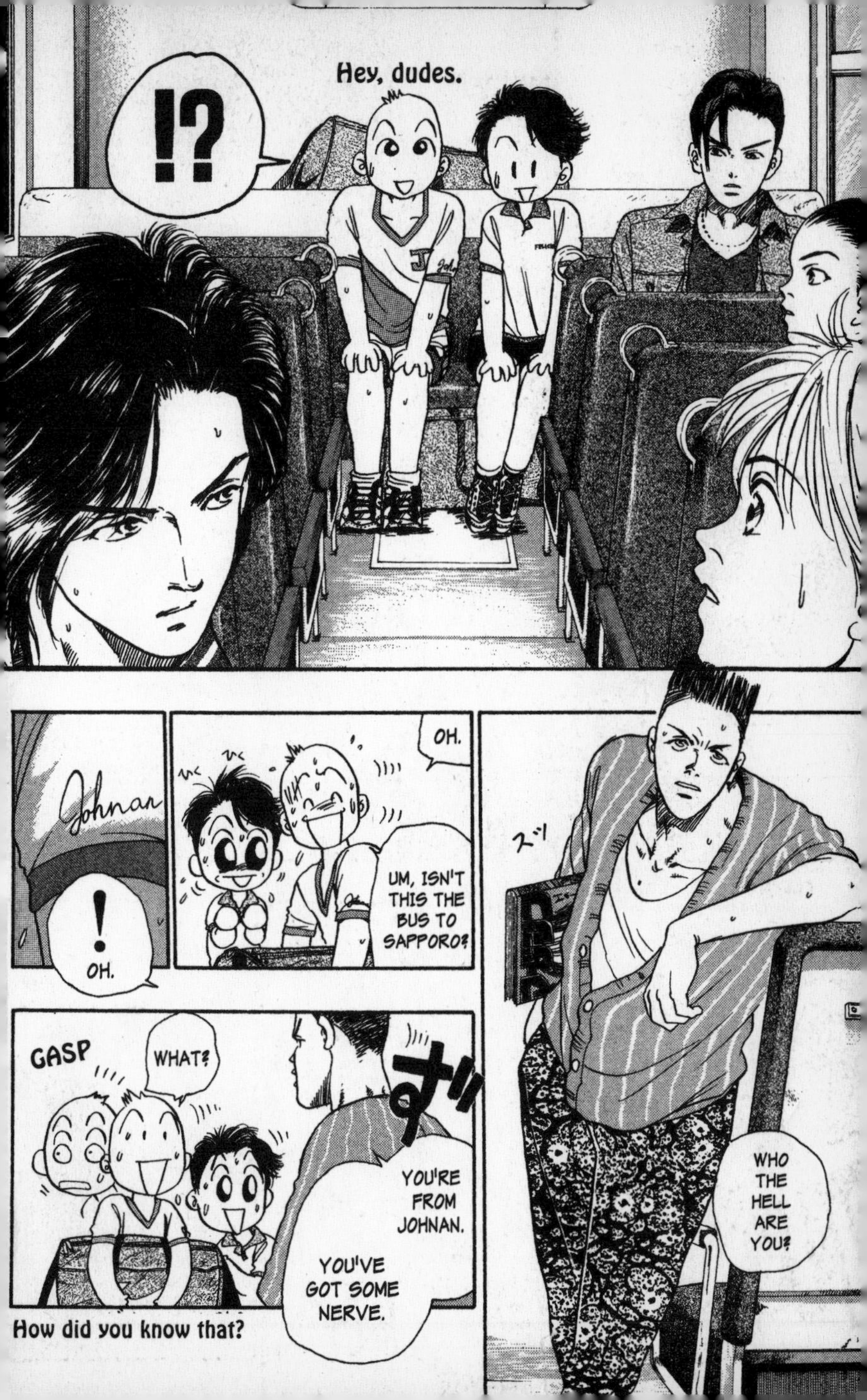
Hey, dudes.
!?
ズッ
WHO THE HELL ARE YOU?
OH.
UM, ISN'T THIS THE BUS TO SAPPORO?
Johnan
!
OH.
YOU'RE FROM JOHNAN.
YOU'VE GOT SOME NERVE.
WHAT?
GASP
How did you know that?

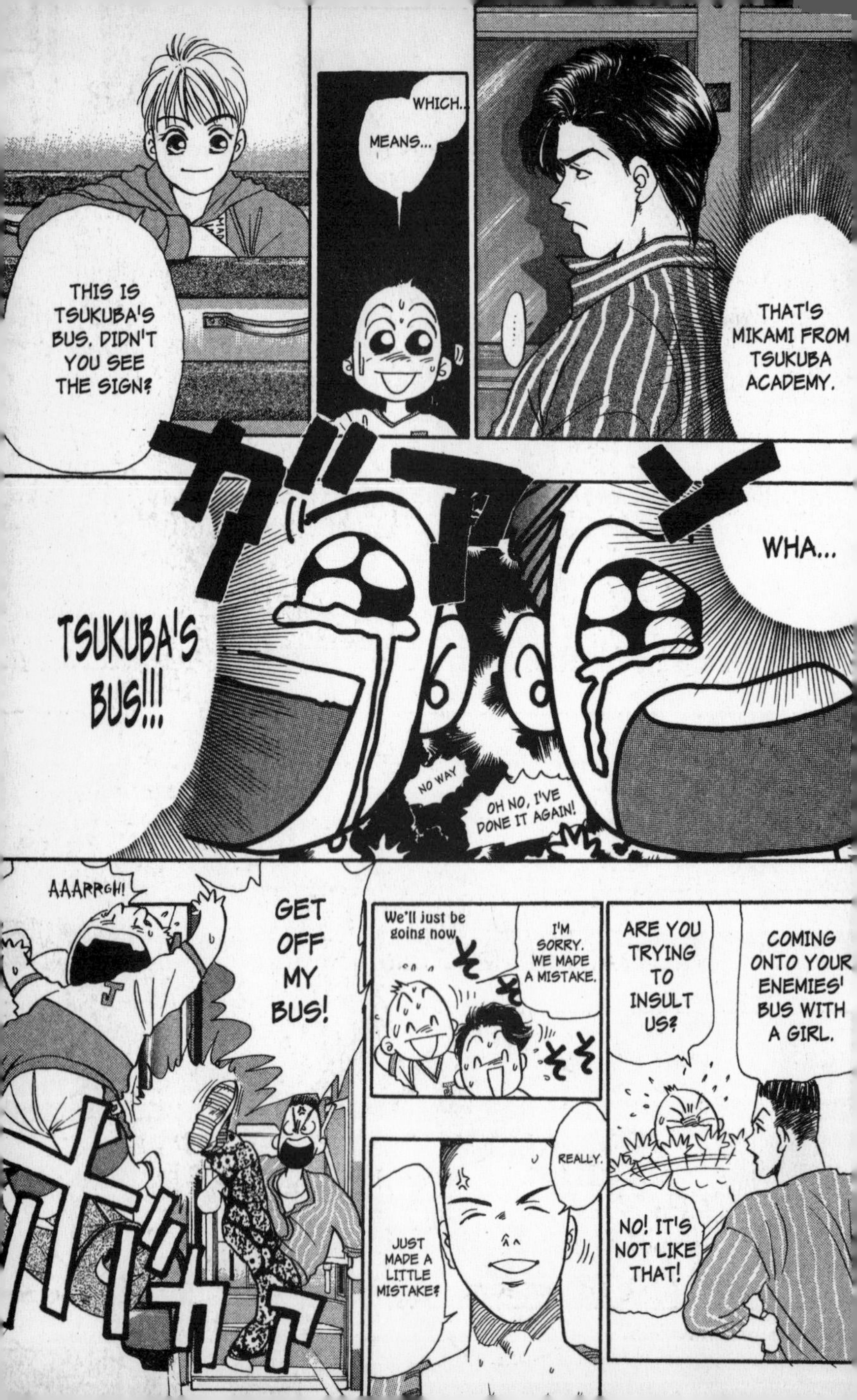
...
THAT'S MIKAMI FROM TSUKUBA ACADEMY.
WHICH...
MEANS...
THIS IS TSUKUBA'S BUS. DIDN'T YOU SEE THE SIGN?
WHA...
TSUKUBA'S BUS!!!
OH NO, I'VE DONE IT AGAIN!
NO WAY
COMING ONTO YOUR ENEMIES' BUS WITH A GIRL.
ARE YOU TRYING TO INSULT US?
NO! IT'S NOT LIKE THAT!
I'M SORRY. WE MADE A MISTAKE.
We'll just be going now.
REALLY.
JUST MADE A LITTLE MISTAKE?
GET OFF MY BUS!
AAARRGH!

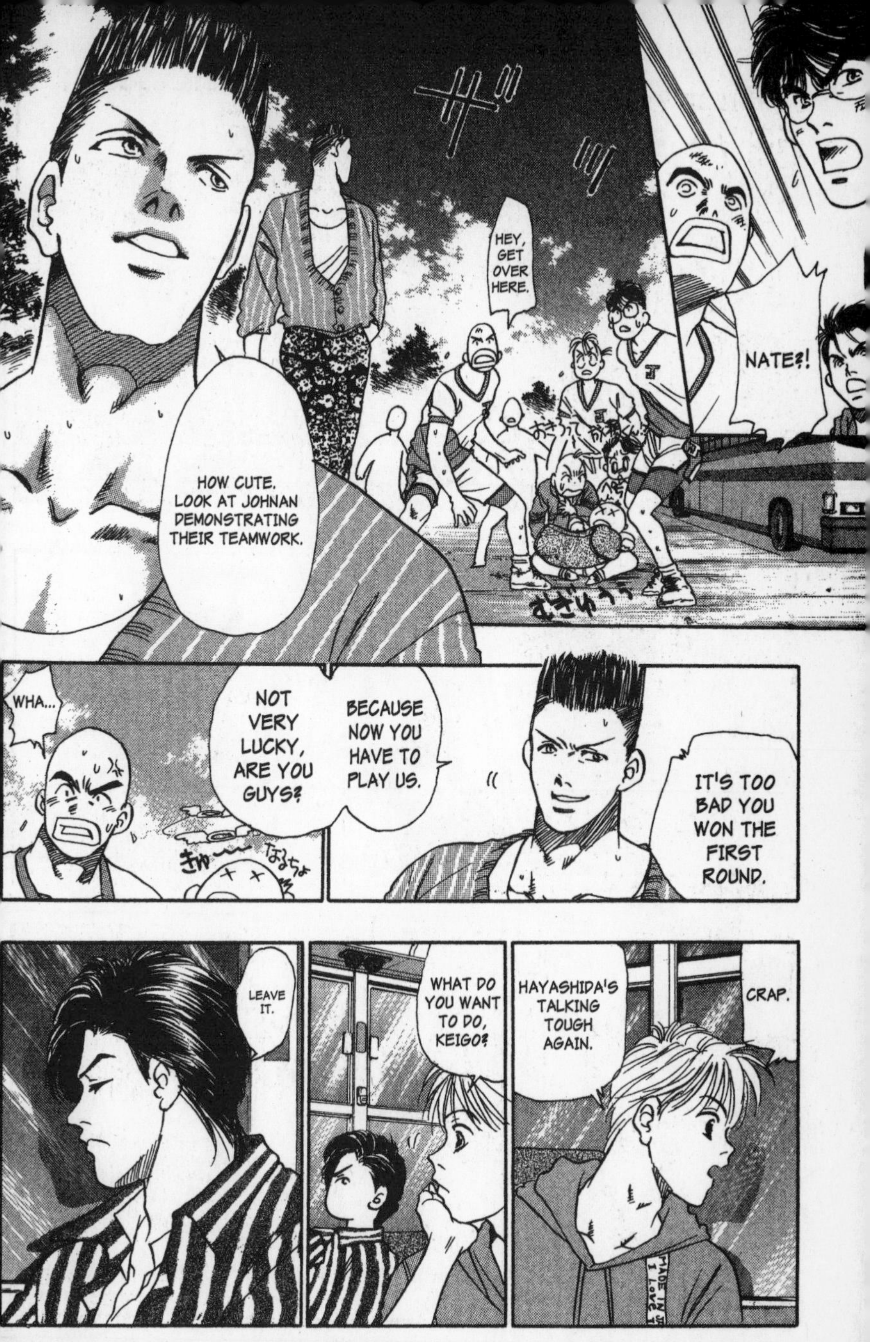
NATE?!
HEY, GET OVER HERE.
HOW CUTE. LOOK AT JOHNAN DEMONSTRATING THEIR TEAMWORK.
IT'S TOO BAD YOU WON THE FIRST ROUND.
BECAUSE NOW YOU HAVE TO PLAY US.
NOT VERY LUCKY, ARE YOU GUYS?
WHA...
CRAP.
HAYASHIDA'S TALKING TOUGH AGAIN.
WHAT DO YOU WANT TO DO, KEIGO?
LEAVE IT.

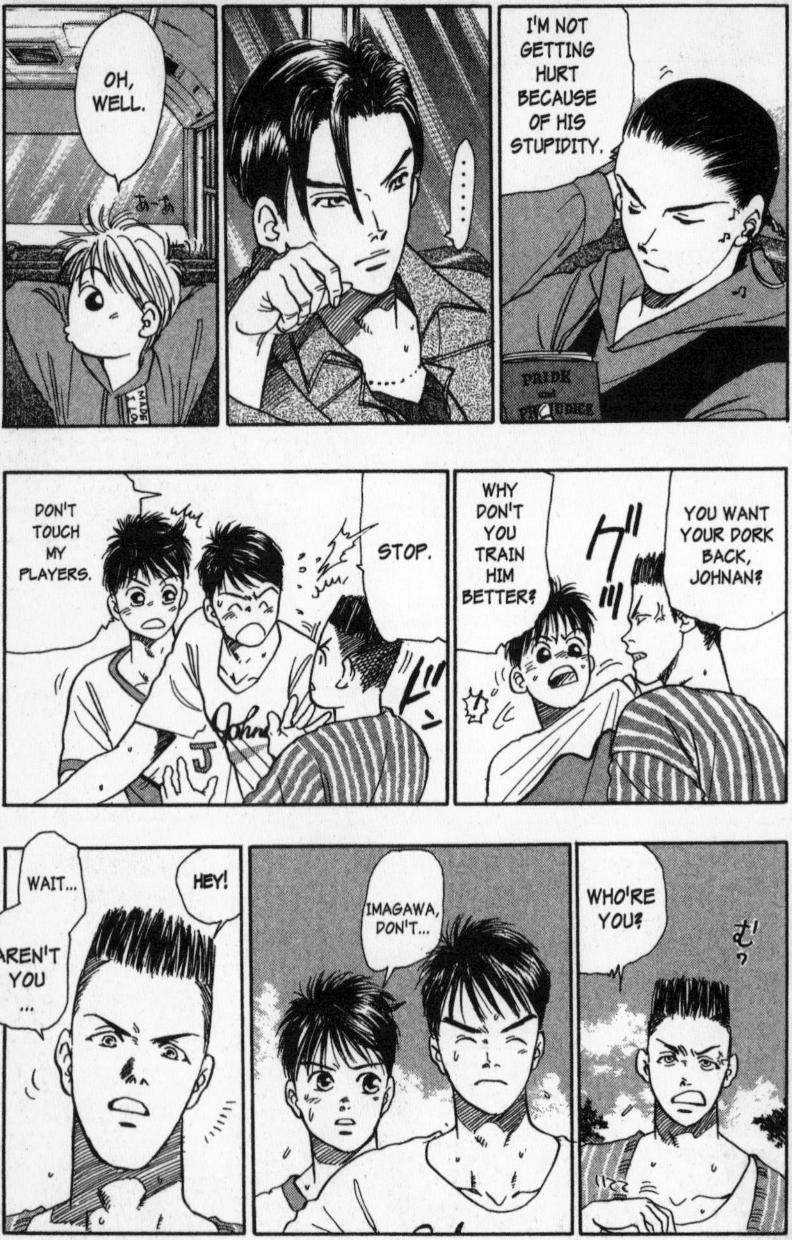
I'M NOT GETTING HURT BECAUSE OF HIS STUPIDITY.
......
OH, WELL.
あ～あ
YOU WANT YOUR DORK BACK, JOHNAN?
WHY DON'T YOU TRAIN HIM BETTER?
STOP.
DON'T TOUCH MY PLAYERS.
WHO'RE YOU?
IMAGAWA, DON'T...
HEY!
WAIT...
AREN'T YOU ...

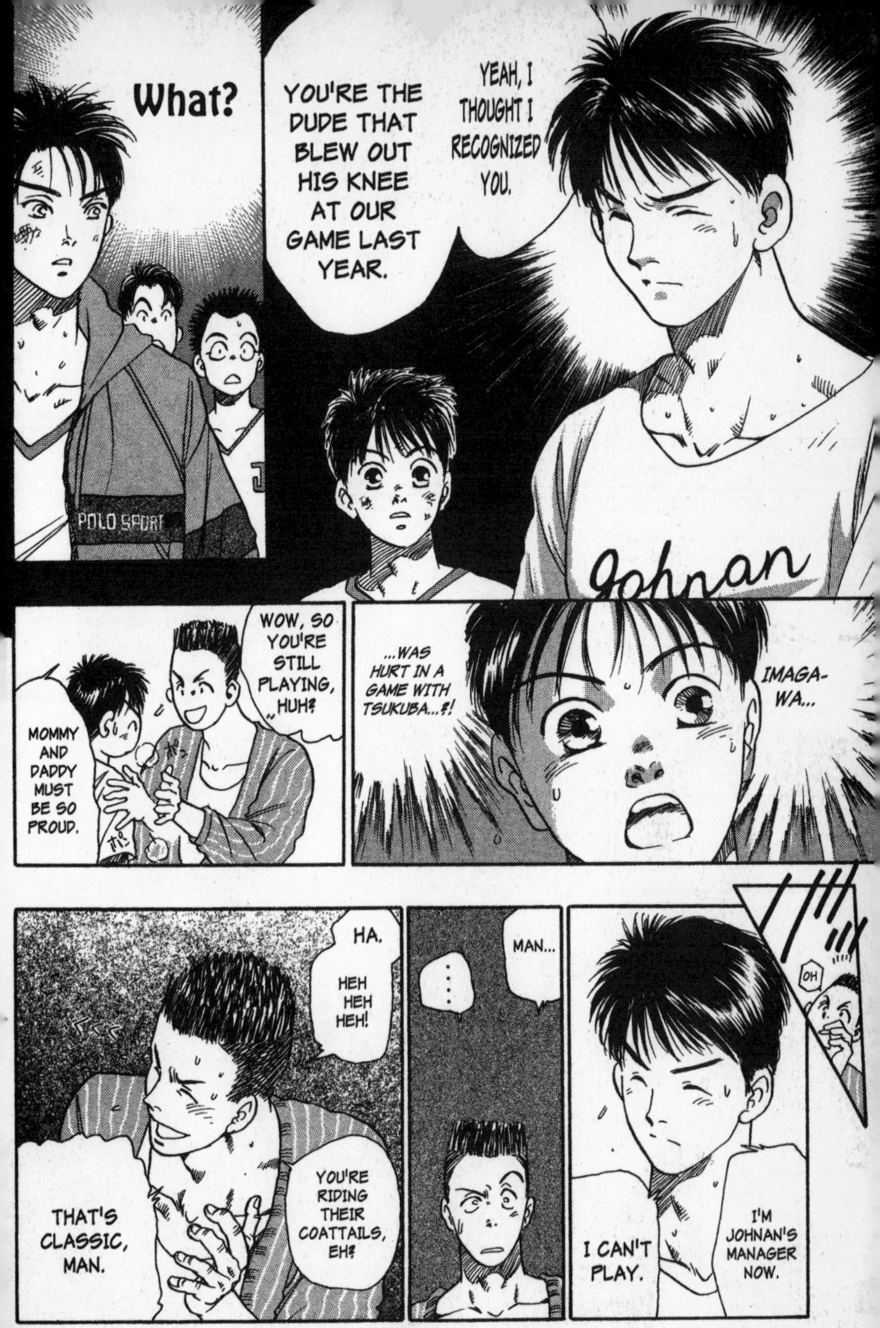
YEAH, I THOUGHT I RECOGNIZED YOU.
YOU'RE THE DUDE THAT BLEW OUT HIS KNEE AT OUR GAME LAST YEAR.
Johnan
What?
POLO SPORT
IMAGA-WA...
...WAS HURT IN A GAME WITH TSUKUBA...?!
WOW, SO YOU'RE STILL PLAYING, HUH?
MOMMY AND DADDY MUST BE SO PROUD.
OH
I'M JOHNAN'S MANAGER NOW.
I CAN'T PLAY.
MAN...
...
HA.
HEH HEH HEH!
YOU'RE RIDING THEIR COATTAILS, EH?
THAT'S CLASSIC, MAN.

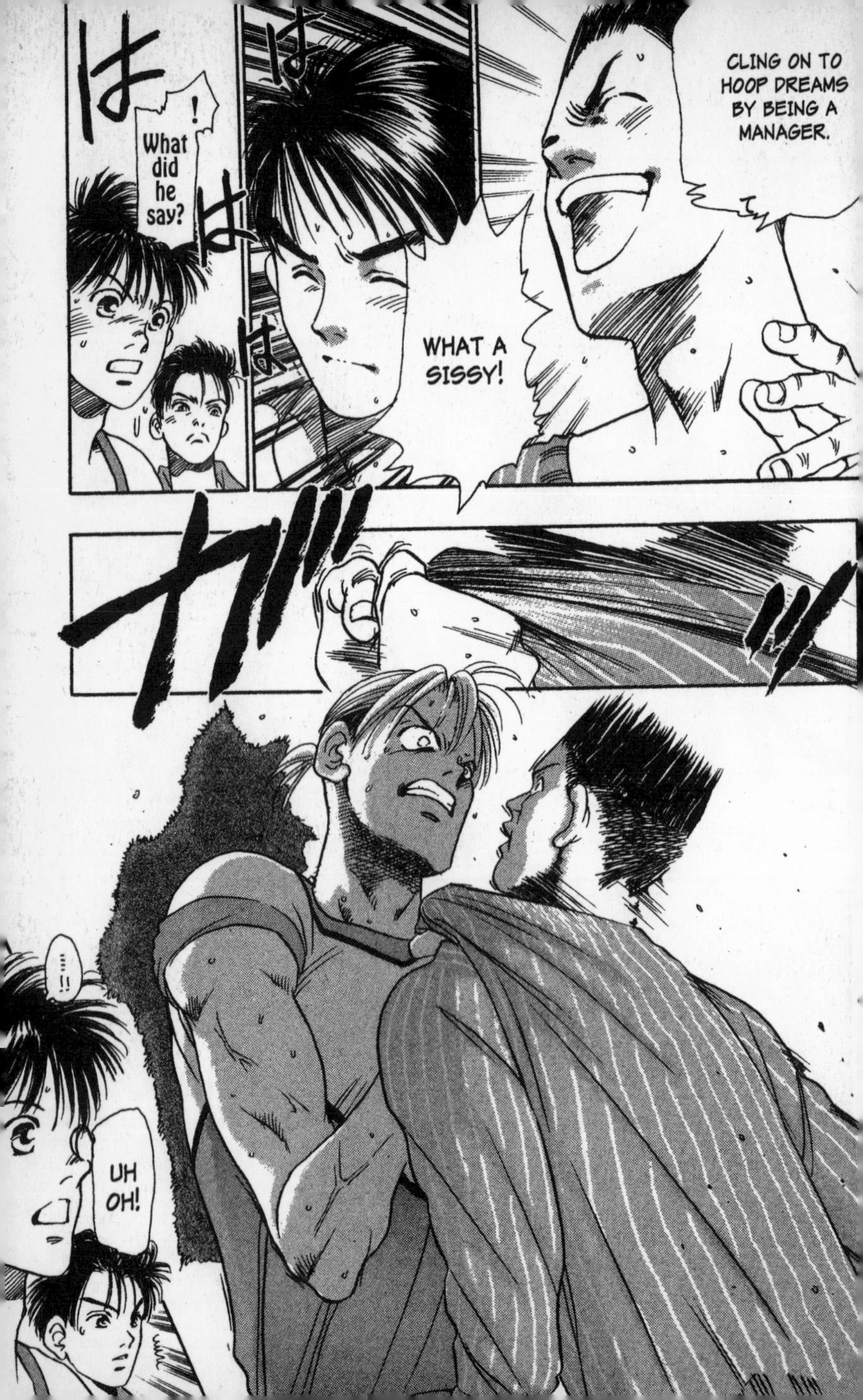

CLING ON TO HOOP DREAMS BY BEING A MANAGER.
WHAT A SISSY!
はははは
!
What did he say?
...!!
UH OH!

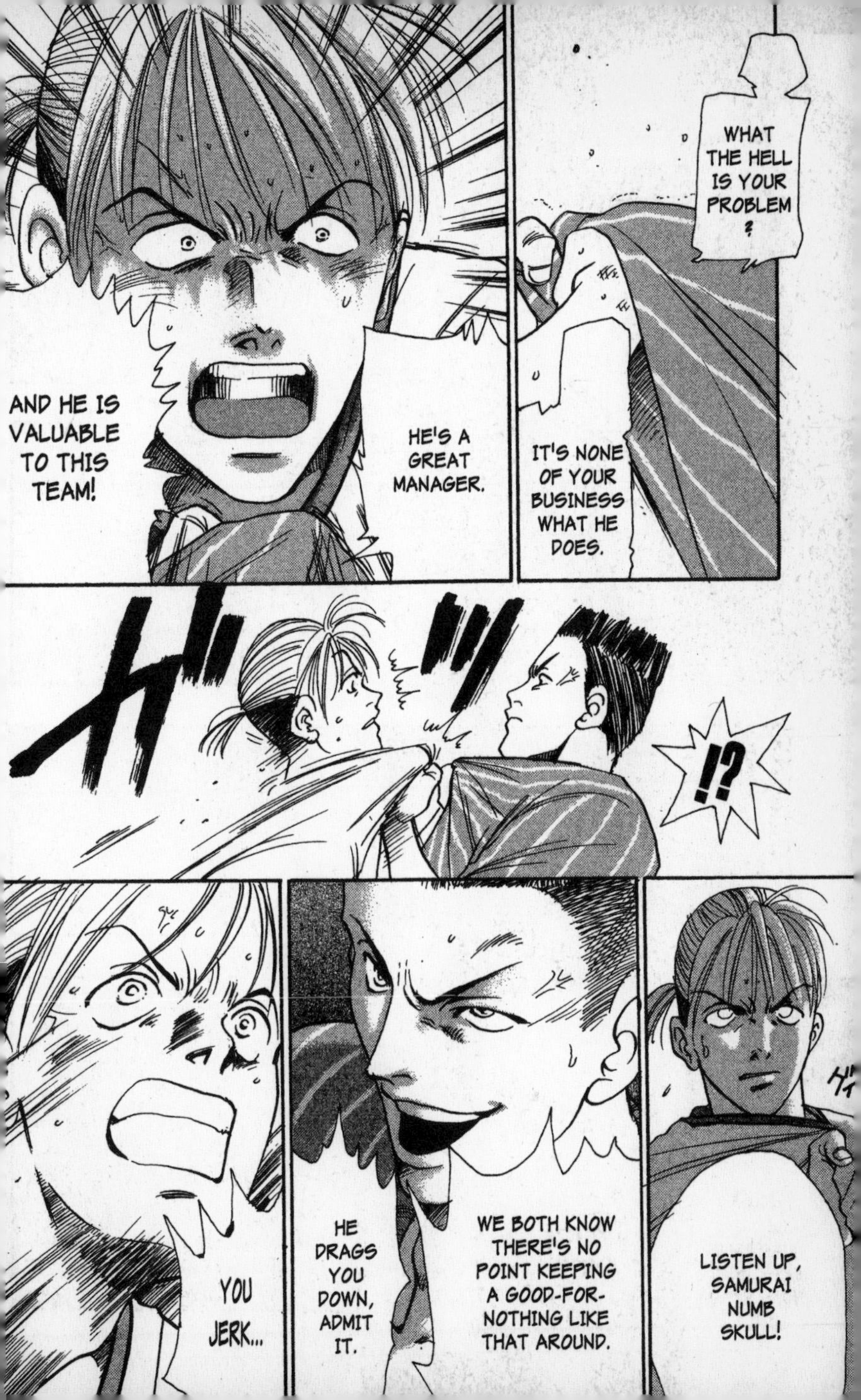
WHAT THE HELL IS YOUR PROBLEM ?
IT'S NONE OF YOUR BUSINESS WHAT HE DOES.
HE'S A GREAT MANAGER.
AND HE IS VALUABLE TO THIS TEAM!
!?
LISTEN UP, SAMURAI NUMB SKULL!
WE BOTH KNOW THERE'S NO POINT KEEPING A GOOD-FOR-NOTHING LIKE THAT AROUND.
HE DRAGS YOU DOWN, ADMIT IT.
YOU JERK...

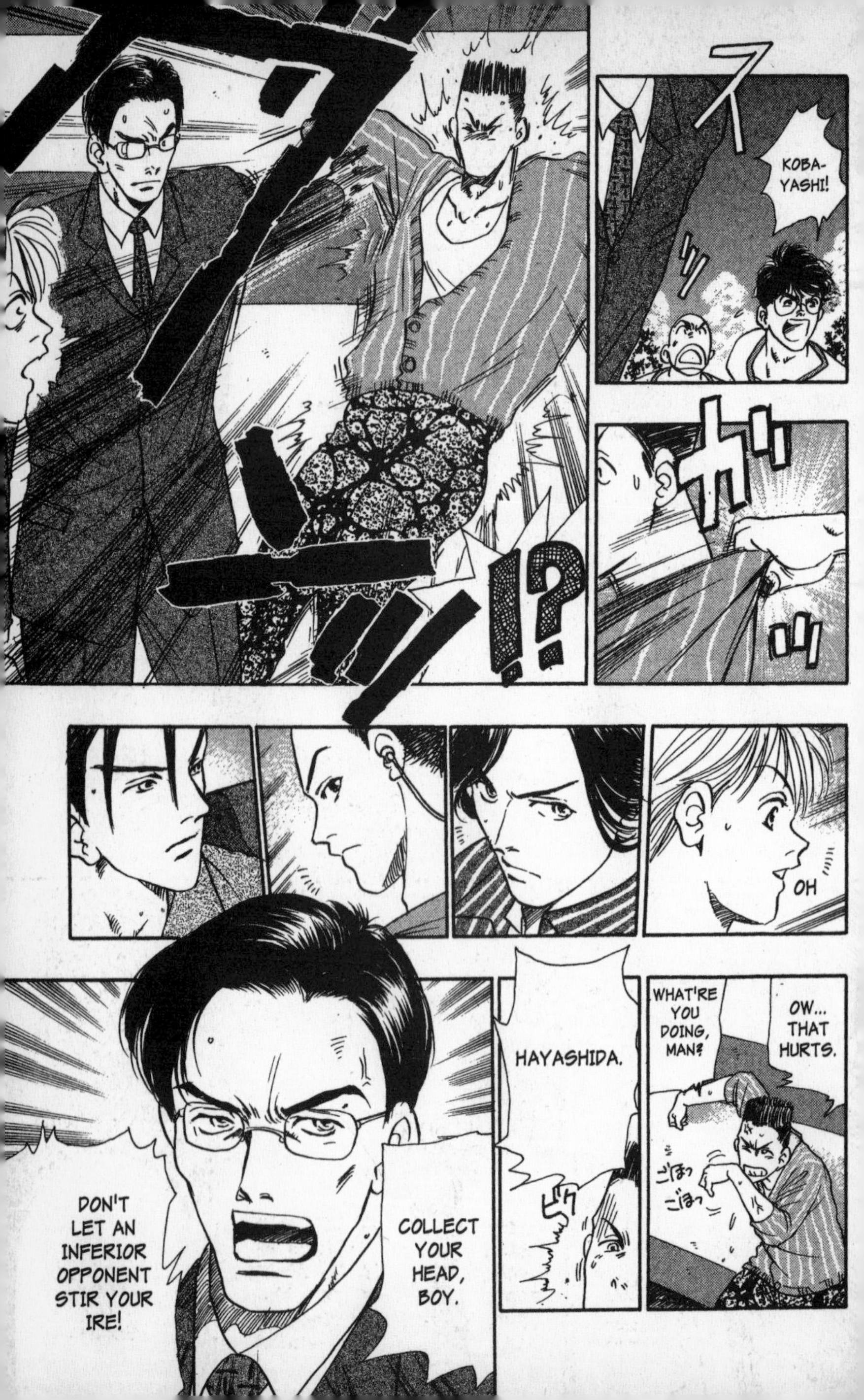
KOBA-
YASHI!
!?
OH
OW... THAT HURTS.
WHAT'RE YOU DOING, MAN?
ごほっ
ごほっ
HAYASHIDA.
COLLECT YOUR HEAD, BOY.
DON'T LET AN INFERIOR OPPONENT STIR YOUR IRE!

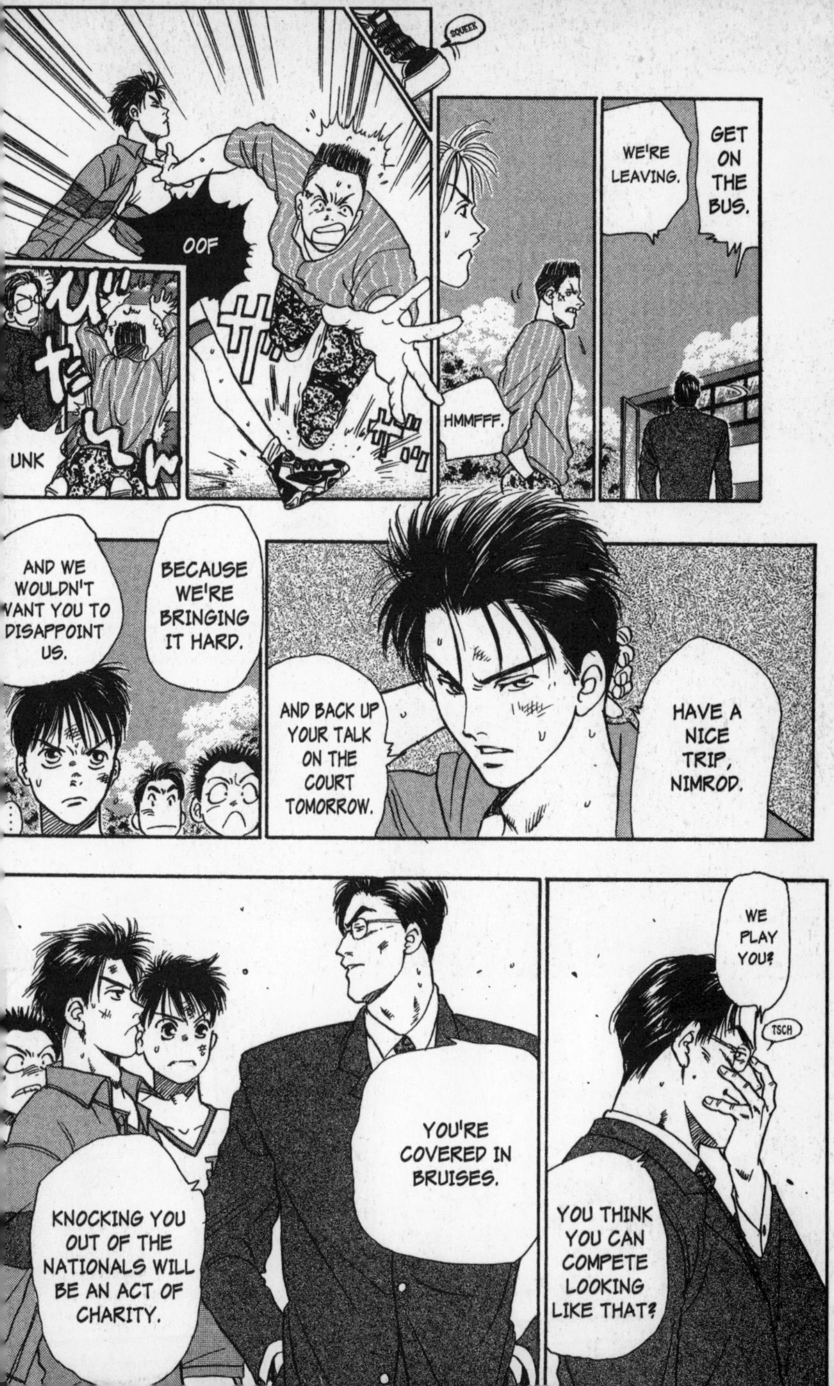
GET ON THE BUS.
WE'RE LEAVING.
HMMFFF.
SQUEEK
OOF
UNK
HAVE A NICE TRIP, NIMROD.
AND BACK UP YOUR TALK ON THE COURT TOMORROW.
BECAUSE WE'RE BRINGING IT HARD.
AND WE WOULDN'T WANT YOU TO DISAPPOINT US.
WE PLAY YOU?
TSCH
YOU THINK YOU CAN COMPETE LOOKING LIKE THAT?
YOU'RE COVERED IN BRUISES.
KNOCKING YOU OUT OF THE NATIONALS WILL BE AN ACT OF CHARITY.

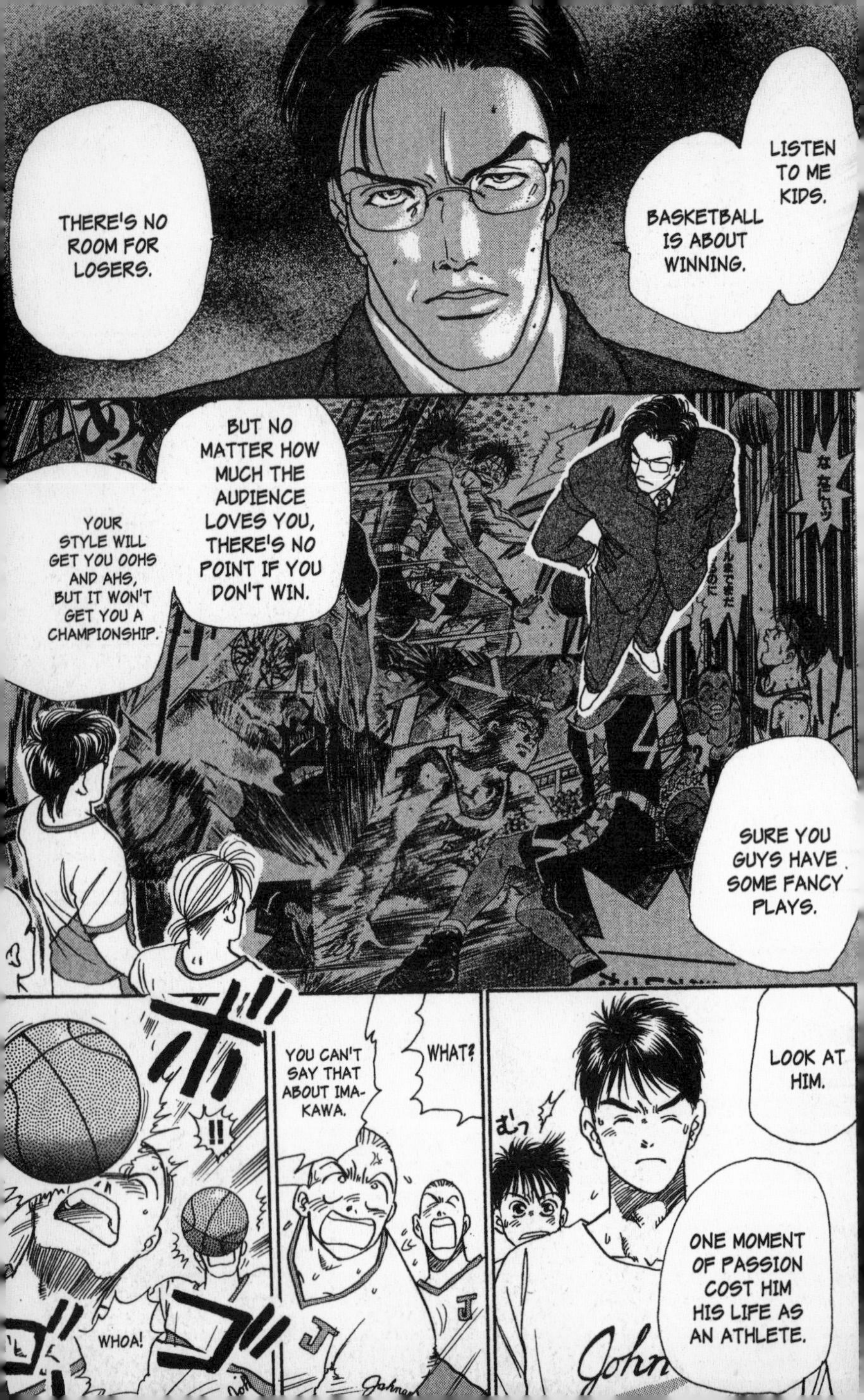
LISTEN TO ME KIDS.
BASKETBALL IS ABOUT WINNING.
THERE'S NO ROOM FOR LOSERS.
SURE YOU GUYS HAVE SOME FANCY PLAYS.
YOUR STYLE WILL GET YOU OOHS AND AHS, BUT IT WON'T GET YOU A CHAMPIONSHIP.
BUT NO MATTER HOW MUCH THE AUDIENCE LOVES YOU, THERE'S NO POINT IF YOU DON'T WIN.
LOOK AT HIM.
ONE MOMENT OF PASSION COST HIM HIS LIFE AS AN ATHLETE.
WHAT?
YOU CAN'T SAY THAT ABOUT IMA-KAWA.
!!
WHOA!

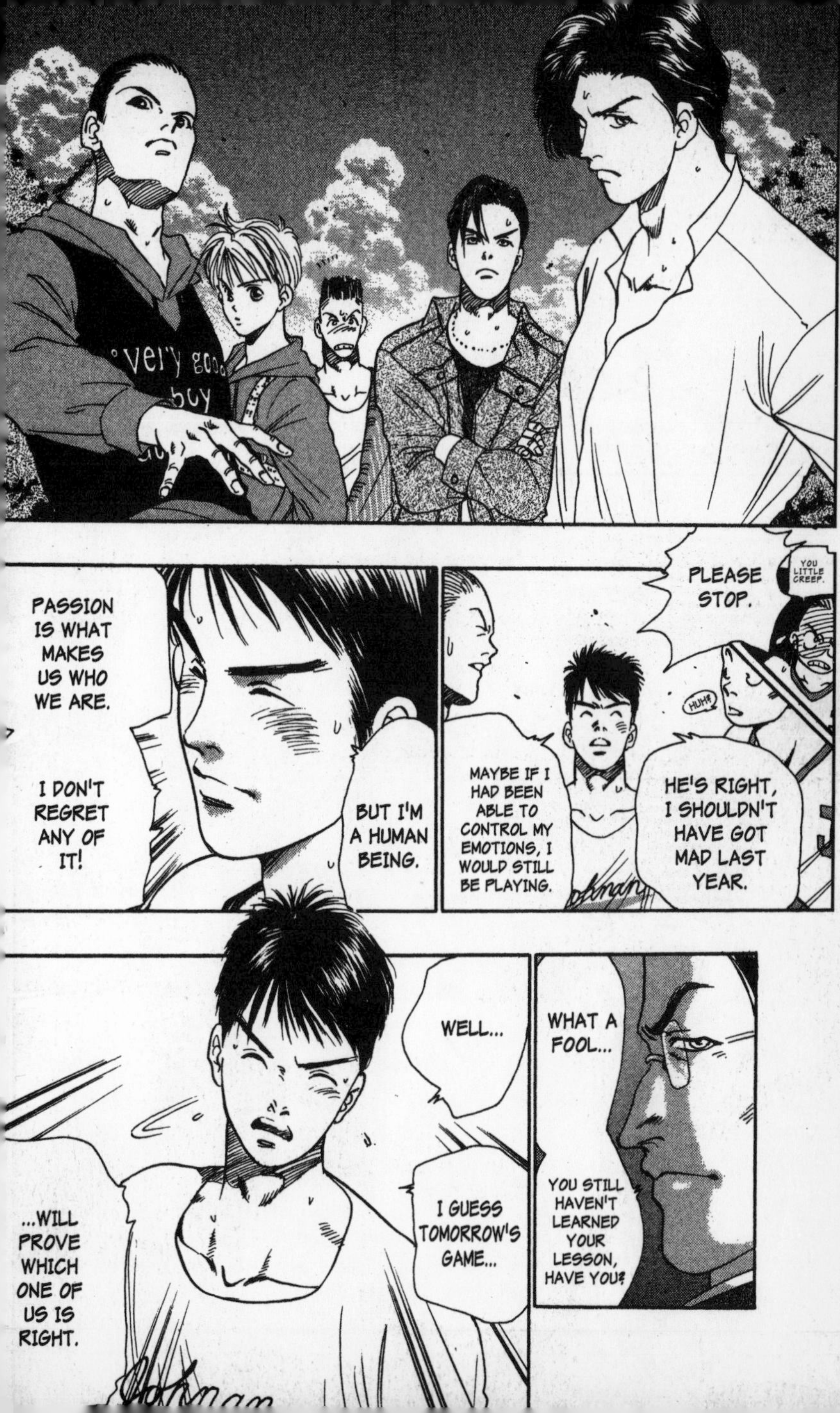

YOU LITTLE CREEP.
PLEASE STOP.
HUH?
HE'S RIGHT, I SHOULDN'T HAVE GOT MAD LAST YEAR.
MAYBE IF I HAD BEEN ABLE TO CONTROL MY EMOTIONS, I WOULD STILL BE PLAYING.
BUT I'M A HUMAN BEING.
PASSION IS WHAT MAKES US WHO WE ARE.
I DON'T REGRET ANY OF IT!
WHAT A FOOL...
YOU STILL HAVEN'T LEARNED YOUR LESSON, HAVE YOU?
WELL...
I GUESS TOMORROW'S GAME...
...WILL PROVE WHICH ONE OF US IS RIGHT.

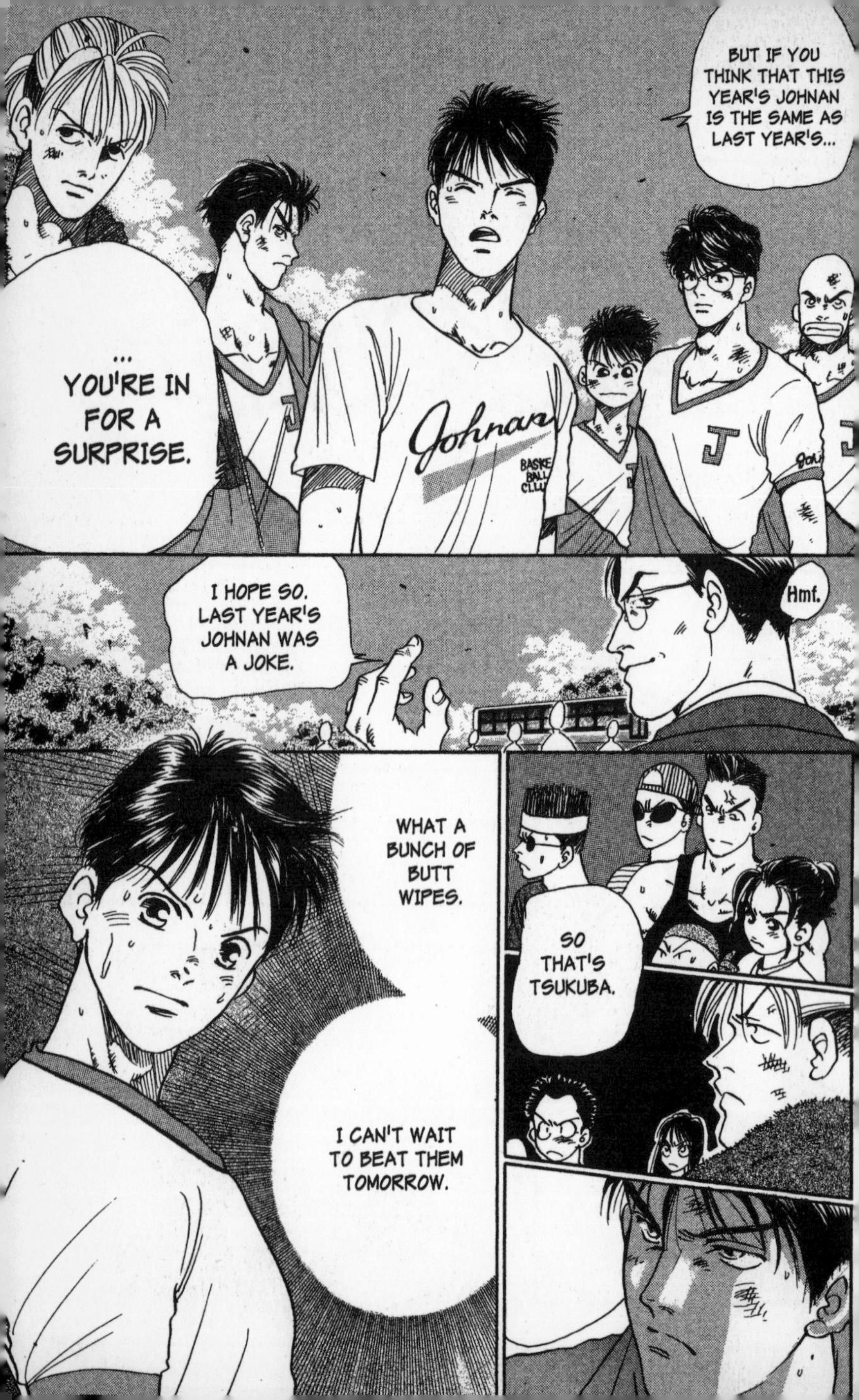
BUT IF YOU THINK THAT THIS YEAR'S JOHNAN IS THE SAME AS LAST YEAR'S...
... YOU'RE IN FOR A SURPRISE.
Johnan
Hmf.
I HOPE SO. LAST YEAR'S JOHNAN WAS A JOKE.
SO THAT'S TSUKUBA.
WHAT A BUNCH OF BUTT WIPES.
I CAN'T WAIT TO BEAT THEM TOMORROW.

REBOUND

HEY, THIS MANGA IS SO MUCH FUN!
I NEED MORE ON-PAGE TIME.
Hopefully you enjoy reading REBOUND as much as they enjoy being in it.
p.62

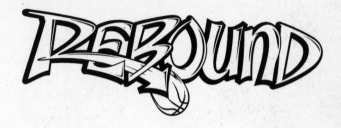

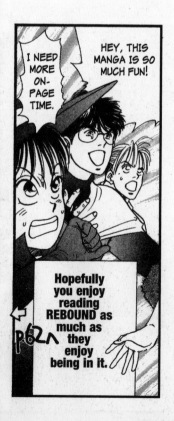

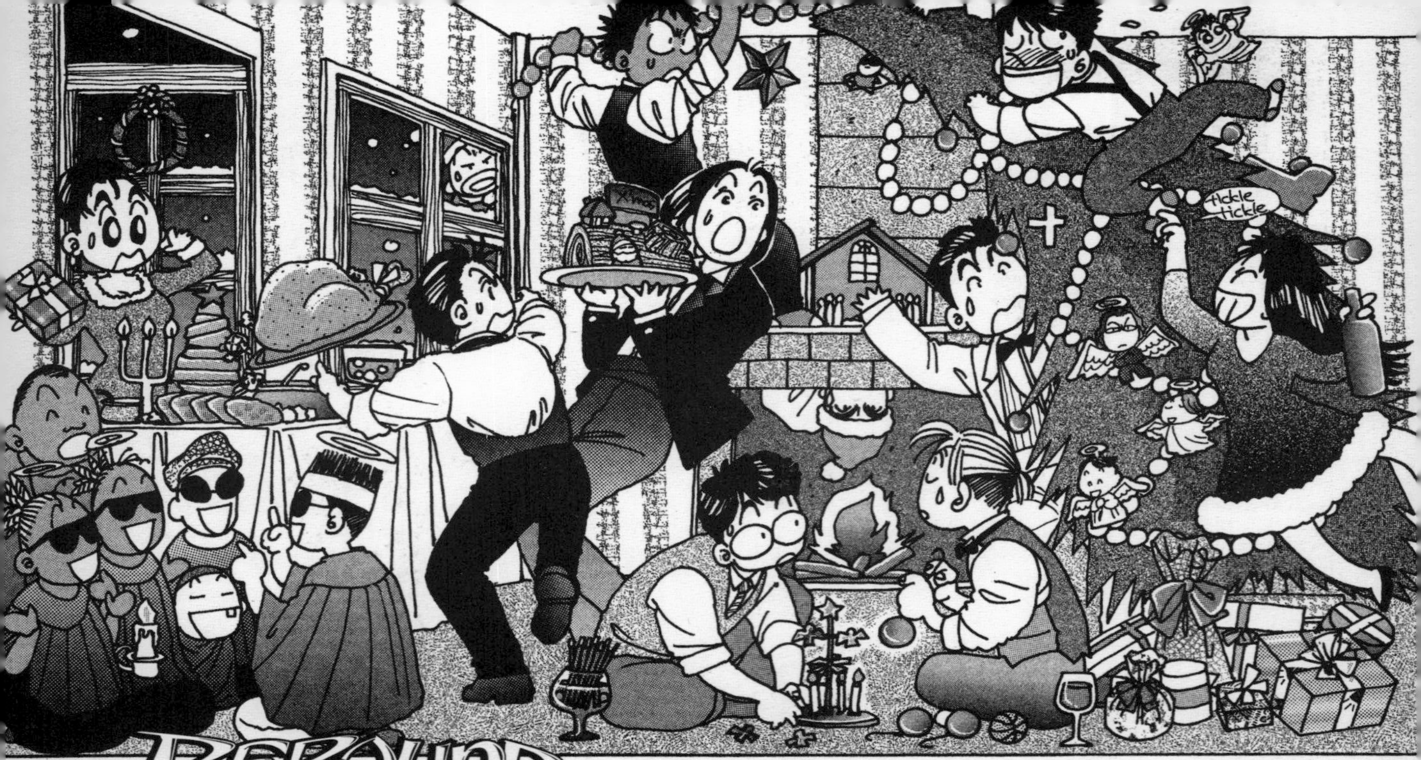
tickle tickle
X'mas

REBOUND

Episode 21: Shape of the Heart

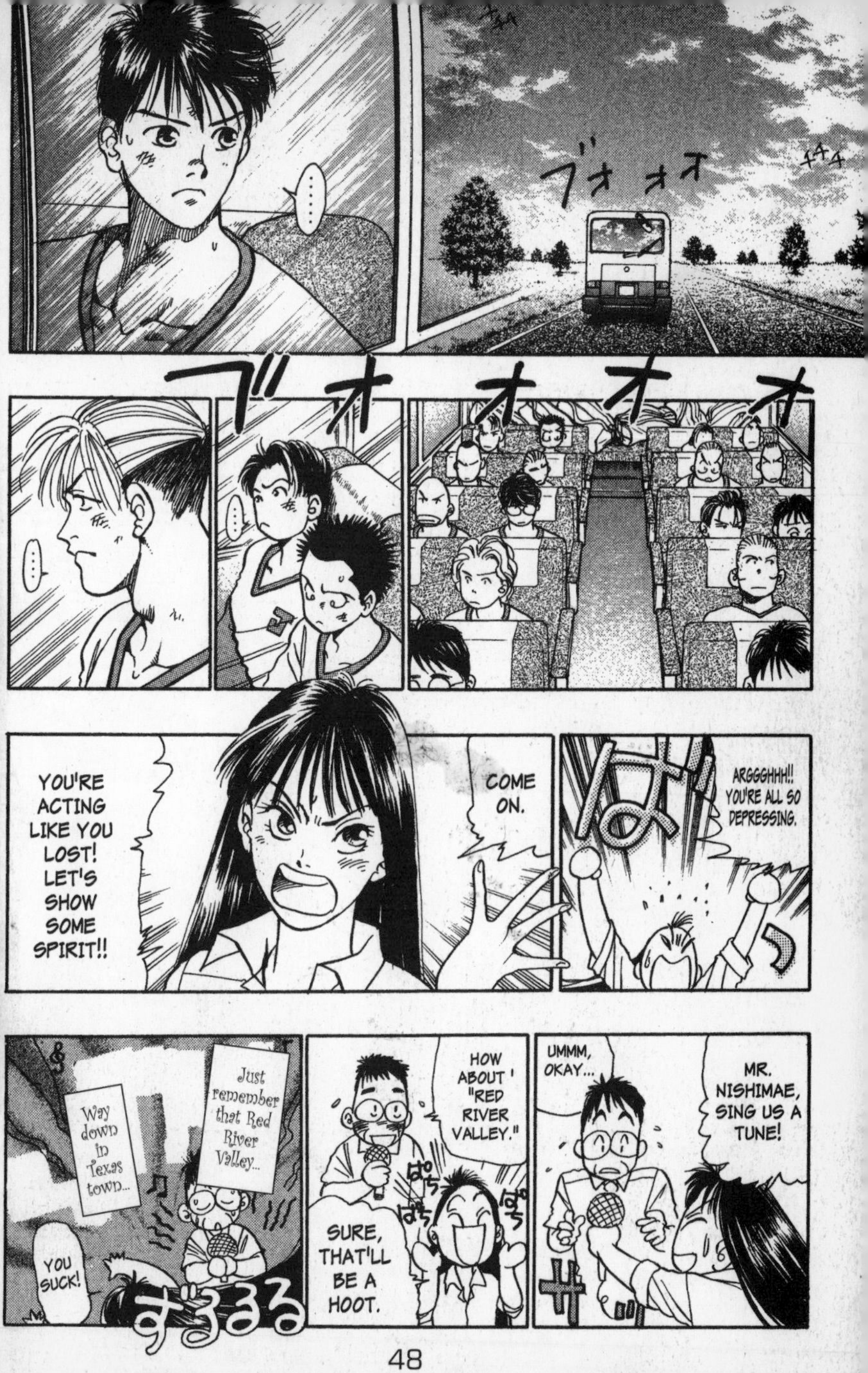
ブオオオ
……
ブオオオオ
……
……
は
ARGGGHHH!! YOU'RE ALL SO DEPRESSING.
COME ON.
YOU'RE ACTING LIKE YOU LOST! LET'S SHOW SOME SPIRIT!!
MR. NISHIMAE, SING US A TUNE!
UMMM, OKAY...
HOW ABOUT "RED RIVER VALLEY."
ぱち
ぱち
ぱち
SURE, THAT'LL BE A HOOT.
Just remember that Red River Valley...
Way down in Texas town...
YOU SUCK!
ずるるる

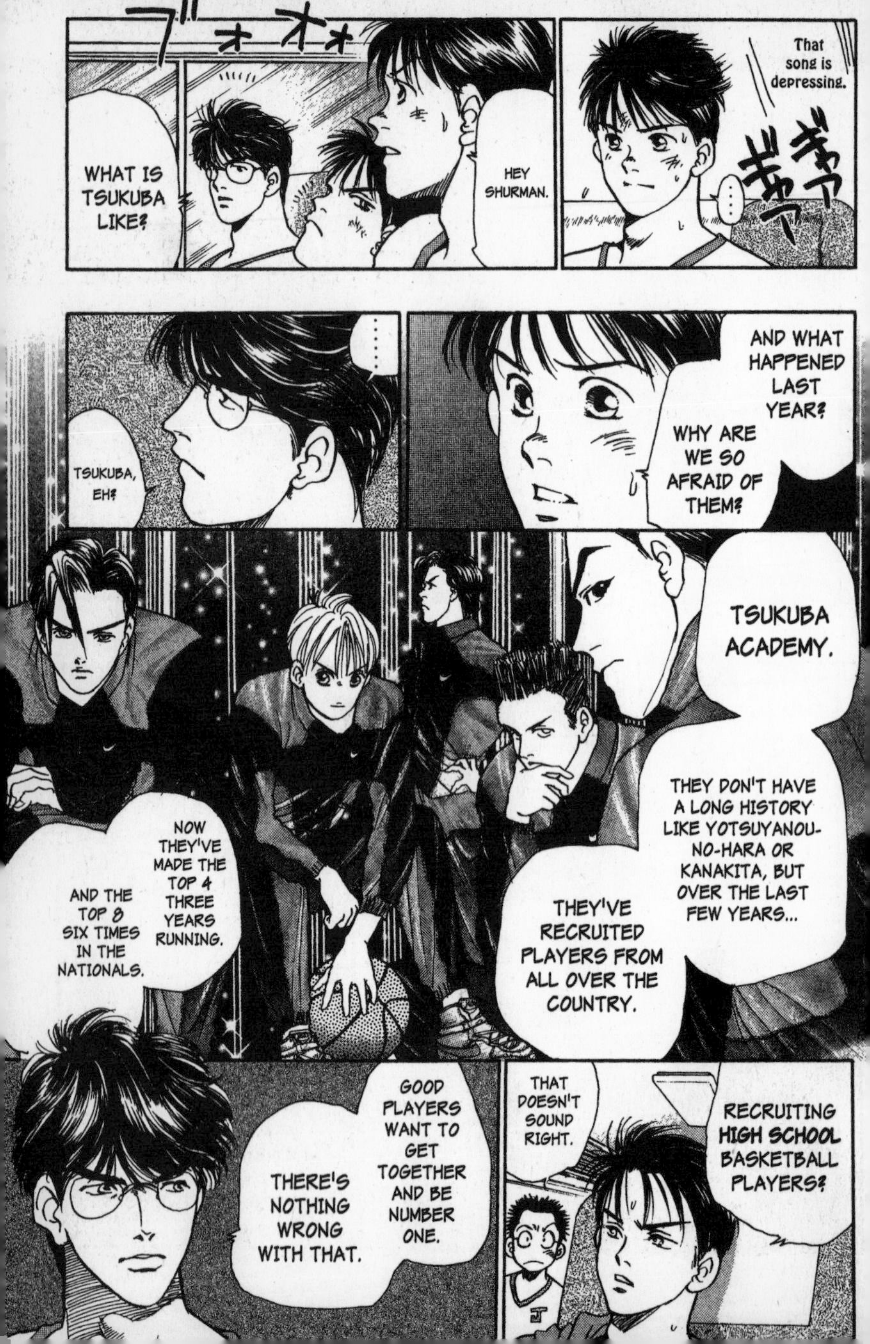
That song is depressing.
...
ギャア ギャア
HEY SHURMAN.
ブォオオ
WHAT IS TSUKUBA LIKE?
AND WHAT HAPPENED LAST YEAR?
WHY ARE WE SO AFRAID OF THEM?
...
TSUKUBA, EH?
TSUKUBA ACADEMY.
THEY DON'T HAVE A LONG HISTORY LIKE YOTSUYANOU-NO-HARA OR KANAKITA, BUT OVER THE LAST FEW YEARS...
THEY'VE RECRUITED PLAYERS FROM ALL OVER THE COUNTRY.
NOW THEY'VE MADE THE TOP 4 THREE YEARS RUNNING.
AND THE TOP 8 SIX TIMES IN THE NATIONALS.
RECRUITING HIGH SCHOOL BASKETBALL PLAYERS?
THAT DOESN'T SOUND RIGHT.
GOOD PLAYERS WANT TO GET TOGETHER AND BE NUMBER ONE.
THERE'S NOTHING WRONG WITH THAT.

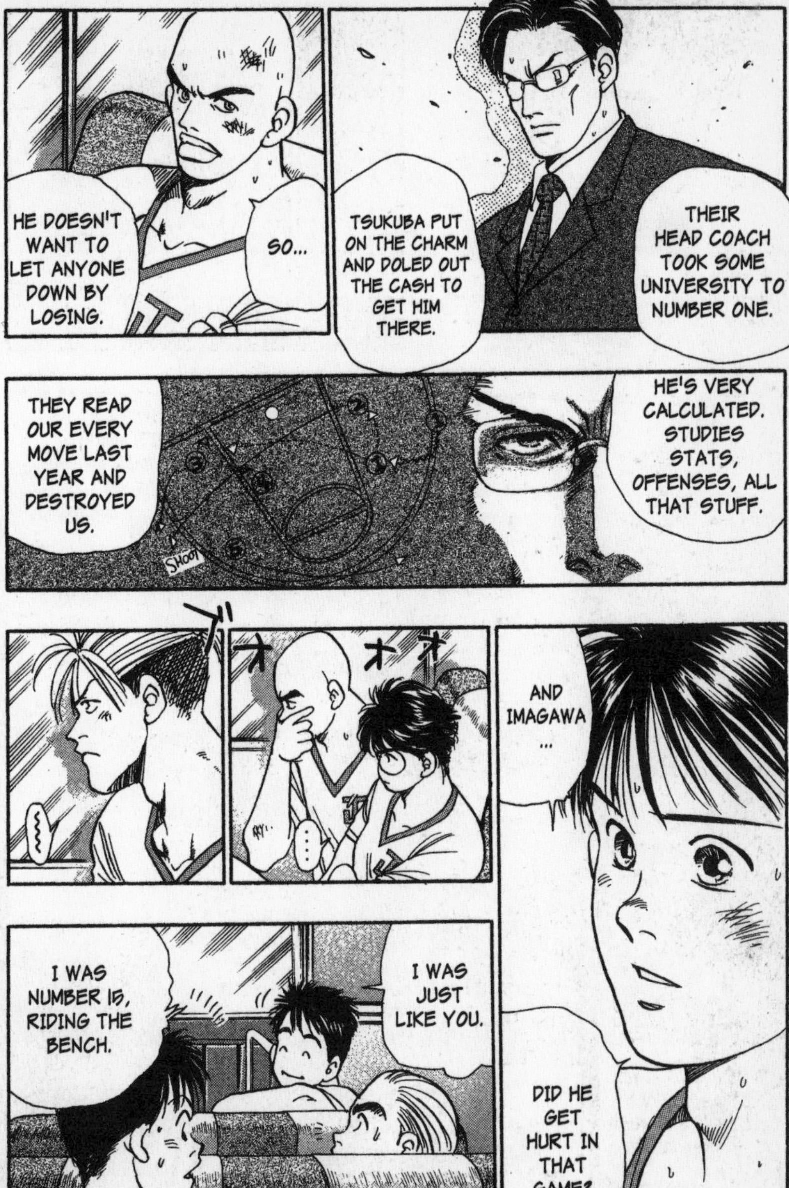
THEIR HEAD COACH TOOK SOME UNIVERSITY TO NUMBER ONE.
TSUKUBA PUT ON THE CHARM AND DOLED OUT THE CASH TO GET HIM THERE.
SO...
HE DOESN'T WANT TO LET ANYONE DOWN BY LOSING.
HE'S VERY CALCULATED. STUDIES STATS, OFFENSES, ALL THAT STUFF.
THEY READ OUR EVERY MOVE LAST YEAR AND DESTROYED US.
SHOOT
AND IMAGAWA ...
DID HE GET HURT IN THAT GAME?
...
...
I WAS JUST LIKE YOU.
I WAS NUMBER 15, RIDING THE BENCH.
WHA?

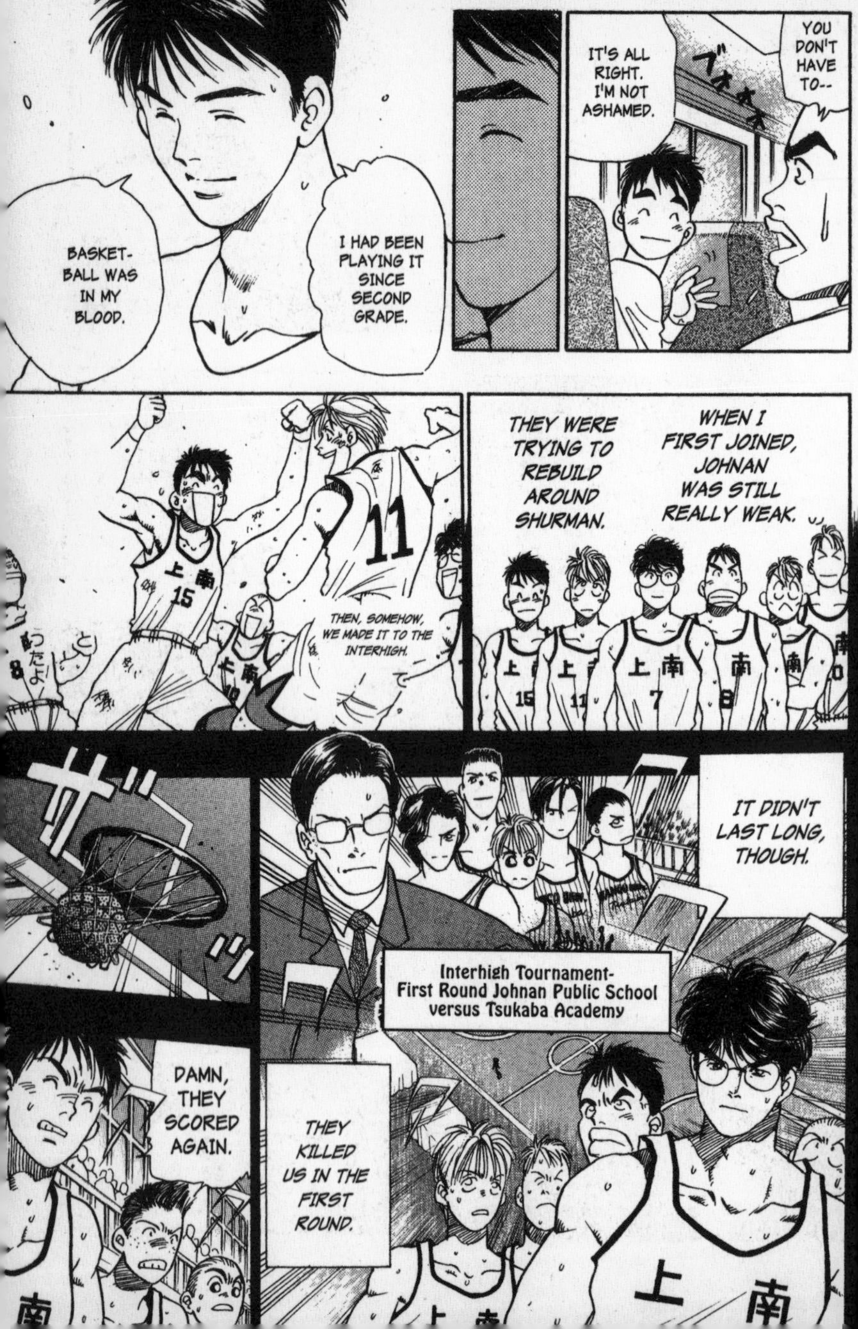
YOU DON'T HAVE TO--
IT'S ALL RIGHT. I'M NOT ASHAMED.
I HAD BEEN PLAYING IT SINCE SECOND GRADE.
BASKET-BALL WAS IN MY BLOOD.
WHEN I FIRST JOINED, JOHNAN WAS STILL REALLY WEAK.
THEY WERE TRYING TO REBUILD AROUND SHURMAN.
THEN, SOMEHOW, WE MADE IT TO THE INTERHIGH.
IT DIDN'T LAST LONG, THOUGH.
Interhigh Tournament-
First Round Johnan Public School
versus Tsukaba Academy
ザッ
THEY KILLED US IN THE FIRST ROUND.
DAMN, THEY SCORED AGAIN.

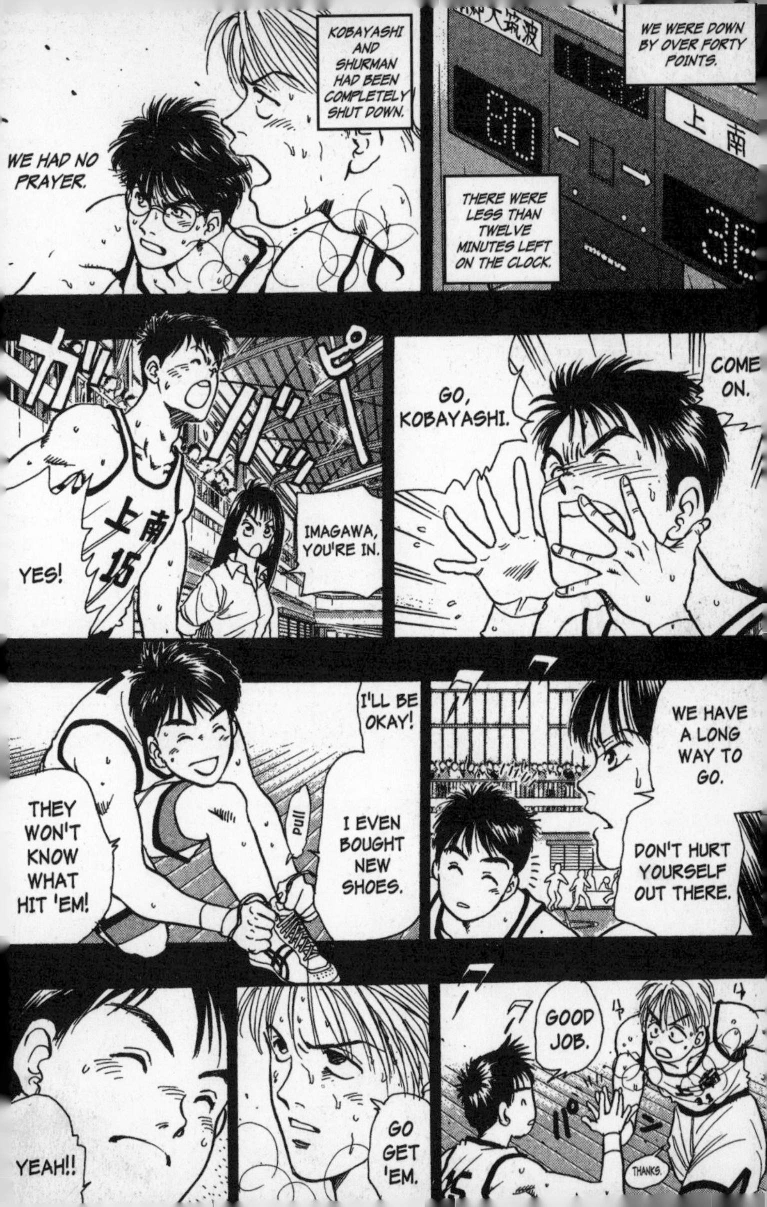
WE WERE DOWN BY OVER FORTY POINTS.
THERE WERE LESS THAN TWELVE MINUTES LEFT ON THE CLOCK.
KOBAYASHI AND SHURMAN HAD BEEN COMPLETELY SHUT DOWN.
WE HAD NO PRAYER.
COME ON.
GO, KOBAYASHI.
IMAGAWA, YOU'RE IN.
YES!
WE HAVE A LONG WAY TO GO.
DON'T HURT YOURSELF OUT THERE.
I'LL BE OKAY!
I EVEN BOUGHT NEW SHOES.
PULL
THEY WON'T KNOW WHAT HIT 'EM!
GOOD JOB.
THANKS.
GO GET 'EM.
YEAH!!

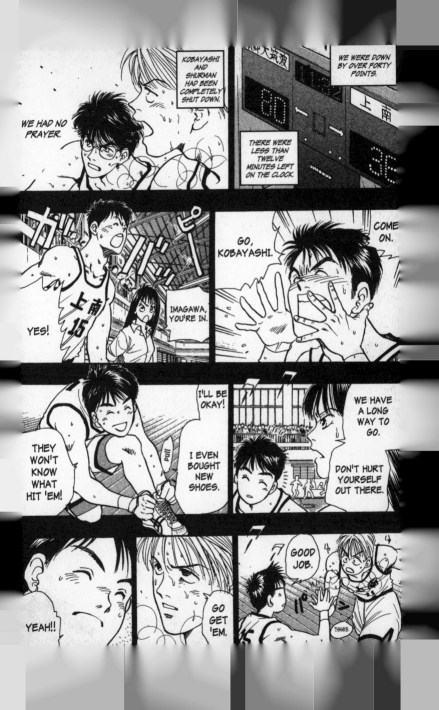

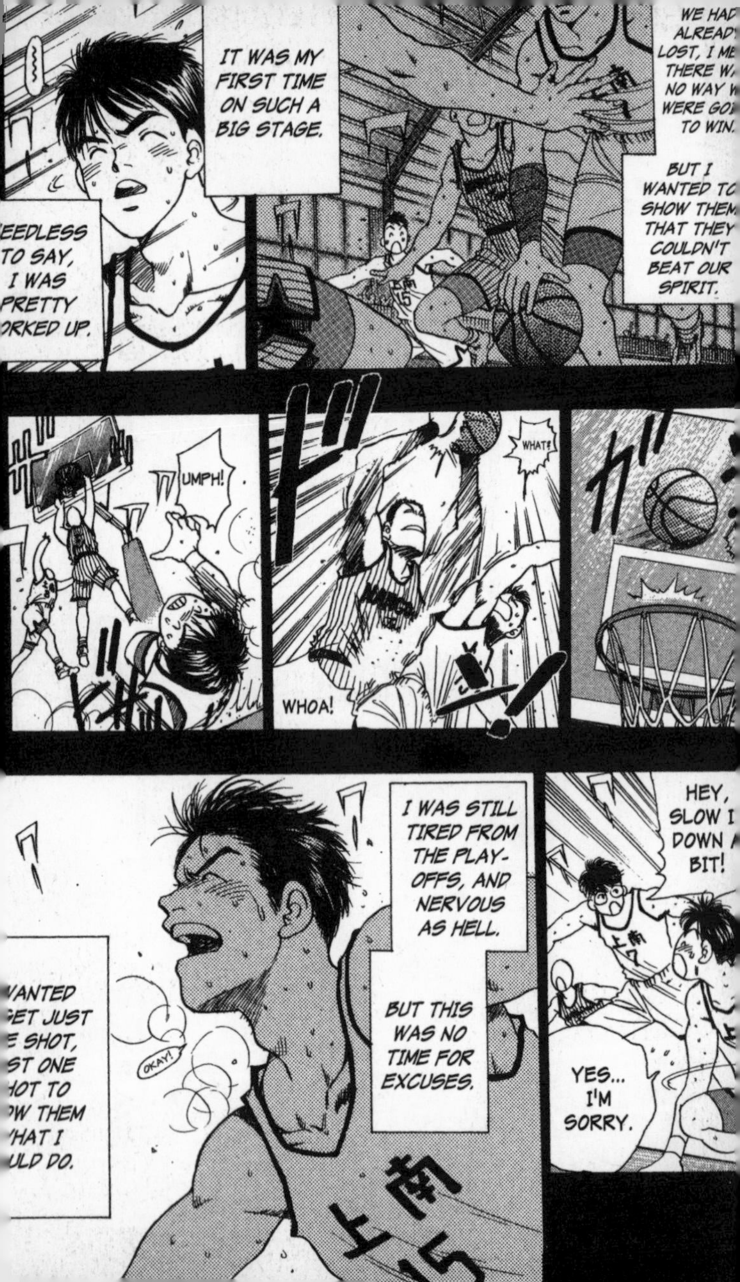

WE HAD ALREADY LOST, I ME THERE W NO WAY W WERE GO TO WIN.
BUT I WANTED TO SHOW THEM THAT THEY COULDN'T BEAT OUR SPIRIT.
IT WAS MY FIRST TIME ON SUCH A BIG STAGE.
...
EEDLESS TO SAY, I WAS PRETTY ORKED UP.
WHAT!?
WHOA!
UMPH!
HEY, SLOW I DOWN A BIT!
YES... I'M SORRY.
I WAS STILL TIRED FROM THE PLAY-OFFS, AND NERVOUS AS HELL.
BUT THIS WAS NO TIME FOR EXCUSES.
OKAY!
VANTED GET JUST E SHOT, ST ONE HOT TO OW THEM VHAT I ULD DO.

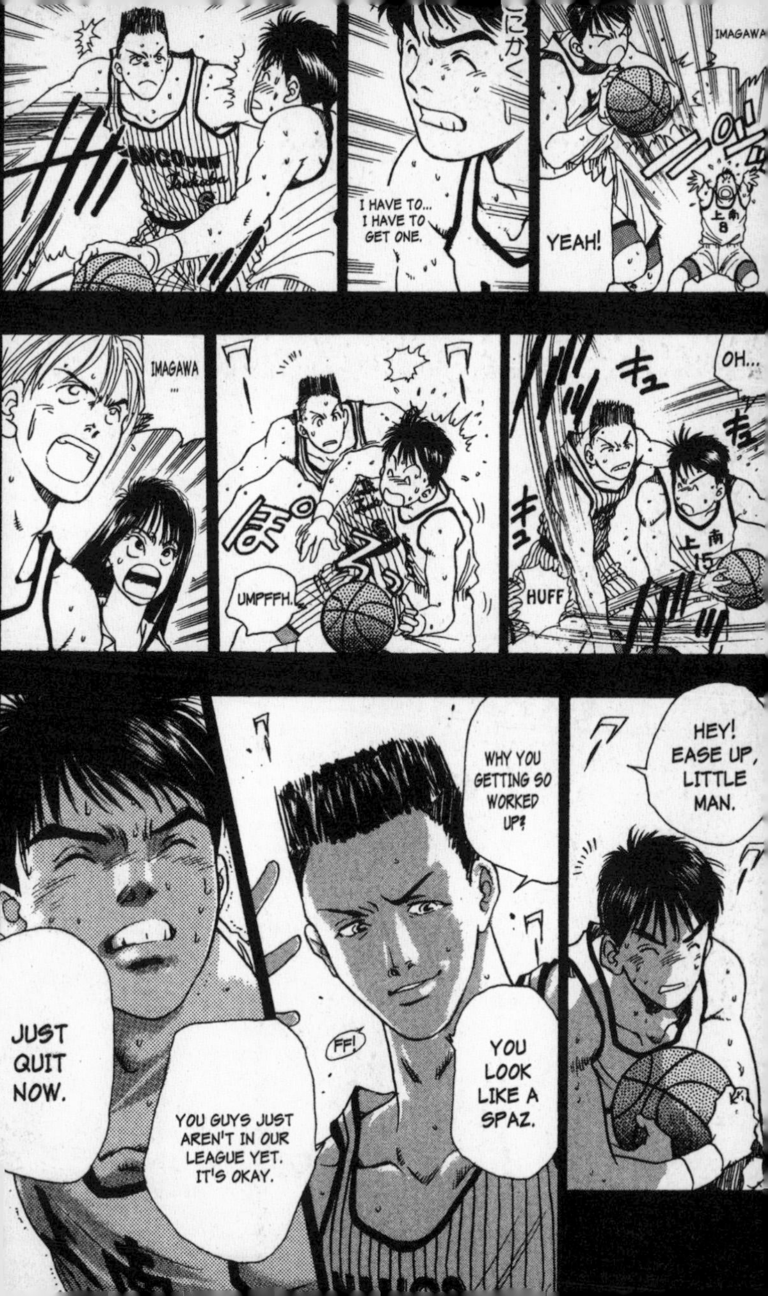
IMAGAWA
YEAH!
にかく
I HAVE TO... I HAVE TO GET ONE.
OH...
HUFF
UMPFFH.
IMAGAWA ...
HEY! EASE UP, LITTLE MAN.
WHY YOU GETTING SO WORKED UP?
YOU LOOK LIKE A SPAZ.
FF!
JUST QUIT NOW.
YOU GUYS JUST AREN'T IN OUR LEAGUE YET. IT'S OKAY.

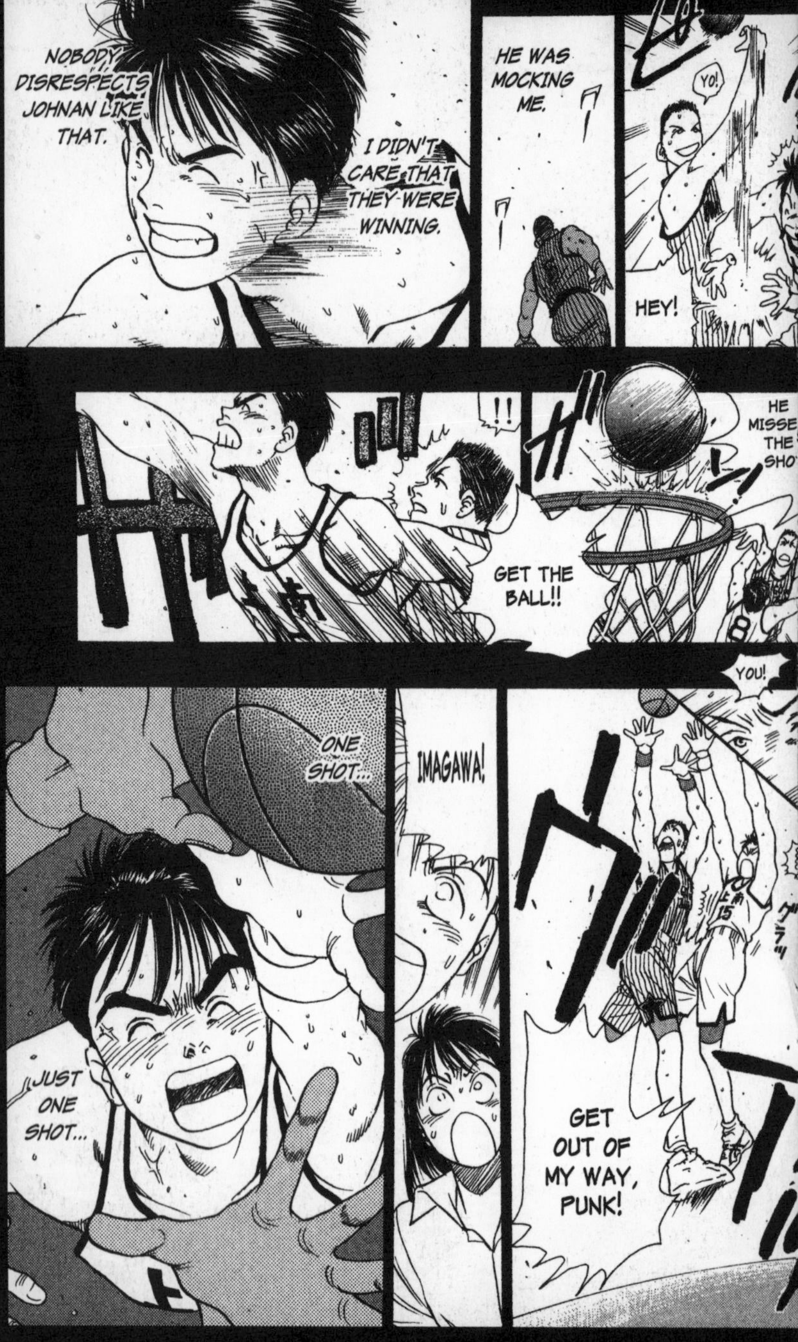
YO!
HEY!
HE WAS MOCKING ME.
NOBODY DISRESPECTS JOHNAN LIKE THAT.
I DIDN'T CARE THAT THEY WERE WINNING.
HE MISSE THE SHO
!!
GET THE BALL!!
YOU!
GET OUT OF MY WAY, PUNK!
IMAGAWA!
ONE SHOT...
JUST ONE SHOT...

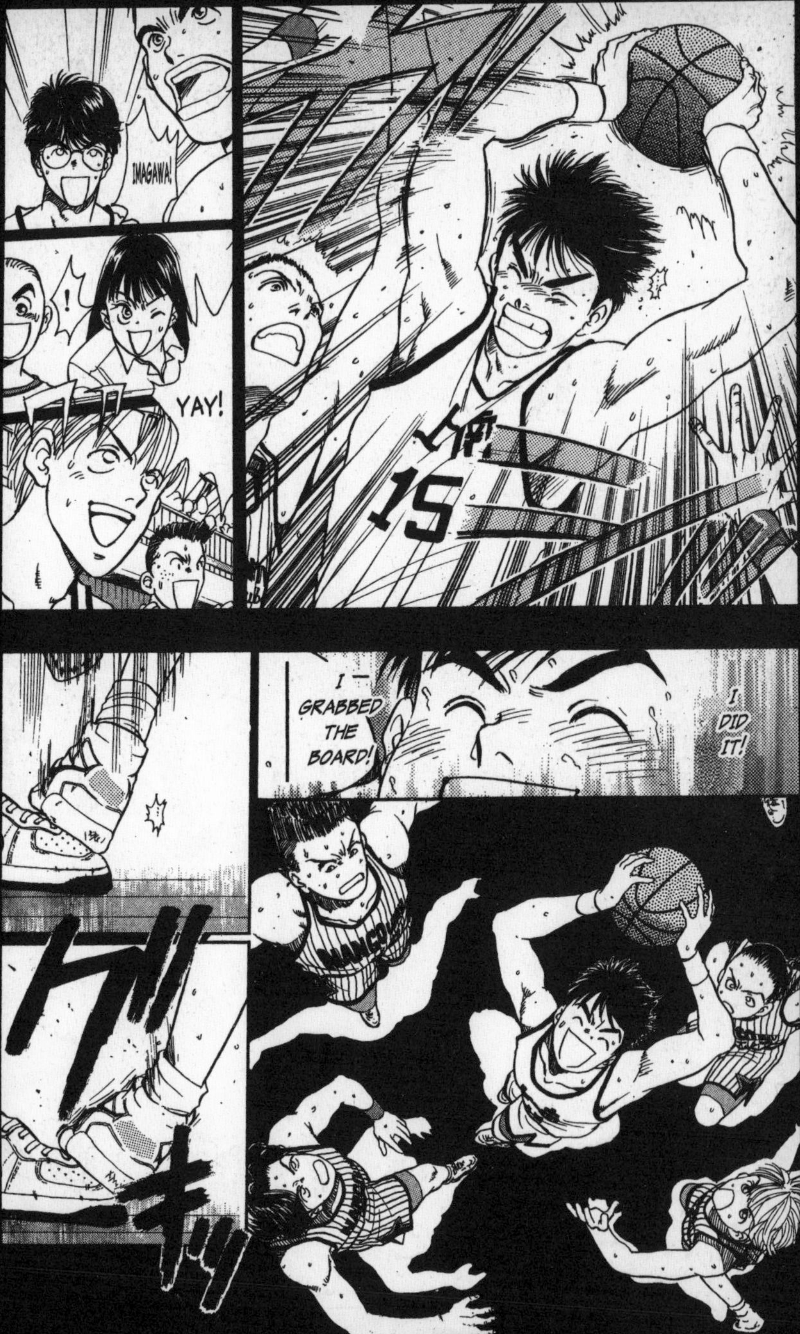
IMAGAWA!
!
YAY!
I DID IT!
I — GRABBED THE BOARD!
!

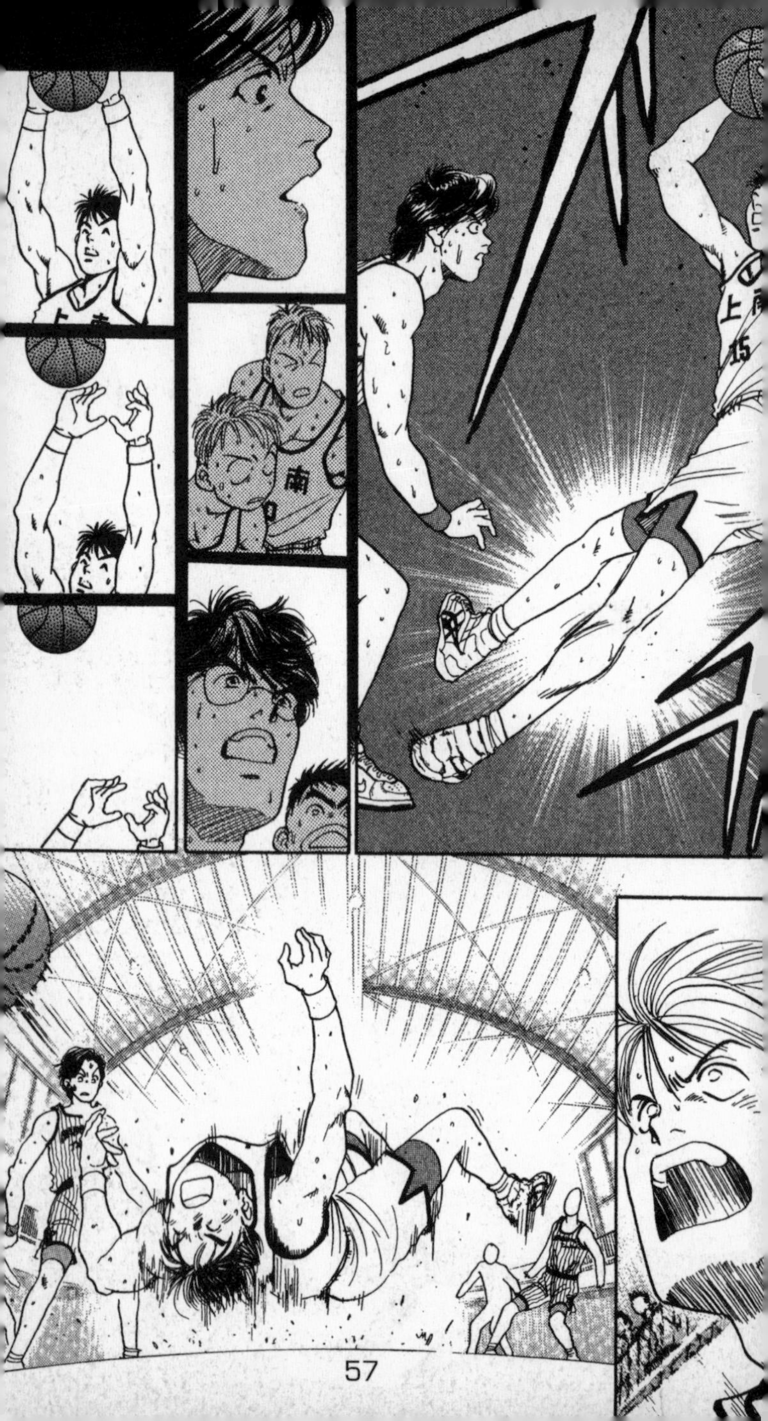

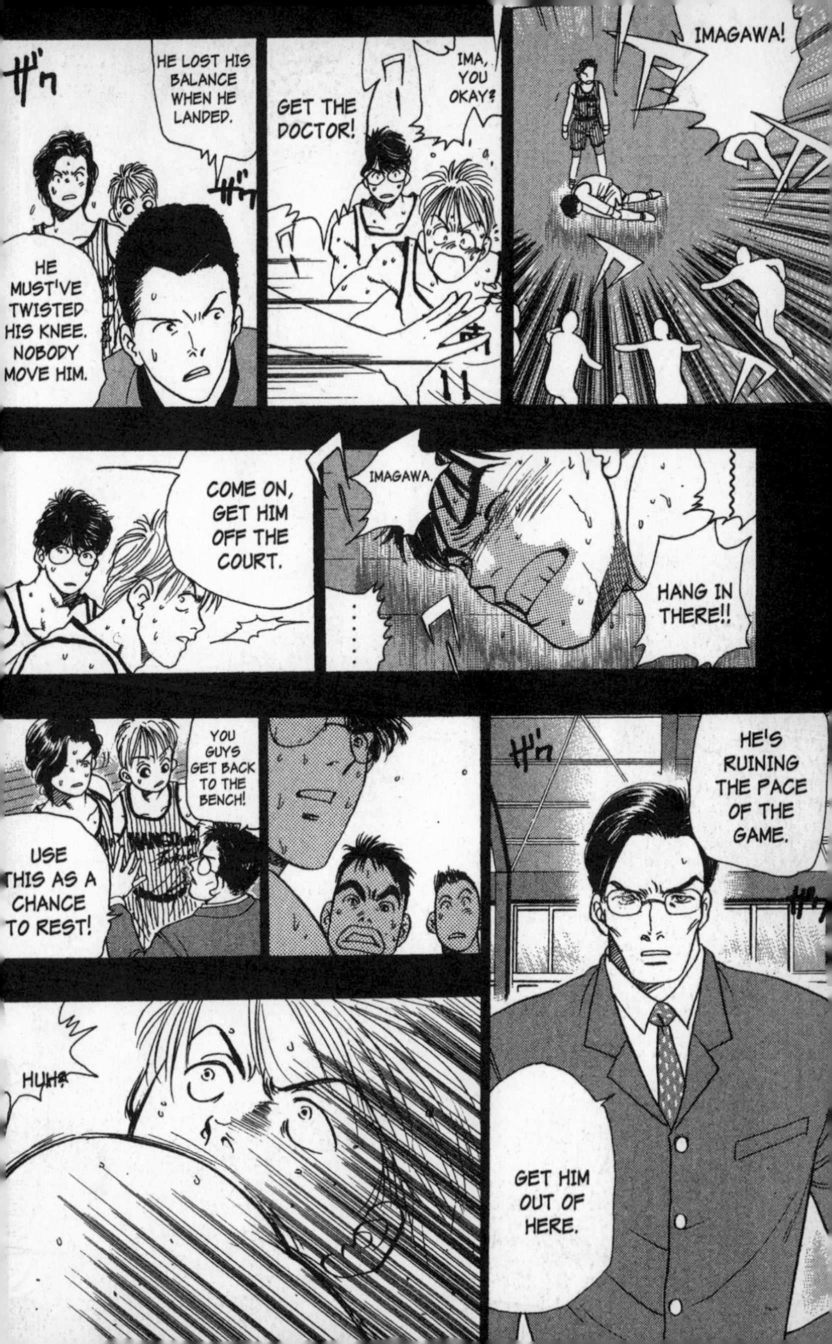
IMAGAWA!
IMA, YOU OKAY?
GET THE DOCTOR!
ザワ
HE LOST HIS BALANCE WHEN HE LANDED.
ザワ
HE MUST'VE TWISTED HIS KNEE. NOBODY MOVE HIM.
IMAGAWA.
HANG IN THERE!!
.....
COME ON, GET HIM OFF THE COURT.
ザワ
HE'S RUINING THE PACE OF THE GAME.
ザワ
GET HIM OUT OF HERE.
YOU GUYS GET BACK TO THE BENCH!
USE THIS AS A CHANCE TO REST!
HUH?

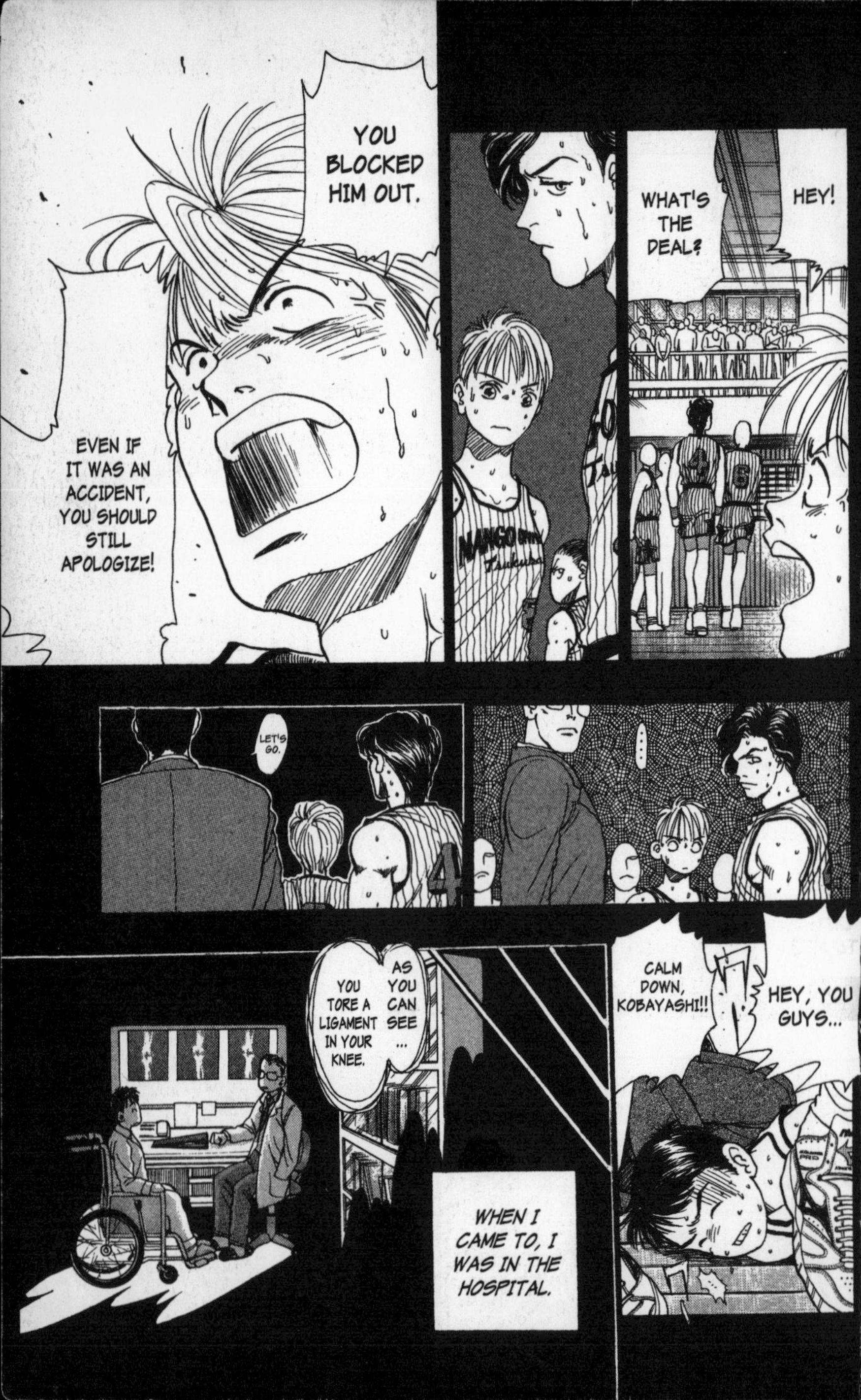
HEY!
WHAT'S THE DEAL?
YOU BLOCKED HIM OUT.
EVEN IF IT WAS AN ACCIDENT, YOU SHOULD STILL APOLOGIZE!
...
LET'S GO.
HEY, YOU GUYS...
CALM DOWN, KOBAYASHI!!
WHEN I CAME TO, I WAS IN THE HOSPITAL.
AS YOU CAN SEE ...
YOU TORE A LIGAMENT IN YOUR KNEE.

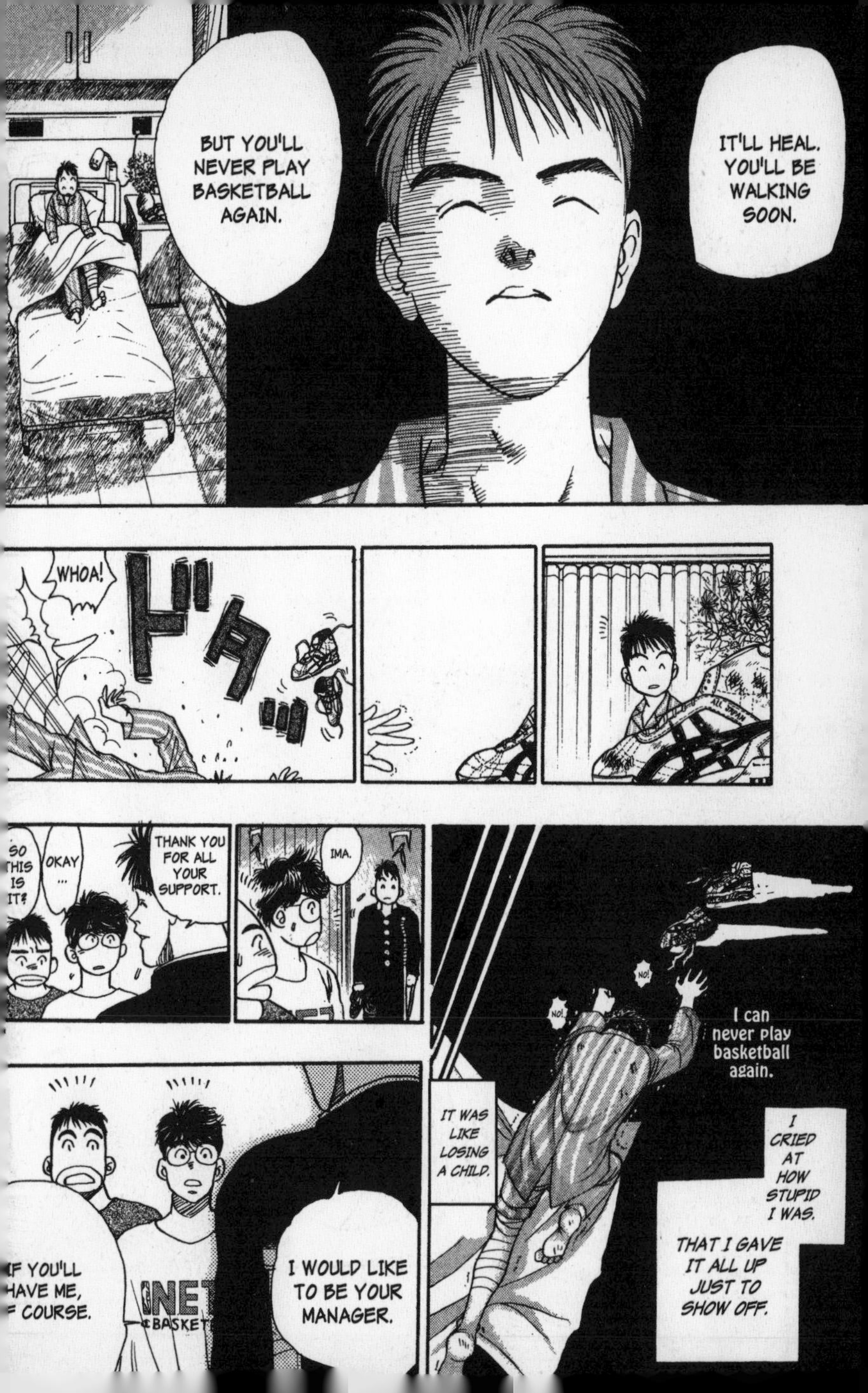
IT'LL HEAL. YOU'LL BE WALKING SOON.
BUT YOU'LL NEVER PLAY BASKETBALL AGAIN.
WHOA!
ドタッ
NO!
NO!
I can never play basketball again.
IT WAS LIKE LOSING A CHILD.
I CRIED AT HOW STUPID I WAS.
THAT I GAVE IT ALL UP JUST TO SHOW OFF.
IMA.
THANK YOU FOR ALL YOUR SUPPORT.
OKAY ...
SO THIS IS IT?
I WOULD LIKE TO BE YOUR MANAGER.
F YOU'LL HAVE ME, F COURSE.

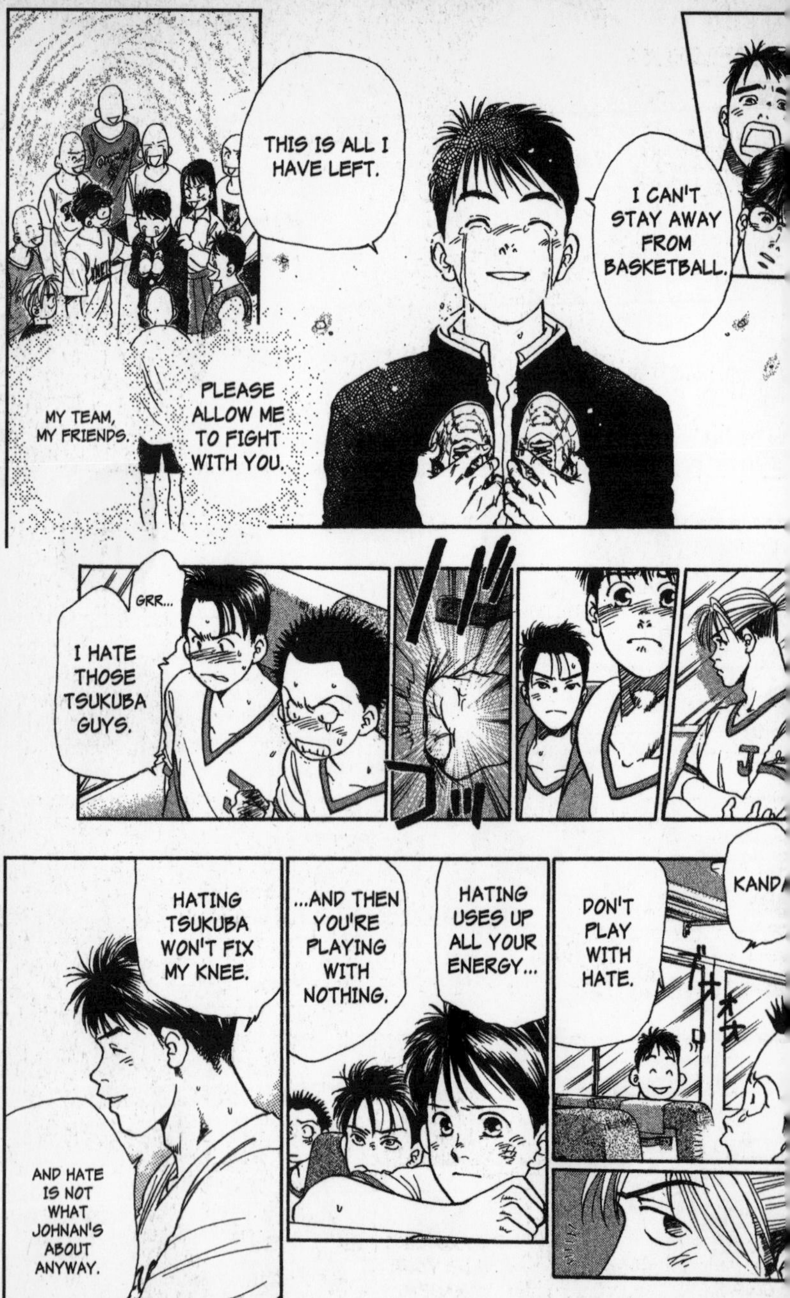
I CAN'T STAY AWAY FROM BASKETBALL.
THIS IS ALL I HAVE LEFT.
PLEASE ALLOW ME TO FIGHT WITH YOU.
MY TEAM, MY FRIENDS.
GRR...
I HATE THOSE TSUKUBA GUYS.
KAND
DON'T PLAY WITH HATE.
HATING USES UP ALL YOUR ENERGY...
...AND THEN YOU'RE PLAYING WITH NOTHING.
HATING TSUKUBA WON'T FIX MY KNEE.
AND HATE IS NOT WHAT JOHNAN'S ABOUT ANYWAY.

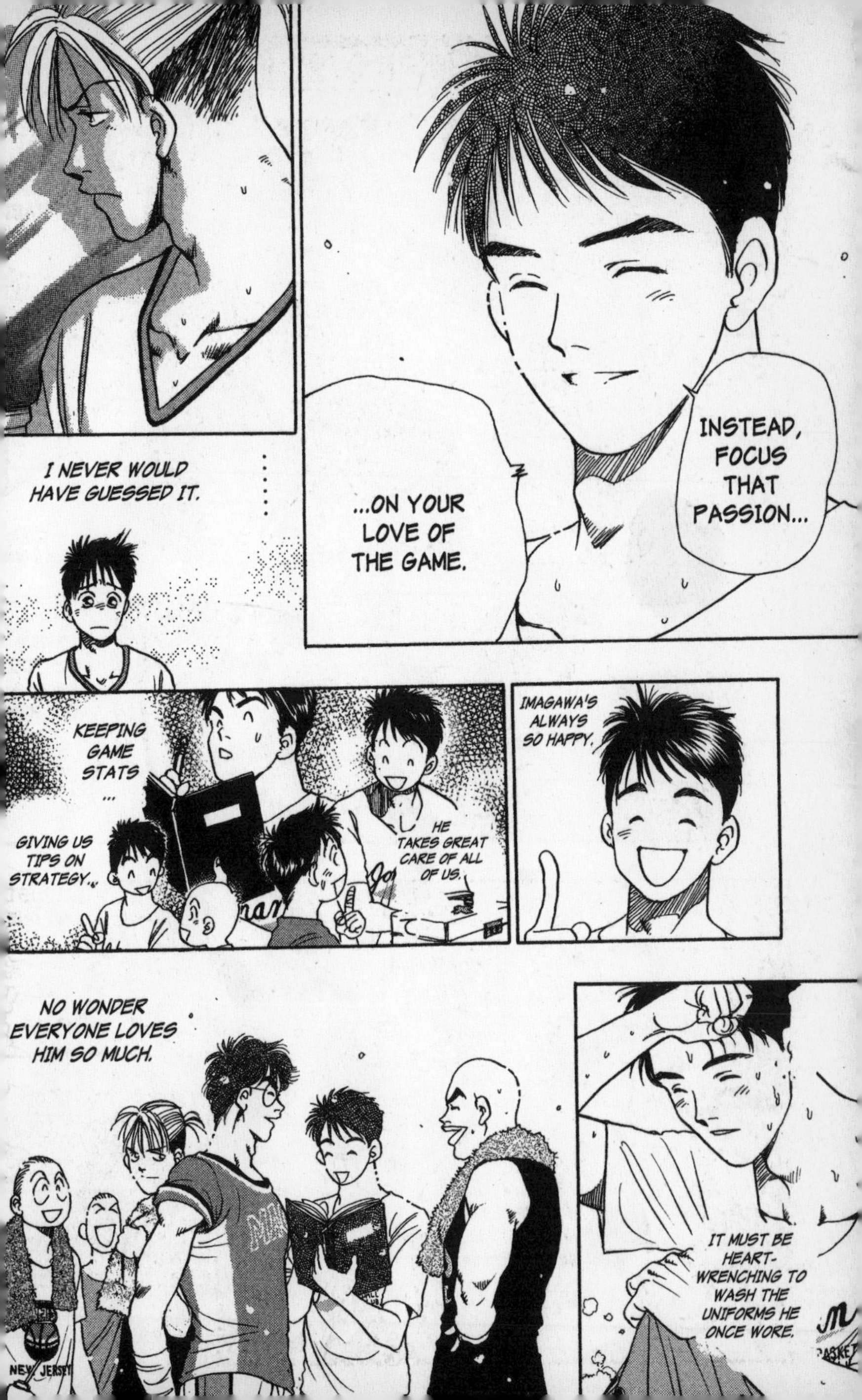
INSTEAD, FOCUS THAT PASSION...
...ON YOUR LOVE OF THE GAME.
I NEVER WOULD HAVE GUESSED IT.
......
IMAGAWA'S ALWAYS SO HAPPY.
KEEPING GAME STATS ...
GIVING US TIPS ON STRATEGY...
HE TAKES GREAT CARE OF ALL OF US.
IT MUST BE HEART-WRENCHING TO WASH THE UNIFORMS HE ONCE WORE.
NO WONDER EVERYONE LOVES HIM SO MUCH.
NEW JERSEY

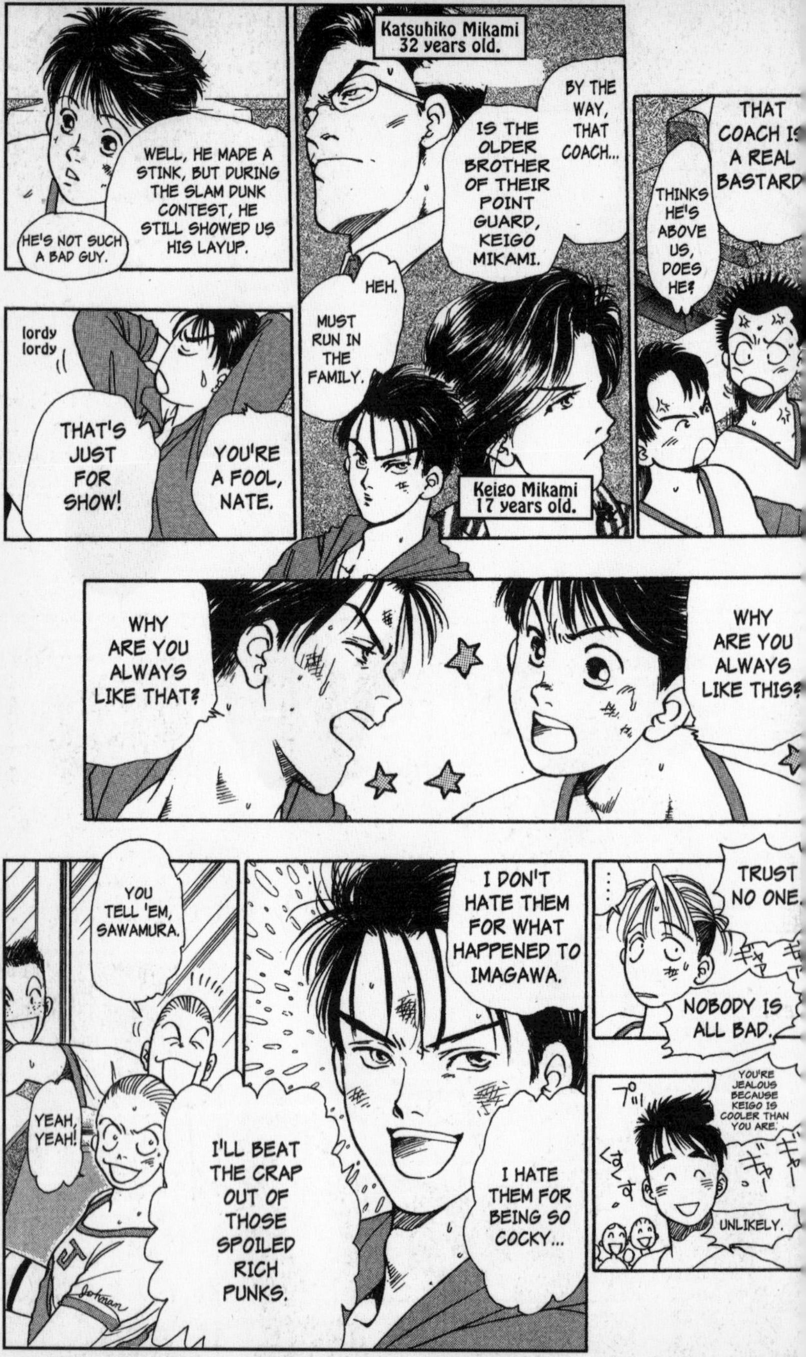
THAT COACH IS A REAL BASTARD
THINKS HE'S ABOVE US, DOES HE?
Katsuhiko Mikami 32 years old.
BY THE WAY, THAT COACH...
IS THE OLDER BROTHER OF THEIR POINT GUARD, KEIGO MIKAMI.
HEH.
MUST RUN IN THE FAMILY.
Keigo Mikami 17 years old.
WELL, HE MADE A STINK, BUT DURING THE SLAM DUNK CONTEST, HE STILL SHOWED US HIS LAYUP.
HE'S NOT SUCH A BAD GUY.
lordy lordy
YOU'RE A FOOL, NATE.
THAT'S JUST FOR SHOW!
WHY ARE YOU ALWAYS LIKE THIS?
WHY ARE YOU ALWAYS LIKE THAT?
...
TRUST NO ONE.
NOBODY IS ALL BAD.
YOU'RE JEALOUS BECAUSE KEIGO IS COOLER THAN YOU ARE.
UNLIKELY.
I DON'T HATE THEM FOR WHAT HAPPENED TO IMAGAWA.
I HATE THEM FOR BEING SO COCKY...
I'LL BEAT THE CRAP OUT OF THOSE SPOILED RICH PUNKS.
YOU TELL 'EM, SAWAMURA.
YEAH, YEAH!

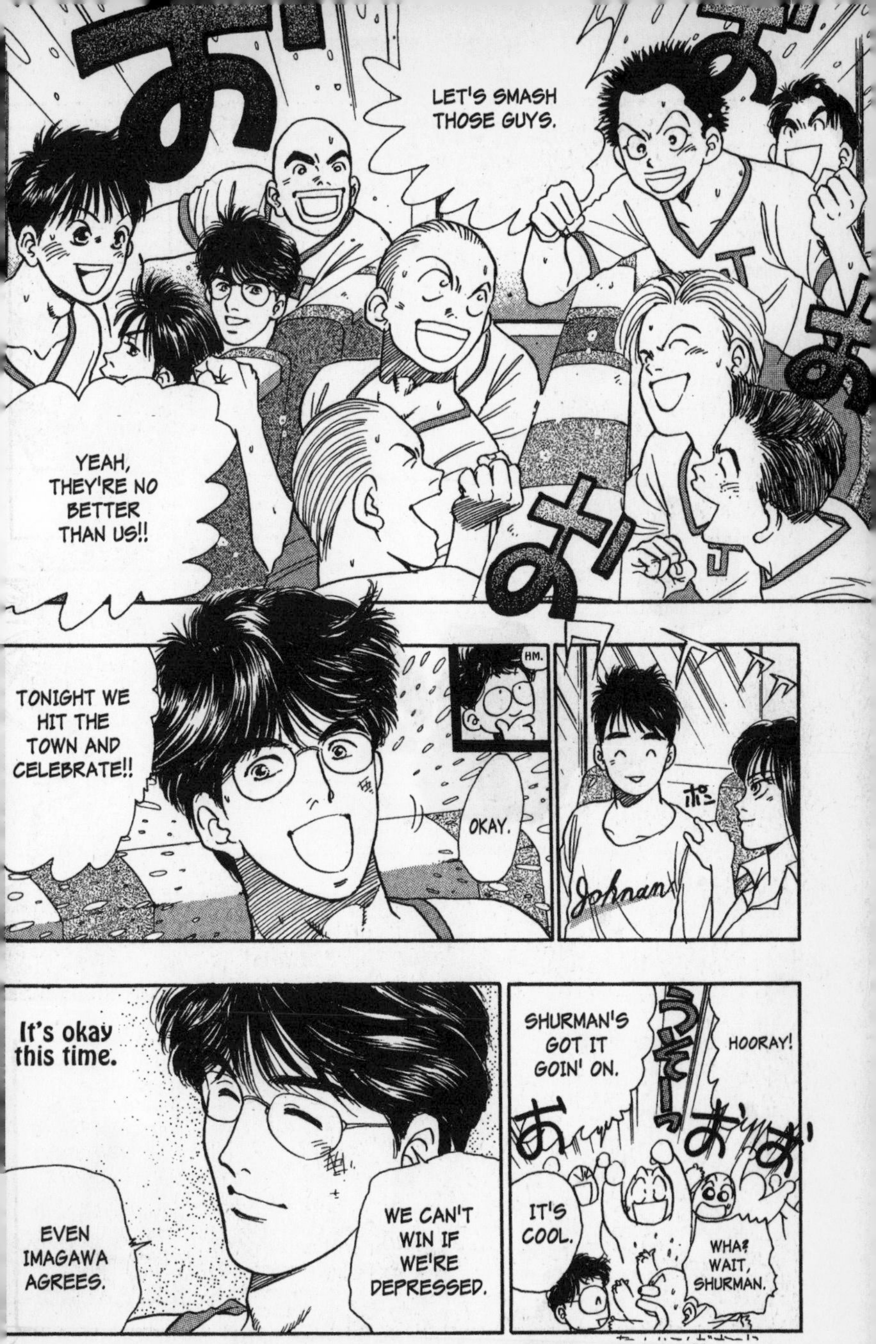
LET'S SMASH THOSE GUYS.
YEAH, THEY'RE NO BETTER THAN US!!
ポン
HM.
TONIGHT WE HIT THE TOWN AND CELEBRATE!!
OKAY.
HOORAY!
SHURMAN'S GOT IT GOIN' ON.
IT'S COOL.
WHA? WAIT, SHURMAN.
What're you saying?!
It's okay this time.
WE CAN'T WIN IF WE'RE DEPRESSED.
EVEN IMAGAWA AGREES.

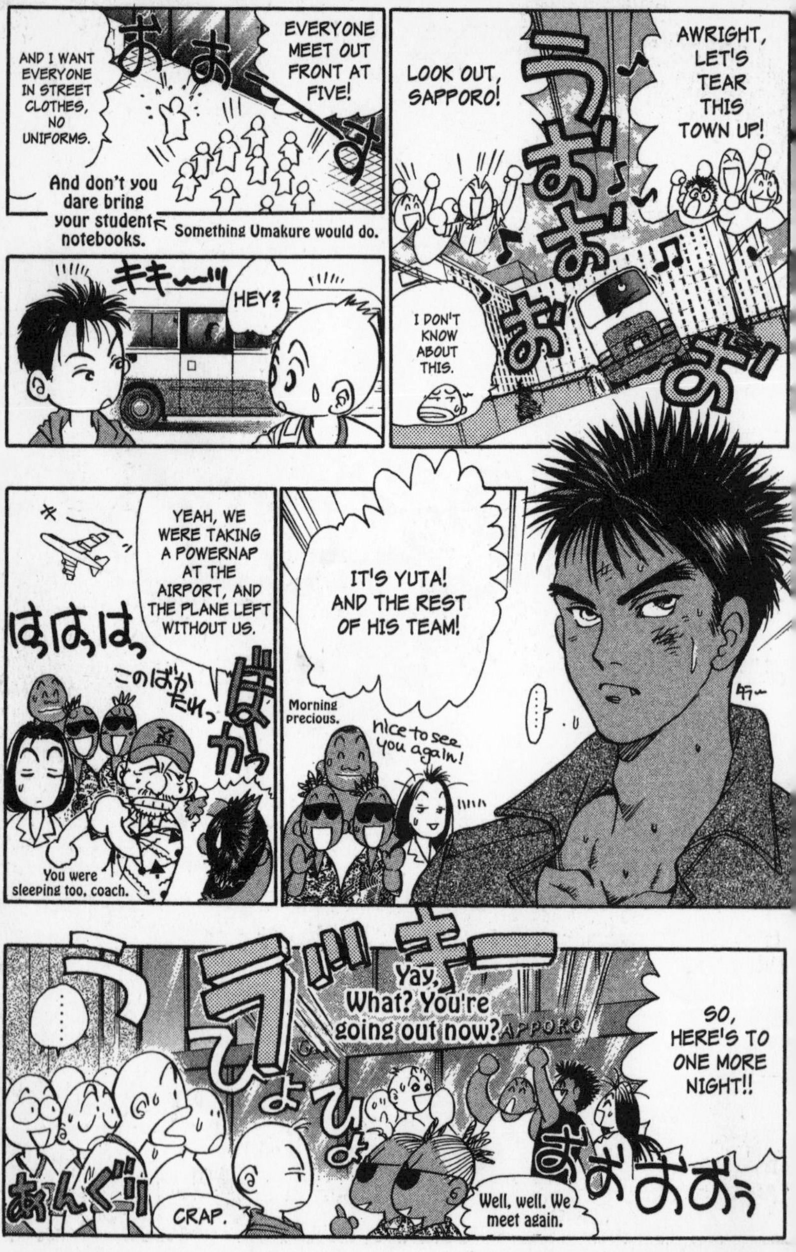
AWRIGHT, LET'S TEAR THIS TOWN UP!
LOOK OUT, SAPPORO!
I DON'T KNOW ABOUT THIS.
EVERYONE MEET OUT FRONT AT FIVE!
AND I WANT EVERYONE IN STREET CLOTHES, NO UNIFORMS.
And don't you dare bring your student notebooks.
Something Umakure would do.
HEY?
IT'S YUTA! AND THE REST OF HIS TEAM!
…
Morning precious.
nice to see you again!
YEAH, WE WERE TAKING A POWERNAP AT THE AIRPORT, AND THE PLANE LEFT WITHOUT US.
ははは
このばかたれっ
You were sleeping too, coach.
SO, HERE'S TO ONE MORE NIGHT!!
Yay, What? You're going out now?
APPORO
……
Well, well. We meet again.
CRAP.

REBOUND

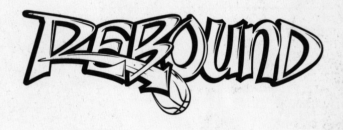

REBOUND

Episode 22: Runner

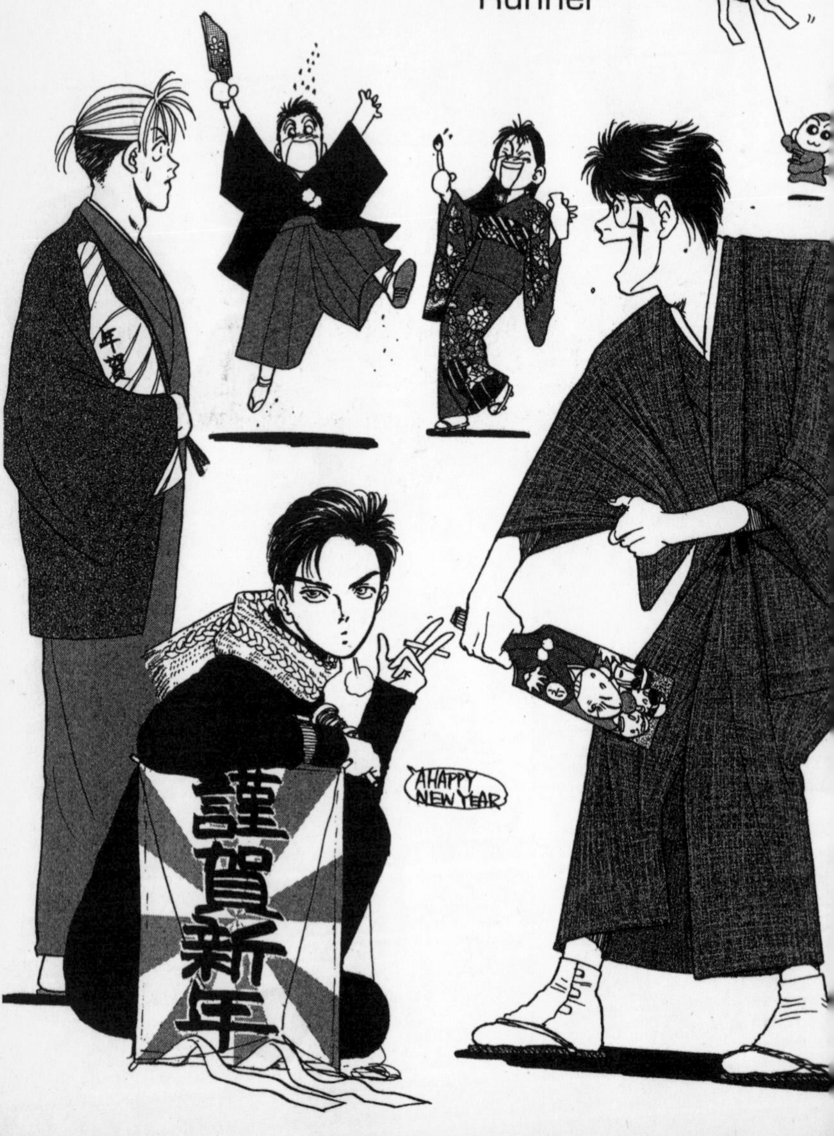
年賀
A HAPPY NEW YEAR
謹賀新年

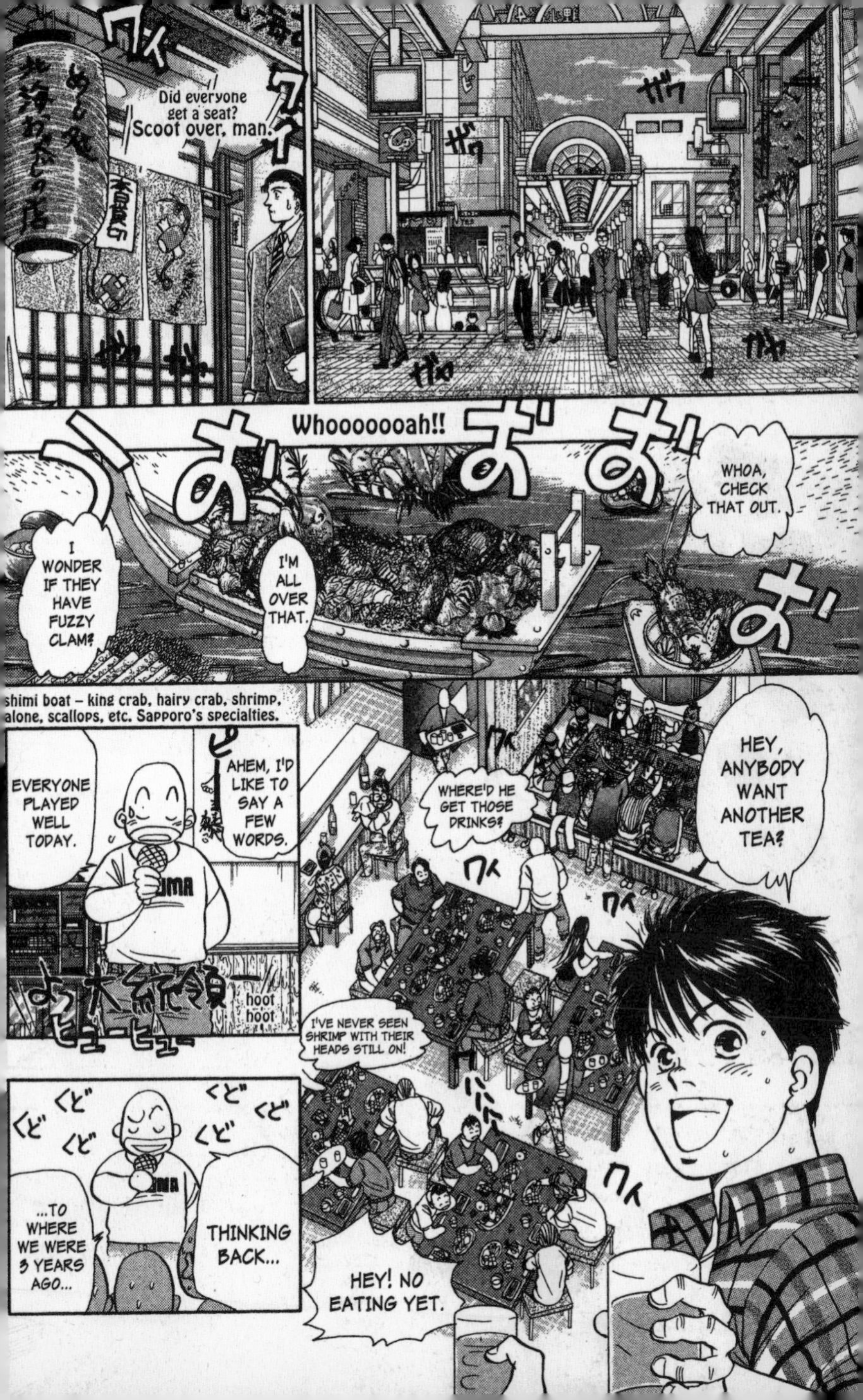

Did everyone get a seat?
Scoot over, man.
Whoooooah!!
WHOA, CHECK THAT OUT.
I'M ALL OVER THAT.
I WONDER IF THEY HAVE FUZZY CLAM?
shimi boat – king crab, hairy crab, shrimp,
alone, scallops, etc. Sapporo's specialties.
HEY, ANYBODY WANT ANOTHER TEA?
WHERE'D HE GET THOSE DRINKS?
I'VE NEVER SEEN SHRIMP WITH THEIR HEADS STILL ON!
HEY! NO EATING YET.
AHEM, I'D LIKE TO SAY A FEW WORDS.
EVERYONE PLAYED WELL TODAY.
hoot hoot
THINKING BACK...
...TO WHERE WE WERE 3 YEARS AGO...

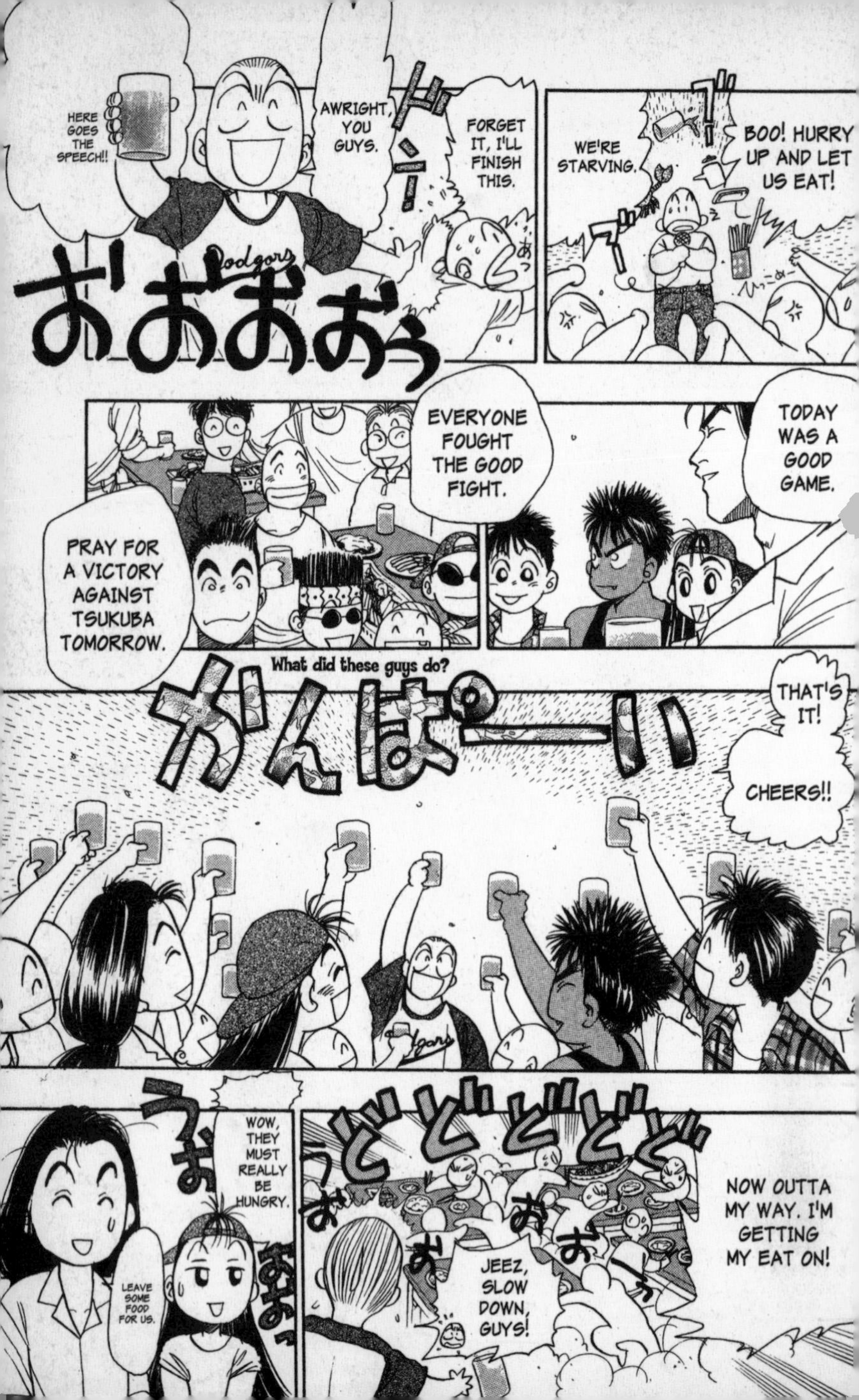
BOO! HURRY UP AND LET US EAT!
WE'RE STARVING.
FORGET IT, I'LL FINISH THIS.
AWRIGHT, YOU GUYS.
HERE GOES THE SPEECH!!
おおおおぉ
TODAY WAS A GOOD GAME.
EVERYONE FOUGHT THE GOOD FIGHT.
PRAY FOR A VICTORY AGAINST TSUKUBA TOMORROW.
What did these guys do?
THAT'S IT!
CHEERS!!
かんぱーい
NOW OUTTA MY WAY. I'M GETTING MY EAT ON!
JEEZ, SLOW DOWN, GUYS!
WOW, THEY MUST REALLY BE HUNGRY.
LEAVE SOME FOOD FOR US.

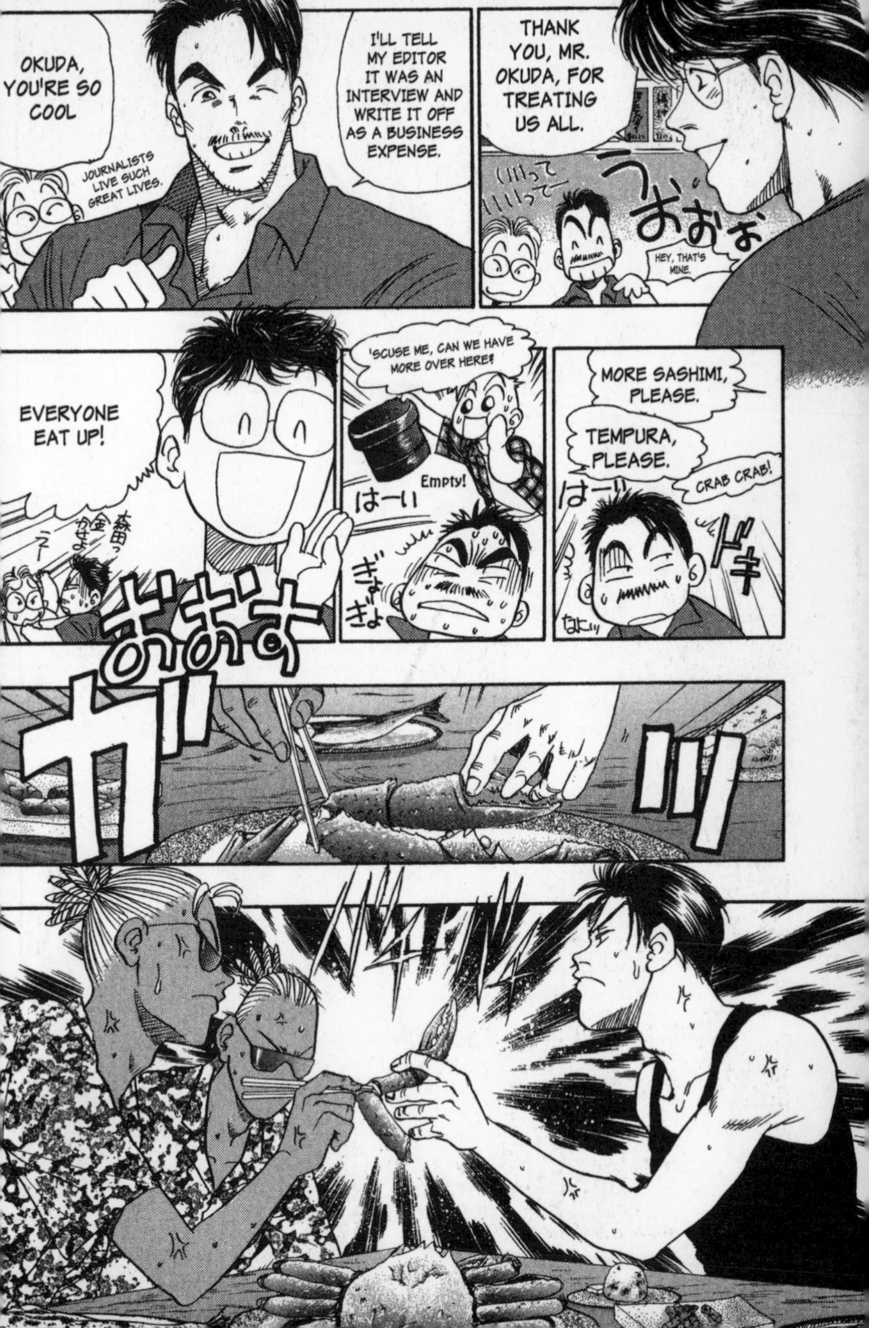
THANK YOU, MR. OKUDA, FOR TREATING US ALL.
うおぉぉ
いいって いいって
HEY, THAT'S MINE.
I'LL TELL MY EDITOR IT WAS AN INTERVIEW AND WRITE IT OFF AS A BUSINESS EXPENSE.
OKUDA, YOU'RE SO COOL
JOURNALISTS LIVE SUCH GREAT LIVES.
MORE SASHIMI, PLEASE.
TEMPURA, PLEASE.
CRAB CRAB!
はーい
ドキ
なにッ
'SCUSE ME, CAN WE HAVE MORE OVER HERE?
Empty!
はーい
ぎょぎょ
EVERYONE EAT UP!
森田っ
金かせよ
えー
おおす
ガッ

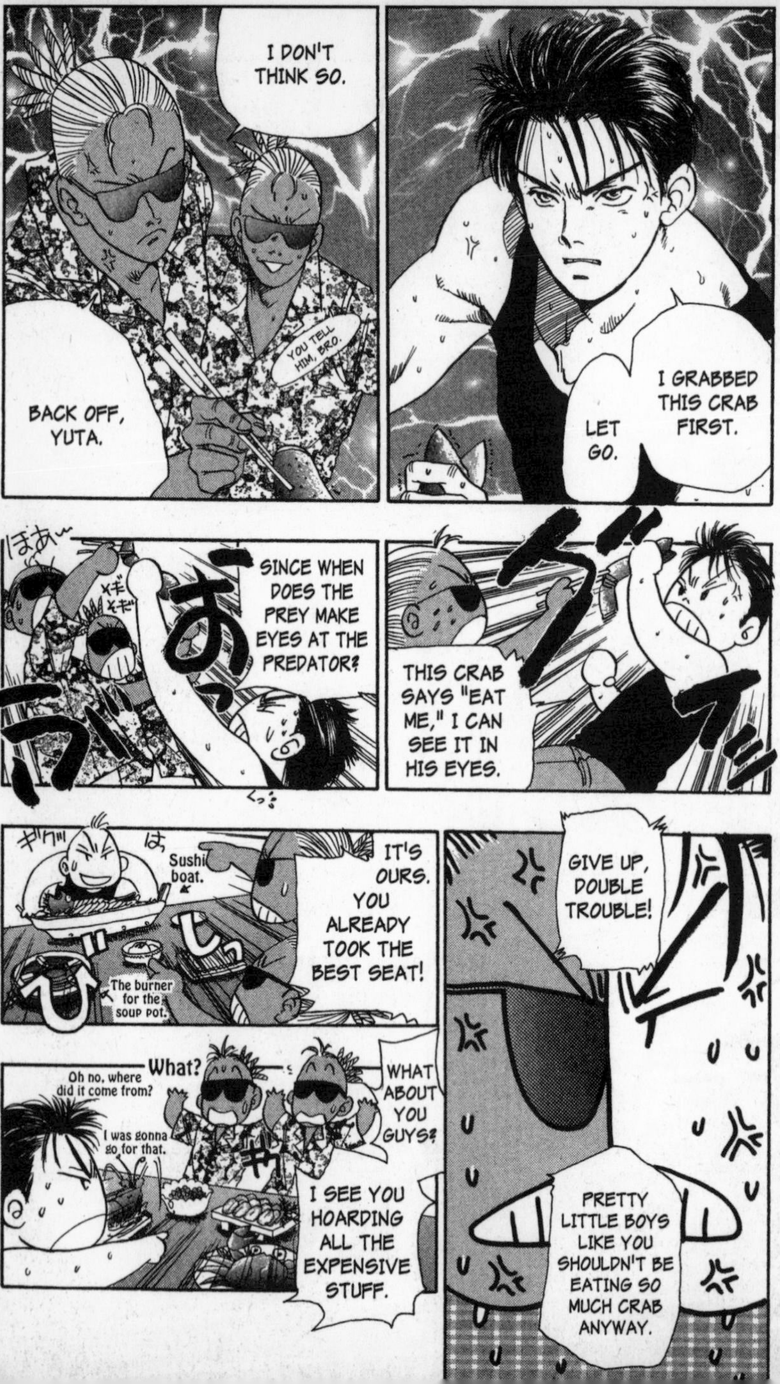
I GRABBED THIS CRAB FIRST.
LET GO.
I DON'T THINK SO.
YOU TELL HIM, BRO.
BACK OFF, YUTA.
THIS CRAB SAYS "EAT ME," I CAN SEE IT IN HIS EYES.
SINCE WHEN DOES THE PREY MAKE EYES AT THE PREDATOR?
GIVE UP, DOUBLE TROUBLE!
PRETTY LITTLE BOYS LIKE YOU SHOULDN'T BE EATING SO MUCH CRAB ANYWAY.
IT'S OURS. YOU ALREADY TOOK THE BEST SEAT!
Sushi boat.
The burner for the soup pot.
WHAT ABOUT YOU GUYS?
I SEE YOU HOARDING ALL THE EXPENSIVE STUFF.
What?
Oh no, where did it come from?
I was gonna go for that.

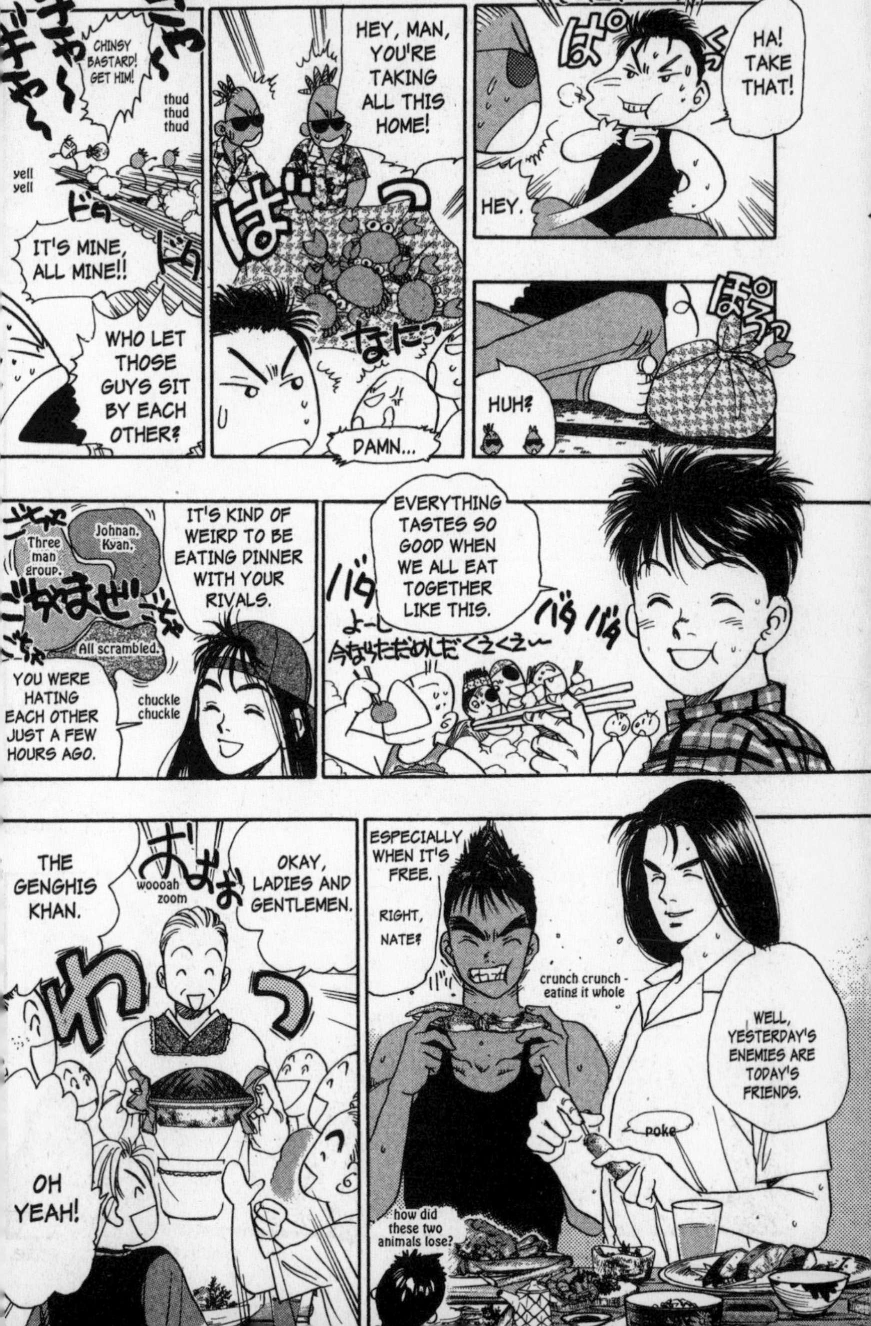
いただきっ
ぱく
HA! TAKE THAT!
HEY.
ぽろっ
HUH?
HEY, MAN, YOU'RE TAKING ALL THIS HOME!
ばっ
なにっ
DAMN...
CHINSY BASTARD! GET HIM!
thud thud thud
yell yell
IT'S MINE, ALL MINE!!
WHO LET THOSE GUYS SIT BY EACH OTHER?
EVERYTHING TASTES SO GOOD WHEN WE ALL EAT TOGETHER LIKE THIS.
バタ バタ
IT'S KIND OF WEIRD TO BE EATING DINNER WITH YOUR RIVALS.
Johnan. Kyan.
Three man group.
All scrambled.
YOU WERE HATING EACH OTHER JUST A FEW HOURS AGO.
chuckle chuckle
ESPECIALLY WHEN IT'S FREE.
RIGHT, NATE?
crunch crunch - eating it whole
WELL, YESTERDAY'S ENEMIES ARE TODAY'S FRIENDS.
poke
how did these two animals lose?
OKAY, LADIES AND GENTLEMEN.
THE GENGHIS KHAN.
woooah zoom
わっ
OH YEAH!

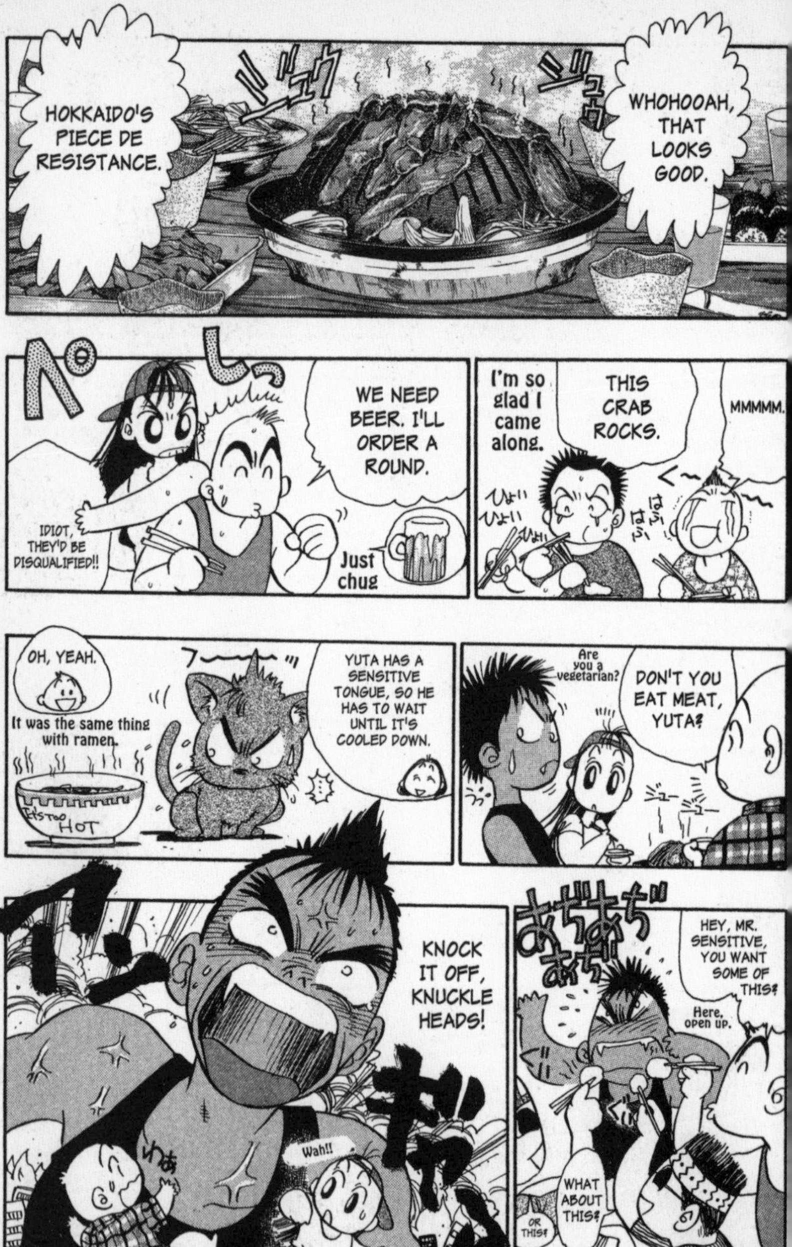
WHOHOOAH, THAT LOOKS GOOD.
HOKKAIDO'S PIECE DE RESISTANCE.
MMMMM.
THIS CRAB ROCKS.
I'm so glad I came along.
WE NEED BEER. I'LL ORDER A ROUND.
Just chug
IDIOT, THEY'D BE DISQUALIFIED!!
DON'T YOU EAT MEAT, YUTA?
Are you a vegetarian?
YUTA HAS A SENSITIVE TONGUE, SO HE HAS TO WAIT UNTIL IT'S COOLED DOWN.
OH, YEAH.
It was the same thing with ramen.
IT'S TOO HOT
HEY, MR. SENSITIVE, YOU WANT SOME OF THIS?
Here, open up.
WHAT ABOUT THIS?
OR THIS?
KNOCK IT OFF, KNUCKLE HEADS!
Wah!!

Don't do this at home.

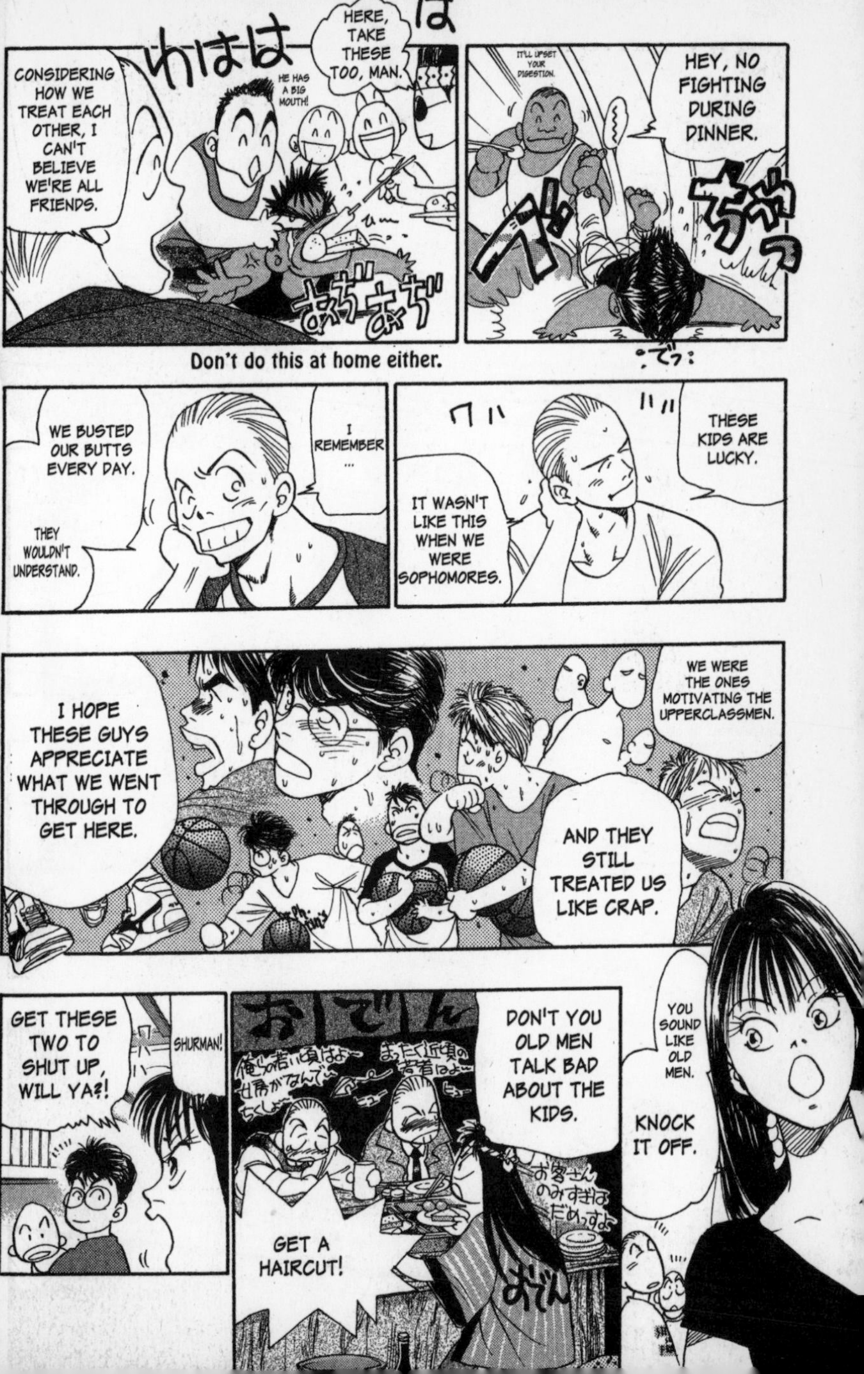
IT'LL UPSET YOUR DIGESTION.
HEY, NO FIGHTING DURING DINNER.
は
HERE, TAKE THESE TOO, MAN.
HE HAS A BIG MOUTH!
わはは
CONSIDERING HOW WE TREAT EACH OTHER, I CAN'T BELIEVE WE'RE ALL FRIENDS.
あぢあぢ
Don't do this at home either.
THESE KIDS ARE LUCKY.
IT WASN'T LIKE THIS WHEN WE WERE SOPHOMORES.
I REMEMBER...
WE BUSTED OUR BUTTS EVERY DAY.
THEY WOULDN'T UNDERSTAND.
WE WERE THE ONES MOTIVATING THE UPPERCLASSMEN.
AND THEY STILL TREATED US LIKE CRAP.
I HOPE THESE GUYS APPRECIATE WHAT WE WENT THROUGH TO GET HERE.
YOU SOUND LIKE OLD MEN.
KNOCK IT OFF.
DON'T YOU OLD MEN TALK BAD ABOUT THE KIDS.
おでん
まったく近頃の若者はよー
俺らの若い頃はよー
女房がなんでぃ ちくしょー
お客さん のみすぎは だめっすよ
GET A HAIRCUT!
おでん
SHURMAN!
GET THESE TWO TO SHUT UP, WILL YA?!

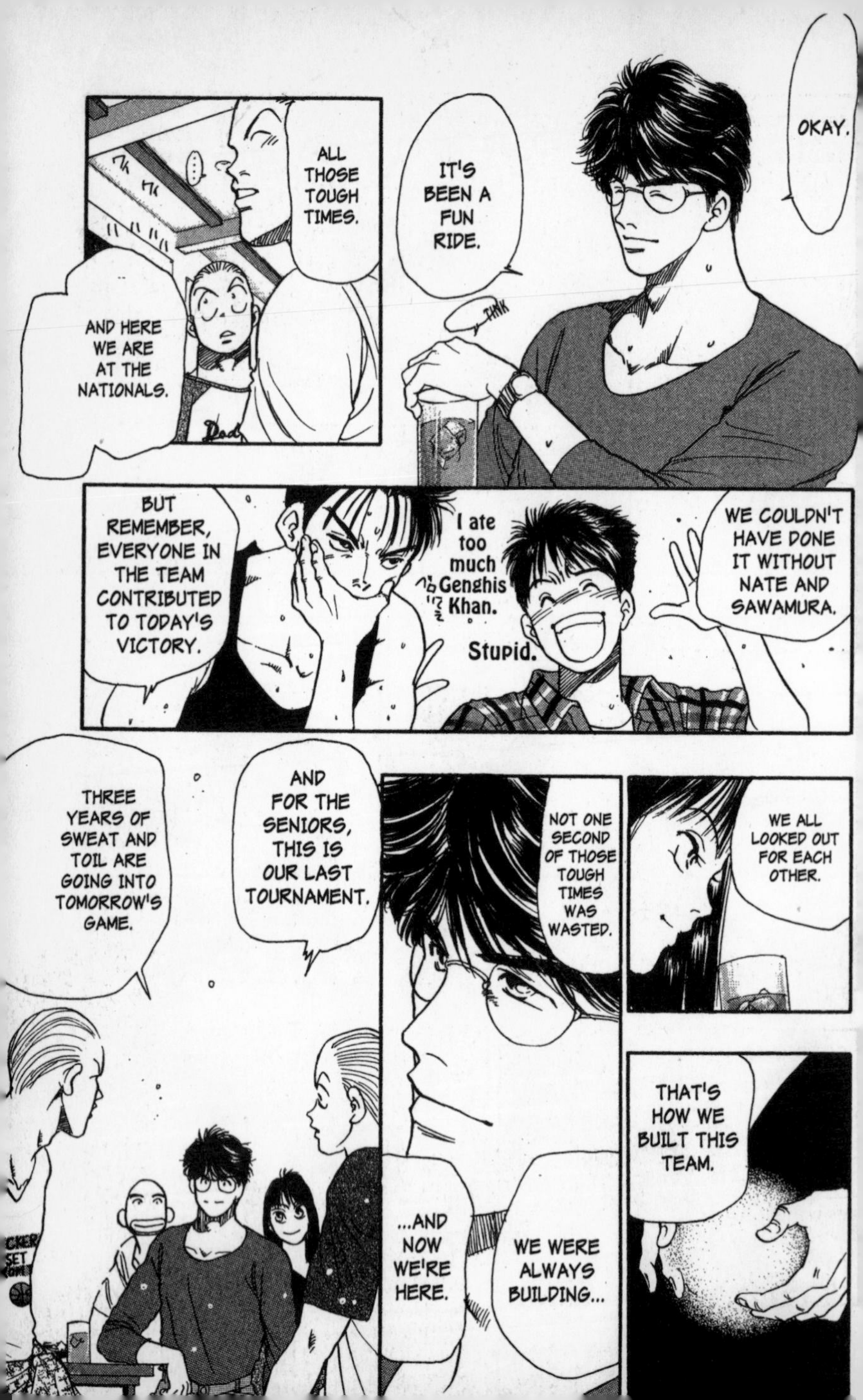
OKAY.
IT'S BEEN A FUN RIDE.
THNK
ALL THOSE TOUGH TIMES.
...
AND HERE WE ARE AT THE NATIONALS.
WE COULDN'T HAVE DONE IT WITHOUT NATE AND SAWAMURA.
I ate too much Genghis Khan.
Stupid.
BUT REMEMBER, EVERYONE IN THE TEAM CONTRIBUTED TO TODAY'S VICTORY.
WE ALL LOOKED OUT FOR EACH OTHER.
THAT'S HOW WE BUILT THIS TEAM.
NOT ONE SECOND OF THOSE TOUGH TIMES WAS WASTED.
WE WERE ALWAYS BUILDING...
...AND NOW WE'RE HERE.
AND FOR THE SENIORS, THIS IS OUR LAST TOURNAMENT.
THREE YEARS OF SWEAT AND TOIL ARE GOING INTO TOMORROW'S GAME.

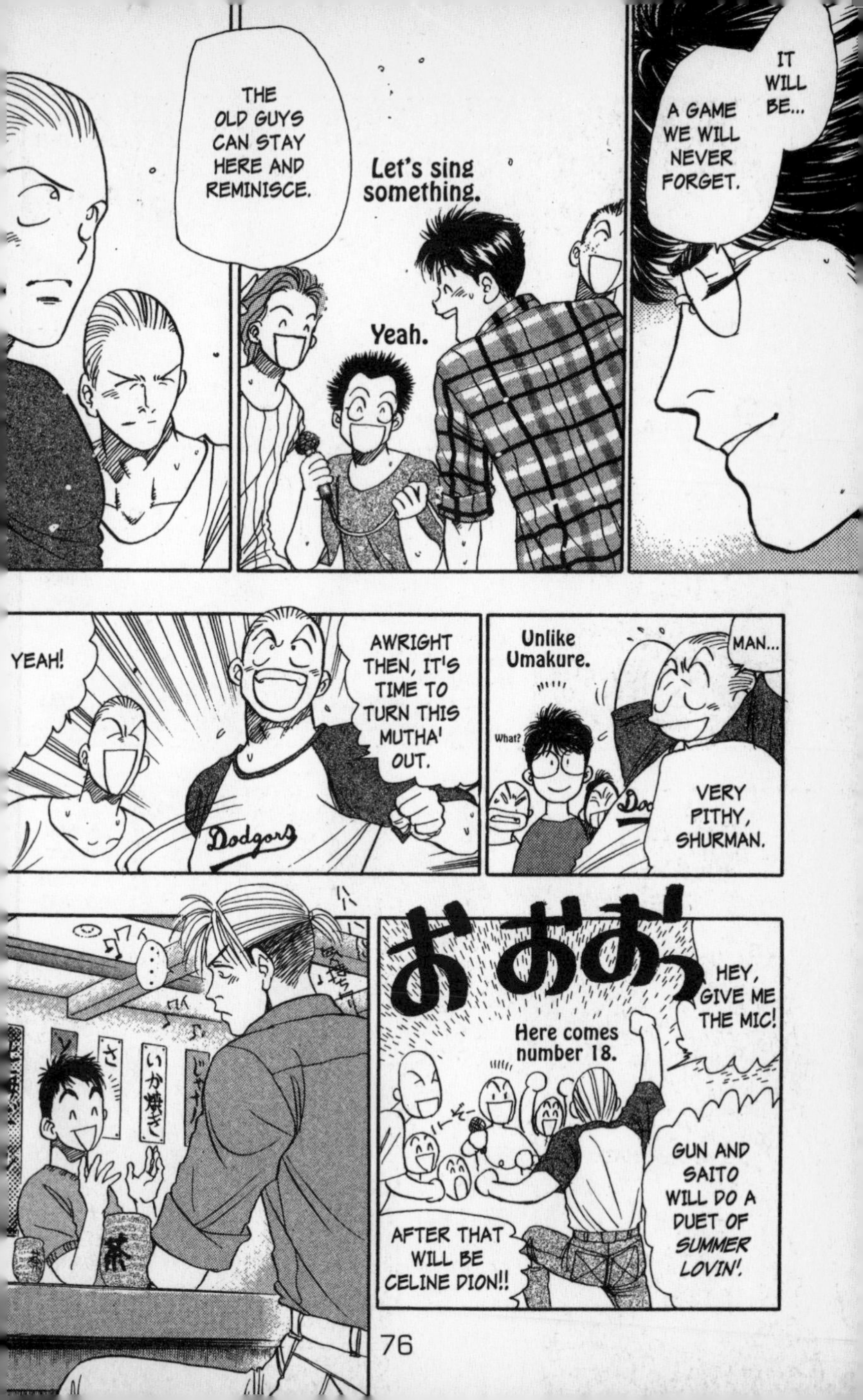
IT WILL BE...
A GAME WE WILL NEVER FORGET.
THE OLD GUYS CAN STAY HERE AND REMINISCE.
Let's sing something.
Yeah.
MAN...
Unlike Umakure.
What?
VERY PITHY, SHURMAN.
AWRIGHT THEN, IT'S TIME TO TURN THIS MUTHA' OUT.
YEAH!
おおおっ
HEY, GIVE ME THE MIC!
Here comes number 18.
GUN AND SAITO WILL DO A DUET OF *SUMMER LOVIN'*.
AFTER THAT WILL BE CELINE DION!!
さ
いか焼き

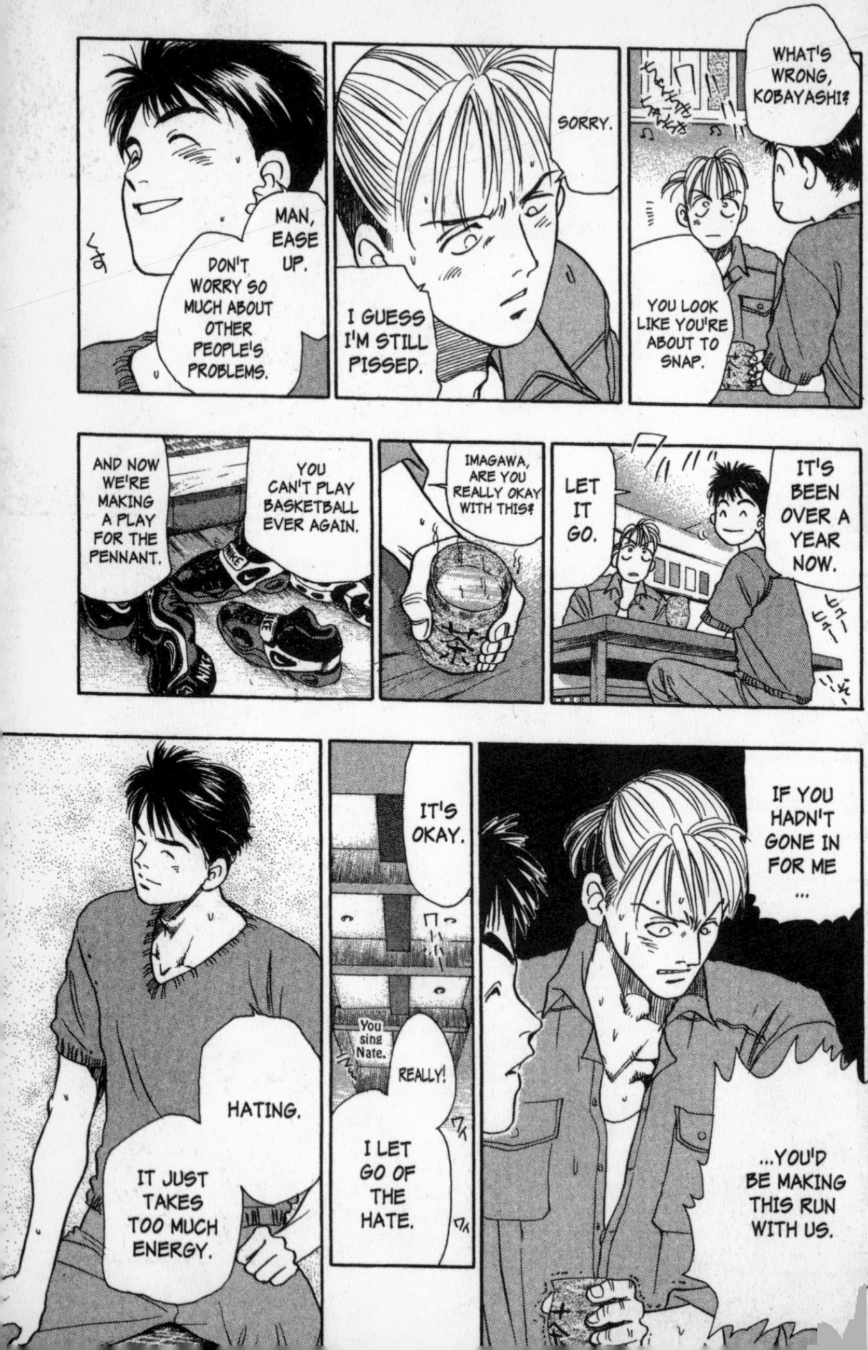
WHAT'S WRONG, KOBAYASHI?
YOU LOOK LIKE YOU'RE ABOUT TO SNAP.
SORRY.
I GUESS I'M STILL PISSED.
MAN, EASE UP.
DON'T WORRY SO MUCH ABOUT OTHER PEOPLE'S PROBLEMS.
IT'S BEEN OVER A YEAR NOW.
LET IT GO.
IMAGAWA, ARE YOU REALLY OKAY WITH THIS?
YOU CAN'T PLAY BASKETBALL EVER AGAIN.
AND NOW WE'RE MAKING A PLAY FOR THE PENNANT.
IF YOU HADN'T GONE IN FOR ME ...
...YOU'D BE MAKING THIS RUN WITH US.
IT'S OKAY.
You sing Nate.
REALLY!
I LET GO OF THE HATE.
HATING.
IT JUST TAKES TOO MUCH ENERGY.

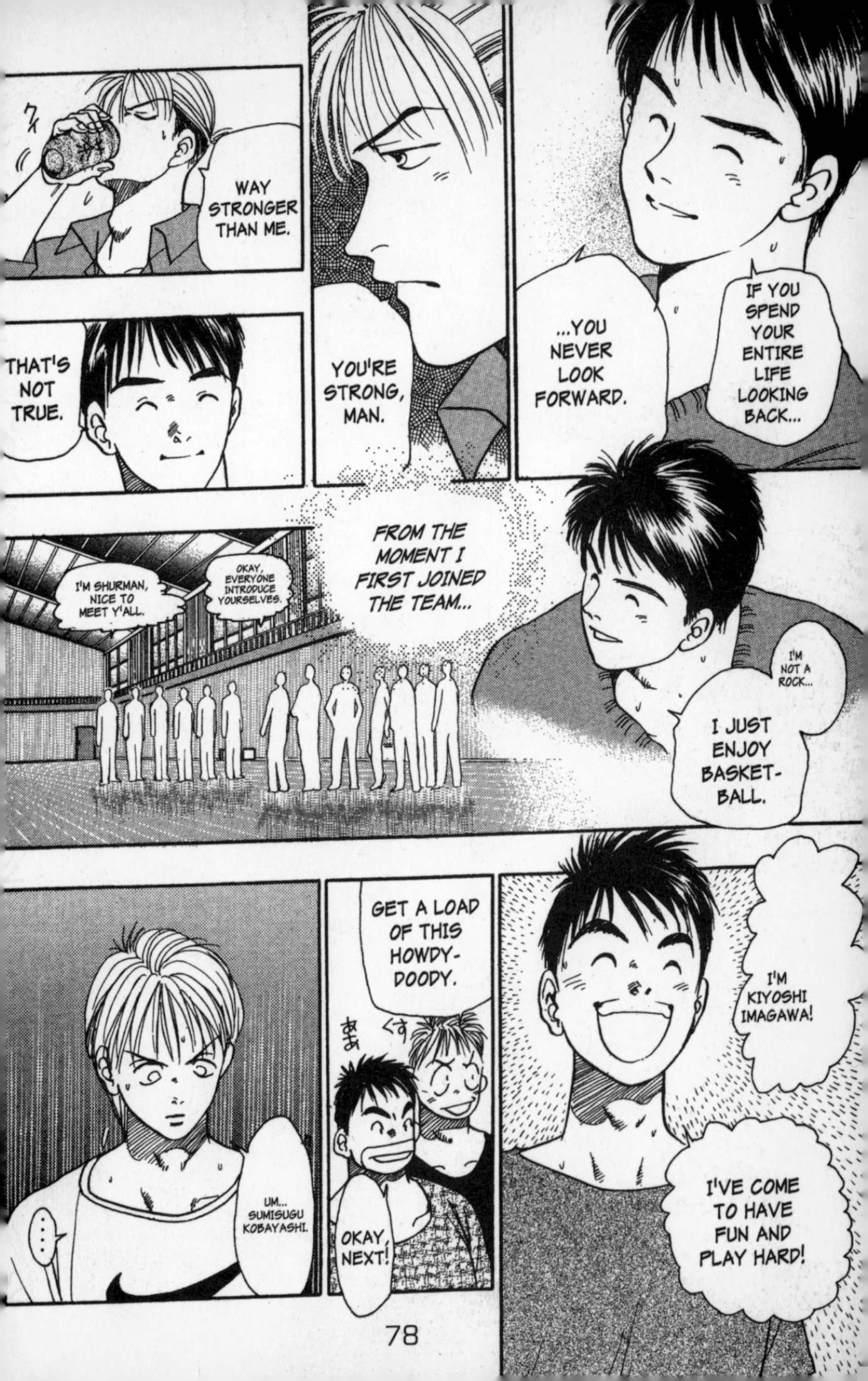

IF YOU SPEND YOUR ENTIRE LIFE LOOKING BACK...
...YOU NEVER LOOK FORWARD.
YOU'RE STRONG, MAN.
クイ
WAY STRONGER THAN ME.
THAT'S NOT TRUE.
I'M NOT A ROCK...
I JUST ENJOY BASKET-BALL.
FROM THE MOMENT I FIRST JOINED THE TEAM...
OKAY, EVERYONE INTRODUCE YOURSELVES.
I'M SHURMAN, NICE TO MEET Y'ALL.
I'M KIYOSHI IMAGAWA!
I'VE COME TO HAVE FUN AND PLAY HARD!
GET A LOAD OF THIS HOWDY-DOODY.
くす
OKAY, NEXT!
UM... SUMISUGU KOBAYASHI.
...

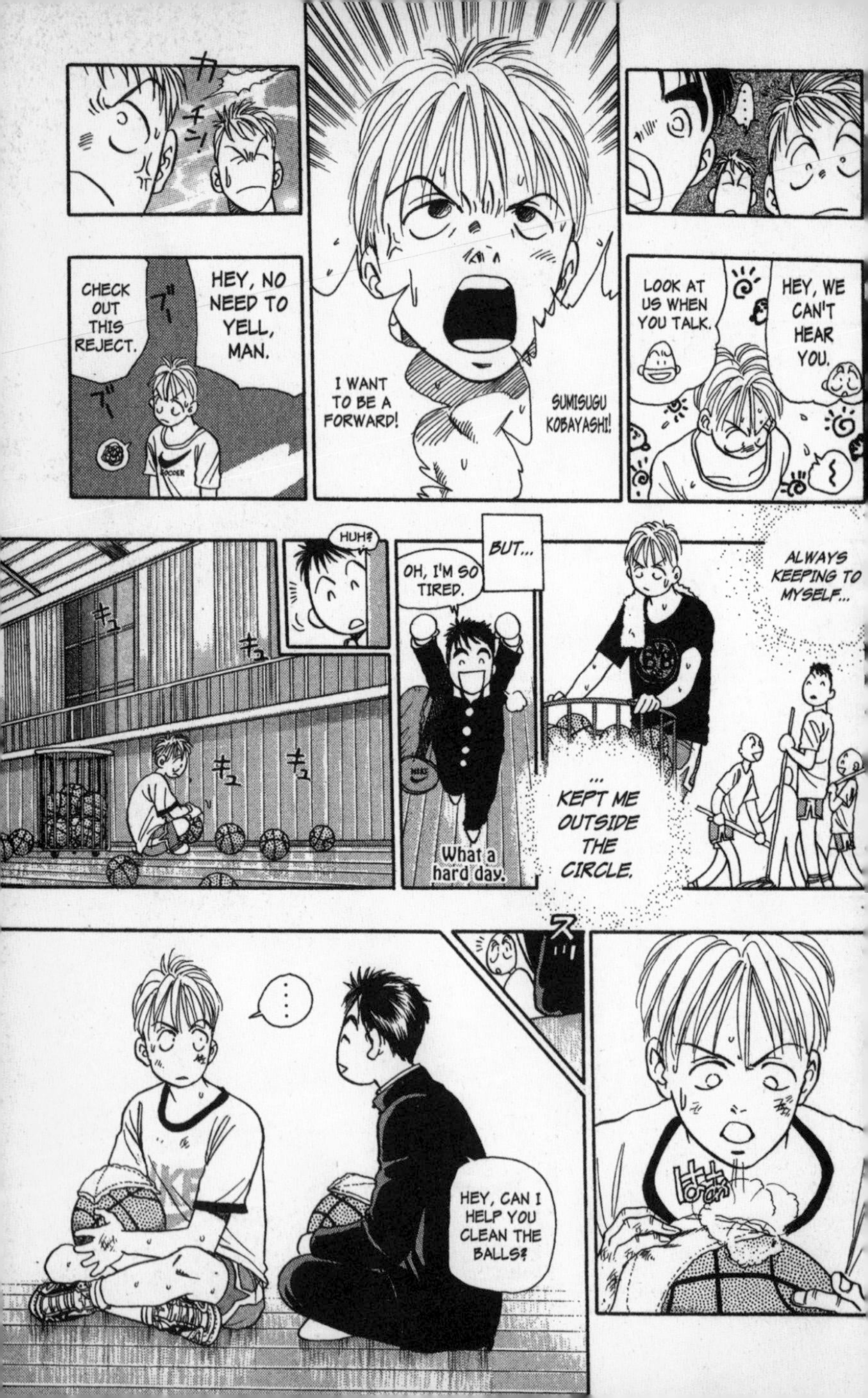
HEY, WE CAN'T HEAR YOU.
LOOK AT US WHEN YOU TALK.
SUMISUGU KOBAYASHI!
I WANT TO BE A FORWARD!
カチン
HEY, NO NEED TO YELL, MAN.
CHECK OUT THIS REJECT.
ALWAYS KEEPING TO MYSELF...
... KEPT ME OUTSIDE THE CIRCLE.
BUT...
OH, I'M SO TIRED.
What a hard day.
HUH?
キュ
キュ
キュ
キュ
ス
HEY, CAN I HELP YOU CLEAN THE BALLS?
.....

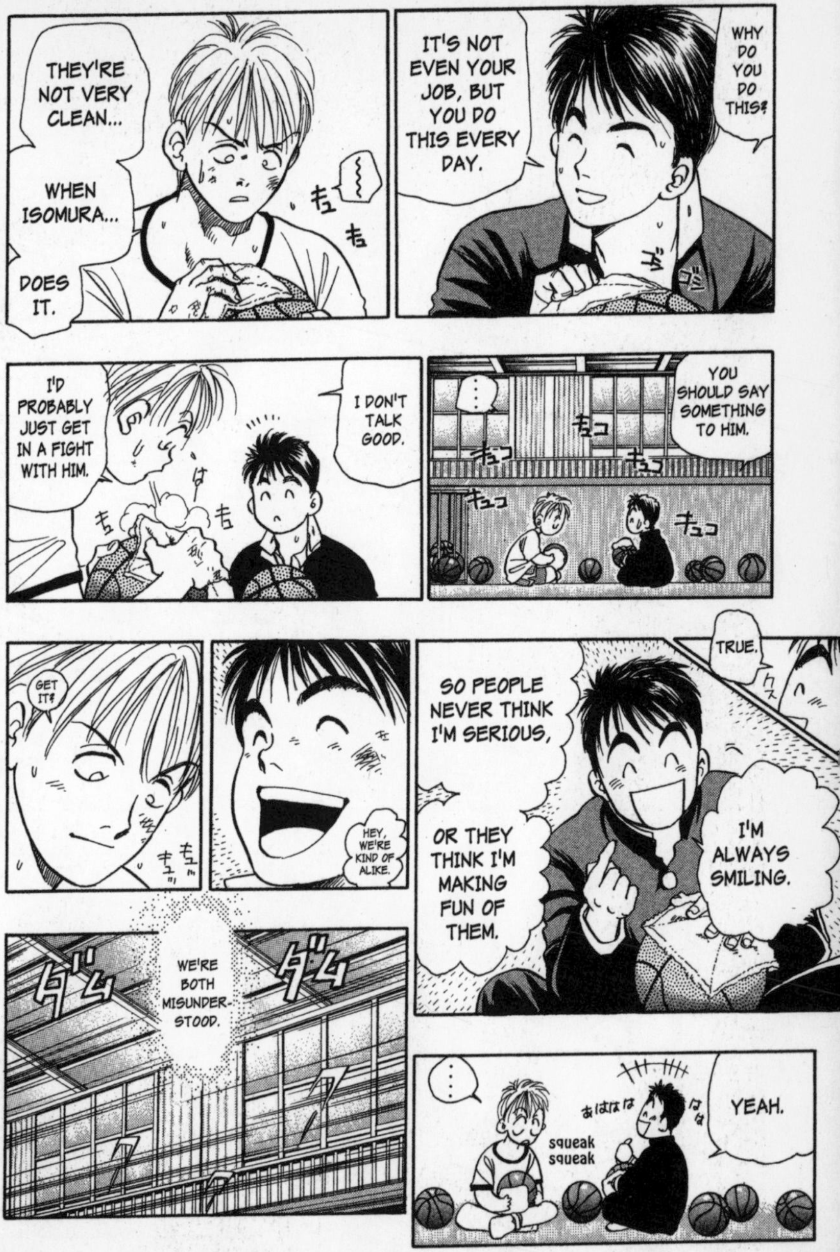
WHY DO YOU DO THIS?
IT'S NOT EVEN YOUR JOB, BUT YOU DO THIS EVERY DAY.
THEY'RE NOT VERY CLEAN...
WHEN ISOMURA...
DOES IT.
YOU SHOULD SAY SOMETHING TO HIM.
...
I DON'T TALK GOOD.
I'D PROBABLY JUST GET IN A FIGHT WITH HIM.
TRUE.
I'M ALWAYS SMILING.
SO PEOPLE NEVER THINK I'M SERIOUS,
OR THEY THINK I'M MAKING FUN OF THEM.
HEY, WE'RE KIND OF ALIKE.
GET IT?
WE'RE BOTH MISUNDERSTOOD.
YEAH.
あははは
...
squeak squeak

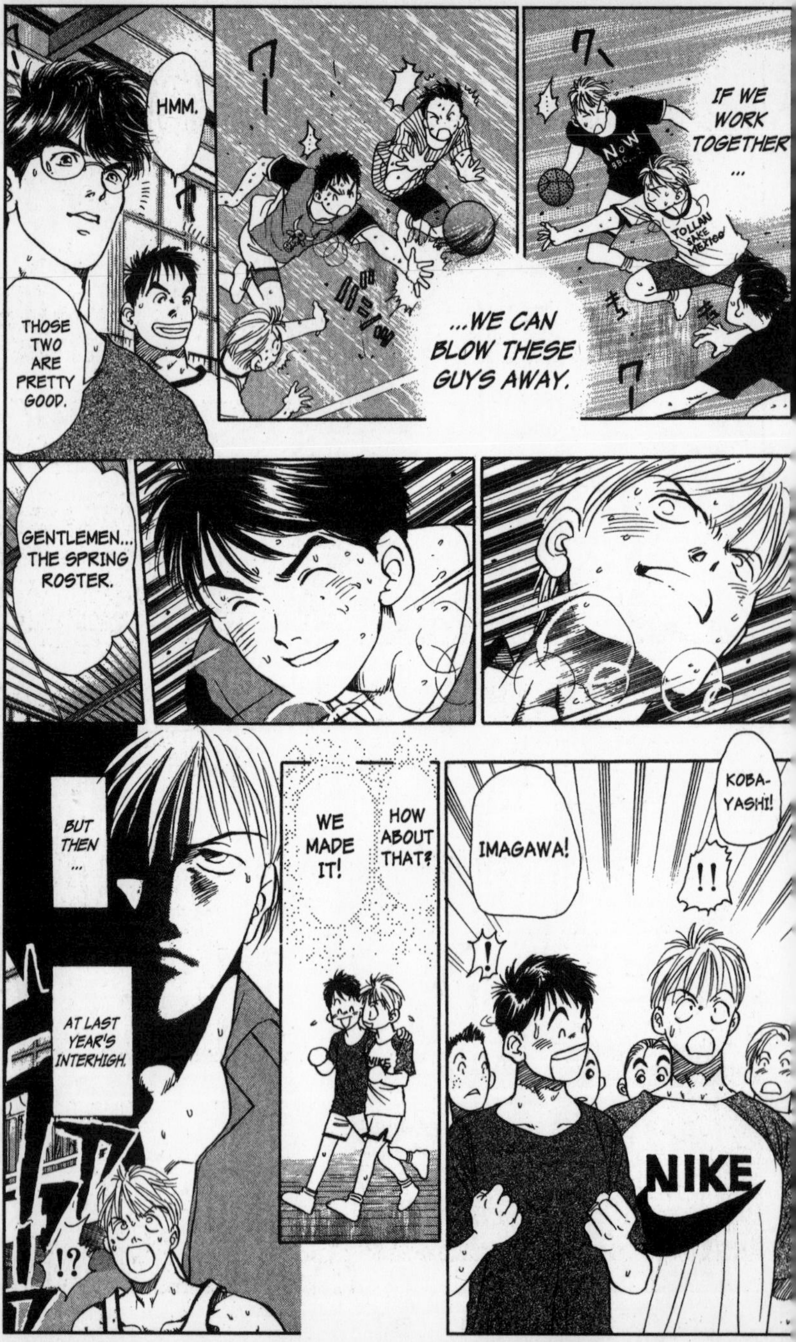
IF WE WORK TOGETHER ...
...WE CAN BLOW THESE GUYS AWAY.
HMM.
THOSE TWO ARE PRETTY GOOD.
GENTLEMEN... THE SPRING ROSTER.
KOBA-YASHI!
!!
IMAGAWA!
!
HOW ABOUT THAT?
WE MADE IT!
BUT THEN ...
AT LAST YEAR'S INTERHIGH.
!?

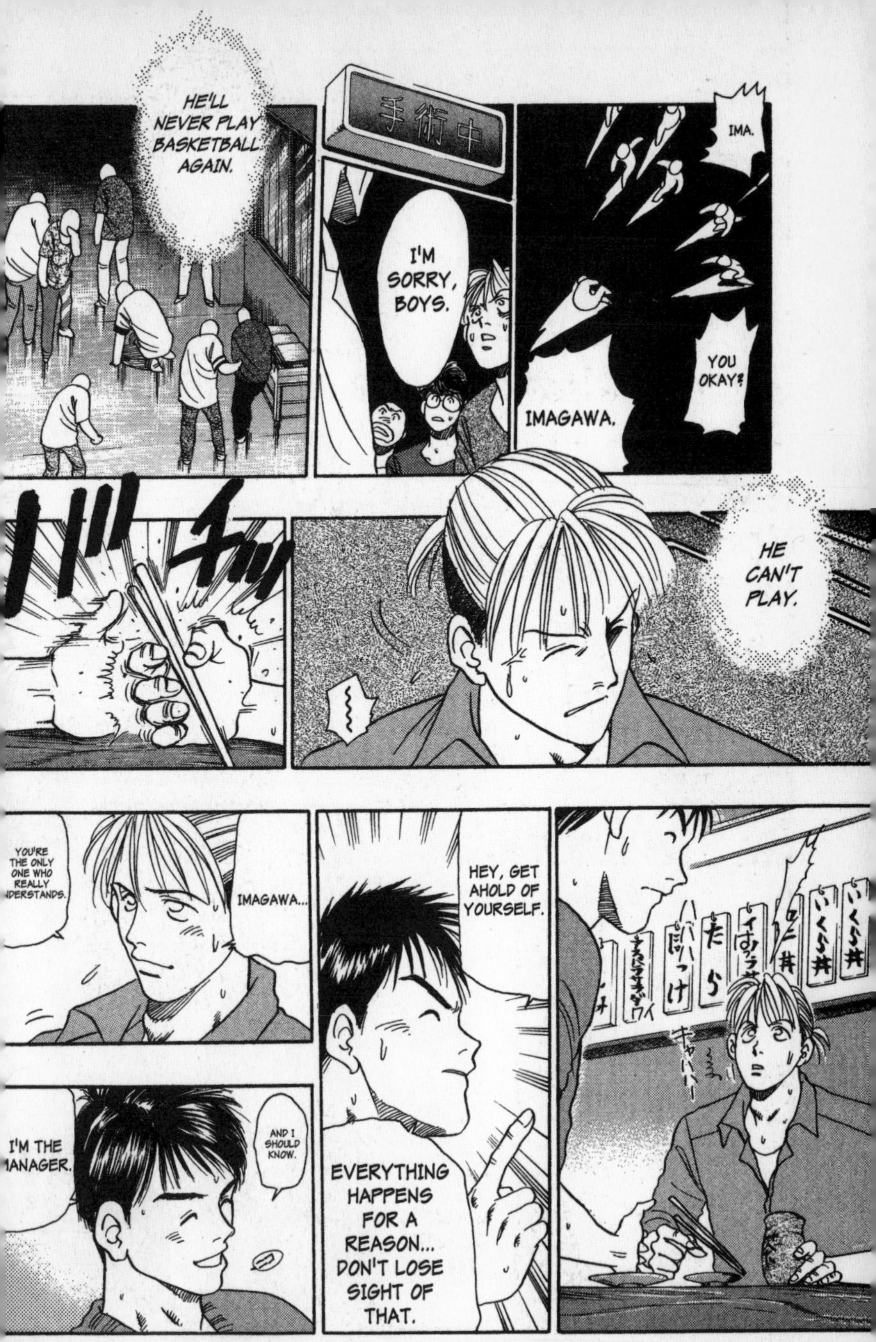
IMA.
YOU OKAY?
IMAGAWA.
手術中
I'M SORRY, BOYS.
HE'LL NEVER PLAY BASKETBALL AGAIN.
HE CAN'T PLAY.
いくら丼
いくら丼
HEY, GET AHOLD OF YOURSELF.
EVERYTHING HAPPENS FOR A REASON... DON'T LOSE SIGHT OF THAT.
YOU'RE THE ONLY ONE WHO REALLY NDERSTANDS.
IMAGAWA...
I'M THE ANAGER.
AND I SHOULD KNOW.

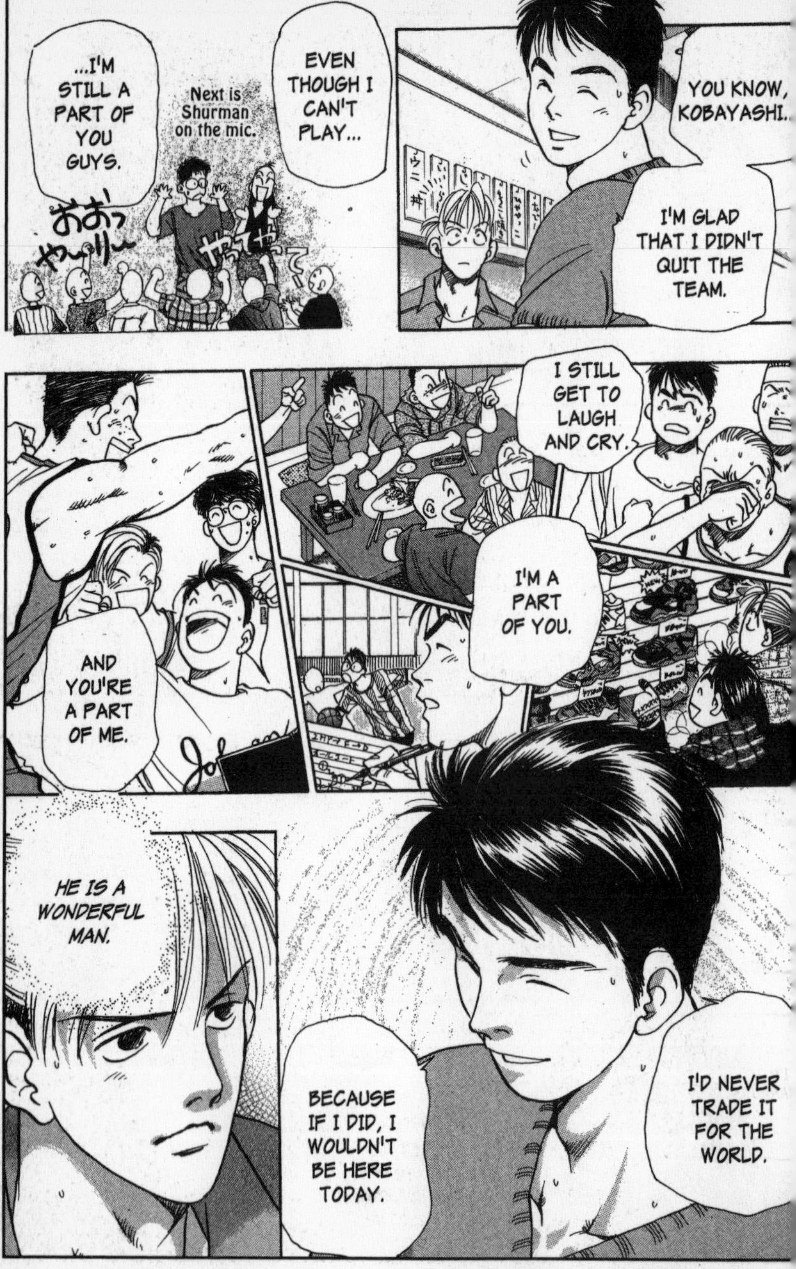
YOU KNOW, KOBAYASHI...
I'M GLAD THAT I DIDN'T QUIT THE TEAM.
EVEN THOUGH I CAN'T PLAY...
Next is Shurman on the mic.
...I'M STILL A PART OF YOU GUYS.
おおっ
I STILL GET TO LAUGH AND CRY.
I'M A PART OF YOU.
AND YOU'RE A PART OF ME.
I'D NEVER TRADE IT FOR THE WORLD.
BECAUSE IF I DID, I WOULDN'T BE HERE TODAY.
HE IS A WONDERFUL MAN.

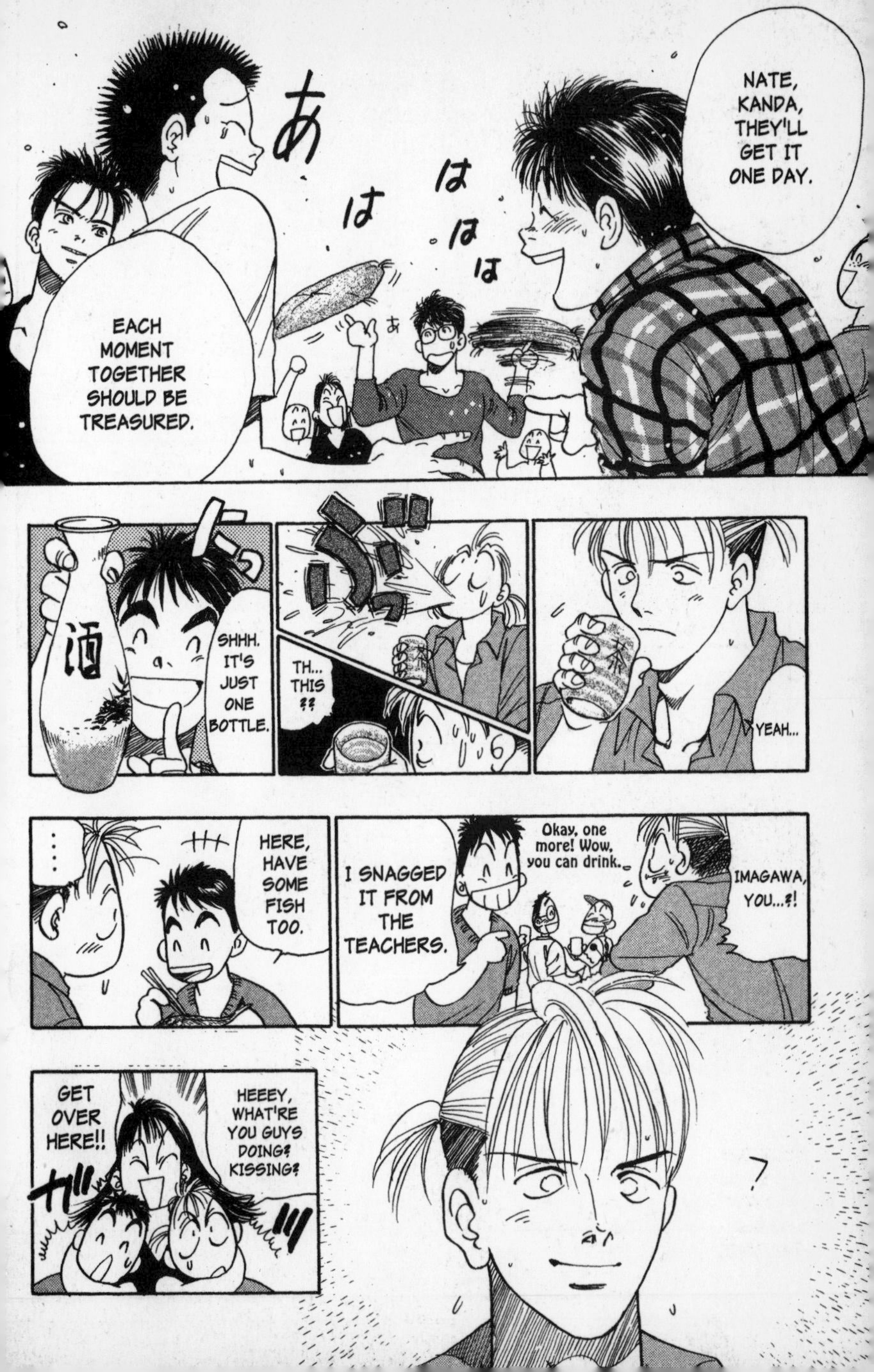
NATE, KANDA, THEY'LL GET IT ONE DAY.
あははは
あ
EACH MOMENT TOGETHER SHOULD BE TREASURED.
YEAH...
TH... THIS ??
酒
SHHH. IT'S JUST ONE BOTTLE.
IMAGAWA, YOU...?!
Okay, one more! Wow, you can drink.
I SNAGGED IT FROM THE TEACHERS.
HERE, HAVE SOME FISH TOO.
....
HEEEY, WHAT'RE YOU GUYS DOING? KISSING?
GET OVER HERE!!

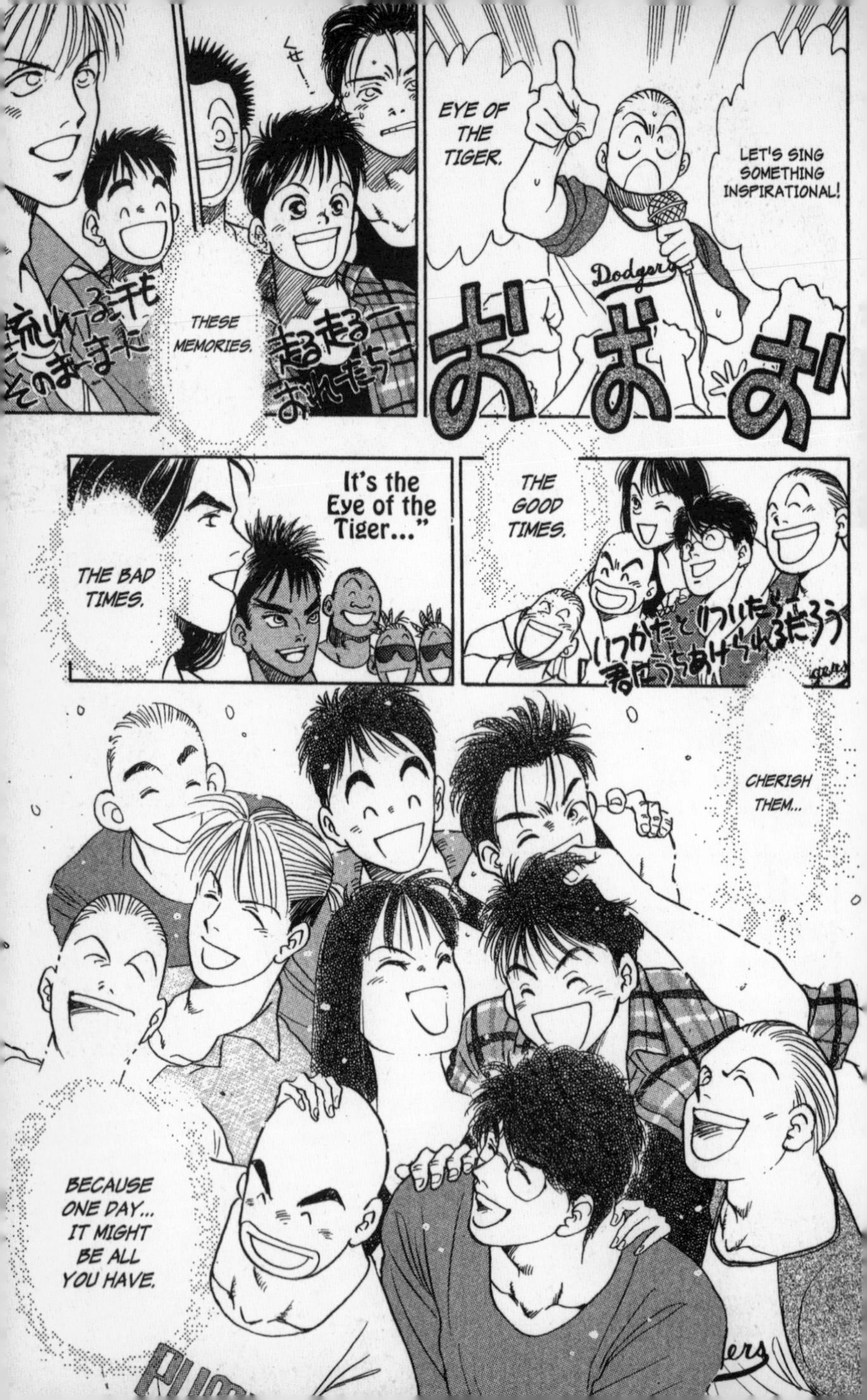
LET'S SING SOMETHING INSPIRATIONAL!
EYE OF THE TIGER.
おおお
くせー…!
走る走るー おれたち
THESE MEMORIES.
流れーる汗も そのまーまーに
THE GOOD TIMES.
いつかたどりついたら 君にうちあけられるだろう
It's the Eye of the Tiger..."
THE BAD TIMES.
CHERISH THEM...
BECAUSE ONE DAY... IT MIGHT BE ALL YOU HAVE.

今川聖

Nate... well, Nate. What can we say? He's sweet, he's neat, got a great smile and clean feet. Wants to be the best and studies hard to pass that test. Now only if he could get the girls as good as he can slam the net, then maybe Nate will soon be taking another kind of test.

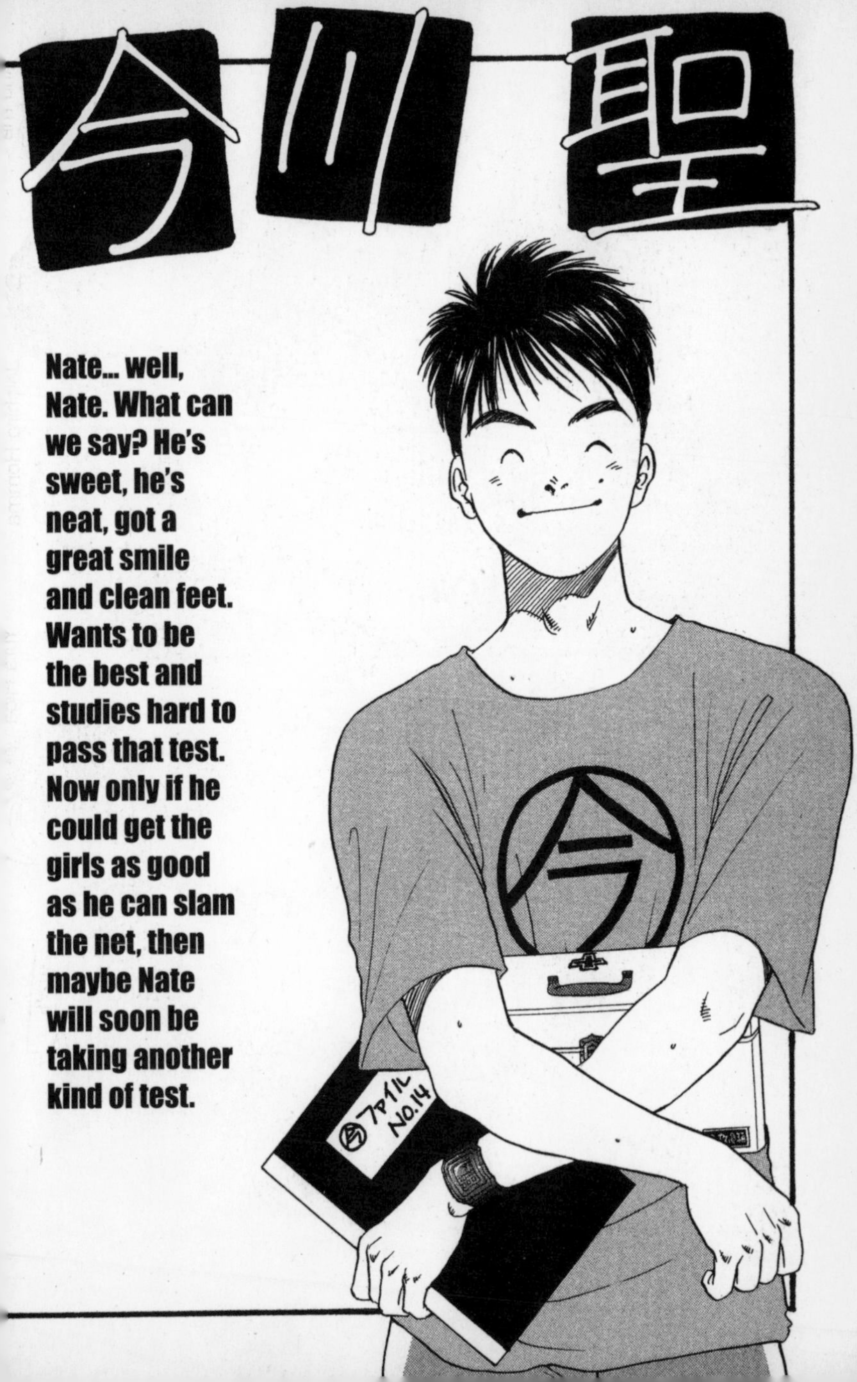

今 ファイル
No.14

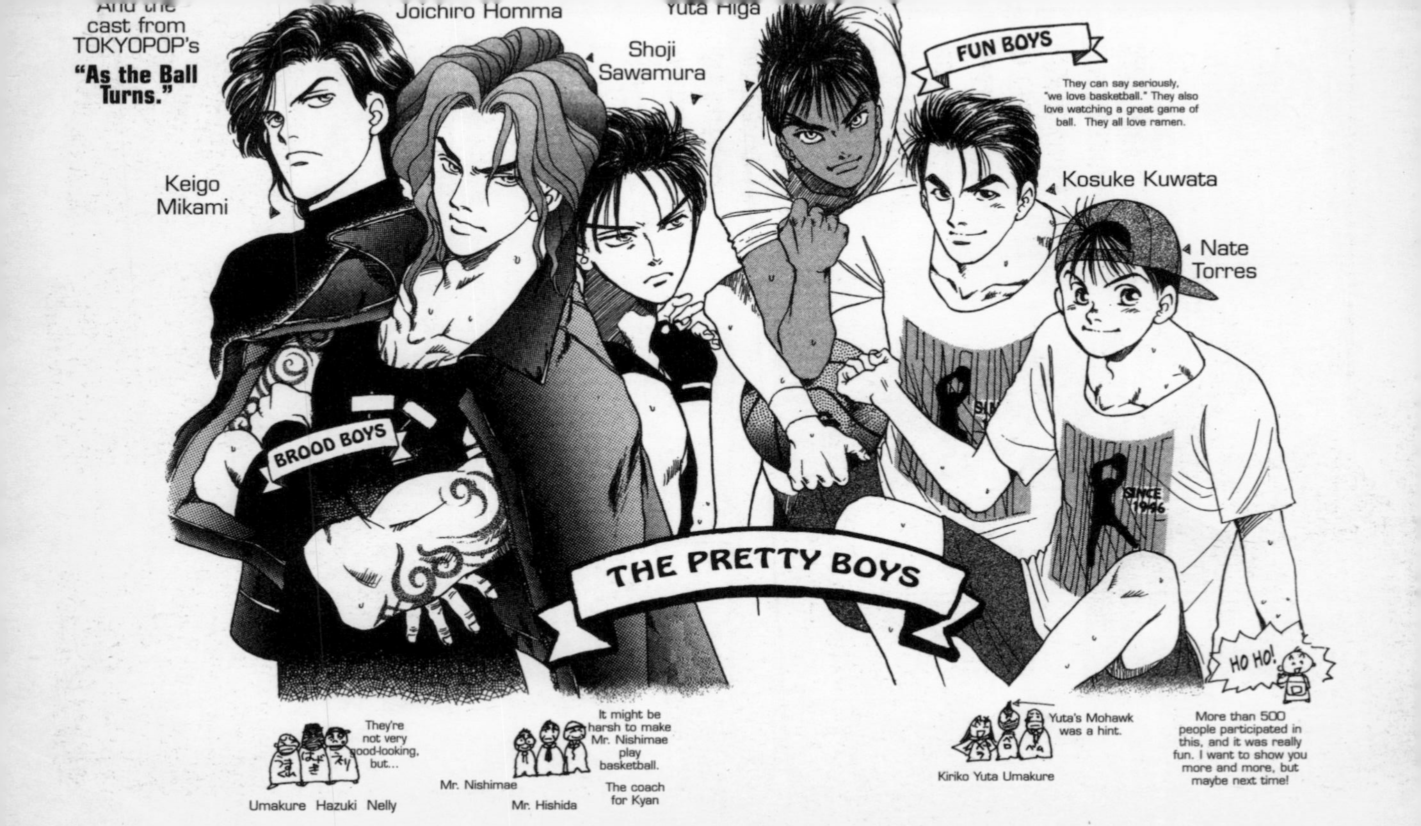
And the cast from TOKYOPOP's
"As the Ball Turns."
Keigo Mikami
Joichiro Homma
Shoji Sawamura
Yuta Higa
FUN BOYS
They can say seriously, "we love basketball." They also love watching a great game of ball. They all love ramen.
Kosuke Kuwata
Nate Torres
BROOD BOYS
THE PRETTY BOYS
HO HO!
They're not very good-looking, but...
Umakure Hazuki Nelly
It might be harsh to make Mr. Nishimae play basketball.
Mr. Nishimae
Mr. Hishida
The coach for Kyan
Yuta's Mohawk was a hint.
Kiriko Yuta Umakure
More than 500 people participated in this, and it was really fun. I want to show you more and more, but maybe next time!

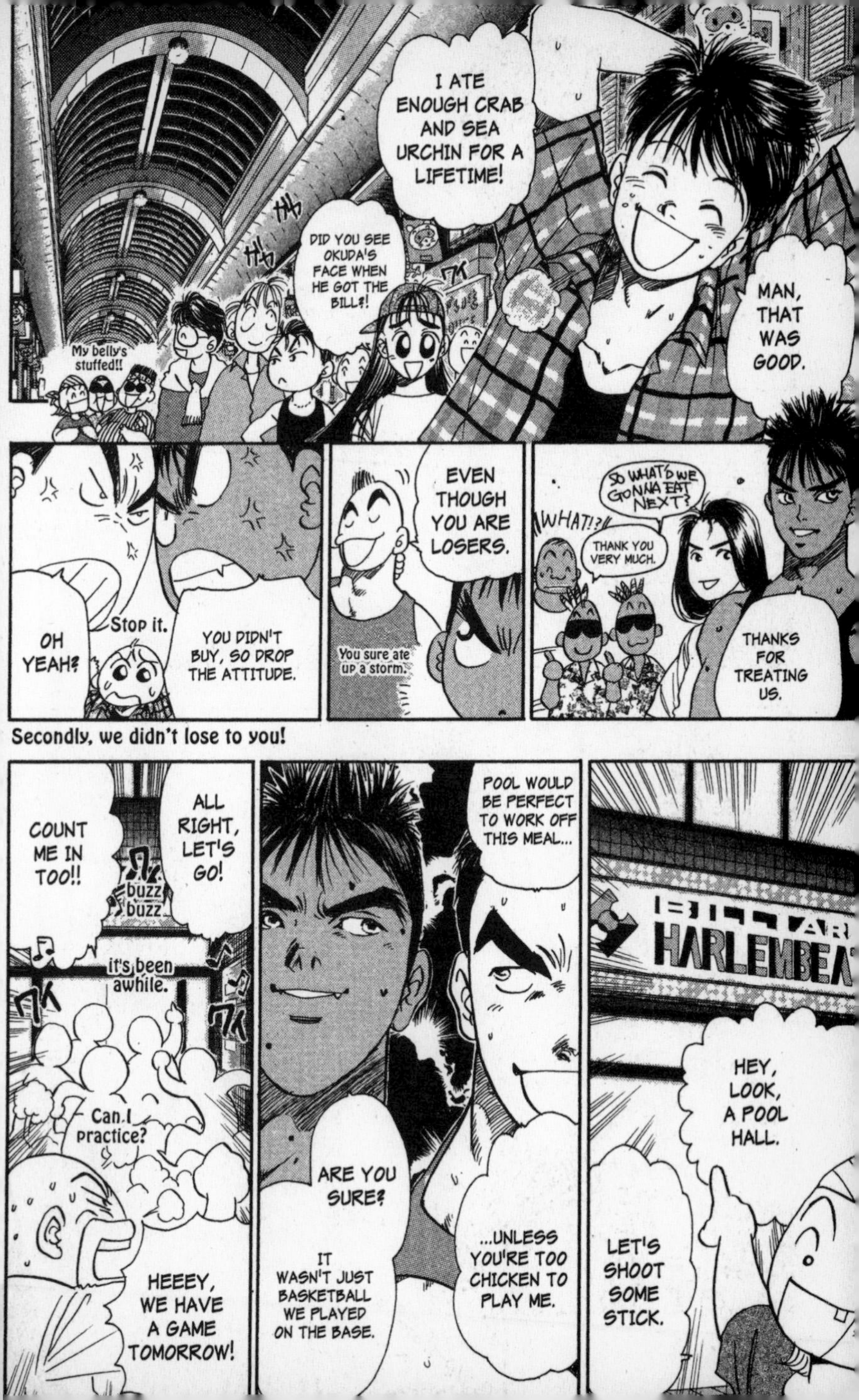
MAN, THAT WAS GOOD.
I ATE ENOUGH CRAB AND SEA URCHIN FOR A LIFETIME!
DID YOU SEE OKUDA'S FACE WHEN HE GOT THE BILL?!
My belly's stuffed!!
THANKS FOR TREATING US.
SO WHAT'D WE GONNA EAT NEXT?
THANK YOU VERY MUCH.
WHAT!?
EVEN THOUGH YOU ARE LOSERS.
You sure ate up a storm.
YOU DIDN'T BUY, SO DROP THE ATTITUDE.
Stop it.
OH YEAH?
Secondly, we didn't lose to you!
HEY, LOOK, A POOL HALL.
LET'S SHOOT SOME STICK.
POOL WOULD BE PERFECT TO WORK OFF THIS MEAL...
...UNLESS YOU'RE TOO CHICKEN TO PLAY ME.
ARE YOU SURE?
IT WASN'T JUST BASKETBALL WE PLAYED ON THE BASE.
ALL RIGHT, LET'S GO!
COUNT ME IN TOO!!
buzz buzz
it's been awhile.
Can I practice?
HEEEY, WE HAVE A GAME TOMORROW!

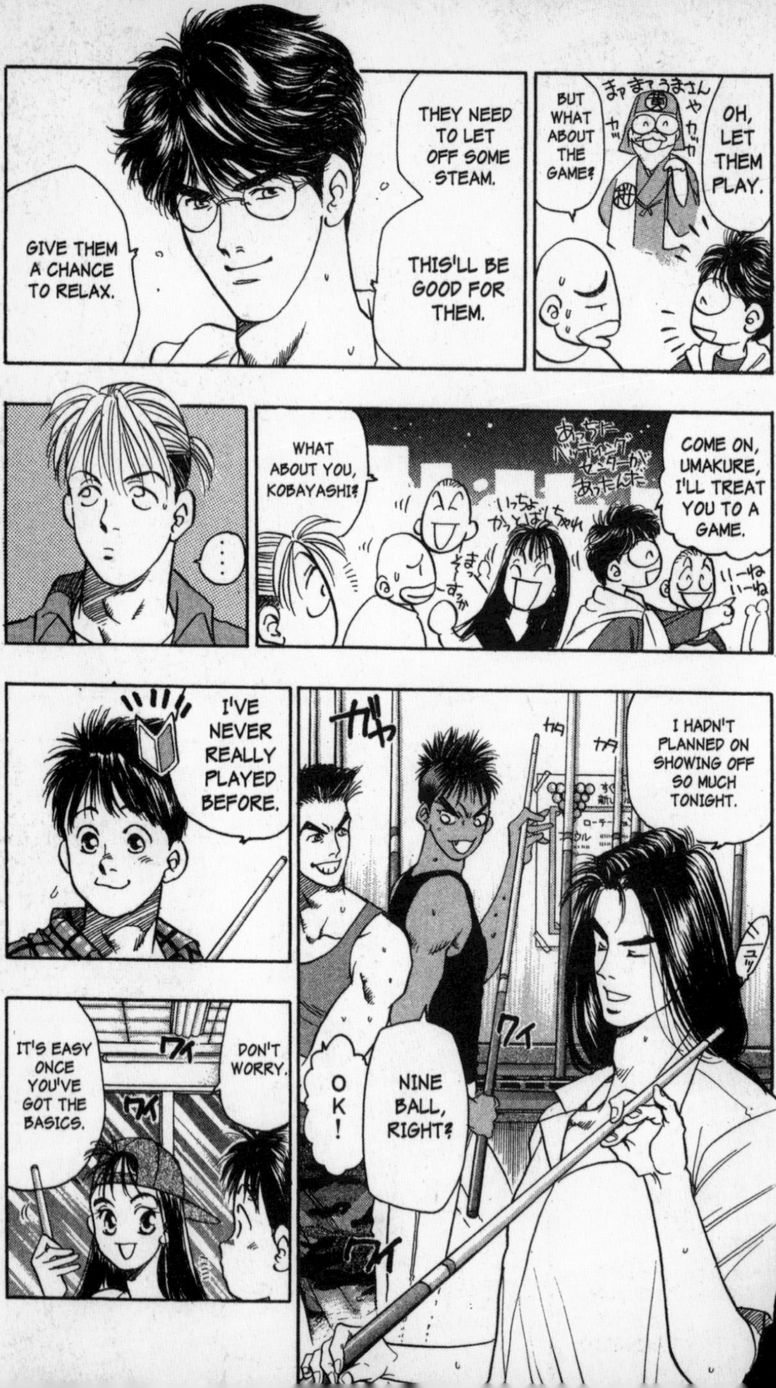
OH, LET THEM PLAY.
BUT WHAT ABOUT THE GAME?
THEY NEED TO LET OFF SOME STEAM.
THIS'LL BE GOOD FOR THEM.
GIVE THEM A CHANCE TO RELAX.
COME ON, UMAKURE, I'LL TREAT YOU TO A GAME.
WHAT ABOUT YOU, KOBAYASHI?
...
I HADN'T PLANNED ON SHOWING OFF SO MUCH TONIGHT.
ガヤ
NINE BALL, RIGHT?
OK!
I'VE NEVER REALLY PLAYED BEFORE.
DON'T WORRY.
IT'S EASY ONCE YOU'VE GOT THE BASICS.

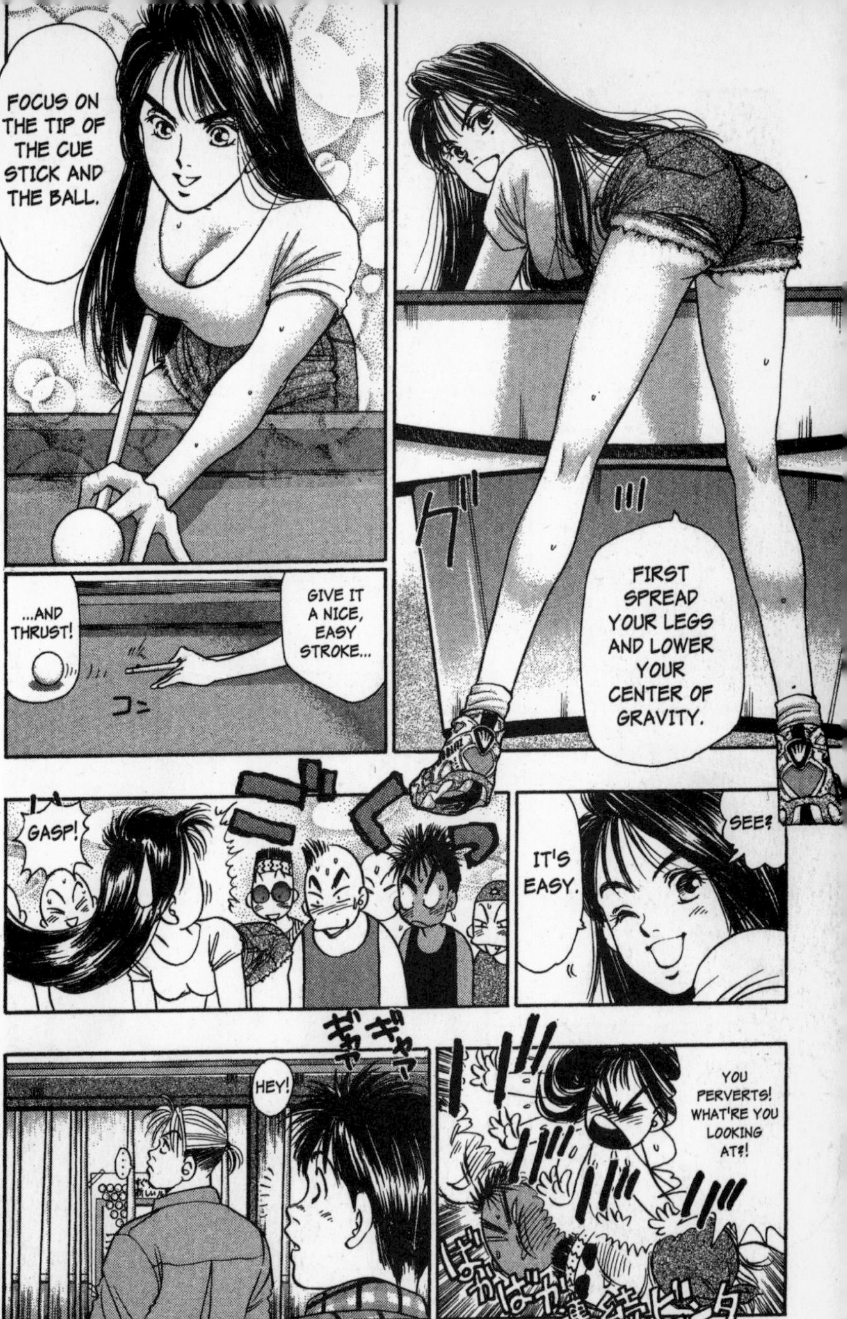

FIRST SPREAD YOUR LEGS AND LOWER YOUR CENTER OF GRAVITY.
FOCUS ON THE TIP OF THE CUE STICK AND THE BALL.
GIVE IT A NICE, EASY STROKE...
...AND THRUST!
SEE?
IT'S EASY.
GASP!
YOU PERVERTS! WHAT'RE YOU LOOKING AT?!
HEY!
...

Ah, more beatings.

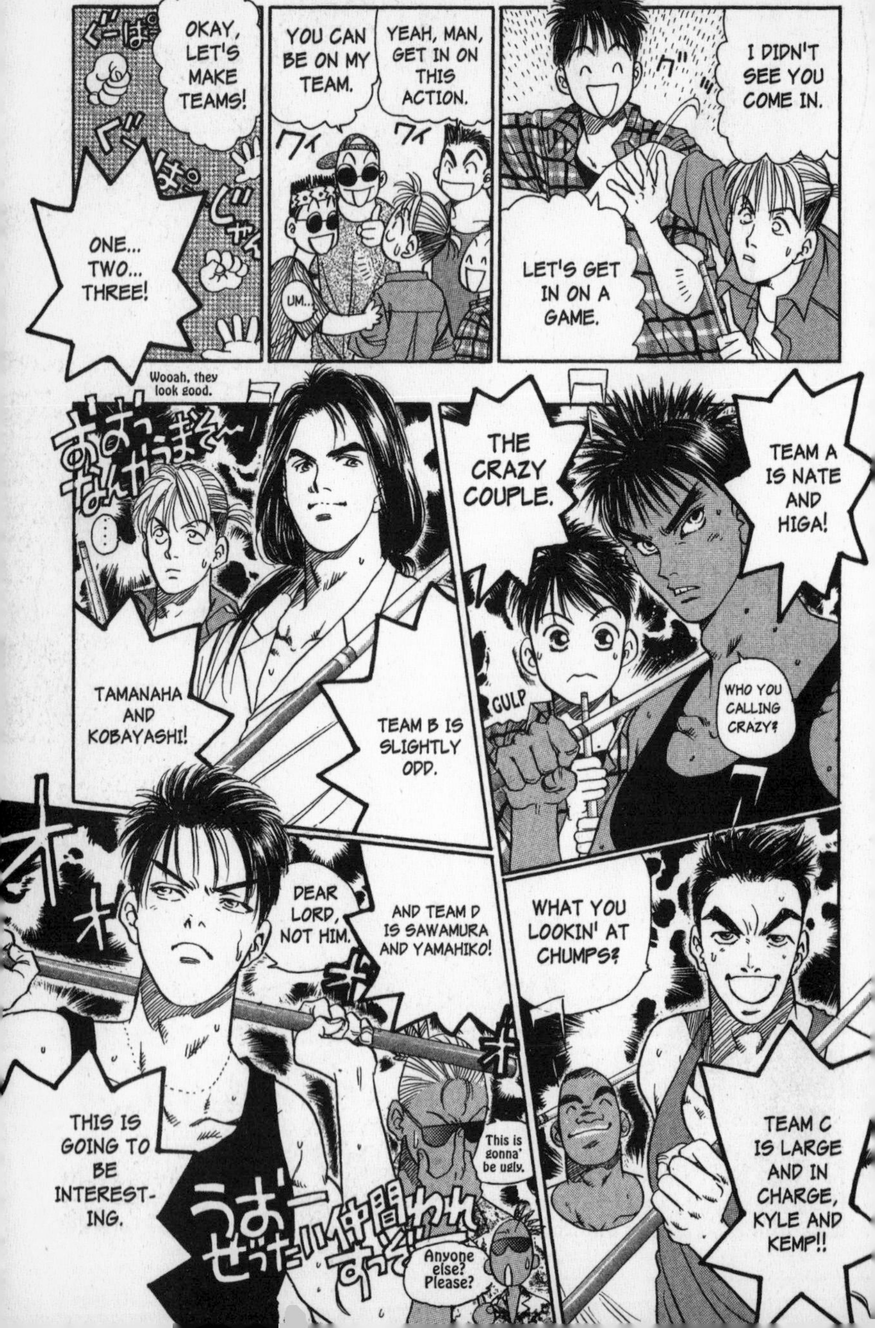
I DIDN'T SEE YOU COME IN.
LET'S GET IN ON A GAME.
YEAH, MAN, GET IN ON THIS ACTION.
YOU CAN BE ON MY TEAM.
UM...
OKAY, LET'S MAKE TEAMS!
ONE... TWO... THREE!
Wooah, they look good.
TEAM A IS NATE AND HIGA!
THE CRAZY COUPLE.
WHO YOU CALLING CRAZY?
GULP
TEAM B IS SLIGHTLY ODD.
TAMANAHA AND KOBAYASHI!
...
TEAM C IS LARGE AND IN CHARGE, KYLE AND KEMP!!
WHAT YOU LOOKIN' AT CHUMPS?
AND TEAM D IS SAWAMURA AND YAMAHIKO!
DEAR LORD, NOT HIM.
This is gonna' be ugly.
THIS IS GOING TO BE INTEREST-ING.
Anyone else? Please?

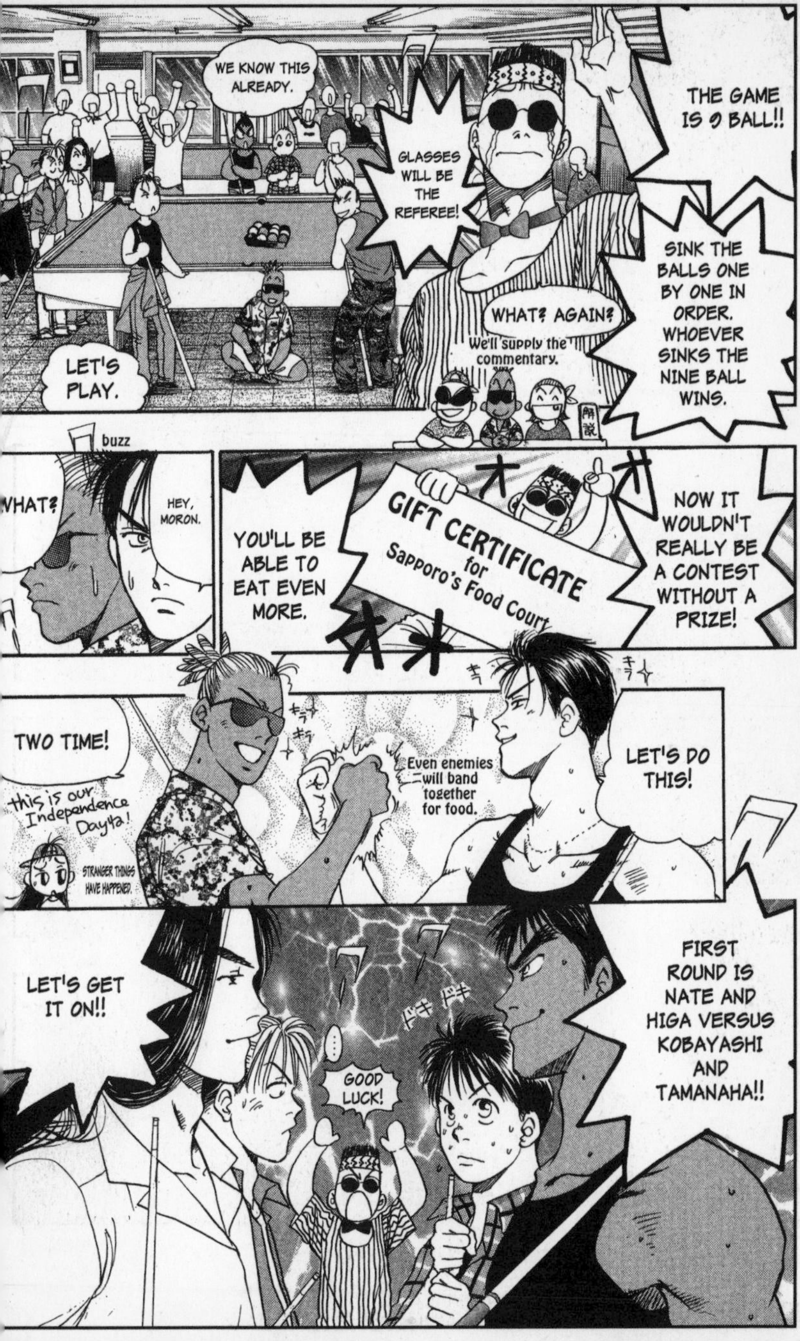
THE GAME IS 9 BALL!!
GLASSES WILL BE THE REFEREE!
SINK THE BALLS ONE BY ONE IN ORDER. WHOEVER SINKS THE NINE BALL WINS.
WE KNOW THIS ALREADY.
WHAT? AGAIN?
We'll supply the commentary.
LET'S PLAY.
NOW IT WOULDN'T REALLY BE A CONTEST WITHOUT A PRIZE!
GIFT CERTIFICATE for Sapporo's Food Court
YOU'LL BE ABLE TO EAT EVEN MORE.
buzz
HEY, MORON.
WHAT?
LET'S DO THIS!
Even enemies will band together for food.
TWO TIME!
this is our Independence Day!
STRANGER THINGS HAVE HAPPENED.
FIRST ROUND IS NATE AND HIGA VERSUS KOBAYASHI AND TAMANAHA!!
GOOD LUCK!
...
LET'S GET IT ON!!

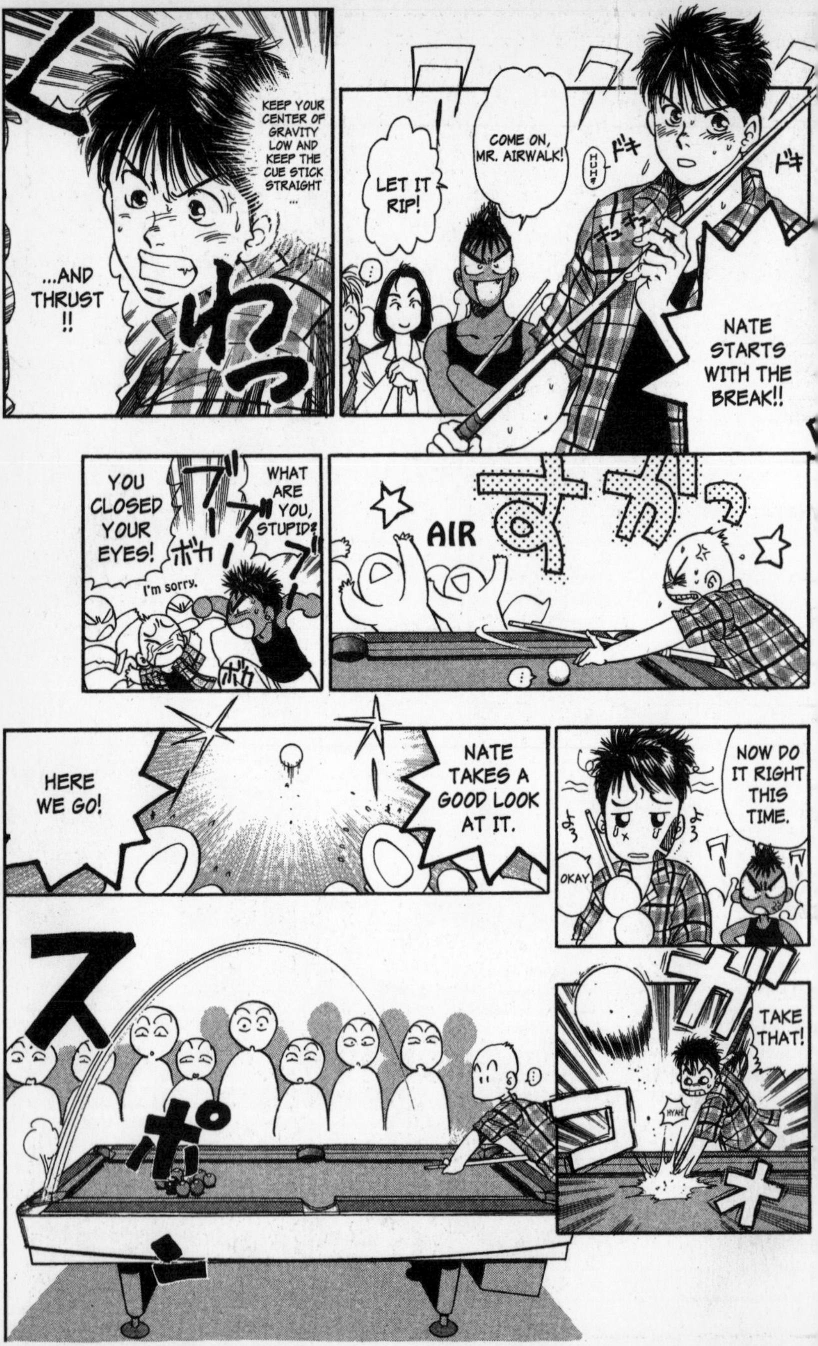
COME ON, MR. AIRWALK!
LET IT RIP!
HUH?
ドキ
ドキ
NATE STARTS WITH THE BREAK!!
KEEP YOUR CENTER OF GRAVITY LOW AND KEEP THE CUE STICK STRAIGHT ...
...AND THRUST !!
AIR
WHAT ARE YOU, STUPID?
YOU CLOSED YOUR EYES!
I'm sorry.
NOW DO IT RIGHT THIS TIME.
OKAY.
NATE TAKES A GOOD LOOK AT IT.
HERE WE GO!
TAKE THAT!
HYAH!

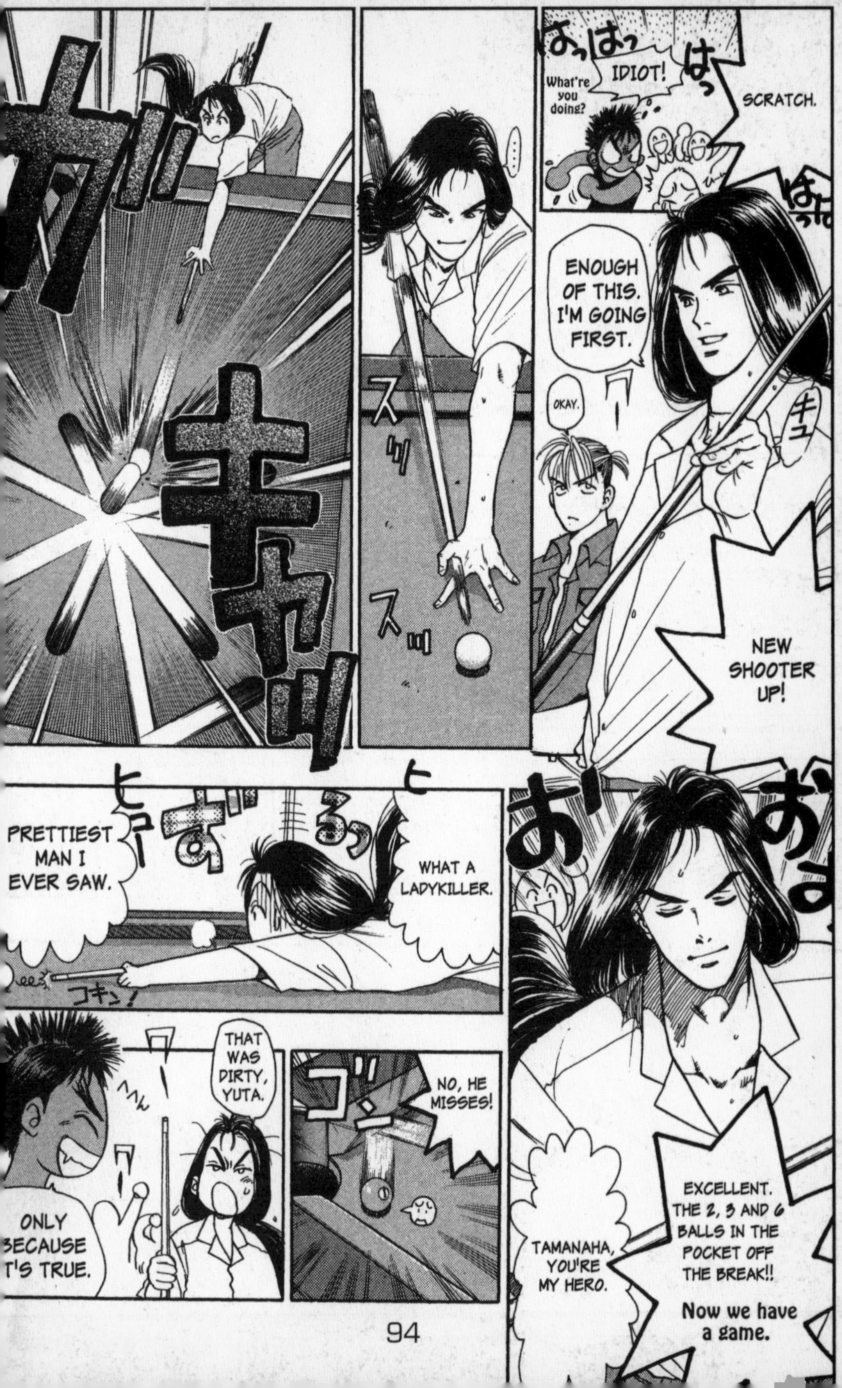
IDIOT!
What're you doing?
SCRATCH.
ENOUGH OF THIS. I'M GOING FIRST.
OKAY.
NEW SHOOTER UP!
EXCELLENT. THE 2, 3 AND 6 BALLS IN THE POCKET OFF THE BREAK!!
TAMANAHA, YOU'RE MY HERO.
Now we have a game.
WHAT A LADYKILLER.
PRETTIEST MAN I EVER SAW.
NO, HE MISSES!
THAT WAS DIRTY, YUTA.
ONLY BECAUSE T'S TRUE.

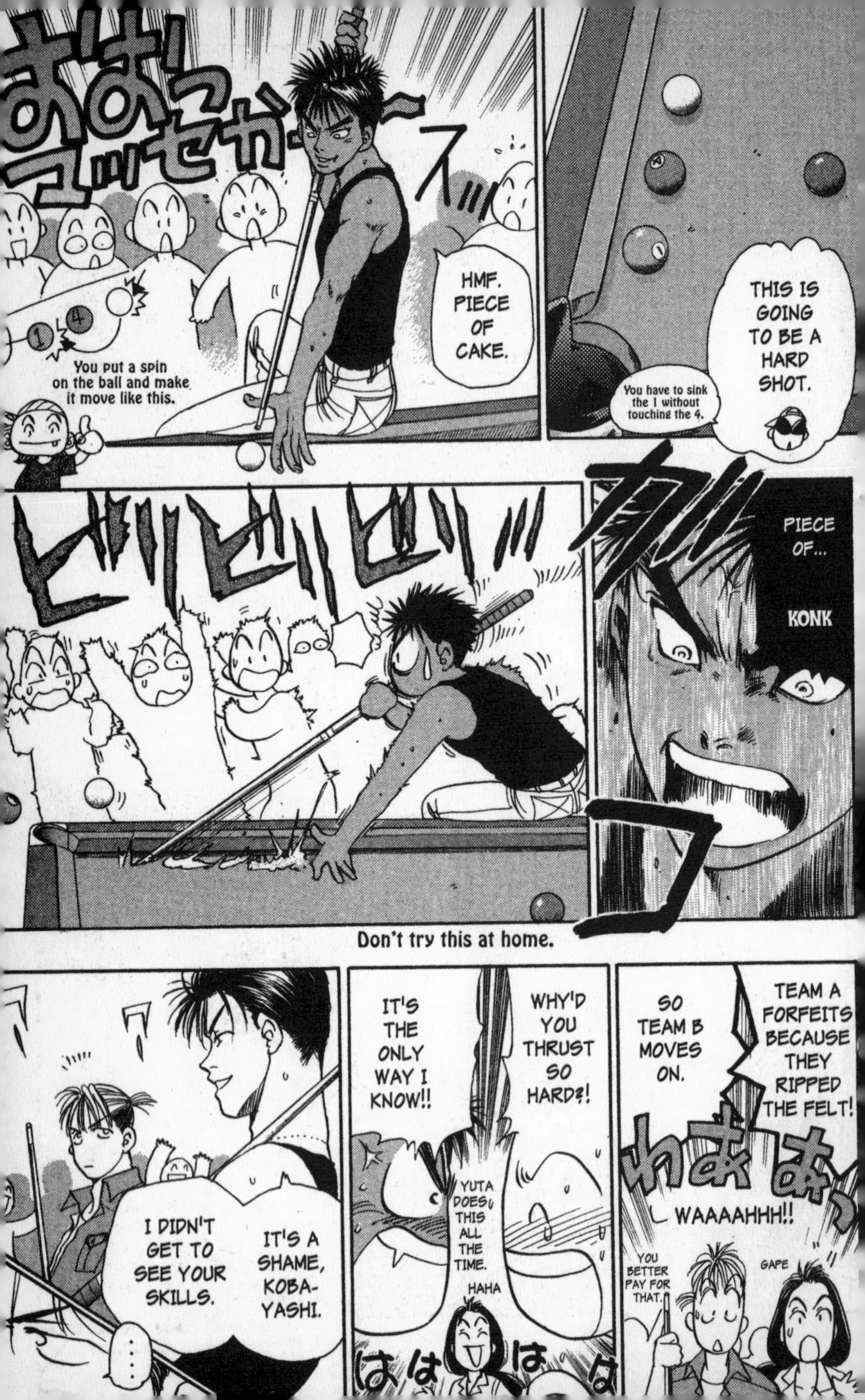
THIS IS GOING TO BE A HARD SHOT.
You have to sink the 1 without touching the 4.
HMF. PIECE OF CAKE.
You put a spin on the ball and make it move like this.
PIECE OF...
KONK
Don't try this at home.
TEAM A FORFEITS BECAUSE THEY RIPPED THE FELT!
SO TEAM B MOVES ON.
WAAAAHHH!!
GAPE
YOU BETTER PAY FOR THAT.
WHY'D YOU THRUST SO HARD?!
IT'S THE ONLY WAY I KNOW!!
YUTA DOES THIS ALL THE TIME.
HAHA
IT'S A SHAME, KOBAYASHI.
I DIDN'T GET TO SEE YOUR SKILLS.
...

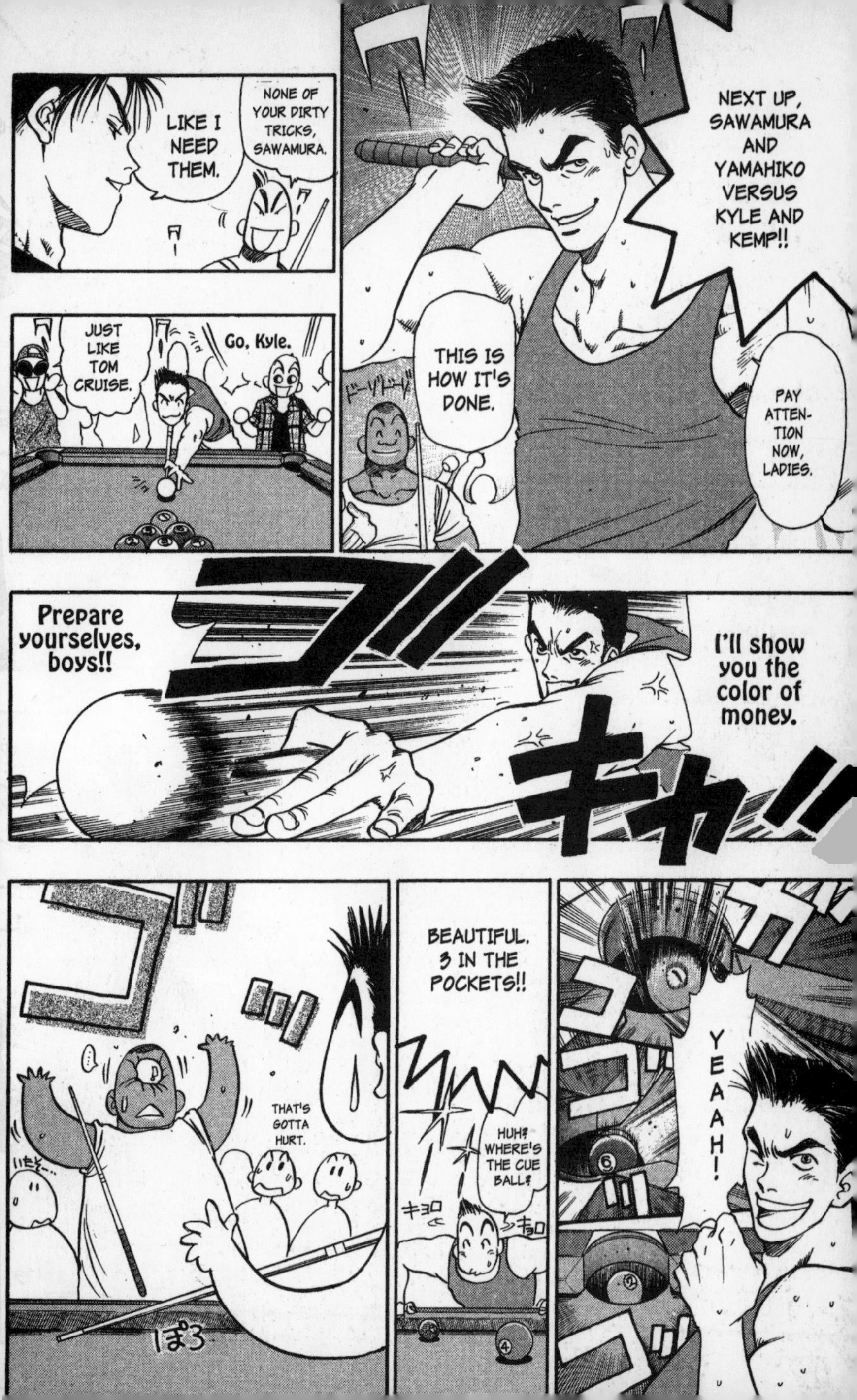
NEXT UP, SAWAMURA AND YAMAHIKO VERSUS KYLE AND KEMP!!
PAY ATTENTION NOW, LADIES.
THIS IS HOW IT'S DONE.
NONE OF YOUR DIRTY TRICKS, SAWAMURA.
LIKE I NEED THEM.
Go, Kyle.
JUST LIKE TOM CRUISE.
I'll show you the color of money.
Prepare yourselves, boys!!
YEAAH!
BEAUTIFUL. 3 IN THE POCKETS!!
HUH? WHERE'S THE CUE BALL?
THAT'S GOTTA HURT.

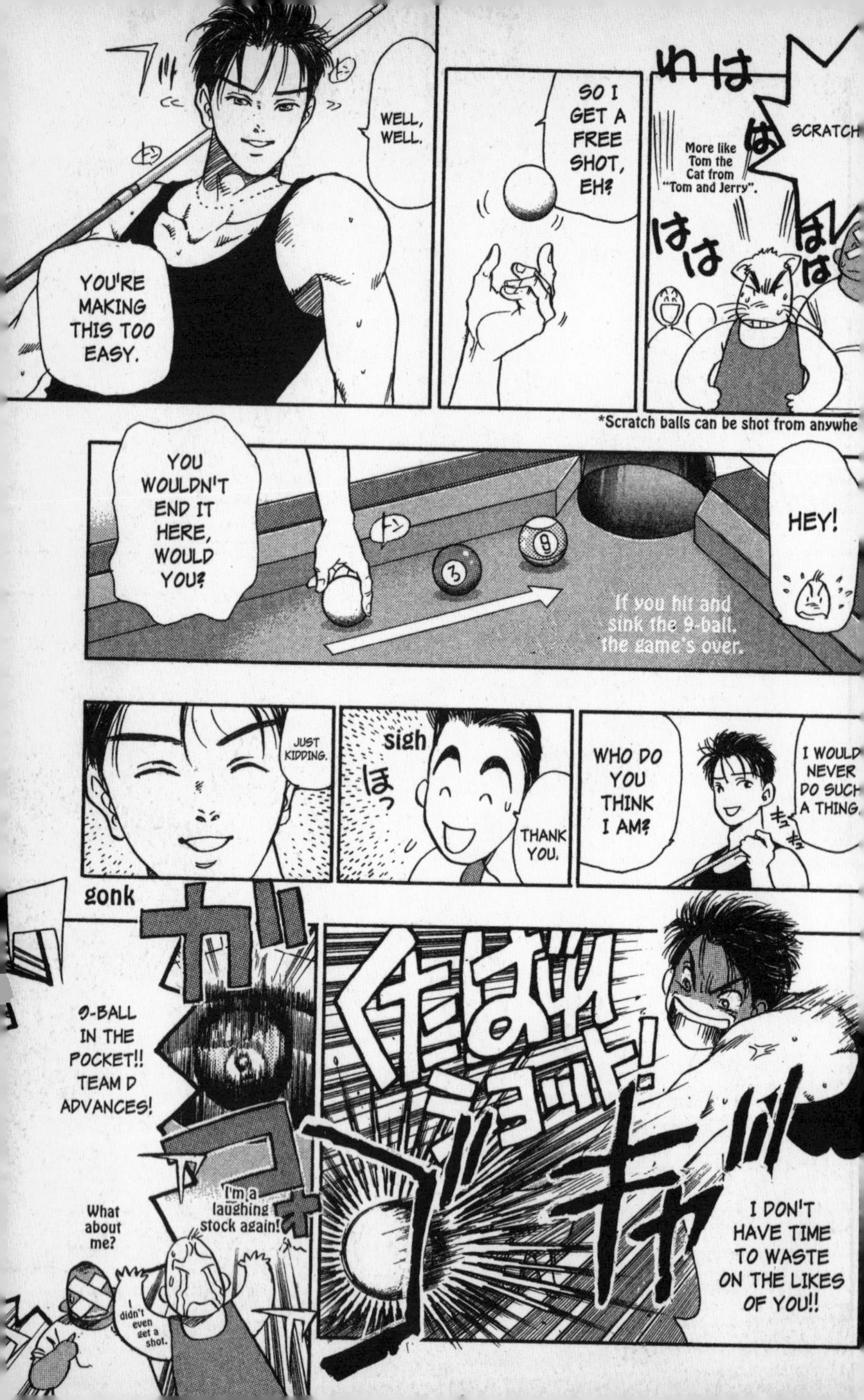
SCRATCH
More like Tom the Cat from "Tom and Jerry".
SO I GET A FREE SHOT, EH?
WELL, WELL.
YOU'RE MAKING THIS TOO EASY.
*Scratch balls can be shot from anywhe
HEY!
YOU WOULDN'T END IT HERE, WOULD YOU?
If you hit and sink the 9-ball, the game's over.
I WOULD NEVER DO SUCH A THING.
WHO DO YOU THINK I AM?
sigh
ほっ
THANK YOU.
JUST KIDDING.
I DON'T HAVE TIME TO WASTE ON THE LIKES OF YOU!!
gonk
9-BALL IN THE POCKET!! TEAM D ADVANCES!
I'm a laughing stock again!
What about me?
I didn't even get a shot.

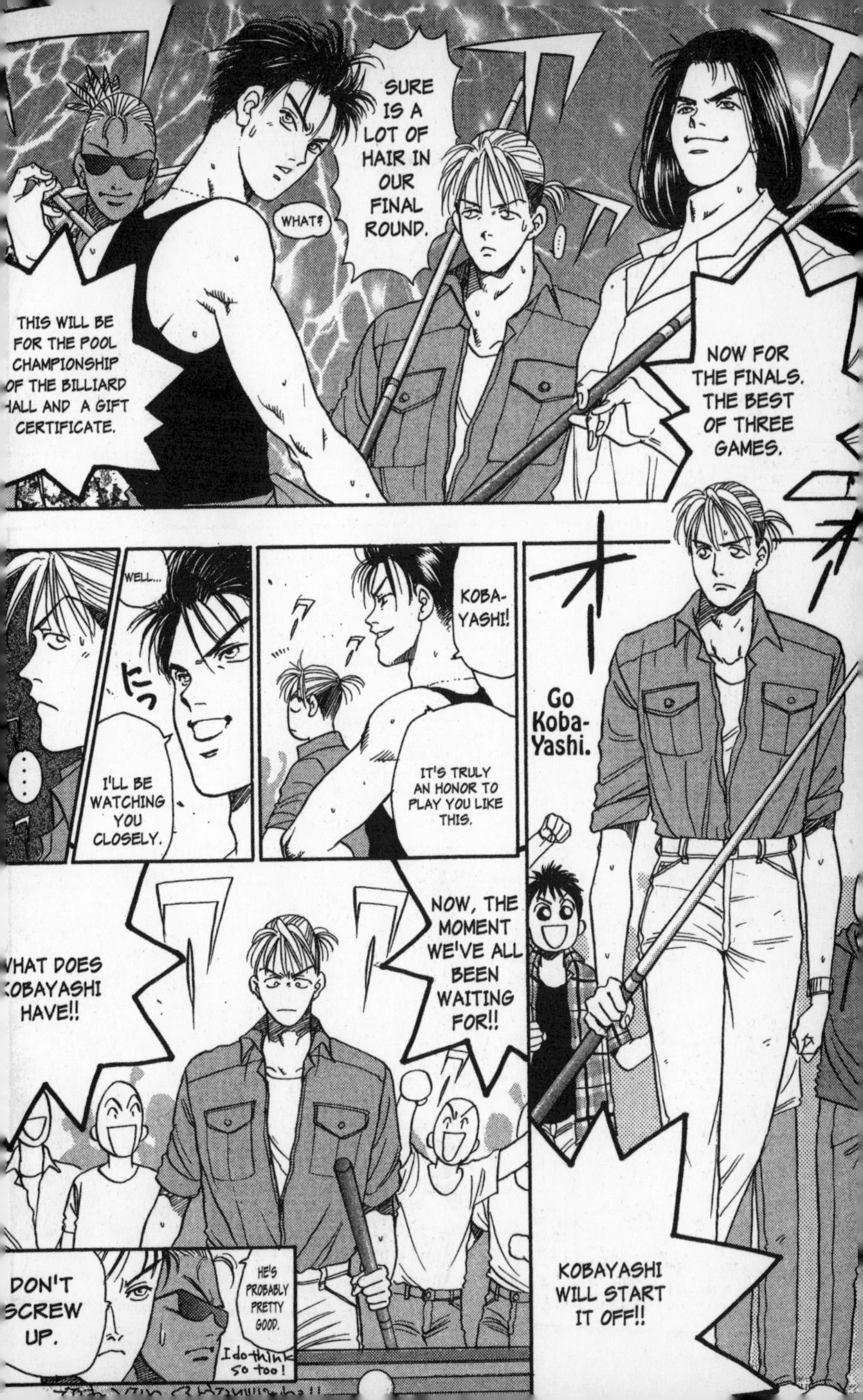
THIS WILL BE FOR THE POOL CHAMPIONSHIP OF THE BILLIARD HALL AND A GIFT CERTIFICATE.
NOW FOR THE FINALS. THE BEST OF THREE GAMES.
SURE IS A LOT OF HAIR IN OUR FINAL ROUND.
WHAT?
...
Go Koba-Yashi.
KOBAYASHI WILL START IT OFF!!
KOBA-YASHI!
IT'S TRULY AN HONOR TO PLAY YOU LIKE THIS.
WELL...
I'LL BE WATCHING YOU CLOSELY.
...
NOW, THE MOMENT WE'VE ALL BEEN WAITING FOR!!
WHAT DOES KOBAYASHI HAVE!!
HE'S PROBABLY PRETTY GOOD.
I do think so too!
DON'T SCREW UP.

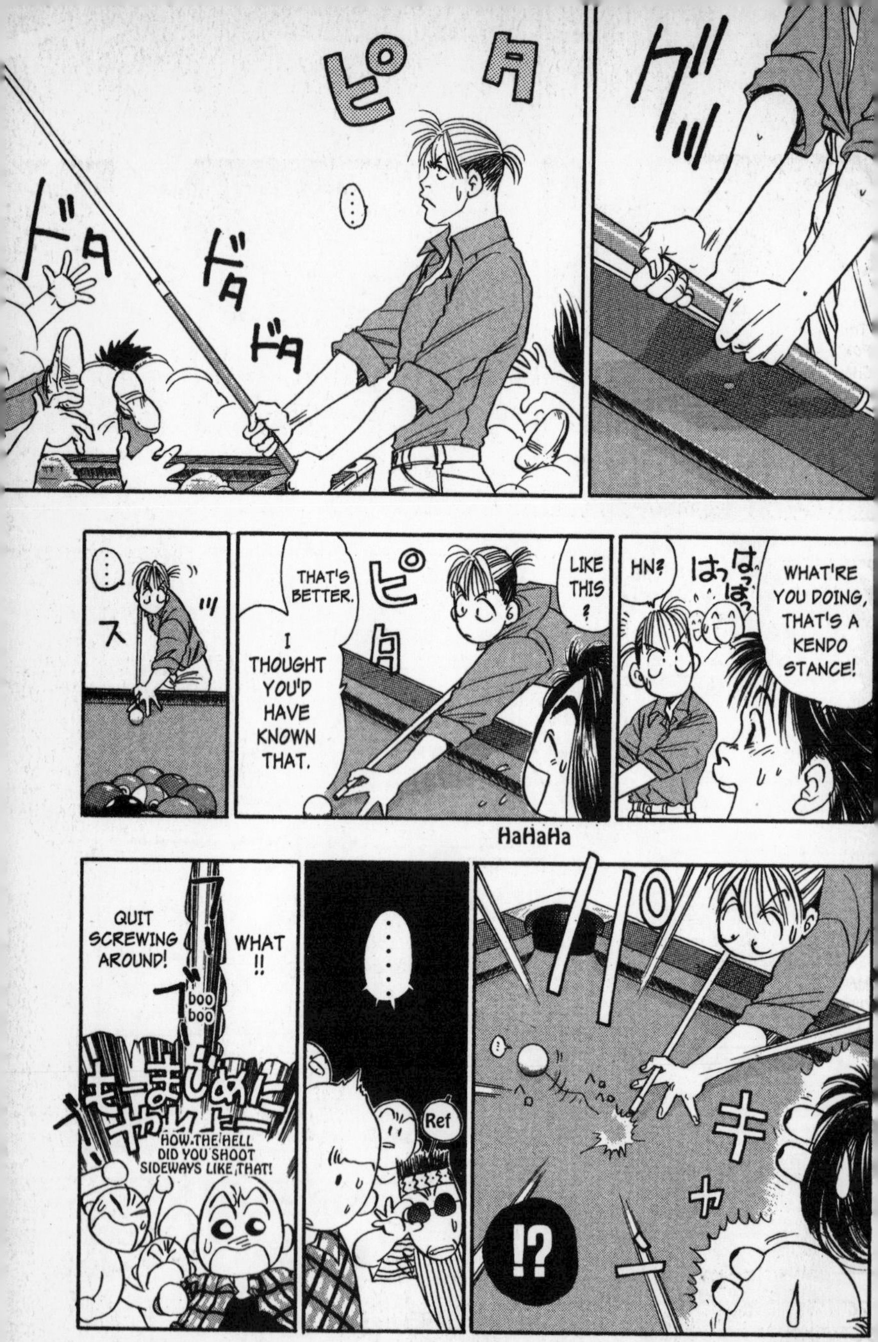
グッ
ピタ
…
ドタ
ドタ
ドタ
WHAT'RE YOU DOING, THAT'S A KENDO STANCE!
はっはっ
はっ
HN?
LIKE THIS?
THAT'S BETTER.
I THOUGHT YOU'D HAVE KNOWN THAT.
ピタ
…
ス
ッ
HaHaHa
パ
キャ
!?
…
Ref
WHAT!!
QUIT SCREWING AROUND!
boo boo
もーまじめにやれよー
HOW THE HELL DID YOU SHOOT SIDEWAYS LIKE THAT!

Nate

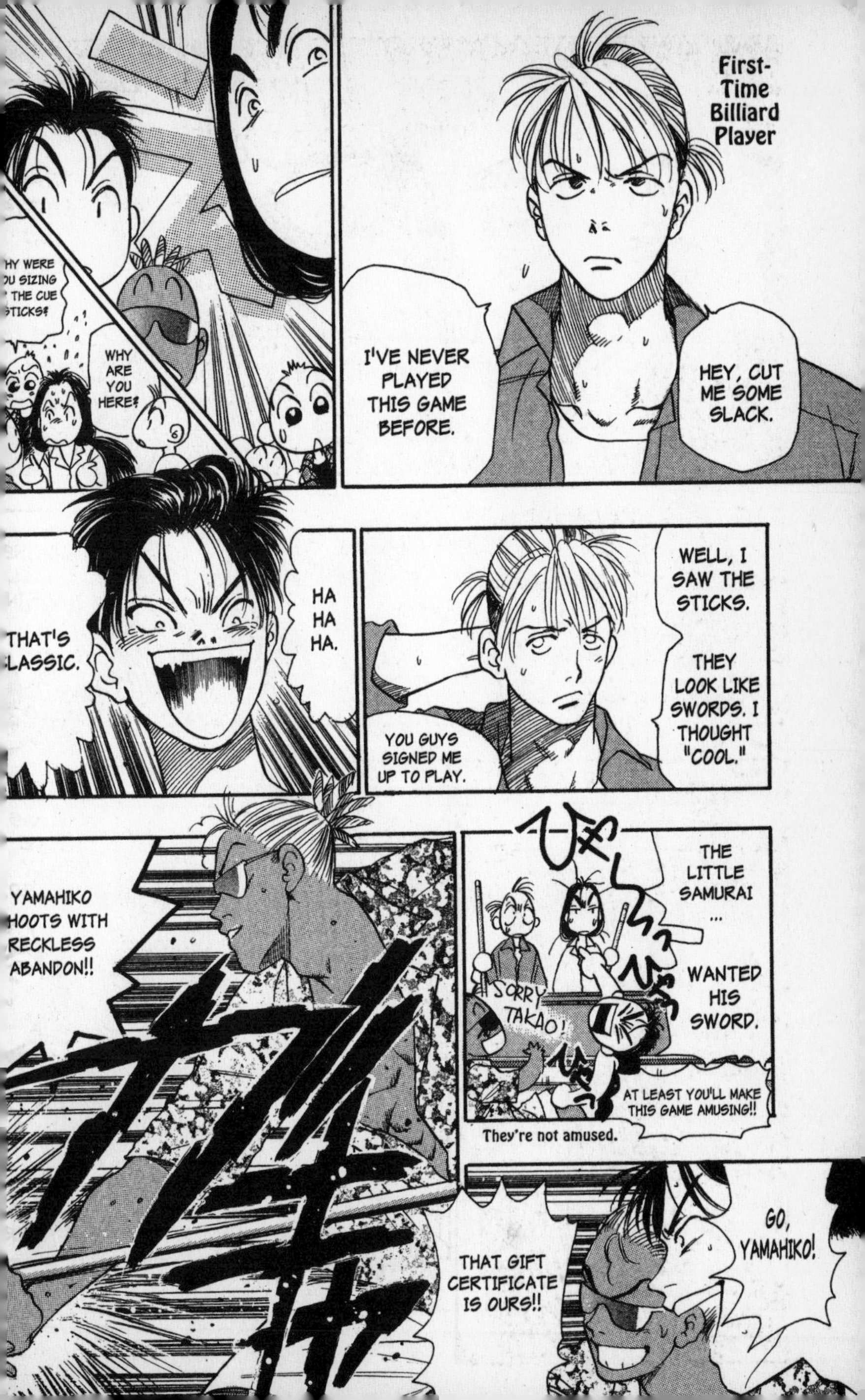
First-Time Billiard Player
HEY, CUT ME SOME SLACK.
I'VE NEVER PLAYED THIS GAME BEFORE.
HY WERE OU SIZING THE CUE TICKS?
WHY ARE YOU HERE?
WELL, I SAW THE STICKS.
THEY LOOK LIKE SWORDS. I THOUGHT "COOL."
YOU GUYS SIGNED ME UP TO PLAY.
HA HA HA.
THAT'S LASSIC.
THE LITTLE SAMURAI ...
WANTED HIS SWORD.
SORRY TAKAO!
AT LEAST YOU'LL MAKE THIS GAME AMUSING!!
They're not amused.
YAMAHIKO HOOTS WITH RECKLESS ABANDON!!
GO, YAMAHIKO!
THAT GIFT CERTIFICATE IS OURS!!

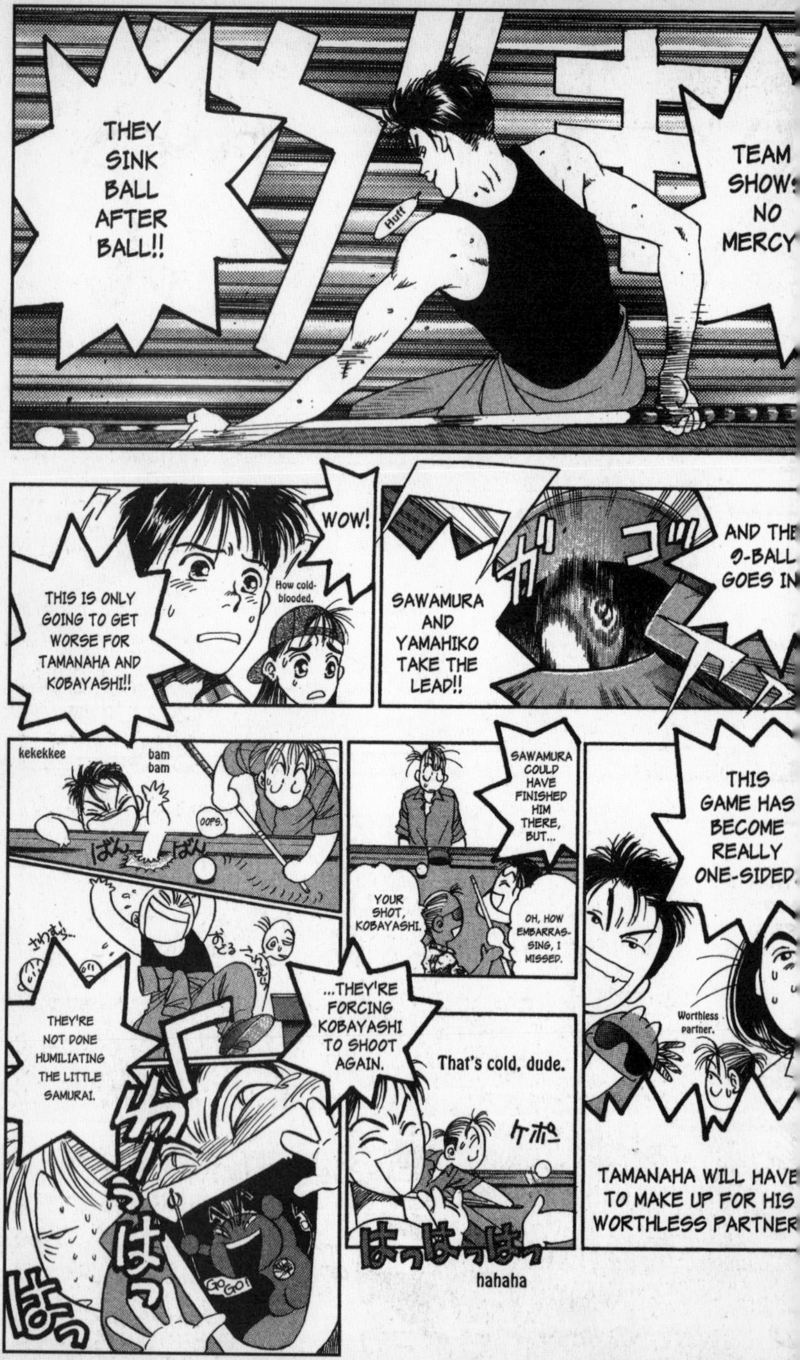

TEAM SHOWS NO MERCY
Huff
THEY SINK BALL AFTER BALL!!
AND THE 9-BALL GOES IN
SAWAMURA AND YAMAHIKO TAKE THE LEAD!!
WOW!
How cold-blooded.
THIS IS ONLY GOING TO GET WORSE FOR TAMANAHA AND KOBAYASHI!!
THIS GAME HAS BECOME REALLY ONE-SIDED.
Worthless partner.
TAMANAHA WILL HAVE TO MAKE UP FOR HIS WORTHLESS PARTNER
SAWAMURA COULD HAVE FINISHED HIM THERE, BUT...
OH, HOW EMBARRAS-SING, I MISSED.
YOUR SHOT, KOBAYASHI.
...THEY'RE FORCING KOBAYASHI TO SHOOT AGAIN.
That's cold, dude.
ケポー
はっはっはっ
hahaha
bam bam
ばん ばん
OOPS.
kekekkee
THEY'RE NOT DONE HUMILIATING THE LITTLE SAMURAI.
GO GO!

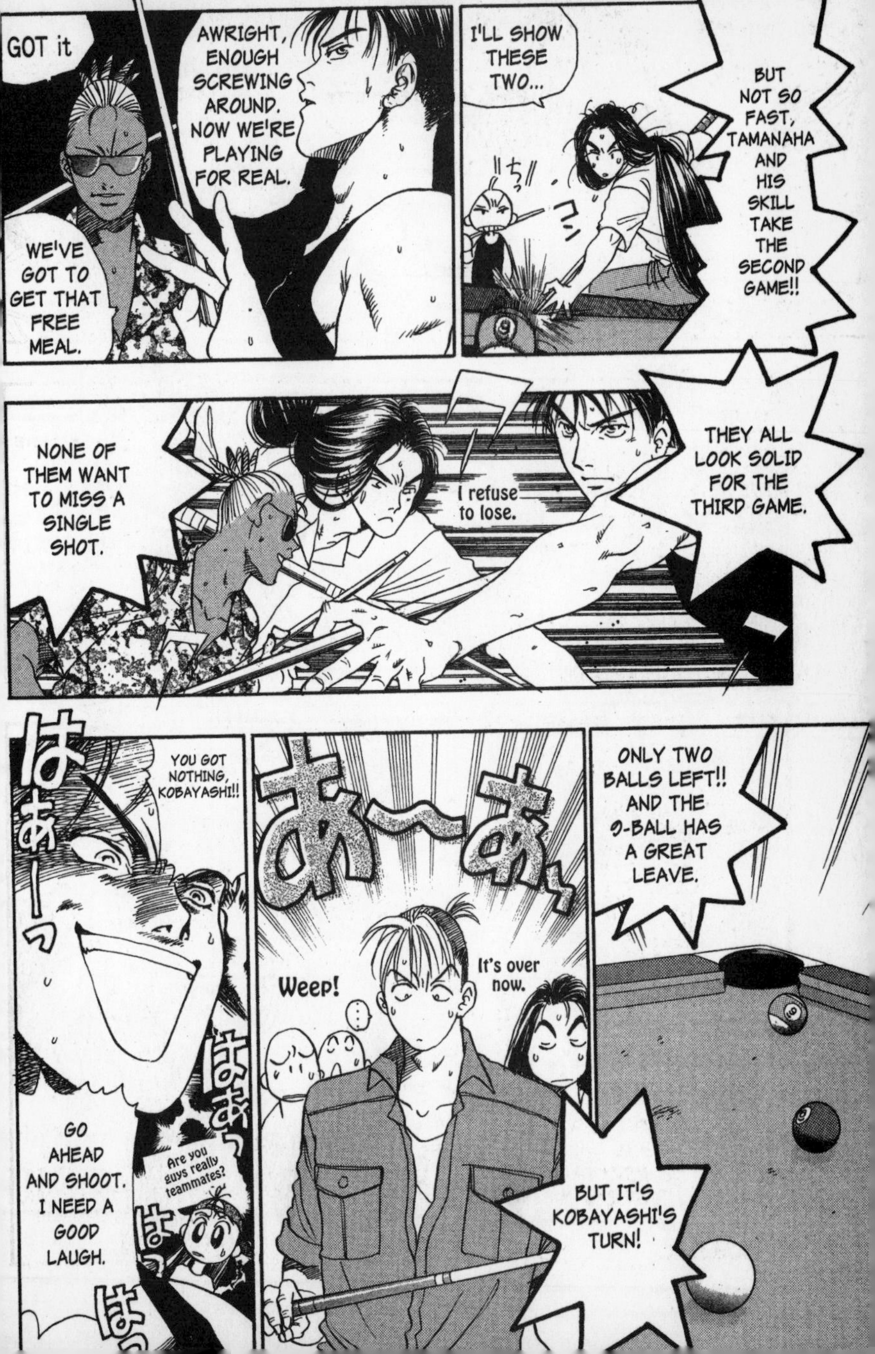
BUT NOT SO FAST, TAMANAHA AND HIS SKILL TAKE THE SECOND GAME!!
I'LL SHOW THESE TWO...
AWRIGHT, ENOUGH SCREWING AROUND. NOW WE'RE PLAYING FOR REAL.
GOT it
WE'VE GOT TO GET THAT FREE MEAL.
THEY ALL LOOK SOLID FOR THE THIRD GAME.
I refuse to lose.
NONE OF THEM WANT TO MISS A SINGLE SHOT.
ONLY TWO BALLS LEFT!! AND THE 9-BALL HAS A GREAT LEAVE.
BUT IT'S KOBAYASHI'S TURN!
あ〜あ、
It's over now.
Weep!
はあーっ
YOU GOT NOTHING, KOBAYASHI!!
はあっ
Are you guys really teammates?
GO AHEAD AND SHOOT. I NEED A GOOD LAUGH.
はっ
はっ

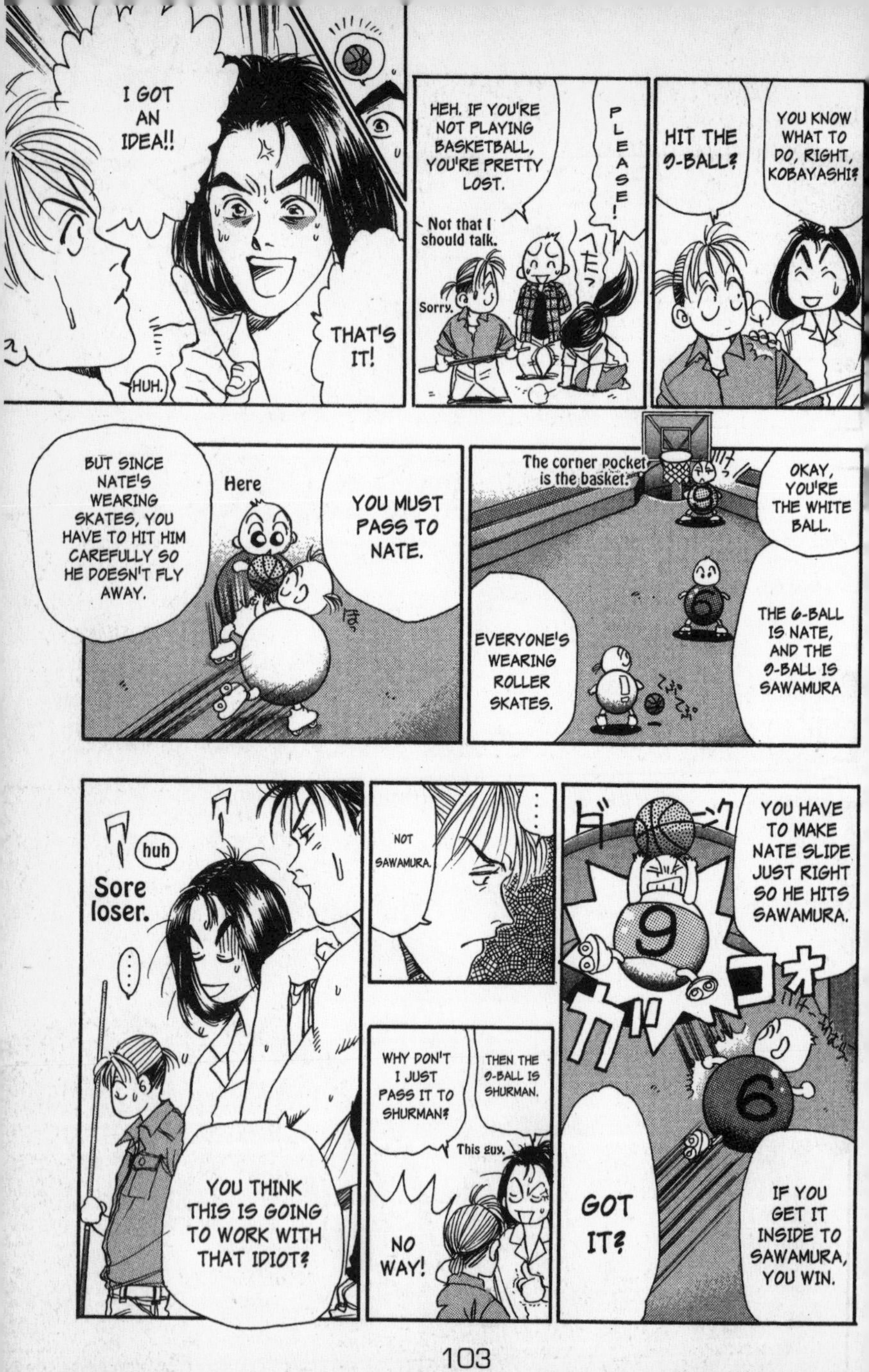
YOU KNOW WHAT TO DO, RIGHT, KOBAYASHI?
HIT THE 9-BALL?
PLEASE!
HEH. IF YOU'RE NOT PLAYING BASKETBALL, YOU'RE PRETTY LOST.
Not that I should talk.
Sorry.
I GOT AN IDEA!!
THAT'S IT!
HUH.
OKAY, YOU'RE THE WHITE BALL.
The corner pocket is the basket.
THE 6-BALL IS NATE, AND THE 9-BALL IS SAWAMURA
EVERYONE'S WEARING ROLLER SKATES.
YOU MUST PASS TO NATE.
Here
BUT SINCE NATE'S WEARING SKATES, YOU HAVE TO HIT HIM CAREFULLY SO HE DOESN'T FLY AWAY.
YOU HAVE TO MAKE NATE SLIDE JUST RIGHT SO HE HITS SAWAMURA.
9
6
IF YOU GET IT INSIDE TO SAWAMURA, YOU WIN.
GOT IT?
...
NOT SAWAMURA.
THEN THE 9-BALL IS SHURMAN.
WHY DON'T I JUST PASS IT TO SHURMAN?
This guy.
NO WAY!
huh
Sore loser.
...
YOU THINK THIS IS GOING TO WORK WITH THAT IDIOT?

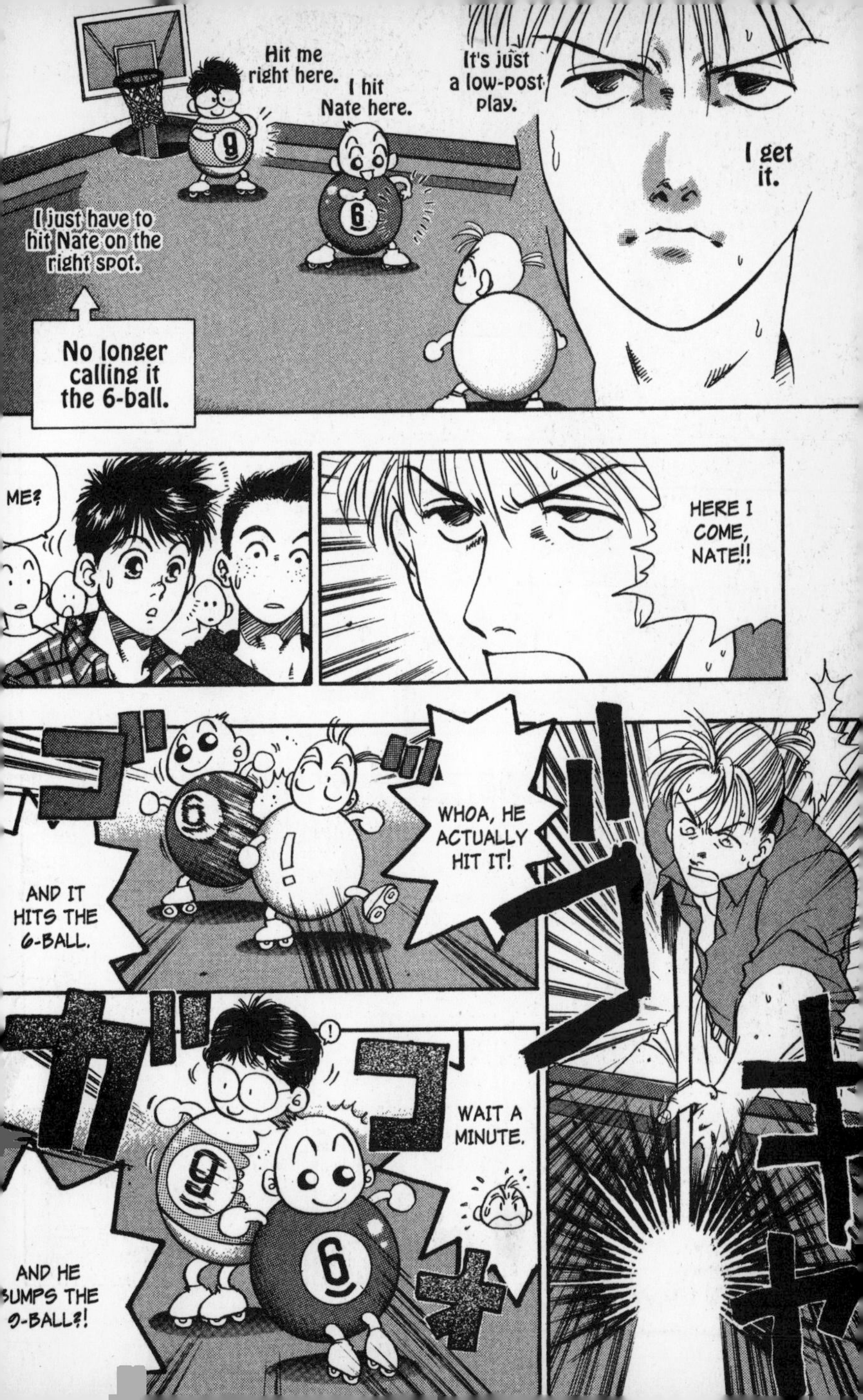
It's just a low-post play.
I get it.
I hit Nate here.
Hit me right here.
I just have to hit Nate on the right spot.
No longer calling it the 6-ball.
HERE I COME, NATE!!
ME?
WHOA, HE ACTUALLY HIT IT!
AND IT HITS THE 6-BALL.
WAIT A MINUTE.
AND HE UMPS THE 9-BALL?!

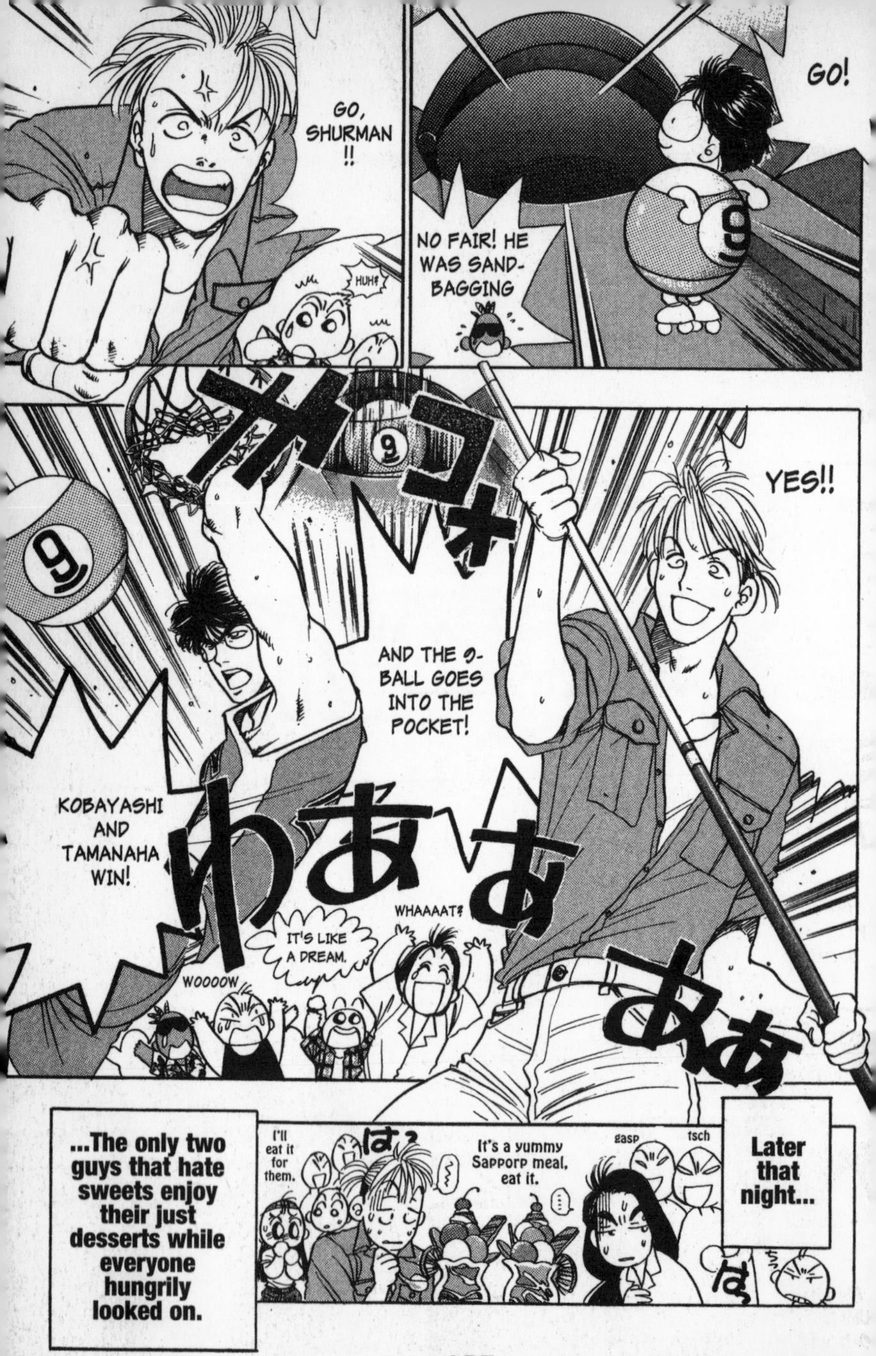
GO!
NO FAIR! HE WAS SAND-BAGGING
GO, SHURMAN !!
HUH?
YES!!
AND THE 9-BALL GOES INTO THE POCKET!
KOBAYASHI AND TAMANAHA WIN!
WHAAAAT?
IT'S LIKE A DREAM.
WOOOOW
Later that night...
tsch
gasp
It's a yummy Sapporp meal, eat it.
I'll eat it for them.
...The only two guys that hate sweets enjoy their just desserts while everyone hungrily looked on.

REBOUND

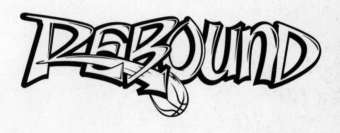

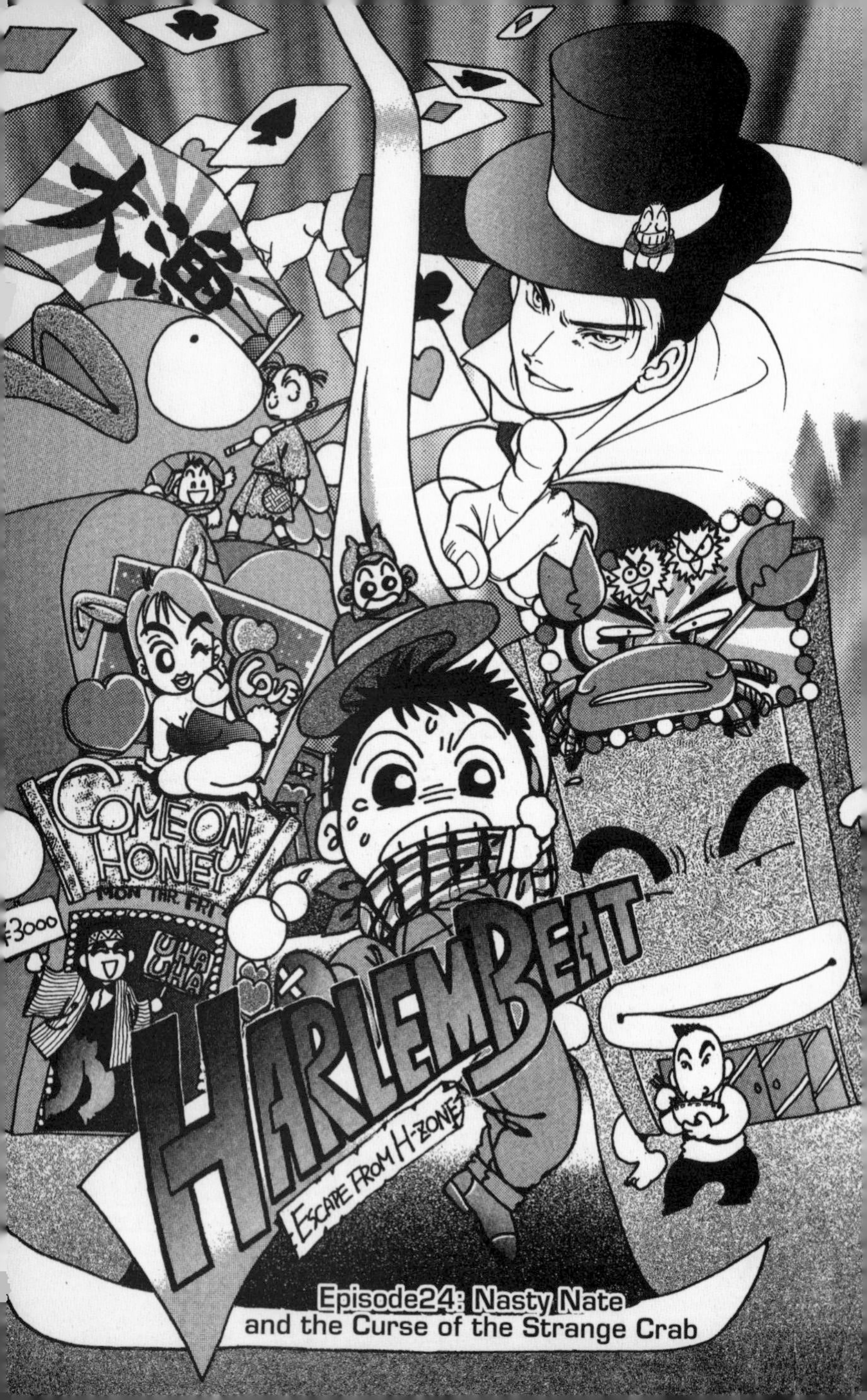

COME ON HONEY
MON THR FRI
¥3000
UHA UHA
LOVE
HARLEM BEAT
ESCAPE FROM H-ZONE
Episode24: Nasty Nate
and the Curse of the Strange Crab

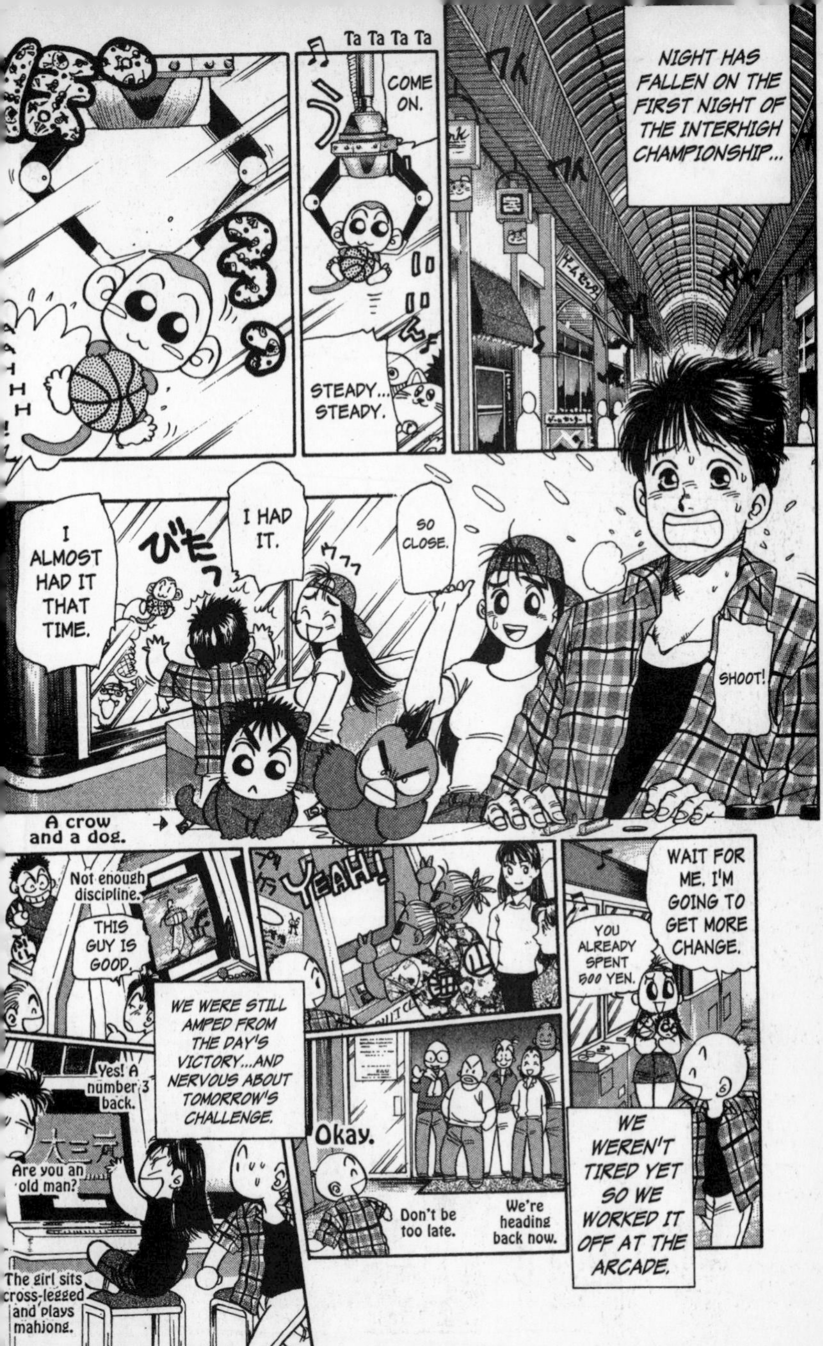
NIGHT HAS FALLEN ON THE FIRST NIGHT OF THE INTERHIGH CHAMPIONSHIP...
Ta Ta Ta Ta
COME ON.
STEADY... STEADY.
SHOOT!
SO CLOSE.
I HAD IT.
I ALMOST HAD IT THAT TIME.
A crow and a dog.
WAIT FOR ME. I'M GOING TO GET MORE CHANGE.
YOU ALREADY SPENT 500 YEN.
WE WEREN'T TIRED YET SO WE WORKED IT OFF AT THE ARCADE.
YEAH!
We're heading back now.
Don't be too late.
Okay.
Not enough discipline.
THIS GUY IS GOOD.
WE WERE STILL AMPED FROM THE DAY'S VICTORY...AND NERVOUS ABOUT TOMORROW'S CHALLENGE.
Yes! A number 3 back.
Are you an old man?
The girl sits cross-legged and plays mahjong.

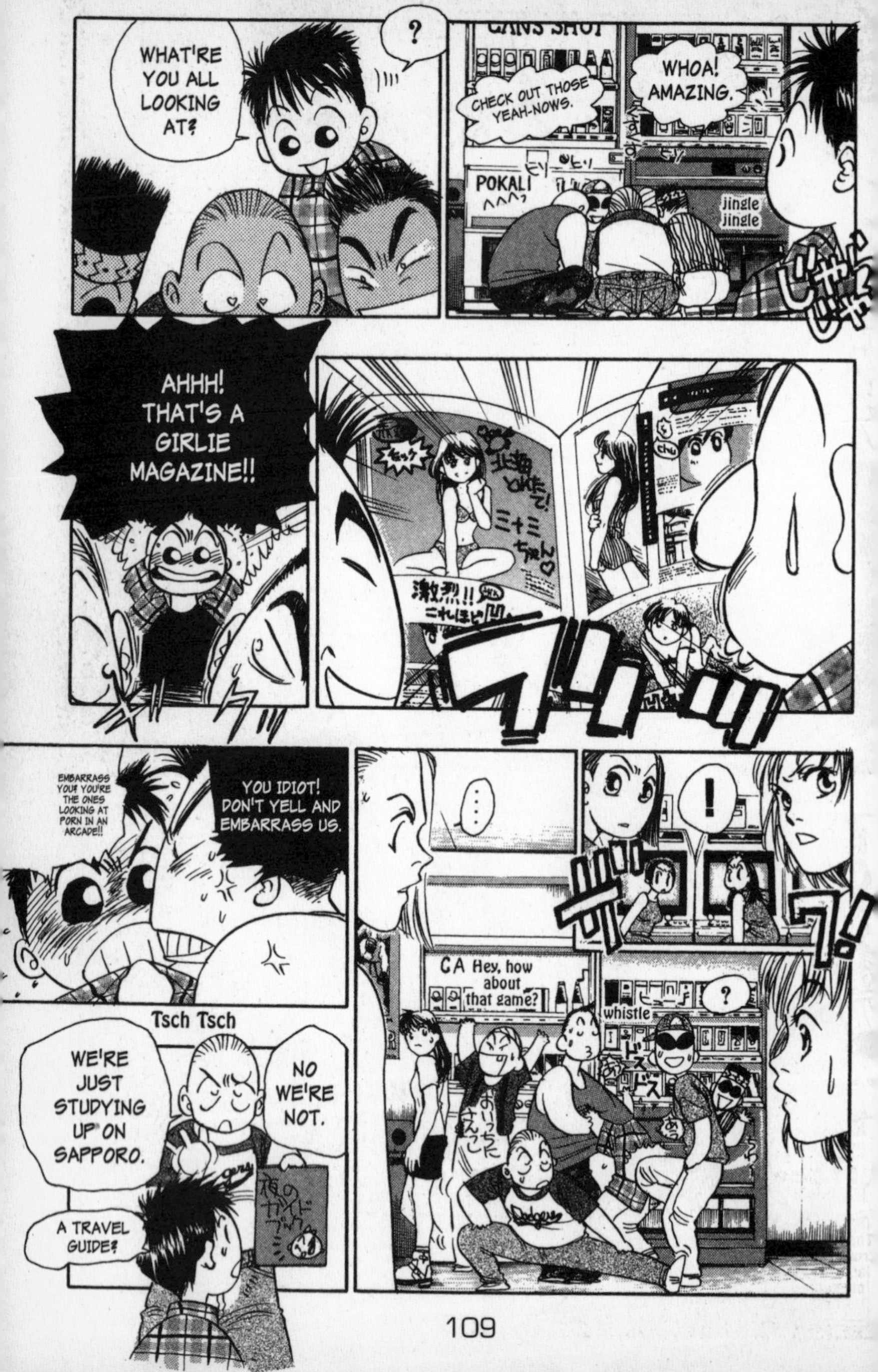
CANS SHOT
WHOA! AMAZING.
CHECK OUT THOSE YEAH-NOWS.
POKALI
jingle jingle
?
WHAT'RE YOU ALL LOOKING AT?
AHHH! THAT'S A GIRLIE MAGAZINE!!
!
...
CA Hey, how about that game?
whistle
?
YOU IDIOT! DON'T YELL AND EMBARRASS US.
EMBARRASS YOU? YOU'RE THE ONES LOOKING AT PORN IN AN ARCADE!!
Tsch Tsch
NO WE'RE NOT.
WE'RE JUST STUDYING UP ON SAPPORO.
A TRAVEL GUIDE?

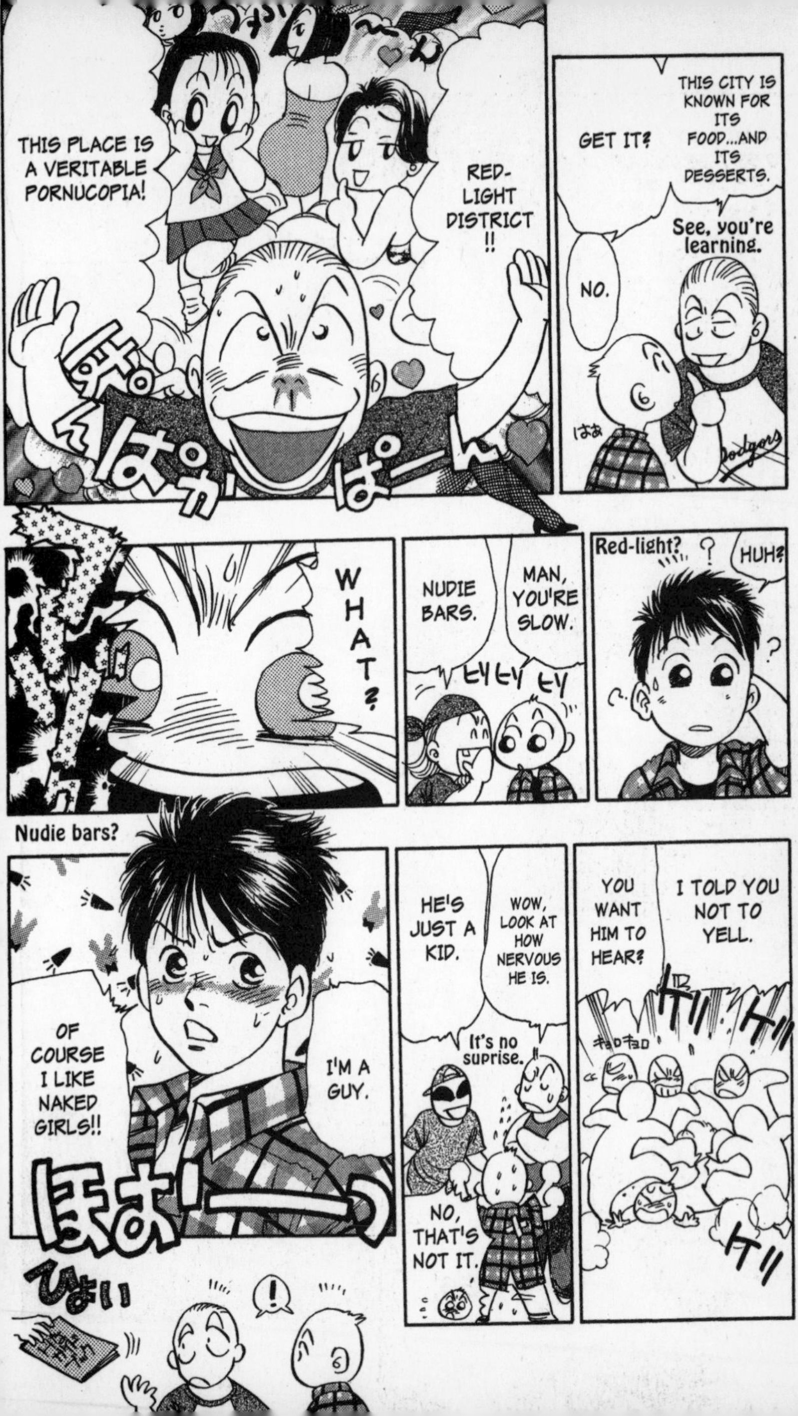

THIS CITY IS KNOWN FOR ITS FOOD...AND ITS DESSERTS.
GET IT?
See, you're learning.
NO.
はあ
RED-LIGHT DISTRICT !!
THIS PLACE IS A VERITABLE PORNUCOPIA!
Red-light?
HUH?
MAN, YOU'RE SLOW.
NUDIE BARS.
ヒソヒソ ヒソ
WHAT?
I TOLD YOU NOT TO YELL.
YOU WANT HIM TO HEAR?
キョロキョロ
WOW, LOOK AT HOW NERVOUS HE IS.
HE'S JUST A KID.
It's no suprise.
NO, THAT'S NOT IT.
Nudie bars?
I'M A GUY.
OF COURSE I LIKE NAKED GIRLS!!
ほおーっ
ひょい

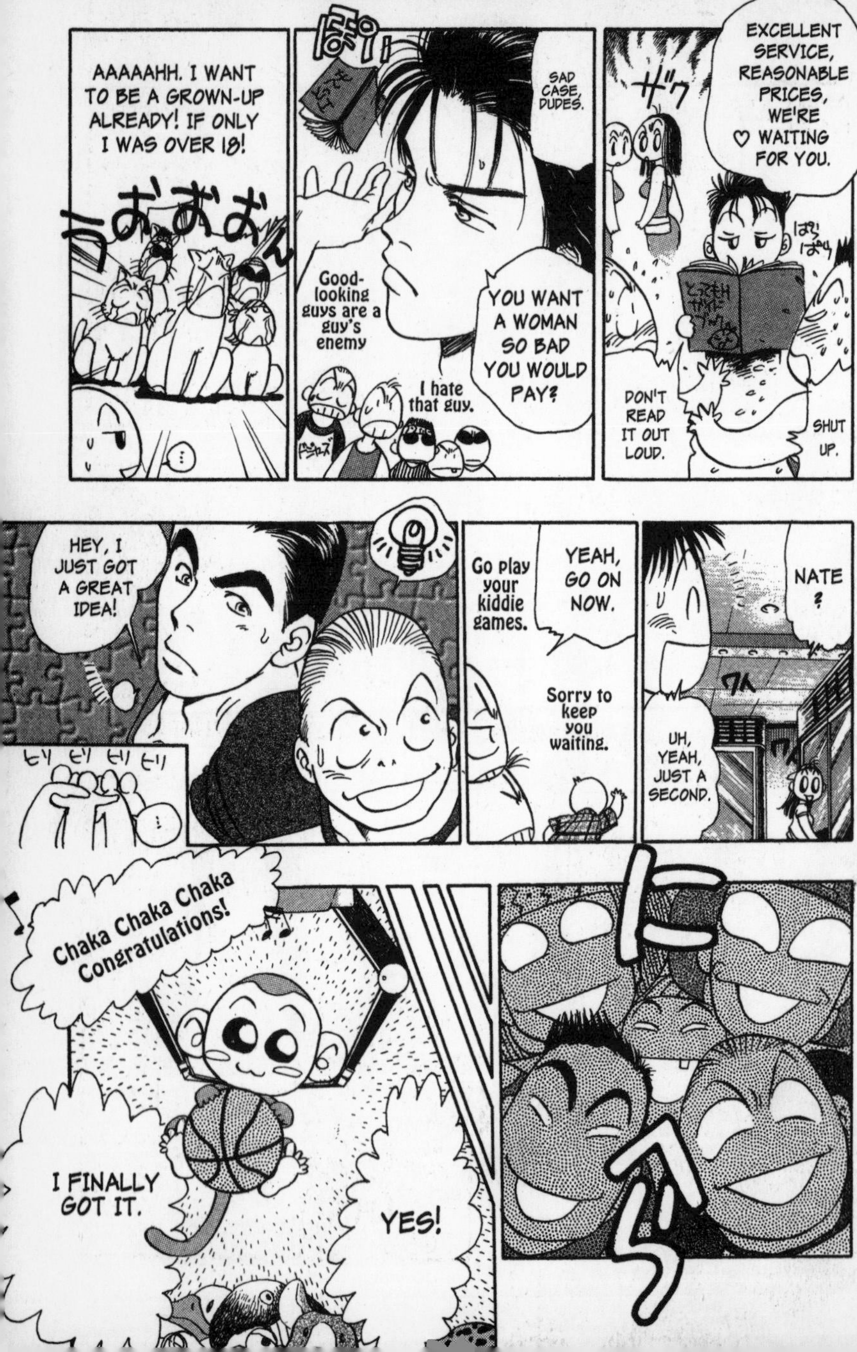
EXCELLENT SERVICE, REASONABLE PRICES, WE'RE ♡ WAITING FOR YOU.
SHUT UP.
DON'T READ IT OUT LOUD.
SAD CASE, DUDES.
YOU WANT A WOMAN SO BAD YOU WOULD PAY?
Good-looking guys are a guy's enemy
I hate that guy.
AAAAAHH. I WANT TO BE A GROWN-UP ALREADY! IF ONLY I WAS OVER 18!
NATE?
UH, YEAH, JUST A SECOND.
YEAH, GO ON NOW.
Go play your kiddie games.
Sorry to keep you waiting.
HEY, I JUST GOT A GREAT IDEA!
Chaka Chaka Chaka Congratulations!
YES!
I FINALLY GOT IT.

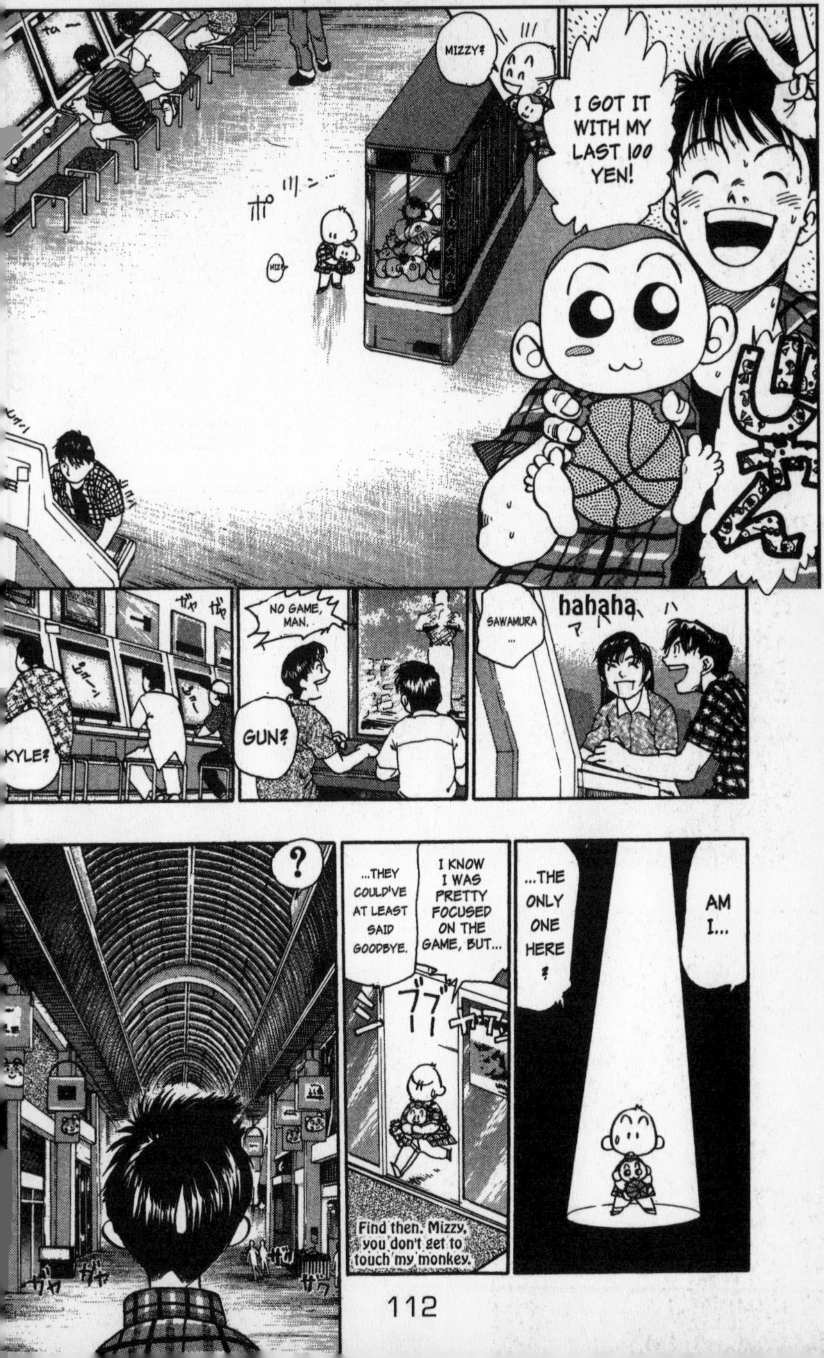

I GOT IT WITH MY LAST 100 YEN!
MIZZY?
hahaha
SAWAMURA ...
NO GAME, MAN.
GUN?
KYLE?
AM I...
...THE ONLY ONE HERE?
I KNOW I WAS PRETTY FOCUSED ON THE GAME, BUT...
...THEY COULD'VE AT LEAST SAID GOODBYE.
Find then. Mizzy, you don't get to touch my monkey.
?

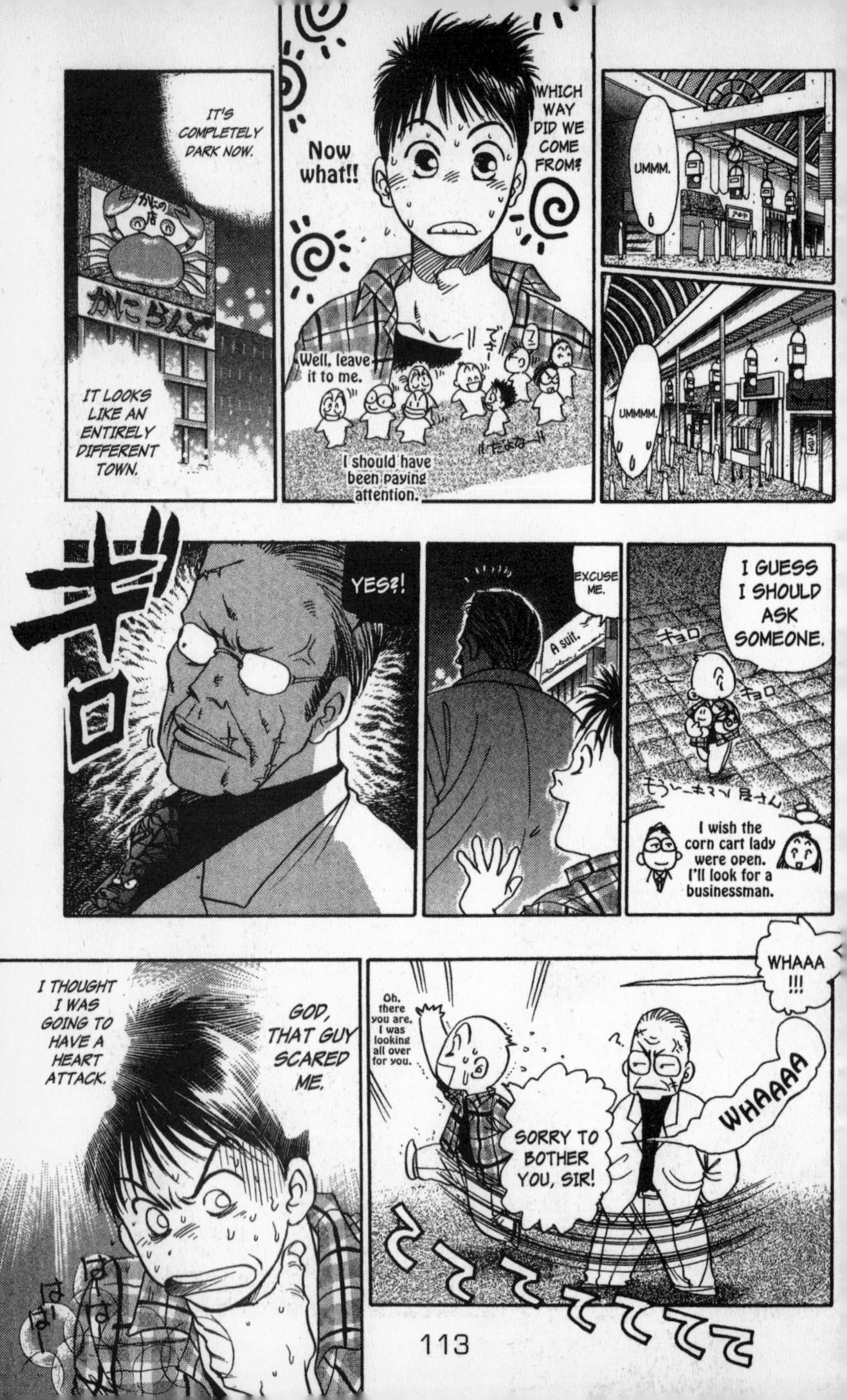
UMMM.
UMMMM.
WHICH WAY DID WE COME FROM?
Now what!!
Well, leave it to me.
I should have been paying attention.
IT'S COMPLETELY DARK NOW.
IT LOOKS LIKE AN ENTIRELY DIFFERENT TOWN.
I GUESS I SHOULD ASK SOMEONE.
I wish the corn cart lady were open. I'll look for a businessman.
EXCUSE ME.
A suit.
YES?!
WHAAA !!!
Oh, there you are. I was looking all over for you.
WHAAAA
SORRY TO BOTHER YOU, SIR!
GOD, THAT GUY SCARED ME.
I THOUGHT I WAS GOING TO HAVE A HEART ATTACK.

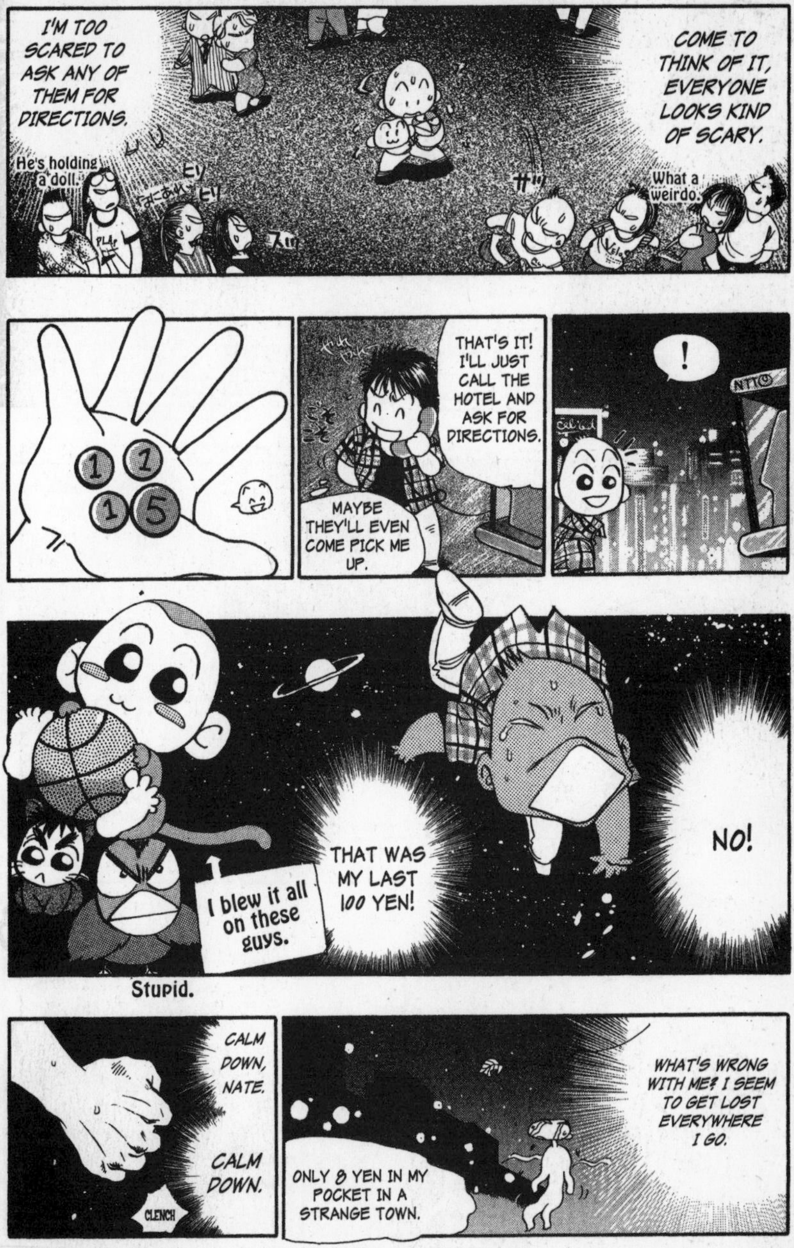
COME TO THINK OF IT, EVERYONE LOOKS KIND OF SCARY.
What a weirdo.
I'M TOO SCARED TO ASK ANY OF THEM FOR DIRECTIONS.
He's holding a doll.
!
THAT'S IT! I'LL JUST CALL THE HOTEL AND ASK FOR DIRECTIONS.
MAYBE THEY'LL EVEN COME PICK ME UP.
NO!
THAT WAS MY LAST 100 YEN!
I blew it all on these guys.
Stupid.
WHAT'S WRONG WITH ME? I SEEM TO GET LOST EVERYWHERE I GO.
ONLY 8 YEN IN MY POCKET IN A STRANGE TOWN.
CALM DOWN, NATE.
CALM DOWN.
CLENCH

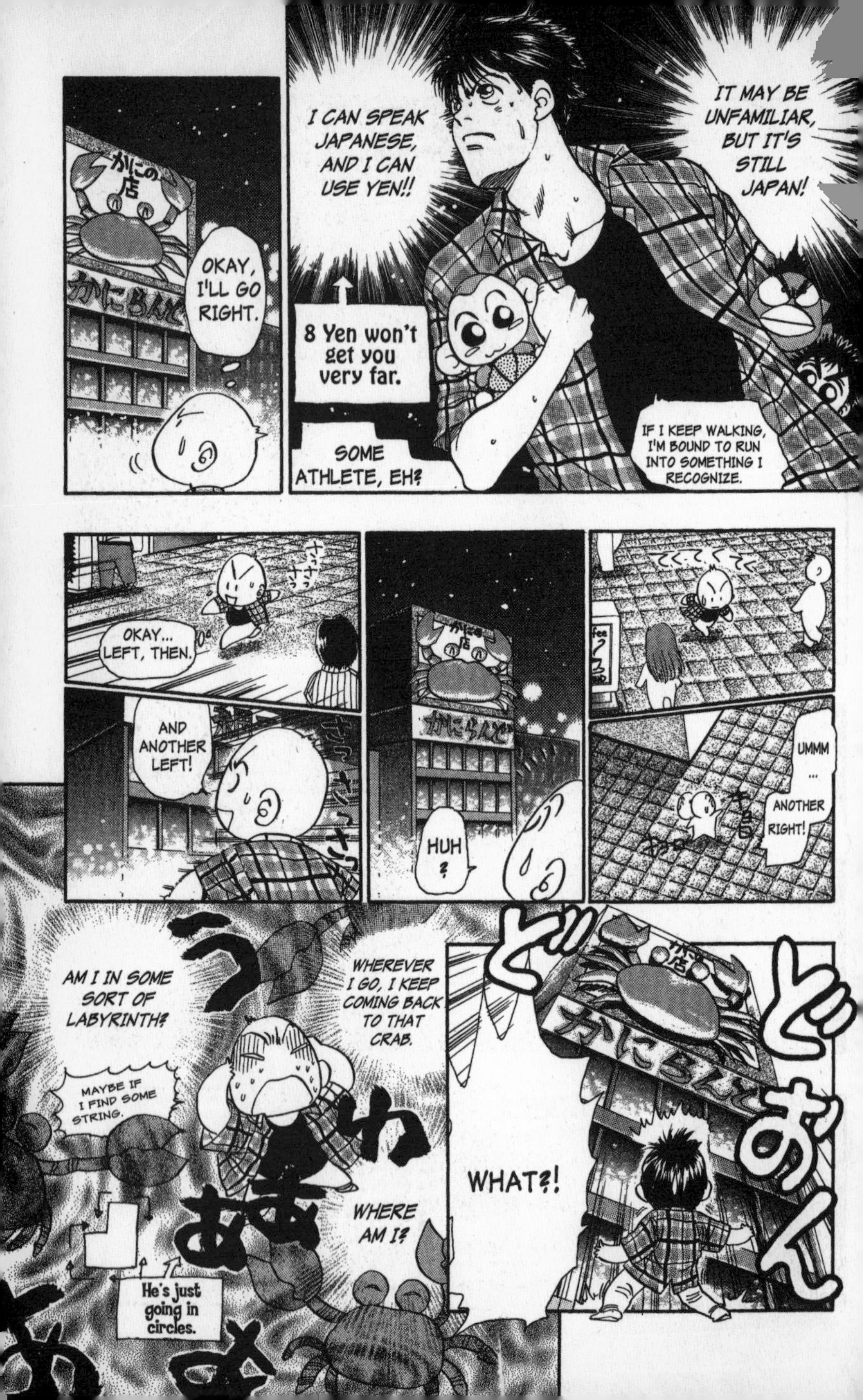
IT MAY BE UNFAMILIAR, BUT IT'S STILL JAPAN!
I CAN SPEAK JAPANESE, AND I CAN USE YEN!!
IF I KEEP WALKING, I'M BOUND TO RUN INTO SOMETHING I RECOGNIZE.
8 Yen won't get you very far.
SOME ATHLETE, EH?
かにの店
かにらんど
OKAY, I'LL GO RIGHT.
UMMM ... ANOTHER RIGHT!
HUH?
OKAY... LEFT, THEN.
AND ANOTHER LEFT!
WHAT?!
かにらんど
WHEREVER I GO, I KEEP COMING BACK TO THAT CRAB.
AM I IN SOME SORT OF LABYRINTH?
MAYBE IF I FIND SOME STRING.
WHERE AM I?
He's just going in circles.

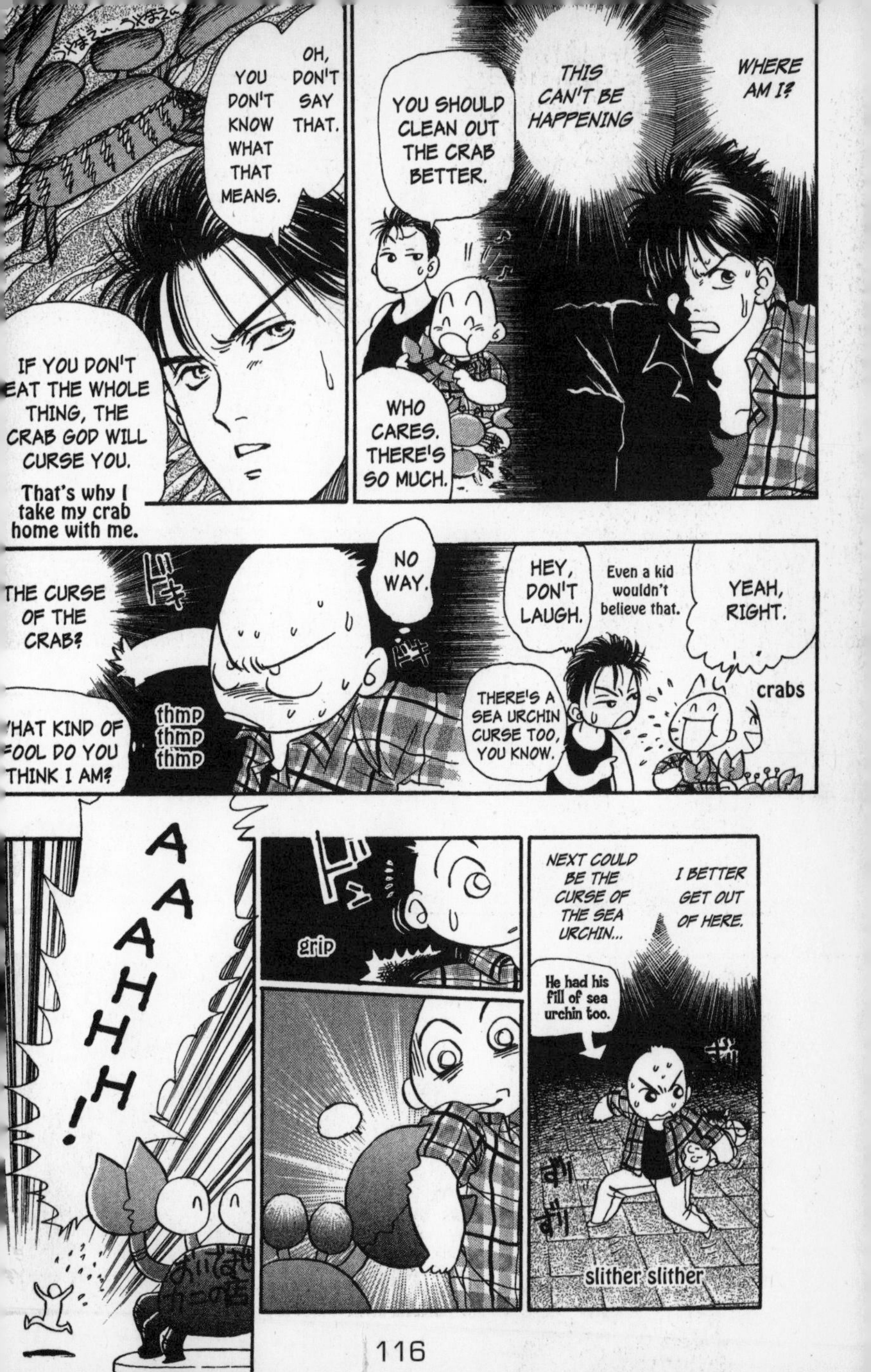
WHERE AM I?
THIS CAN'T BE HAPPENING
YOU SHOULD CLEAN OUT THE CRAB BETTER.
WHO CARES. THERE'S SO MUCH.
OH, DON'T SAY THAT.
YOU DON'T KNOW WHAT THAT MEANS.
IF YOU DON'T EAT THE WHOLE THING, THE CRAB GOD WILL CURSE YOU.
That's why I take my crab home with me.
YEAH, RIGHT.
Even a kid wouldn't believe that.
HEY, DON'T LAUGH.
crabs
THERE'S A SEA URCHIN CURSE TOO, YOU KNOW.
NO WAY.
THE CURSE OF THE CRAB?
thmp thmp thmp
WHAT KIND OF FOOL DO YOU THINK I AM?
I BETTER GET OUT OF HERE.
NEXT COULD BE THE CURSE OF THE SEA URCHIN...
He had his fill of sea urchin too.
slither slither
grip
AAAHHH!

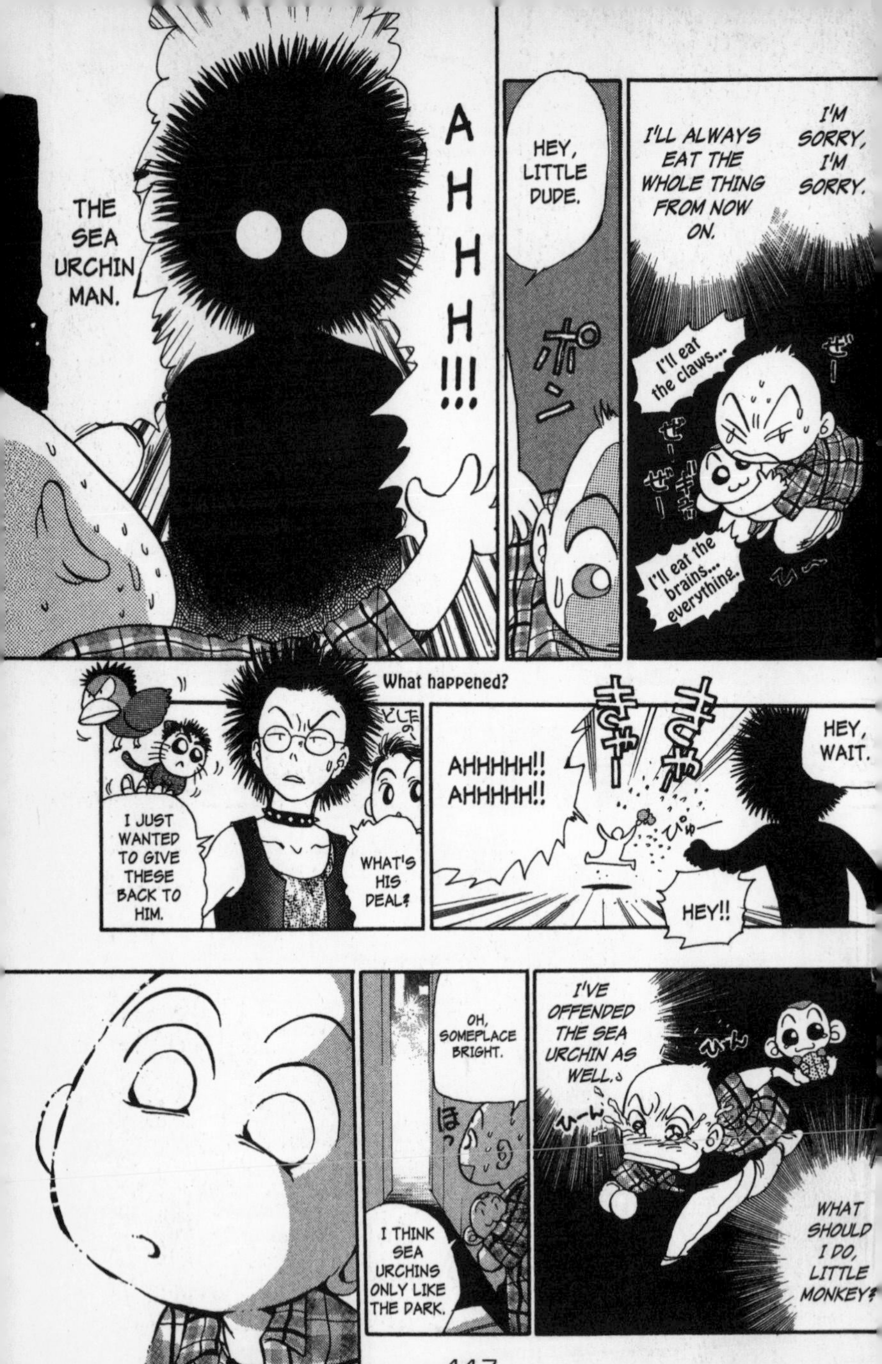
I'M SORRY, I'M SORRY.
I'LL ALWAYS EAT THE WHOLE THING FROM NOW ON.
I'll eat the claws...
I'll eat the brains... everything.
HEY, LITTLE DUDE.
AHHH!!!
THE SEA URCHIN MAN.
HEY, WAIT.
AHHHHH!! AHHHHH!!
HEY!!
What happened?
WHAT'S HIS DEAL?
I JUST WANTED TO GIVE THESE BACK TO HIM.
I'VE OFFENDED THE SEA URCHIN AS WELL.
WHAT SHOULD I DO, LITTLE MONKEY?
OH, SOMEPLACE BRIGHT.
I THINK SEA URCHINS ONLY LIKE THE DARK.

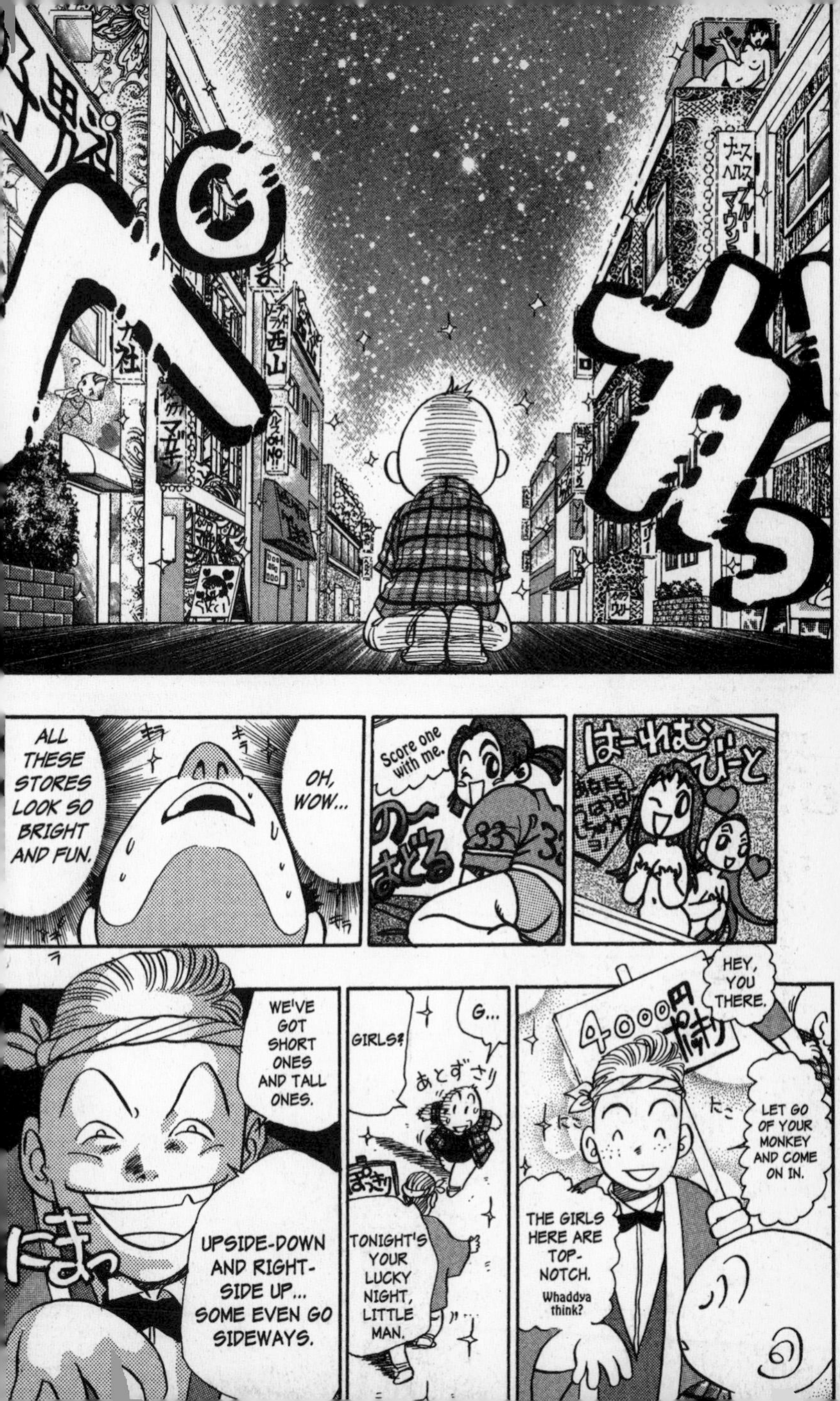
ナースヘルス ブルーマウンテン
西山
OH NO!!
はーれむ びーと
Score one with me.
の〜まどる
OH, WOW...
ALL THESE STORES LOOK SO BRIGHT AND FUN.
キラ
4000円ポッキリ
HEY, YOU THERE.
LET GO OF YOUR MONKEY AND COME ON IN.
THE GIRLS HERE ARE TOP-NOTCH.
Whaddya think?
G...
GIRLS?
あとずさり
TONIGHT'S YOUR LUCKY NIGHT, LITTLE MAN.
WE'VE GOT SHORT ONES AND TALL ONES.
UPSIDE-DOWN AND RIGHT-SIDE UP... SOME EVEN GO SIDEWAYS.
にまっ

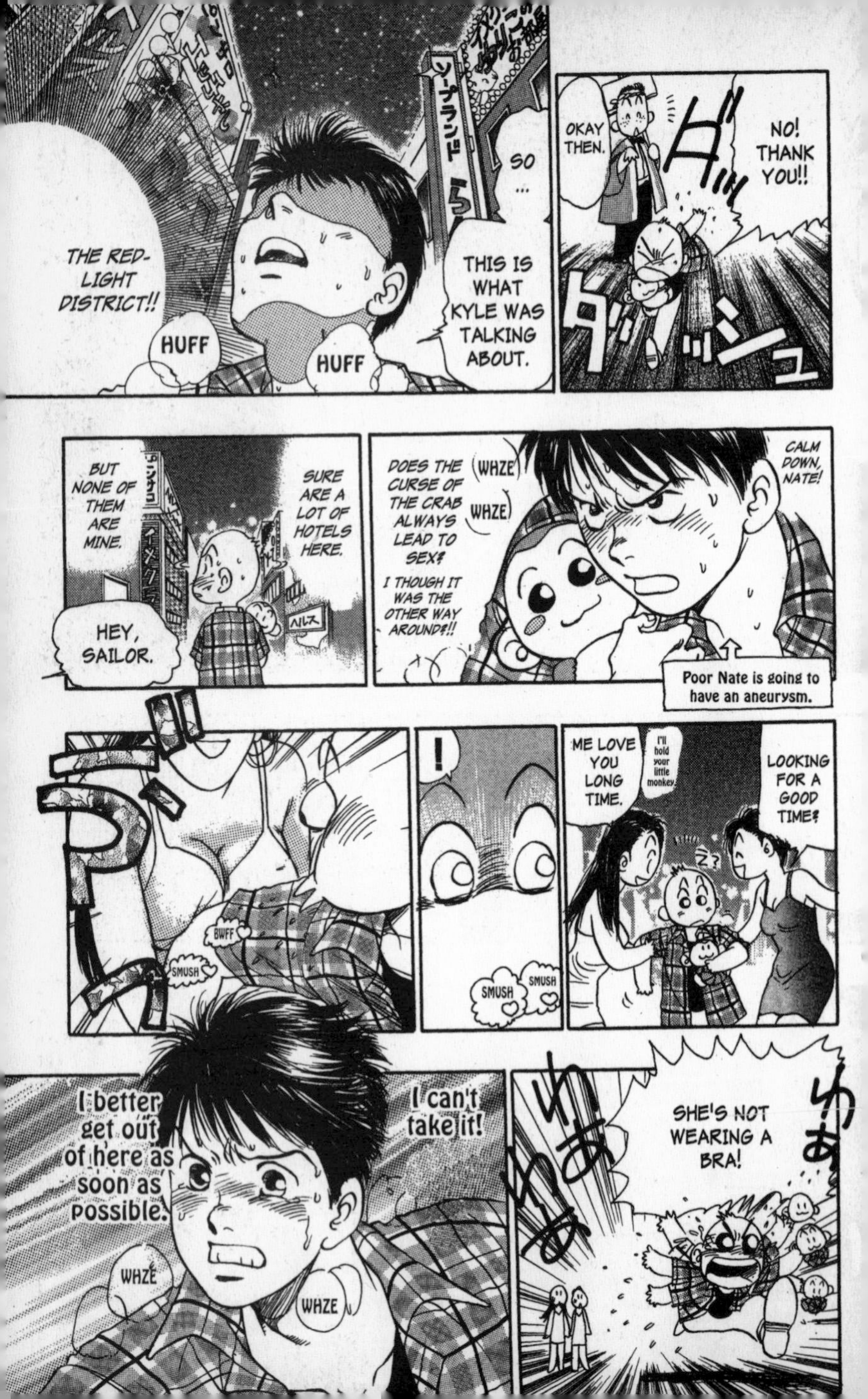
NO! THANK YOU!!
OKAY THEN.
SO ...
THIS IS WHAT KYLE WAS TALKING ABOUT.
ソープランド
THE RED-LIGHT DISTRICT!!
HUFF
HUFF
CALM DOWN, NATE!
DOES THE CURSE OF THE CRAB ALWAYS LEAD TO SEX?
WHZE
WHZE
I THOUGH IT WAS THE OTHER WAY AROUND?!!
Poor Nate is going to have an aneurysm.
SURE ARE A LOT OF HOTELS HERE.
BUT NONE OF THEM ARE MINE.
ヘルス
HEY, SAILOR.
LOOKING FOR A GOOD TIME?
I'll hold your little monkey.
ME LOVE YOU LONG TIME.
!
SMUSH
SMUSH
BWFF
SMUSH
SHE'S NOT WEARING A BRA!
I can't take it!
I better get out of here as soon as possible.
WHZE
WHZE

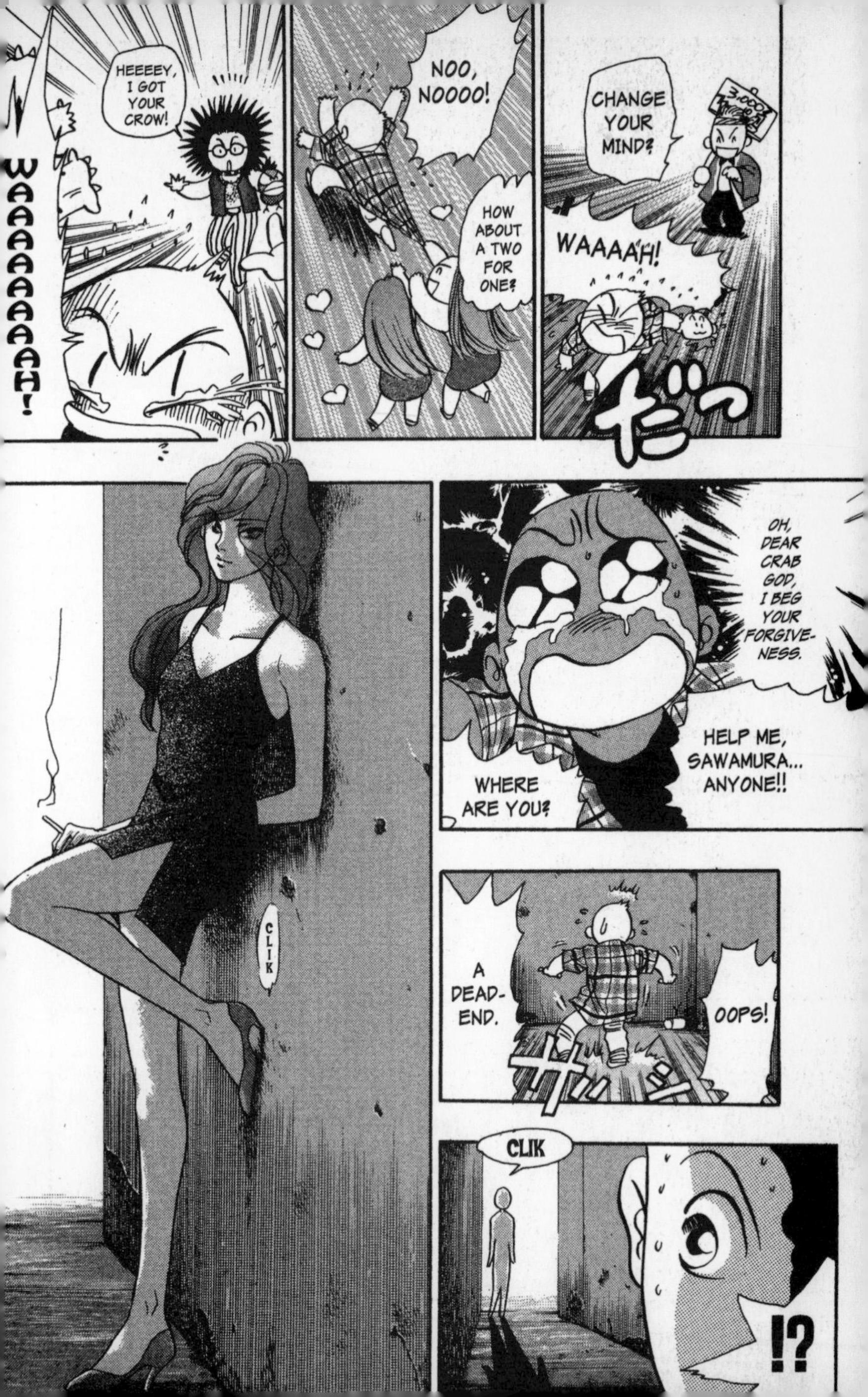
CHANGE YOUR MIND?
WAAAAH!
だっ
NOO, NOOOO!
HOW ABOUT A TWO FOR ONE?
HEEEEY, I GOT YOUR CROW!
WAAAAAAAAAH!
OH, DEAR CRAB GOD, I BEG YOUR FORGIVE-NESS.
HELP ME, SAWAMURA... ANYONE!!
WHERE ARE YOU?
OOPS!
A DEAD-END.
CLIK
!?
CLIK

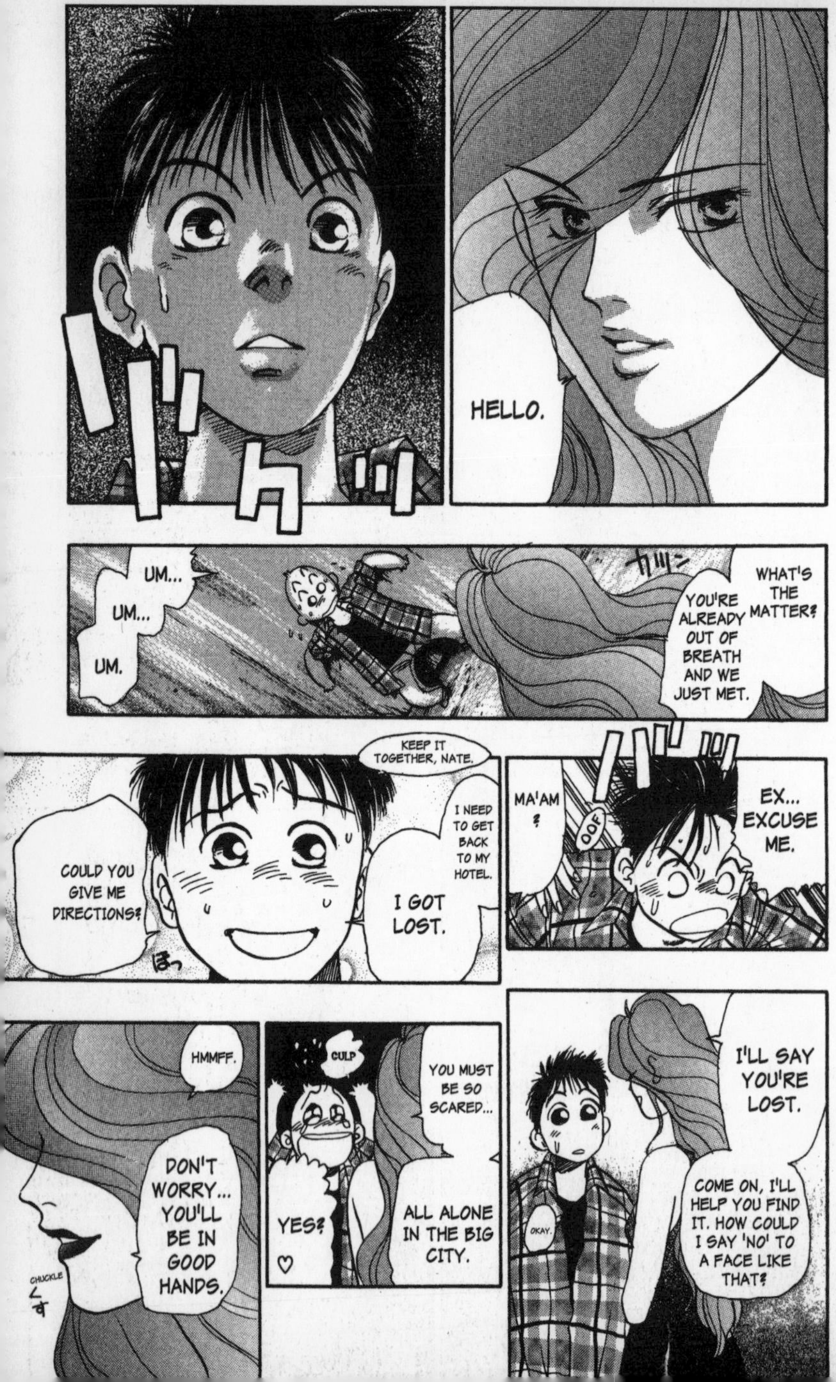
HELLO.
WHAT'S THE MATTER?
YOU'RE ALREADY OUT OF BREATH AND WE JUST MET.
UM...
UM...
UM.
EX... EXCUSE ME.
MA'AM?
OOF
KEEP IT TOGETHER, NATE.
I NEED TO GET BACK TO MY HOTEL.
I GOT LOST.
COULD YOU GIVE ME DIRECTIONS?
ほっ
I'LL SAY YOU'RE LOST.
COME ON, I'LL HELP YOU FIND IT. HOW COULD I SAY 'NO' TO A FACE LIKE THAT?
OKAY.
YOU MUST BE SO SCARED...
CULP
ALL ALONE IN THE BIG CITY.
YES? ♡
HMMFF.
DON'T WORRY... YOU'LL BE IN GOOD HANDS.
CHUCKLE
くす

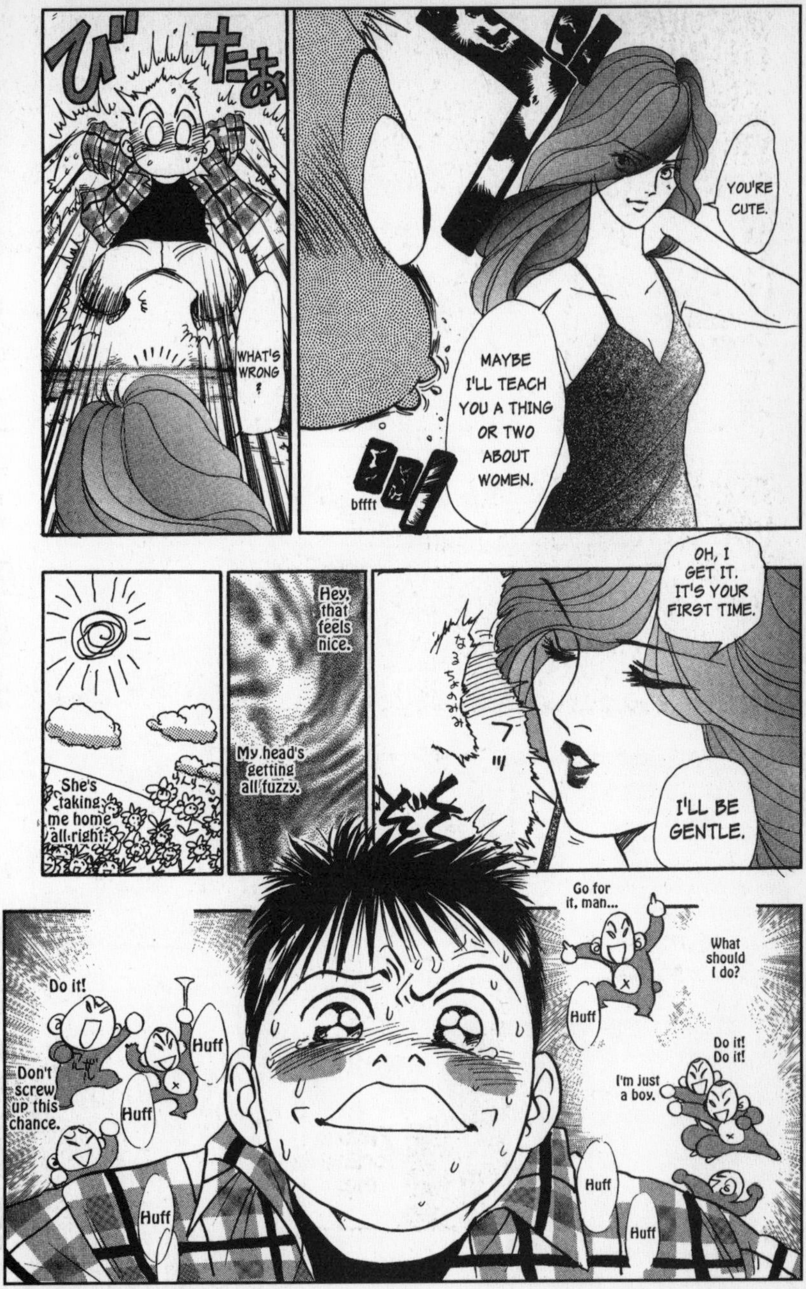
YOU'RE CUTE.
MAYBE I'LL TEACH YOU A THING OR TWO ABOUT WOMEN.
bffft
WHAT'S WRONG?
OH, I GET IT. IT'S YOUR FIRST TIME.
I'LL BE GENTLE.
Hey, that feels nice.
My head's getting all fuzzy.
She's taking me home all right.
Go for it, man...
What should I do?
Huff
Do it! Do it!
I'm just a boy.
Huff
Huff
Do it!
Huff
Don't screw up this chance.
Huff
Huff

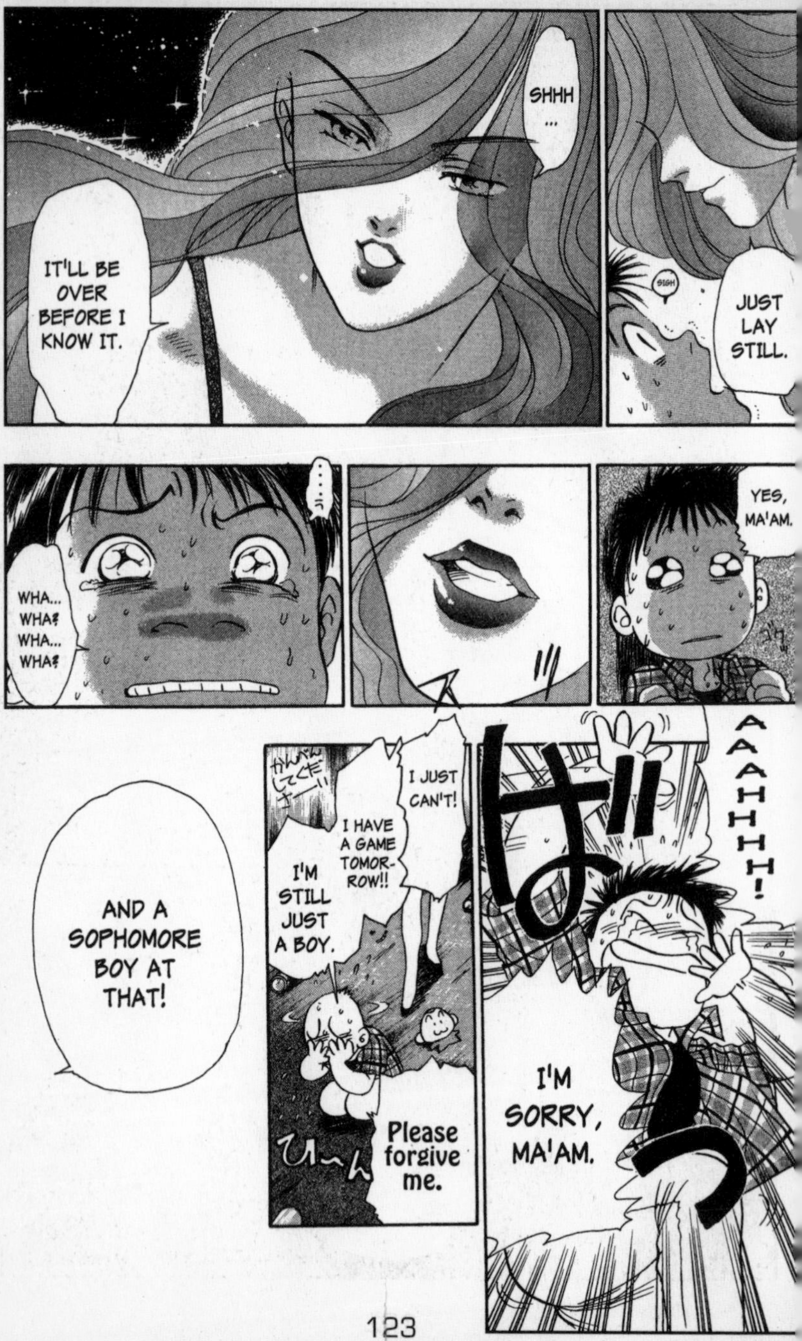
SIGH
JUST LAY STILL.
SHHH ...
IT'LL BE OVER BEFORE I KNOW IT.
YES, MA'AM.
...
WHA... WHA? WHA... WHA?
AAAHHHH!
I'M SORRY, MA'AM.
I JUST CAN'T!
I HAVE A GAME TOMOR-ROW!!
I'M STILL JUST A BOY.
Please forgive me.
AND A SOPHOMORE BOY AT THAT!

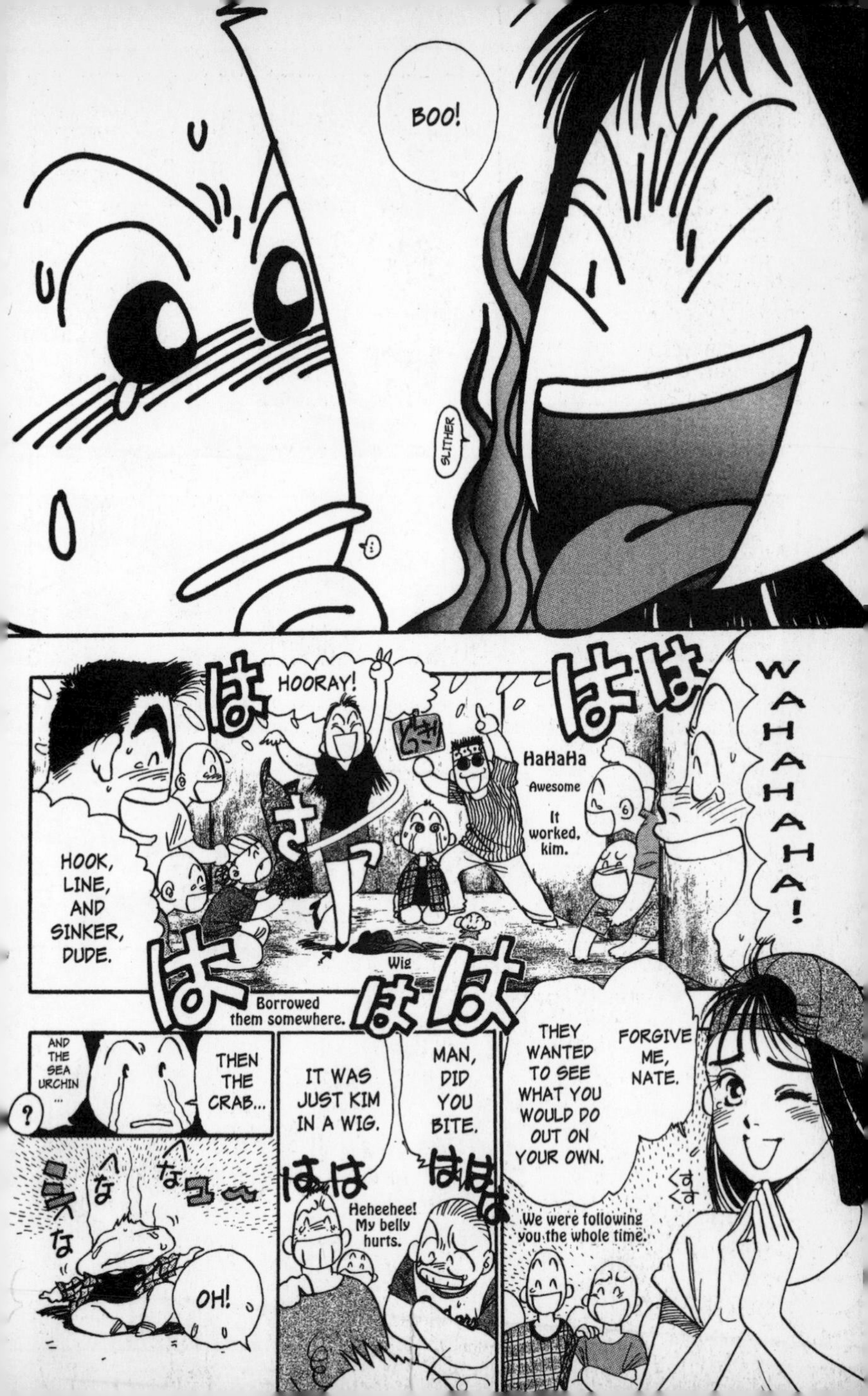
BOO!
SLITHER
WAHAHAHA!
はは
HaHaHa
Awesome
It worked, kim.
HOORAY!
はは
HOOK, LINE, AND SINKER, DUDE.
Wig
Borrowed them somewhere.
FORGIVE ME, NATE.
THEY WANTED TO SEE WHAT YOU WOULD DO OUT ON YOUR OWN.
くすくす
We were following you the whole time.
MAN, DID YOU BITE.
IT WAS JUST KIM IN A WIG.
Heheehee! My belly hurts.
THEN THE CRAB...
AND THE SEA URCHIN...
?
OH!

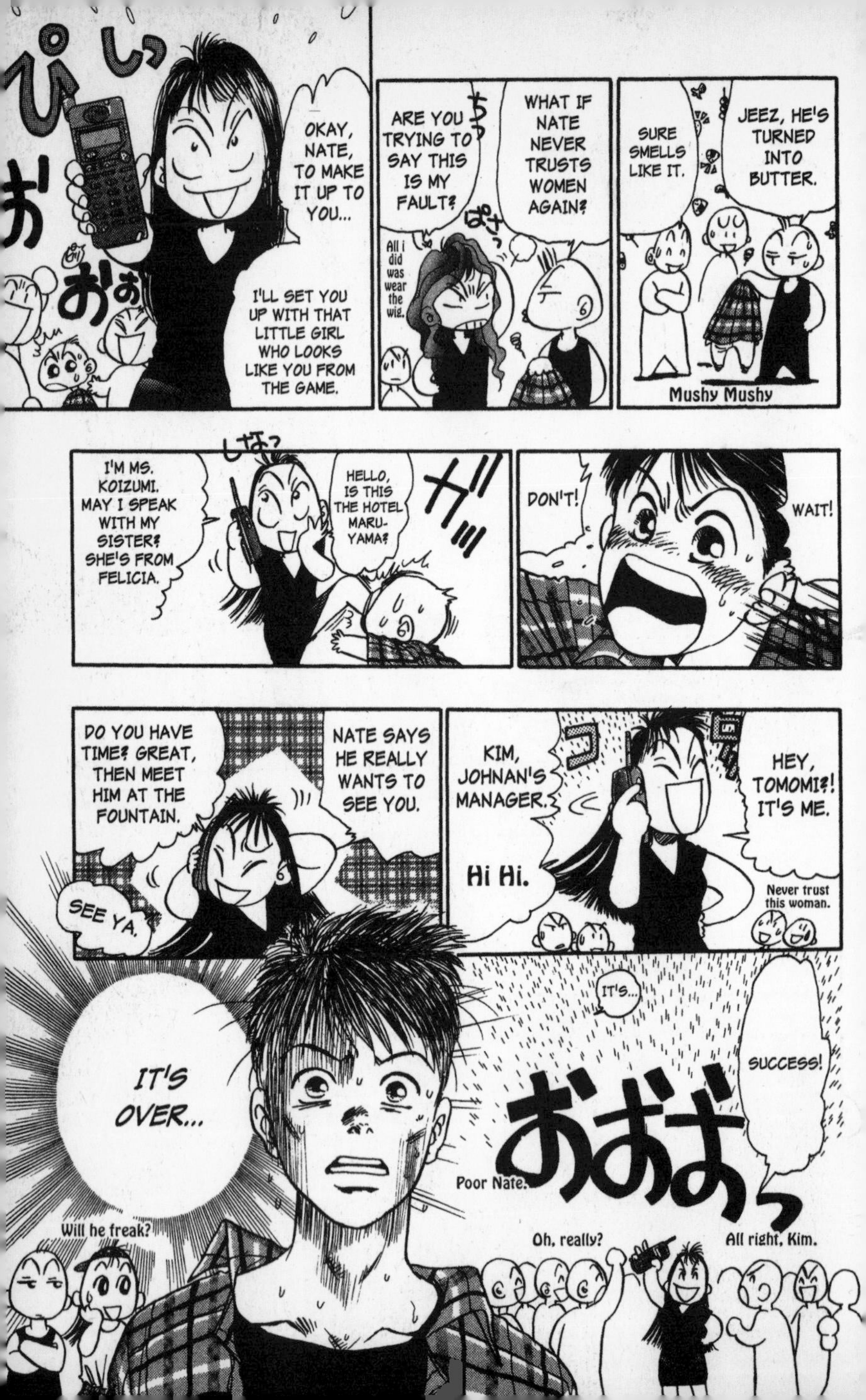
JEEZ, HE'S TURNED INTO BUTTER.
SURE SMELLS LIKE IT.
Mushy Mushy
WHAT IF NATE NEVER TRUSTS WOMEN AGAIN?
ARE YOU TRYING TO SAY THIS IS MY FAULT?
All i did was wear the wig.
OKAY, NATE, TO MAKE IT UP TO YOU...
I'LL SET YOU UP WITH THAT LITTLE GIRL WHO LOOKS LIKE YOU FROM THE GAME.
WAIT!
DON'T!
HELLO, IS THIS THE HOTEL MARU-YAMA?
I'M MS. KOIZUMI. MAY I SPEAK WITH MY SISTER? SHE'S FROM FELICIA.
HEY, TOMOMI?! IT'S ME.
KIM, JOHNAN'S MANAGER.
Hi Hi.
Never trust this woman.
NATE SAYS HE REALLY WANTS TO SEE YOU.
DO YOU HAVE TIME? GREAT, THEN MEET HIM AT THE FOUNTAIN.
SEE YA.
SUCCESS!
IT'S...
IT'S OVER...
All right, Kim.
Oh, really?
Poor Nate.
Will he freak?

REBOUND

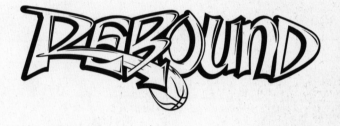

REBOUND

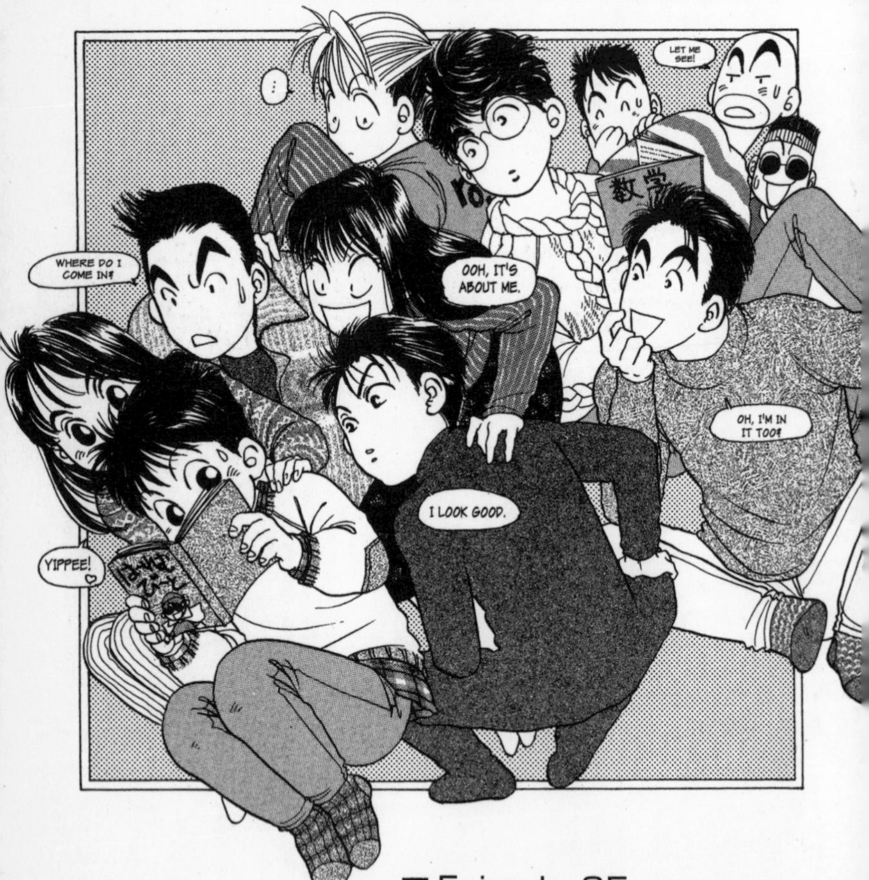
LET ME SEE!
...
数学
OOH, IT'S ABOUT ME.
WHERE DO I COME IN?
OH, I'M IN IT TOO?
I LOOK GOOD.
YIPPEE! ♡

■Episode 25: Beyond the Buzz

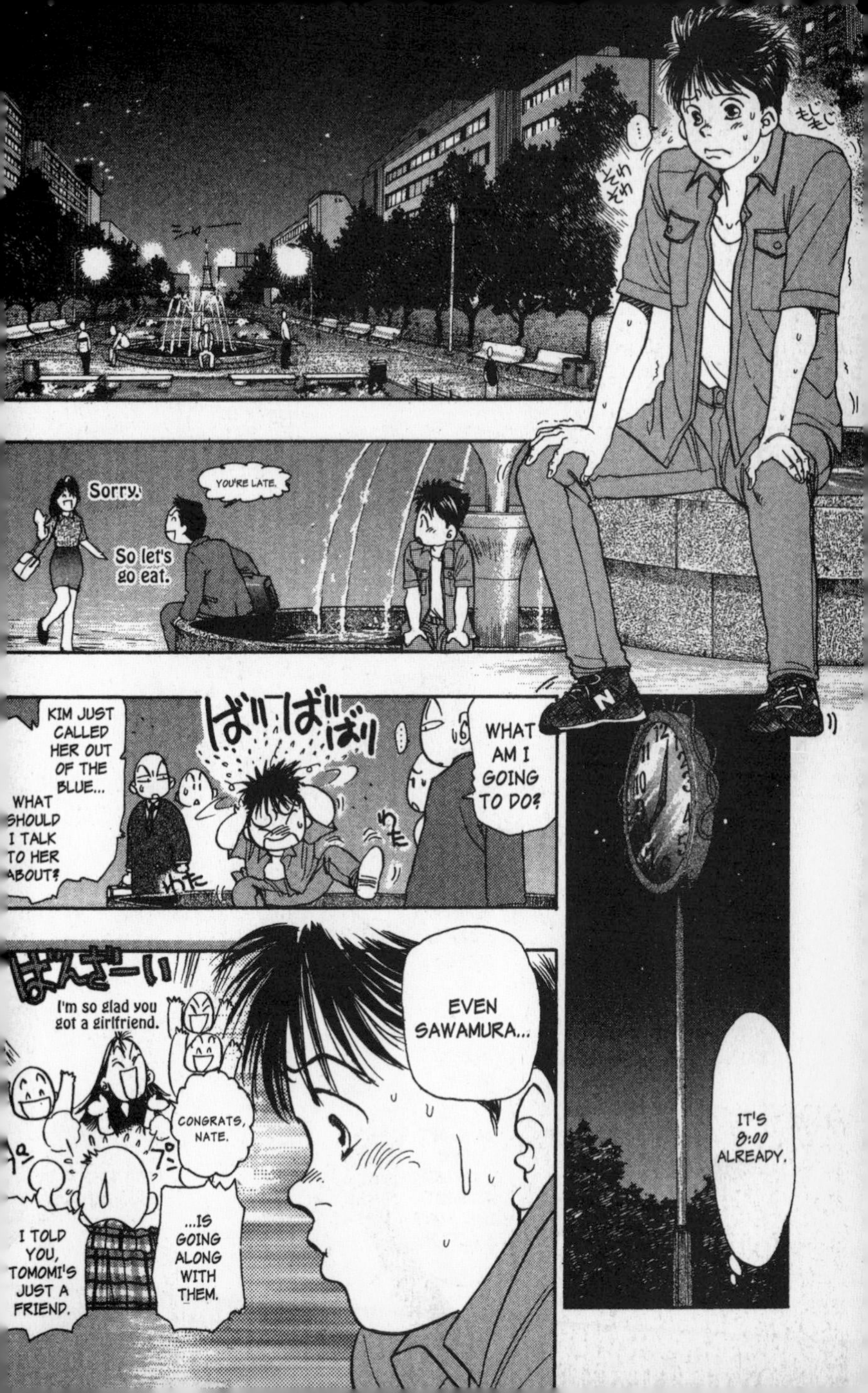
…
そわそわ
もじもじ
YOU'RE LATE.
Sorry.
So let's go eat.
IT'S 8:00 ALREADY.
WHAT AM I GOING TO DO?
…
KIM JUST CALLED HER OUT OF THE BLUE...
WHAT SHOULD I TALK TO HER ABOUT?
EVEN SAWAMURA...
...IS GOING ALONG WITH THEM.
ばんざーい
I'm so glad you got a girlfriend.
CONGRATS, NATE.
I TOLD YOU, TOMOMI'S JUST A FRIEND.

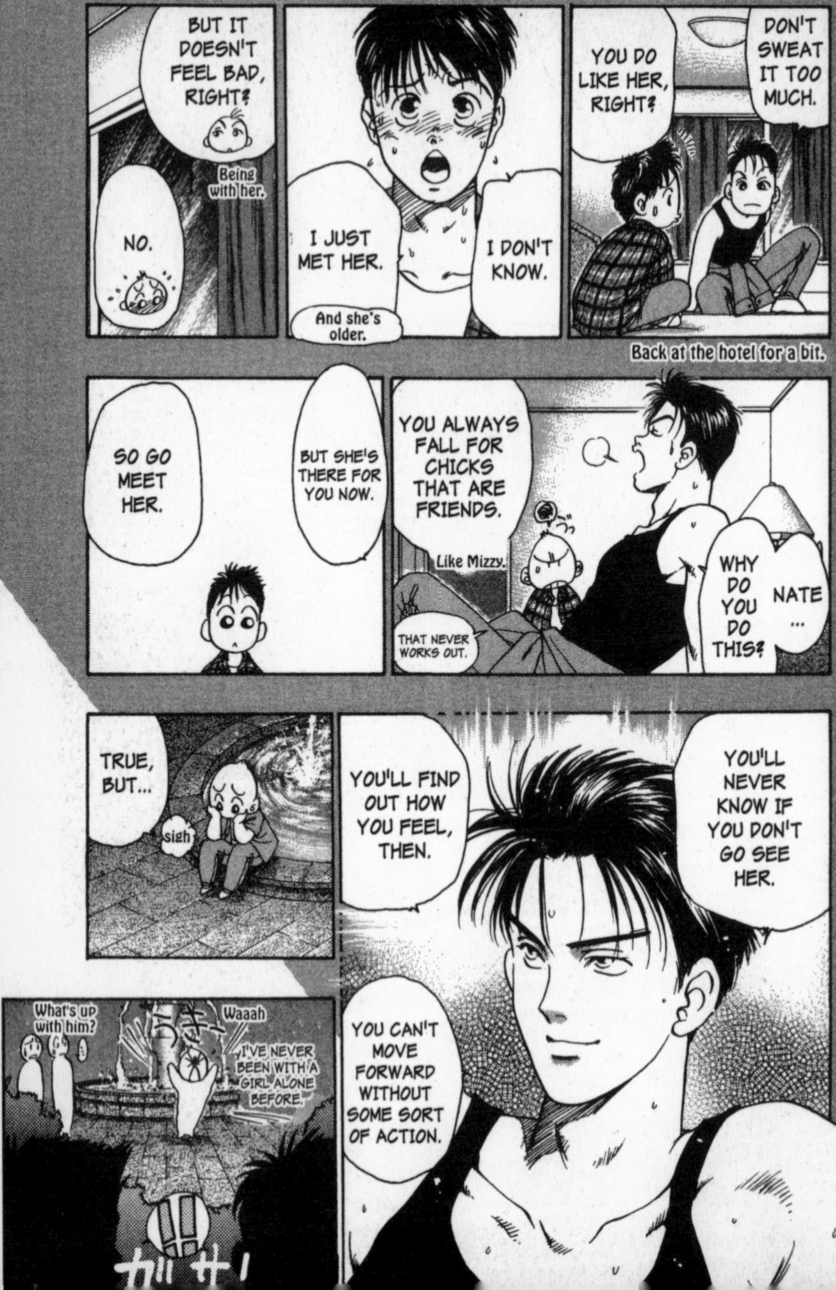
DON'T SWEAT IT TOO MUCH.
YOU DO LIKE HER, RIGHT?
Back at the hotel for a bit.
I DON'T KNOW.
I JUST MET HER.
And she's older.
BUT IT DOESN'T FEEL BAD, RIGHT?
Being with her.
NO.
NATE...
WHY DO YOU DO THIS?
YOU ALWAYS FALL FOR CHICKS THAT ARE FRIENDS.
Like Mizzy.
THAT NEVER WORKS OUT.
BUT SHE'S THERE FOR YOU NOW.
SO GO MEET HER.
YOU'LL NEVER KNOW IF YOU DON'T GO SEE HER.
YOU'LL FIND OUT HOW YOU FEEL, THEN.
YOU CAN'T MOVE FORWARD WITHOUT SOME SORT OF ACTION.
TRUE, BUT...
sigh
Waaah
I'VE NEVER BEEN WITH A GIRL ALONE BEFORE.
What's up with him?

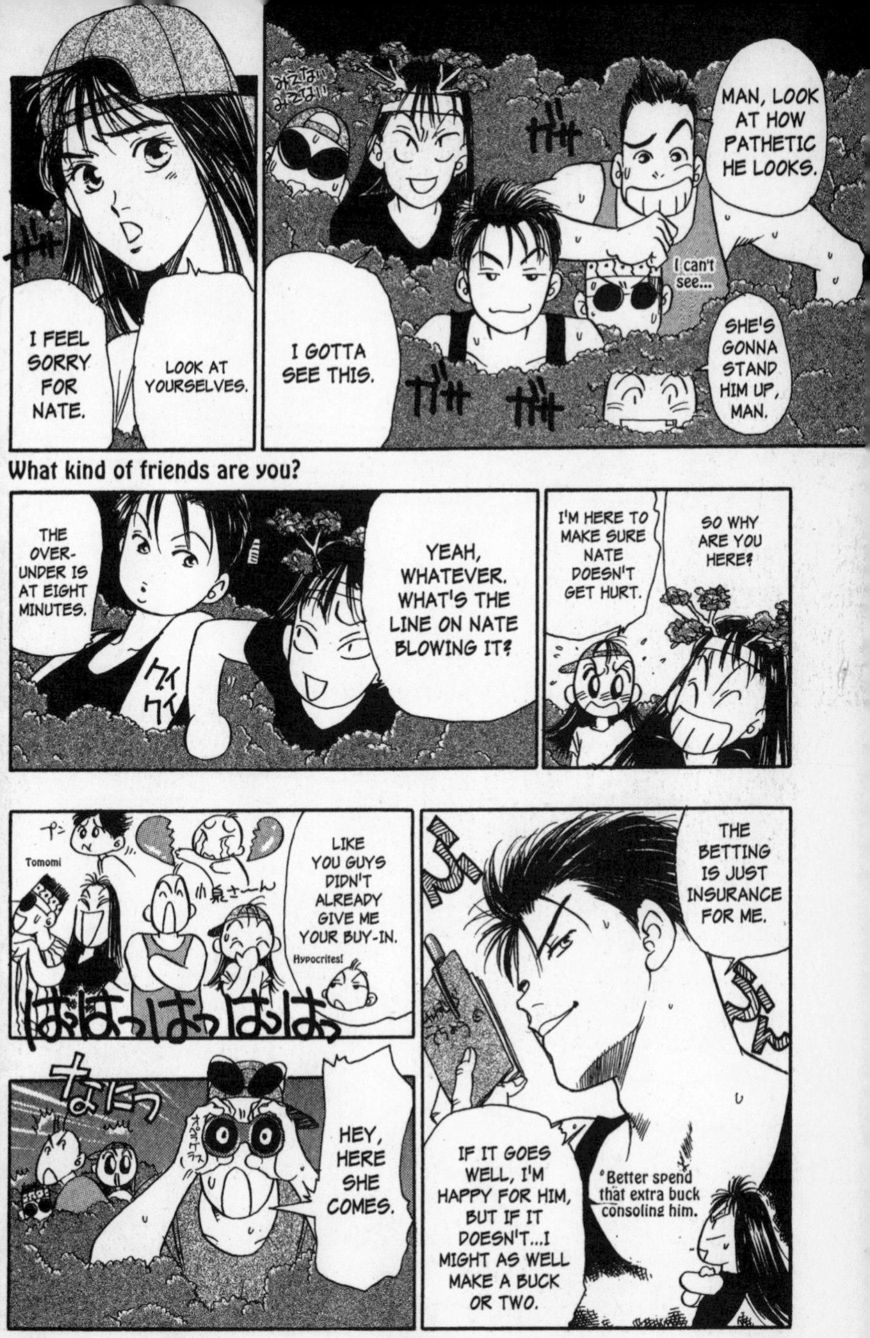
MAN, LOOK AT HOW PATHETIC HE LOOKS.
I can't see...
SHE'S GONNA STAND HIM UP, MAN.
I GOTTA SEE THIS.
LOOK AT YOURSELVES.
I FEEL SORRY FOR NATE.
What kind of friends are you?
SO WHY ARE YOU HERE?
I'M HERE TO MAKE SURE NATE DOESN'T GET HURT.
YEAH, WHATEVER. WHAT'S THE LINE ON NATE BLOWING IT?
THE OVER-UNDER IS AT EIGHT MINUTES.
THE BETTING IS JUST INSURANCE FOR ME.
IF IT GOES WELL, I'M HAPPY FOR HIM, BUT IF IT DOESN'T...I MIGHT AS WELL MAKE A BUCK OR TWO.
Better spend that extra buck consoling him.
Tomomi
LIKE YOU GUYS DIDN'T ALREADY GIVE ME YOUR BUY-IN.
Hypocrites!
HEY, HERE SHE COMES.

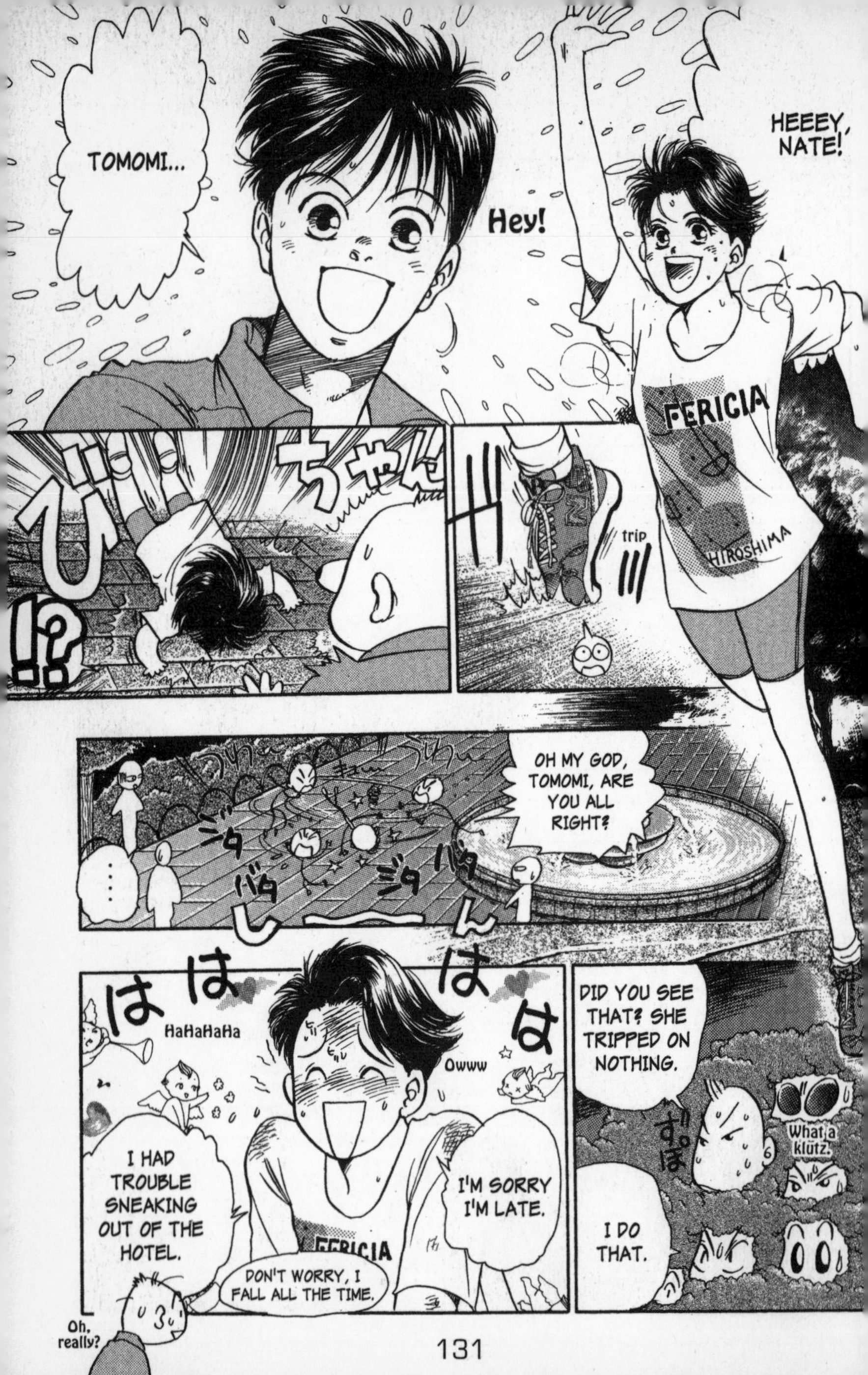
HEEEY, NATE!
FERICIA
HIROSHIMA
Hey!
TOMOMI...
trip
ちゃん
び
!!?
OH MY GOD, TOMOMI, ARE YOU ALL RIGHT?
ジタ
バタ
ジタ
バタ
し
ん
DID YOU SEE THAT? SHE TRIPPED ON NOTHING.
ずぼ
What a klutz.
I DO THAT.
は
は
は
は
HaHaHaHa
Owww
I'M SORRY I'M LATE.
I HAD TROUBLE SNEAKING OUT OF THE HOTEL.
FERICIA
DON'T WORRY, I FALL ALL THE TIME.
Oh, really?

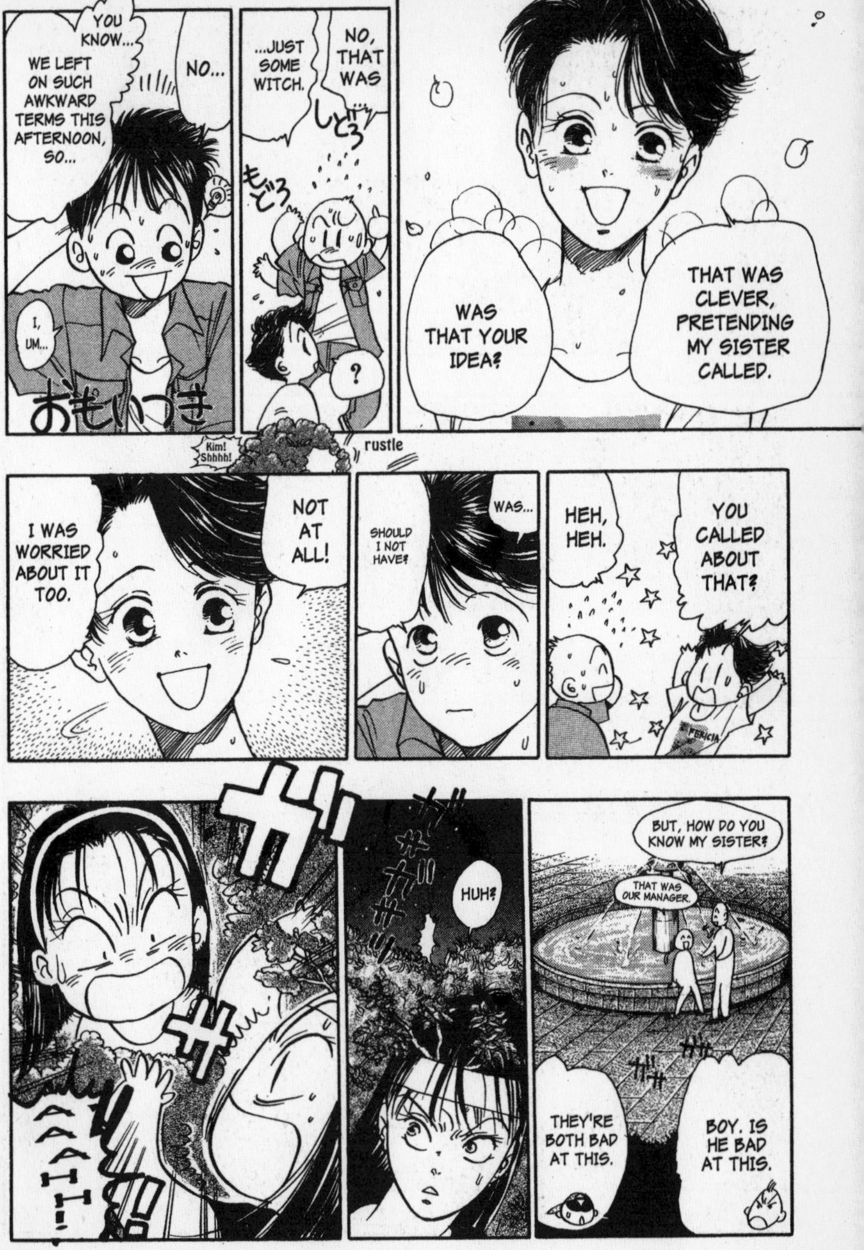
THAT WAS CLEVER, PRETENDING MY SISTER CALLED.
WAS THAT YOUR IDEA?
NO, THAT WAS...
しどろ
...JUST SOME WITCH.
もどろ
?
YOU KNOW...
WE LEFT ON SUCH AWKWARD TERMS THIS AFTERNOON, SO...
NO...
I, UM...
おもいつき
Kim! Shhhh!
rustle
YOU CALLED ABOUT THAT?
HEH, HEH.
WAS...
SHOULD I NOT HAVE?
NOT AT ALL!
I WAS WORRIED ABOUT IT TOO.
BUT, HOW DO YOU KNOW MY SISTER?
THAT WAS OUR MANAGER.
BOY. IS HE BAD AT THIS.
THEY'RE BOTH BAD AT THIS.
HUH?
AAAAH!!

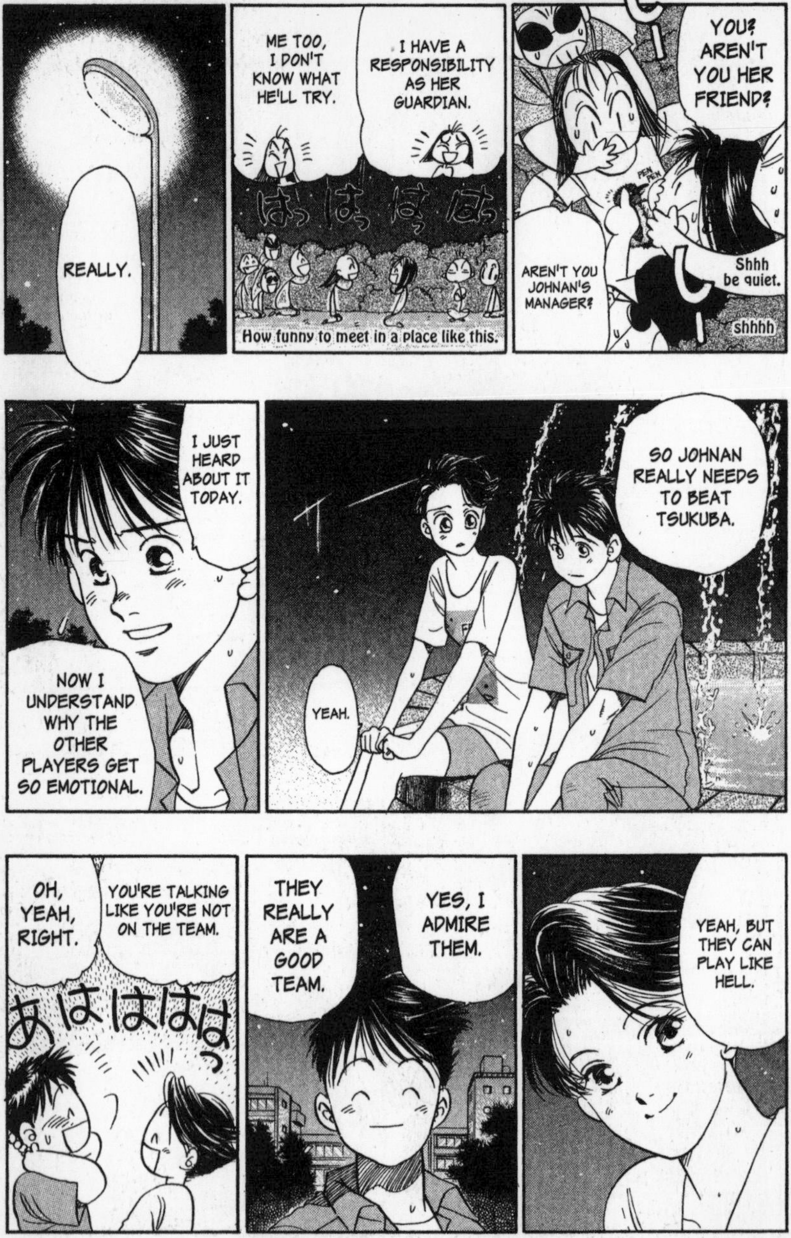
しー
YOU? AREN'T YOU HER FRIEND?
Shhh be quiet.
しー
AREN'T YOU JOHNAN'S MANAGER?
shhhh
I HAVE A RESPONSIBILITY AS HER GUARDIAN.
ME TOO, I DON'T KNOW WHAT HE'LL TRY.
はっはっはっはっ
How funny to meet in a place like this.
REALLY.
SO JOHNAN REALLY NEEDS TO BEAT TSUKUBA.
YEAH.
I JUST HEARD ABOUT IT TODAY.
NOW I UNDERSTAND WHY THE OTHER PLAYERS GET SO EMOTIONAL.
YEAH, BUT THEY CAN PLAY LIKE HELL.
YES, I ADMIRE THEM.
THEY REALLY ARE A GOOD TEAM.
YOU'RE TALKING LIKE YOU'RE NOT ON THE TEAM.
OH, YEAH, RIGHT.
あはははは

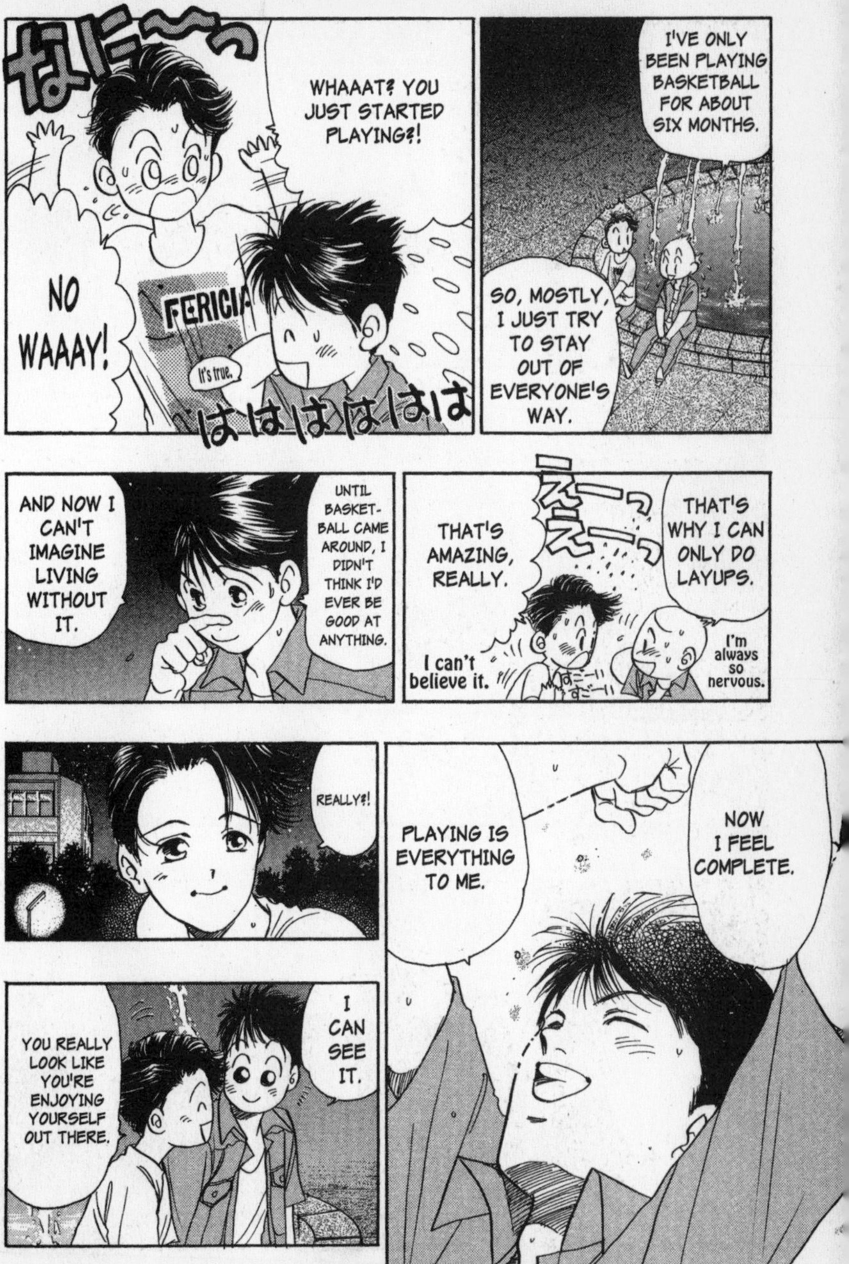
I'VE ONLY BEEN PLAYING BASKETBALL FOR ABOUT SIX MONTHS.
SO, MOSTLY, I JUST TRY TO STAY OUT OF EVERYONE'S WAY.
なに〜っ
WHAAAT? YOU JUST STARTED PLAYING?!
NO WAAAY!
FERICIA
It's true.
はははははは
THAT'S WHY I CAN ONLY DO LAYUPS.
I'm always so nervous.
えーっ えーっ
THAT'S AMAZING, REALLY.
I can't believe it.
UNTIL BASKETBALL CAME AROUND, I DIDN'T THINK I'D EVER BE GOOD AT ANYTHING.
AND NOW I CAN'T IMAGINE LIVING WITHOUT IT.
NOW I FEEL COMPLETE.
PLAYING IS EVERYTHING TO ME.
REALLY?!
I CAN SEE IT.
YOU REALLY LOOK LIKE YOU'RE ENJOYING YOURSELF OUT THERE.

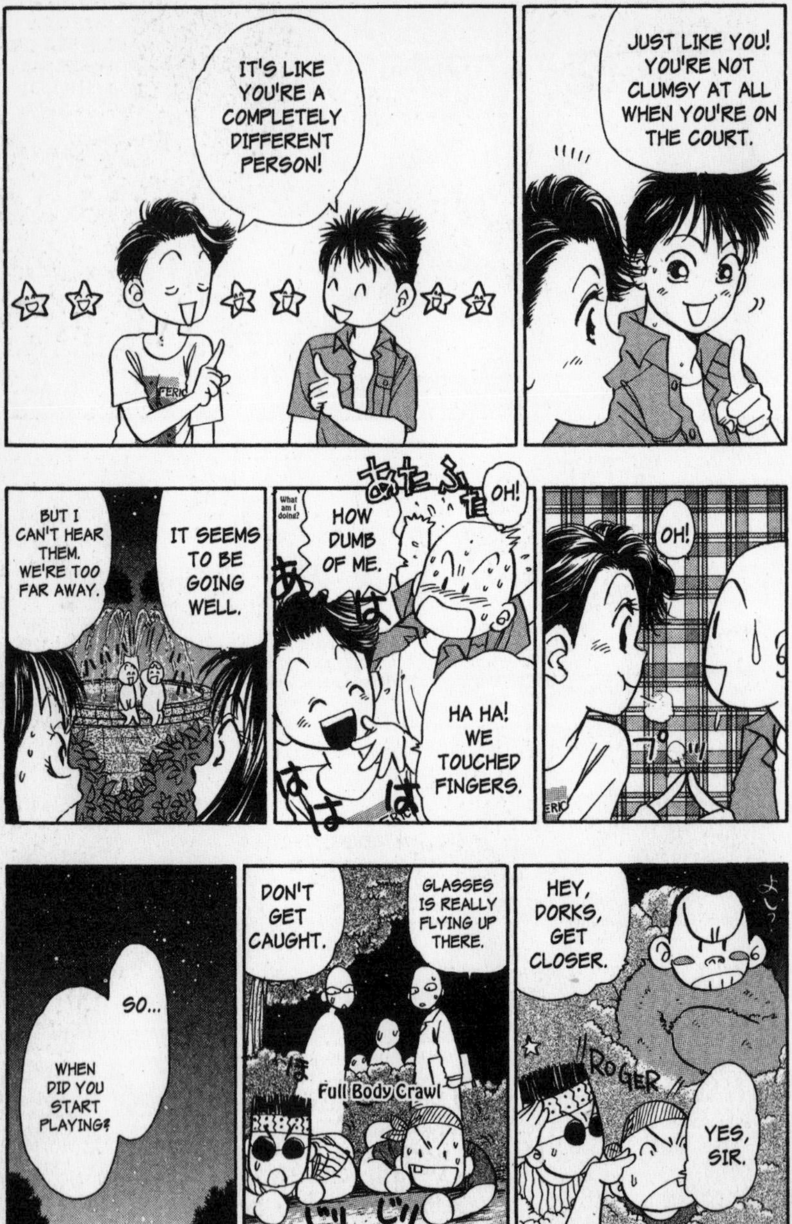
JUST LIKE YOU! YOU'RE NOT CLUMSY AT ALL WHEN YOU'RE ON THE COURT.
IT'S LIKE YOU'RE A COMPLETELY DIFFERENT PERSON!
OH!
OH!
What am I doing?
HOW DUMB OF ME.
HA HA! WE TOUCHED FINGERS.
IT SEEMS TO BE GOING WELL.
BUT I CAN'T HEAR THEM. WE'RE TOO FAR AWAY.
HEY, DORKS, GET CLOSER.
ROGER
YES, SIR.
GLASSES IS REALLY FLYING UP THERE.
DON'T GET CAUGHT.
Full Body Crawl
SO...
WHEN DID YOU START PLAYING?

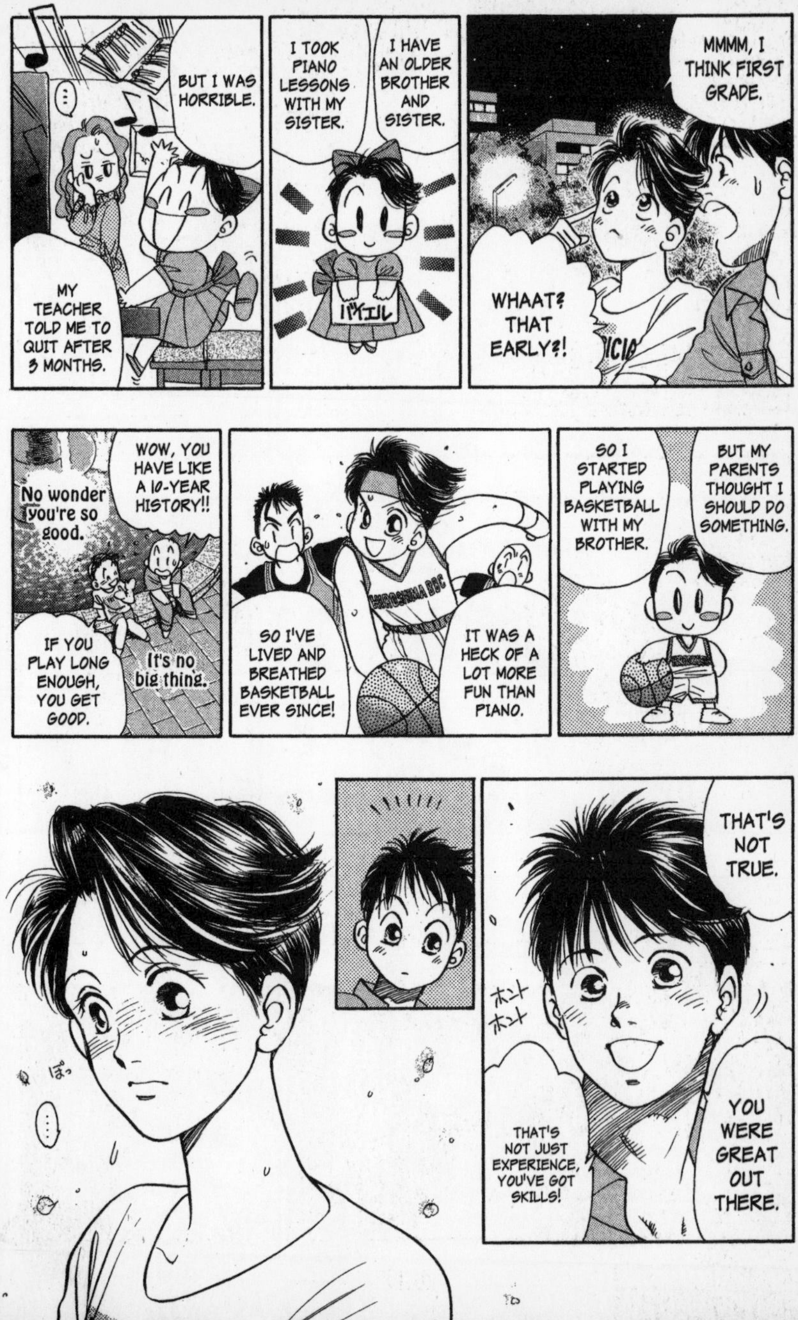
MMMM, I THINK FIRST GRADE.
WHAAT? THAT EARLY?!
I HAVE AN OLDER BROTHER AND SISTER.
I TOOK PIANO LESSONS WITH MY SISTER.
バイエル
BUT I WAS HORRIBLE.
…
MY TEACHER TOLD ME TO QUIT AFTER 3 MONTHS.
BUT MY PARENTS THOUGHT I SHOULD DO SOMETHING.
SO I STARTED PLAYING BASKETBALL WITH MY BROTHER.
IT WAS A HECK OF A LOT MORE FUN THAN PIANO.
SO I'VE LIVED AND BREATHED BASKETBALL EVER SINCE!
WOW, YOU HAVE LIKE A 10-YEAR HISTORY!!
No wonder you're so good.
IF YOU PLAY LONG ENOUGH, YOU GET GOOD.
It's no big thing.
THAT'S NOT TRUE.
ホント ホント
YOU WERE GREAT OUT THERE.
THAT'S NOT JUST EXPERIENCE, YOU'VE GOT SKILLS!
ぽっ
…

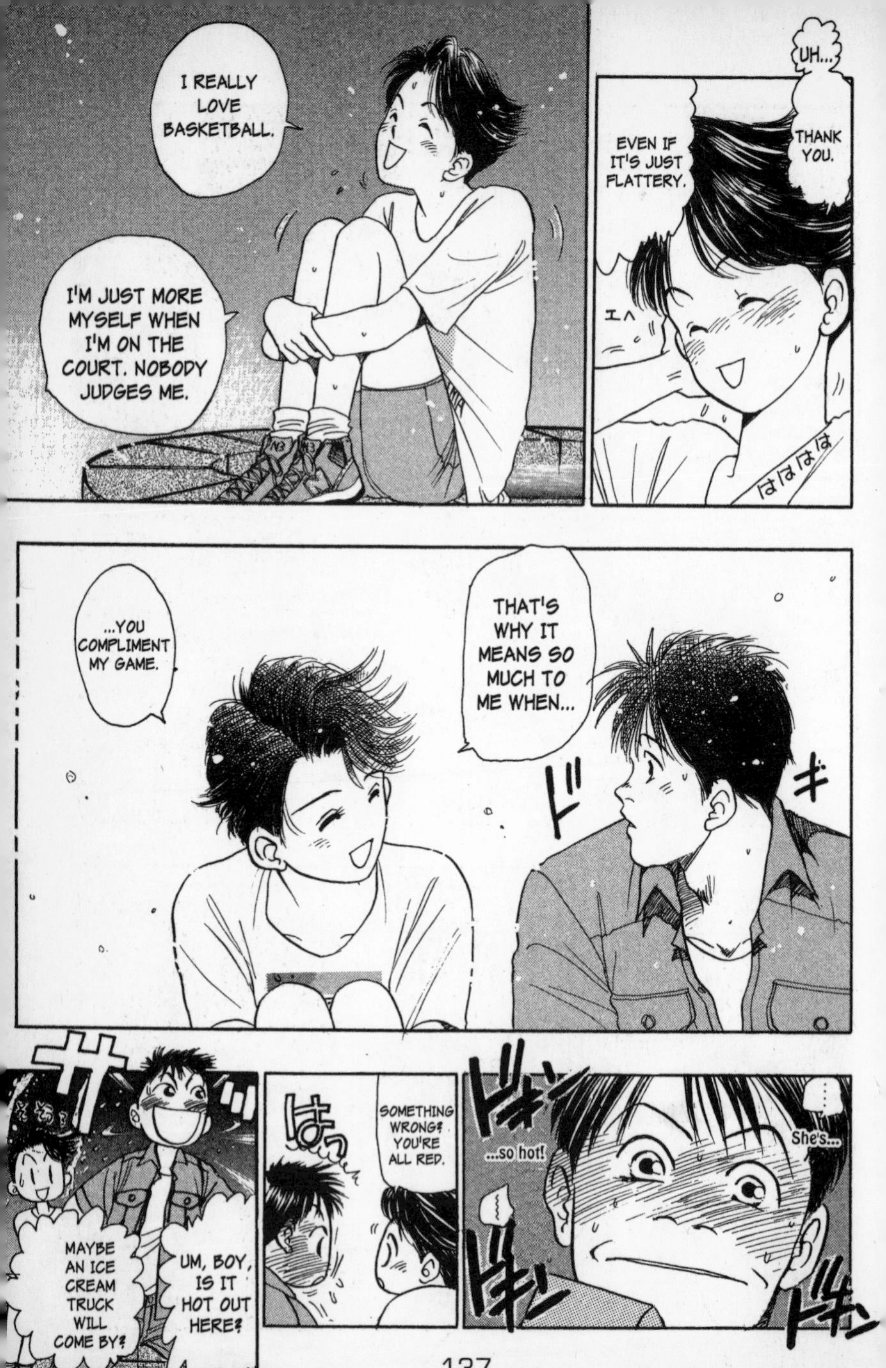
UH...
THANK YOU.
EVEN IF IT'S JUST FLATTERY.
エへ
ははは
I REALLY LOVE BASKETBALL.
I'M JUST MORE MYSELF WHEN I'M ON THE COURT. NOBODY JUDGES ME.
THAT'S WHY IT MEANS SO MUCH TO ME WHEN...
...YOU COMPLIMENT MY GAME.
ドギ
She's...
...so hot!
ドキン
ドキン
ドキン
はっ
SOMETHING WRONG? YOU'RE ALL RED.
サッ
UM, BOY, IS IT HOT OUT HERE?
MAYBE AN ICE CREAM TRUCK WILL COME BY?

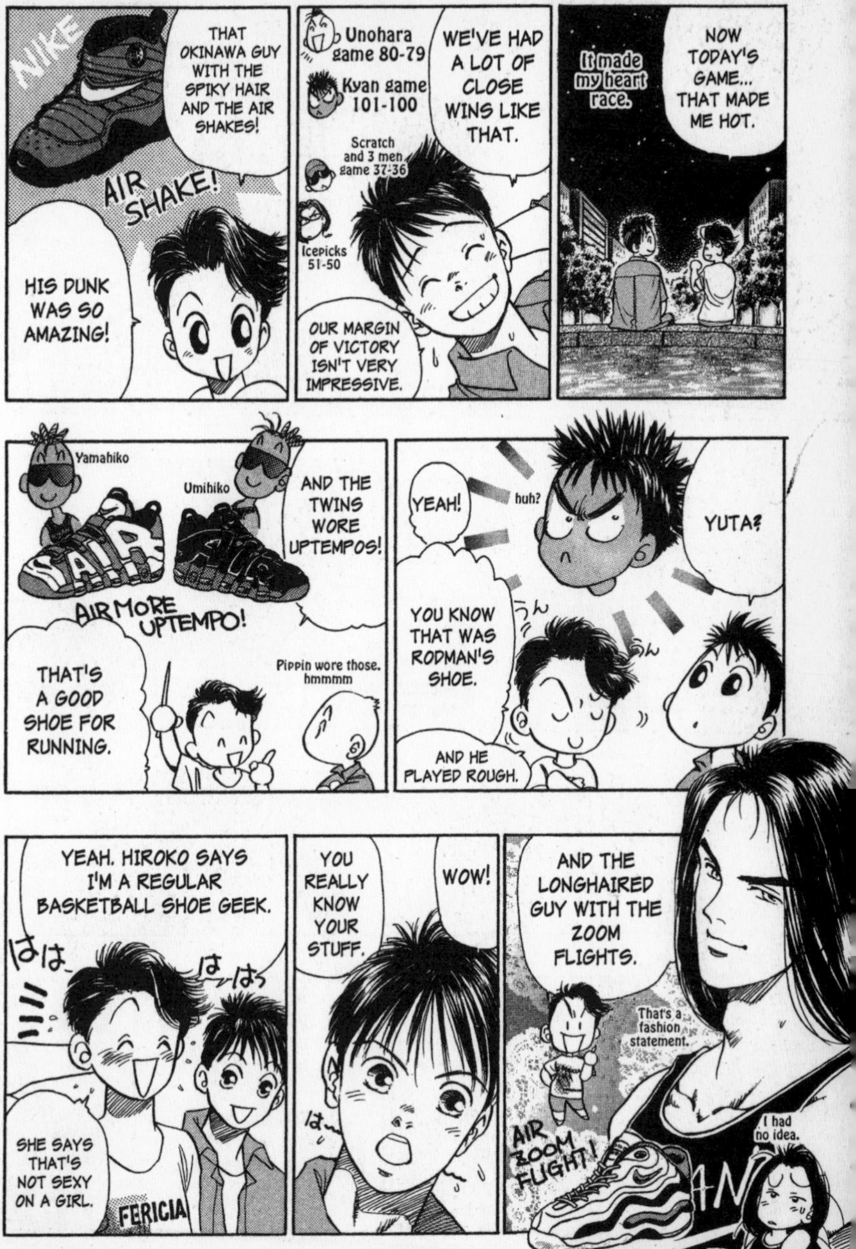
NOW TODAY'S GAME... THAT MADE ME HOT.
It made my heart race.
WE'VE HAD A LOT OF CLOSE WINS LIKE THAT.
Unohara game 80-79
Kyan game 101-100
Scratch and 3 men game 37-36
Icepicks 51-50
OUR MARGIN OF VICTORY ISN'T VERY IMPRESSIVE.
NIKE
THAT OKINAWA GUY WITH THE SPIKY HAIR AND THE AIR SHAKES!
AIR SHAKE!
HIS DUNK WAS SO AMAZING!
YUTA?
huh?
YEAH!
YOU KNOW THAT WAS RODMAN'S SHOE.
うん
うん
AND HE PLAYED ROUGH.
Yamahiko
Umihiko
AND THE TWINS WORE UPTEMPOS!
AIR MORE UPTEMPO!
THAT'S A GOOD SHOE FOR RUNNING.
Pippin wore those. hmmmm
AND THE LONGHAIRED GUY WITH THE ZOOM FLIGHTS.
That's a fashion statement.
AIR ZOOM FLIGHT!
I had no idea.
WOW!
YOU REALLY KNOW YOUR STUFF.
はー
YEAH. HIROKO SAYS I'M A REGULAR BASKETBALL SHOE GEEK.
はは
はっはっ
SHE SAYS THAT'S NOT SEXY ON A GIRL.
FERICIA

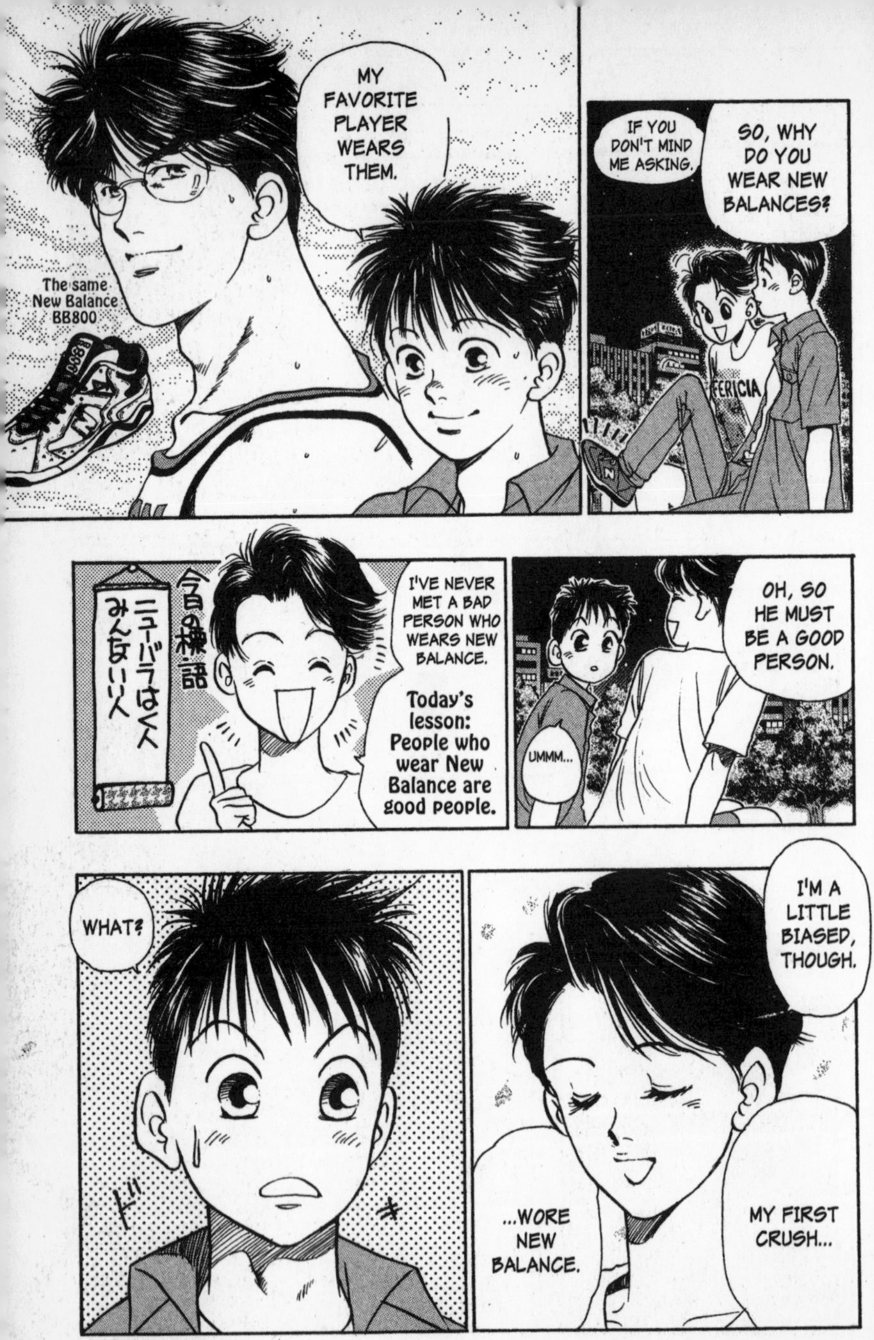
SO, WHY DO YOU WEAR NEW BALANCES?
IF YOU DON'T MIND ME ASKING.
FERICIA
MY FAVORITE PLAYER WEARS THEM.
The same New Balance BB800
OH, SO HE MUST BE A GOOD PERSON.
UMMM...
I'VE NEVER MET A BAD PERSON WHO WEARS NEW BALANCE.
Today's lesson: People who wear New Balance are good people.
今日の標語
ニューバラはく人
みんないい人
I'M A LITTLE BIASED, THOUGH.
MY FIRST CRUSH...
...WORE NEW BALANCE.
WHAT?

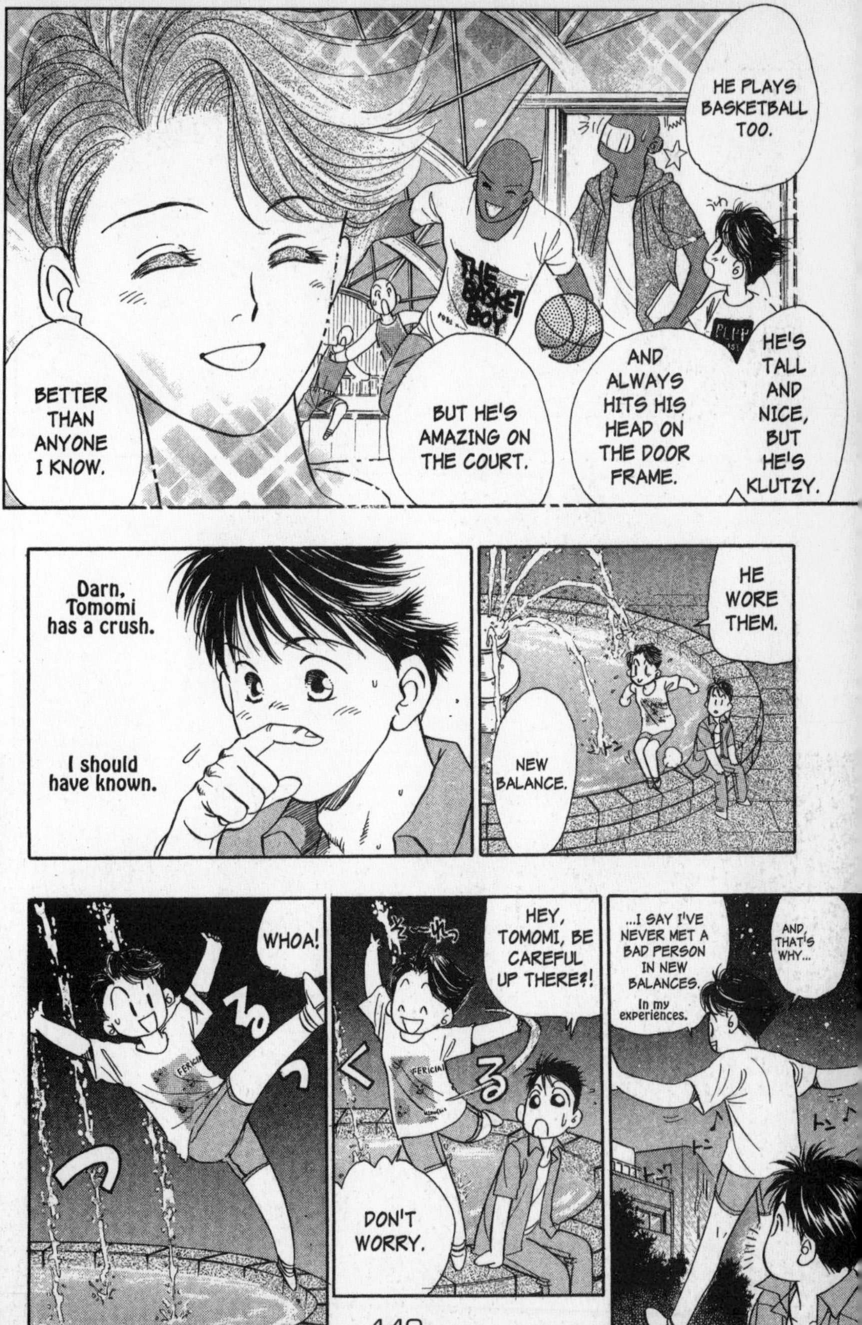
HE PLAYS BASKETBALL TOO.
HE'S TALL AND NICE, BUT HE'S KLUTZY.
AND ALWAYS HITS HIS HEAD ON THE DOOR FRAME.
BUT HE'S AMAZING ON THE COURT.
BETTER THAN ANYONE I KNOW.
HE WORE THEM.
NEW BALANCE.
Darn, Tomomi has a crush.
I should have known.
AND, THAT's WHY...
...I SAY I'VE NEVER MET A BAD PERSON IN NEW BALANCES.
In my experiences.
HEY, TOMOMI, BE CAREFUL UP THERE?!
DON'T WORRY.
WHOA!

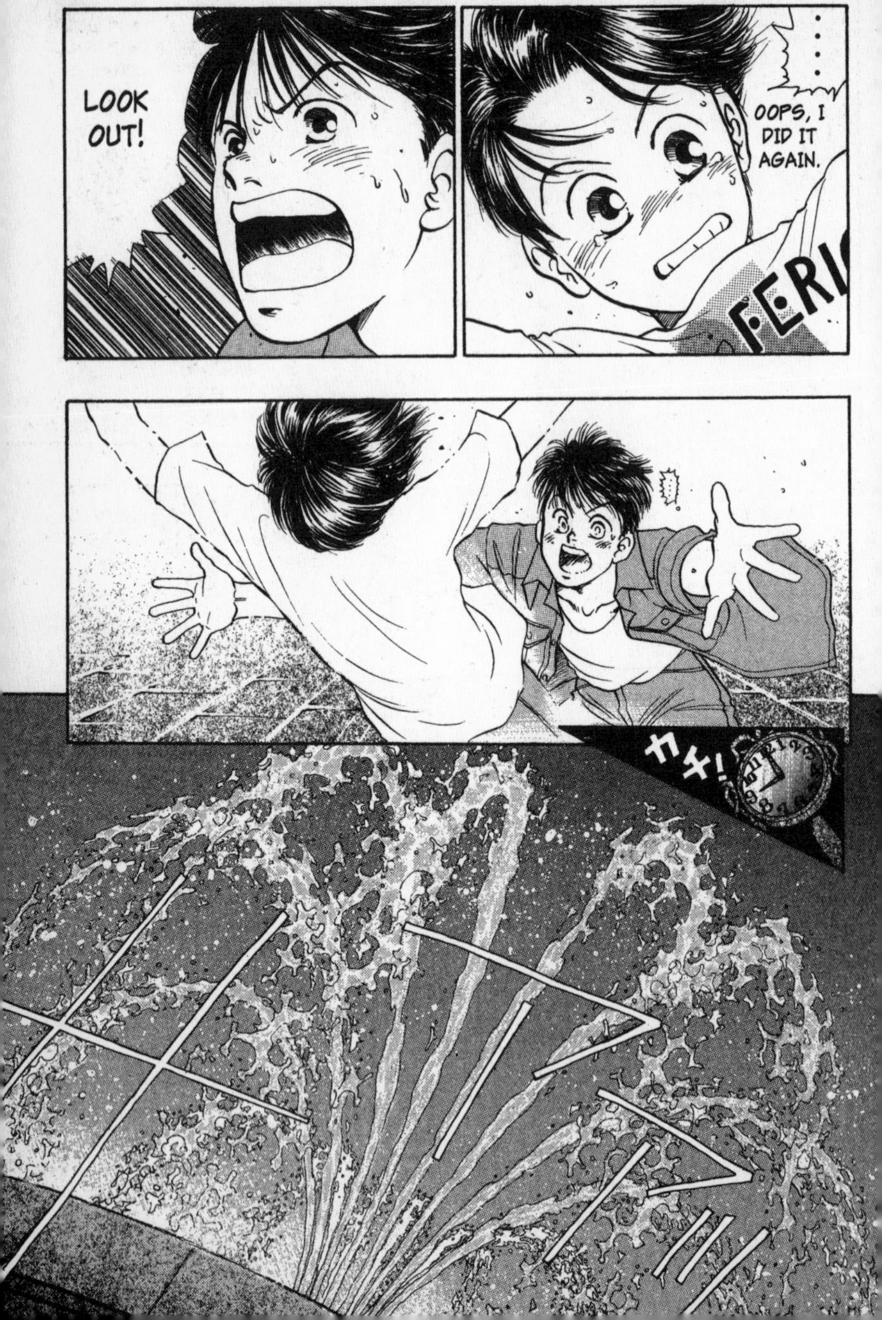
....
OOPS, I DID IT AGAIN.
LOOK OUT!
!...
カチ!

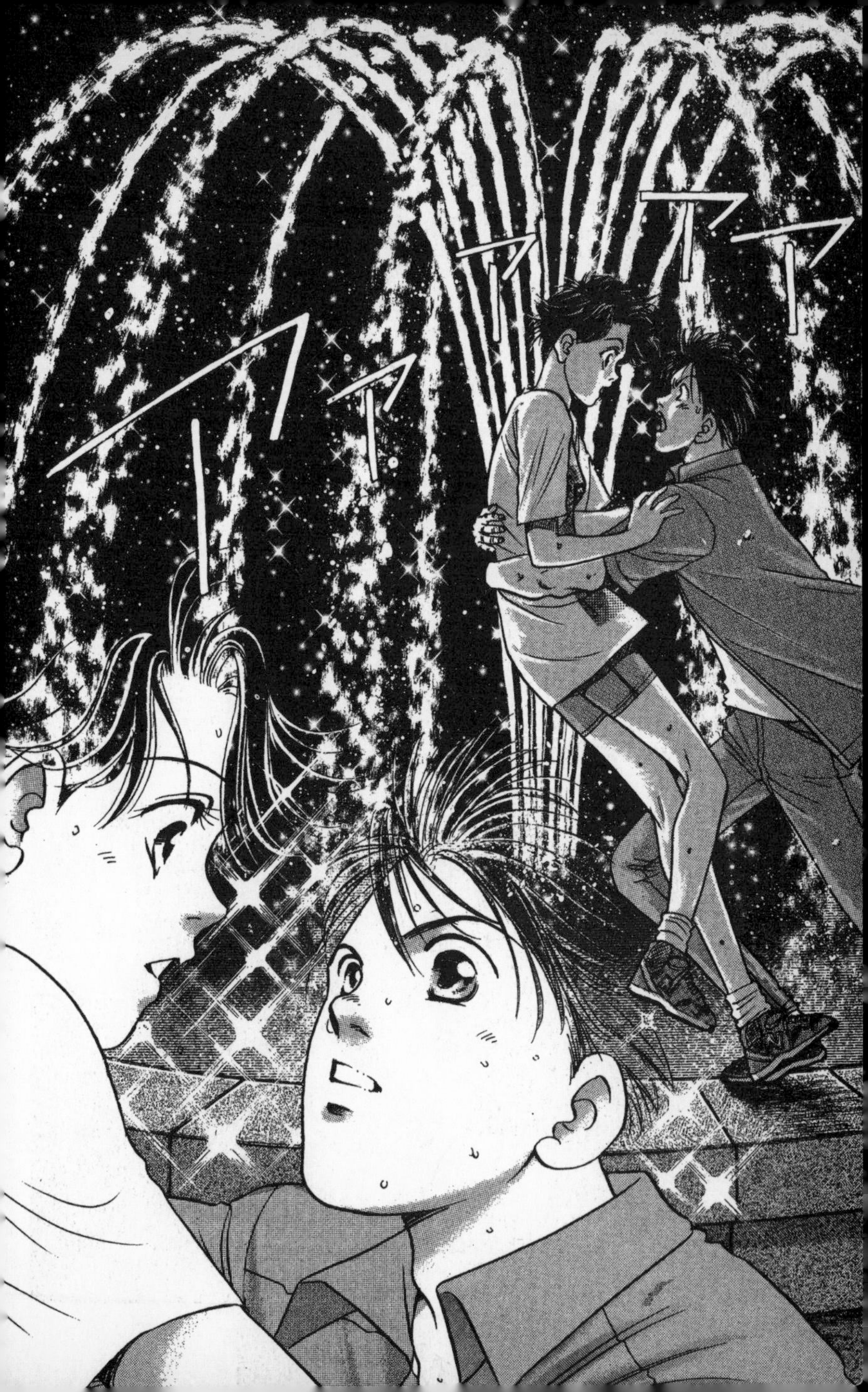
アアア
アア

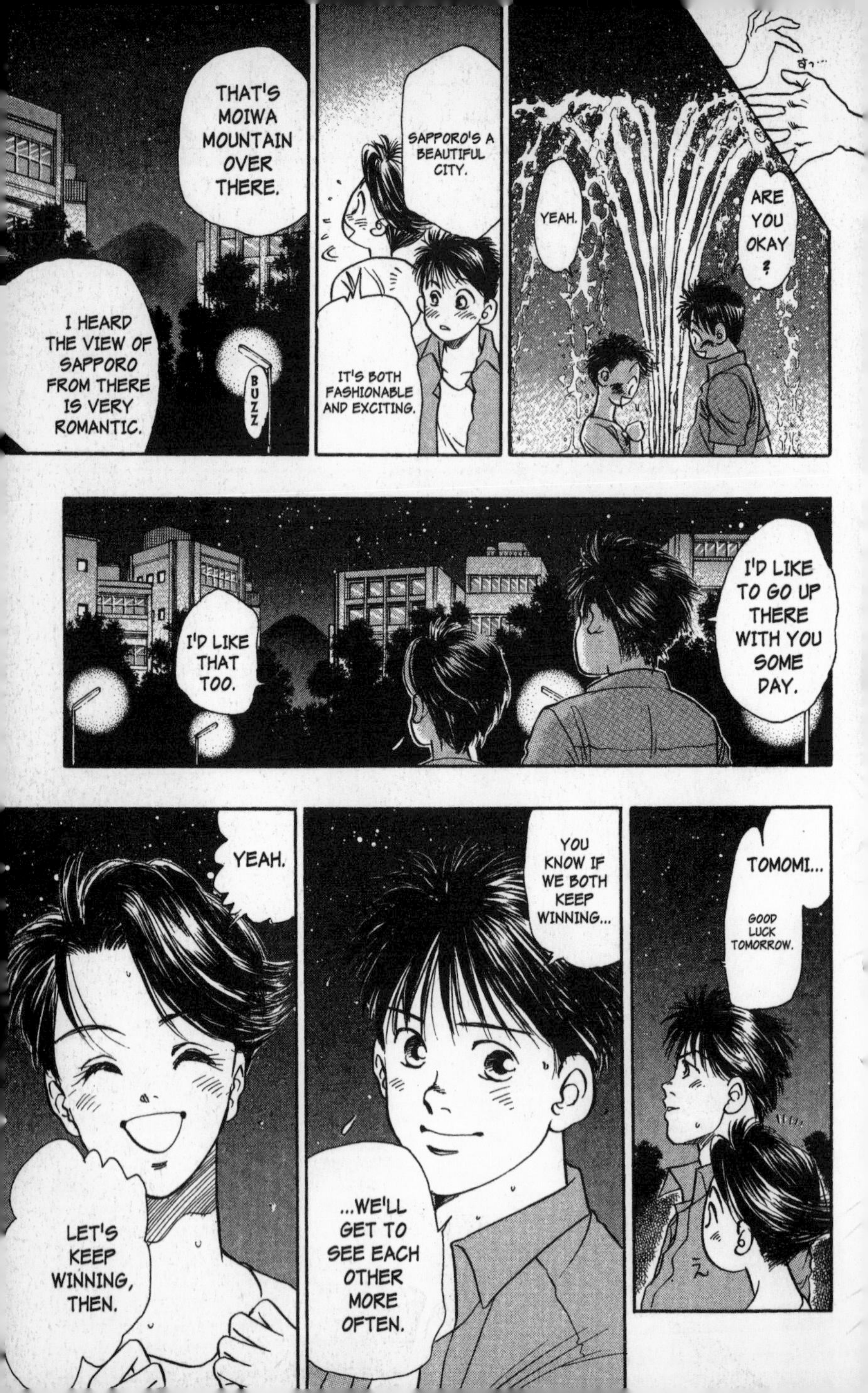

すっ…
ARE YOU OKAY?
YEAH.
SAPPORO'S A BEAUTIFUL CITY.
IT'S BOTH FASHIONABLE AND EXCITING.
THAT'S MOIWA MOUNTAIN OVER THERE.
I HEARD THE VIEW OF SAPPORO FROM THERE IS VERY ROMANTIC.
BUZZ
I'D LIKE TO GO UP THERE WITH YOU SOME DAY.
I'D LIKE THAT TOO.
TOMOMI...
GOOD LUCK TOMORROW.
YOU KNOW IF WE BOTH KEEP WINNING...
...WE'LL GET TO SEE EACH OTHER MORE OFTEN.
YEAH.
LET'S KEEP WINNING, THEN.

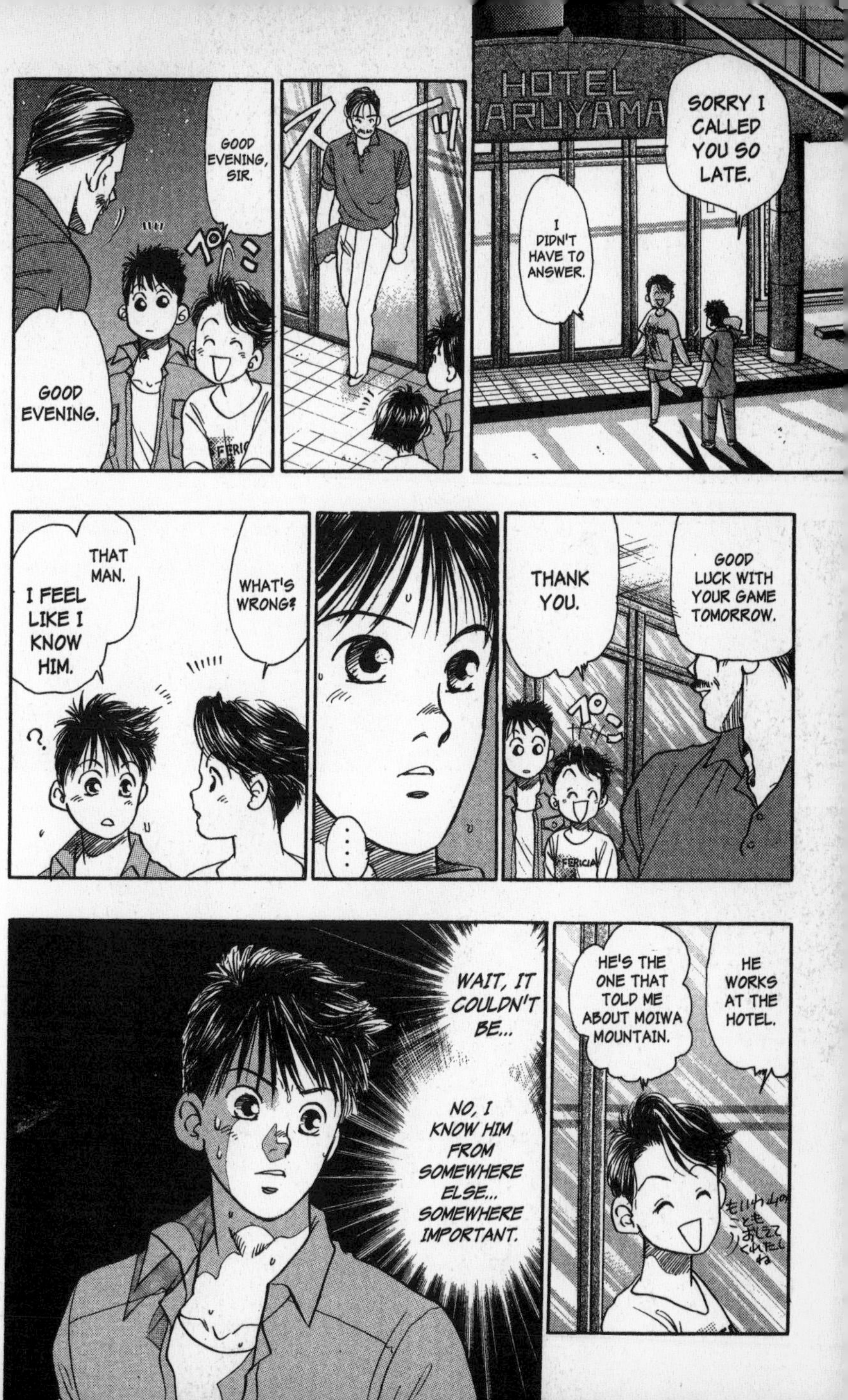
HOTEL
ARUYAMA
SORRY I CALLED YOU SO LATE.
I DIDN'T HAVE TO ANSWER.
スーッ
GOOD EVENING, SIR.
GOOD EVENING.
GOOD LUCK WITH YOUR GAME TOMORROW.
THANK YOU.
....
WHAT'S WRONG?
THAT MAN.
I FEEL LIKE I KNOW HIM.
HE WORKS AT THE HOTEL.
HE'S THE ONE THAT TOLD ME ABOUT MOIWA MOUNTAIN.
もいわ山のこともおしえてくれたしね
WAIT, IT COULDN'T BE...
NO, I KNOW HIM FROM SOMEWHERE ELSE... SOMEWHERE IMPORTANT.

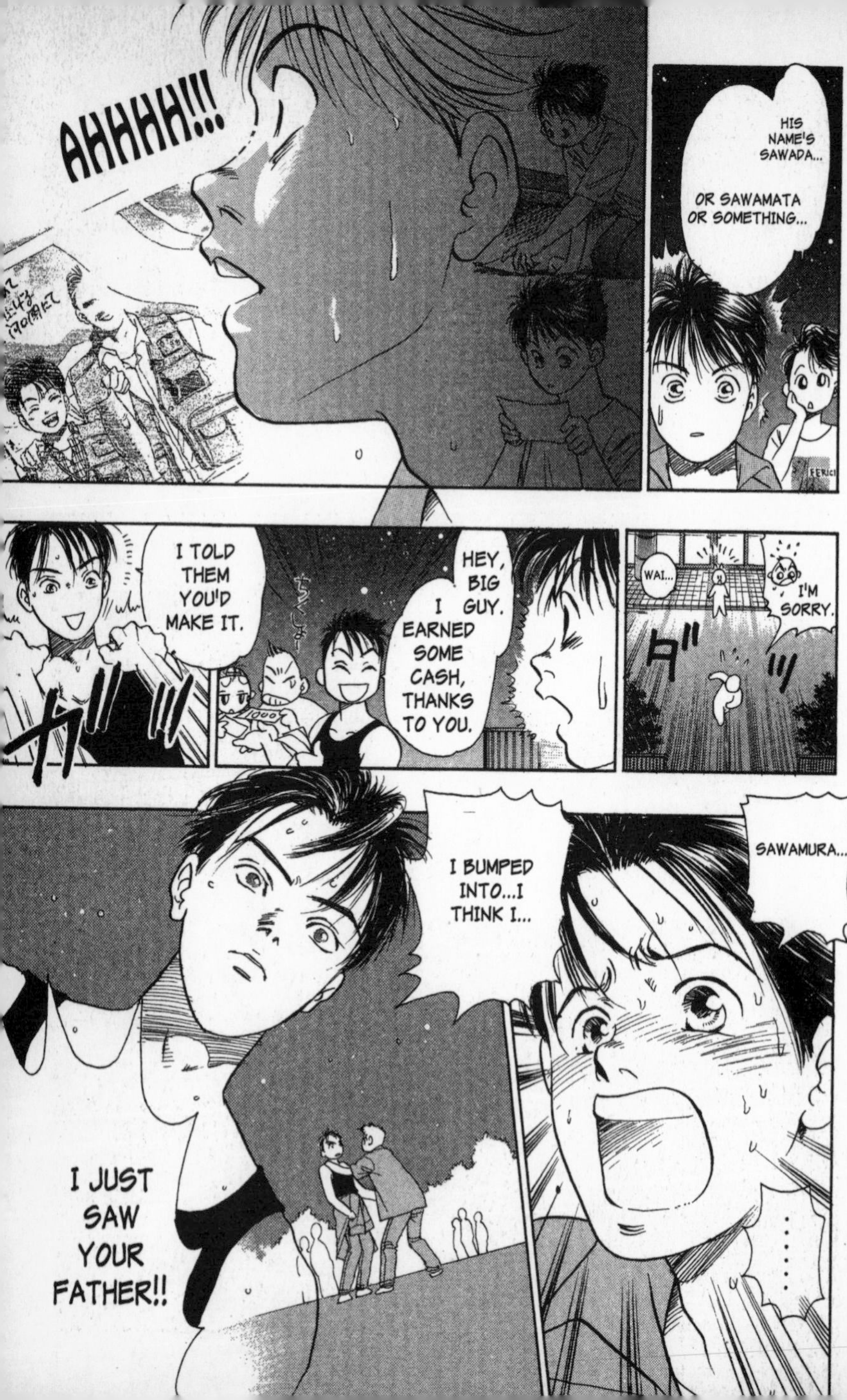
HIS NAME'S SAWADA...
OR SAWAMATA OR SOMETHING...
AHHHH!!!
WAI...
I'M SORRY.
ダッ
HEY, BIG GUY. I EARNED SOME CASH, THANKS TO YOU.
I TOLD THEM YOU'D MAKE IT.
ガッ
SAWAMURA...
I BUMPED INTO...I THINK I...
I JUST SAW YOUR FATHER!!
......

If you don't brush your teeth before bed, the Kim Cavity will come around.

REBOUND

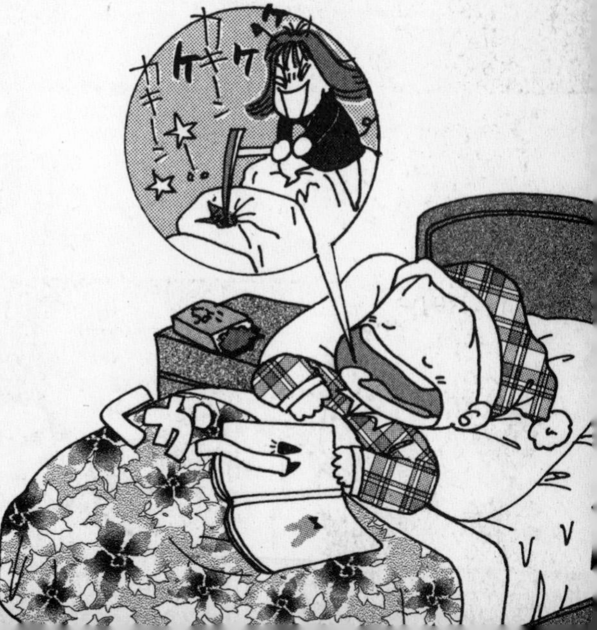

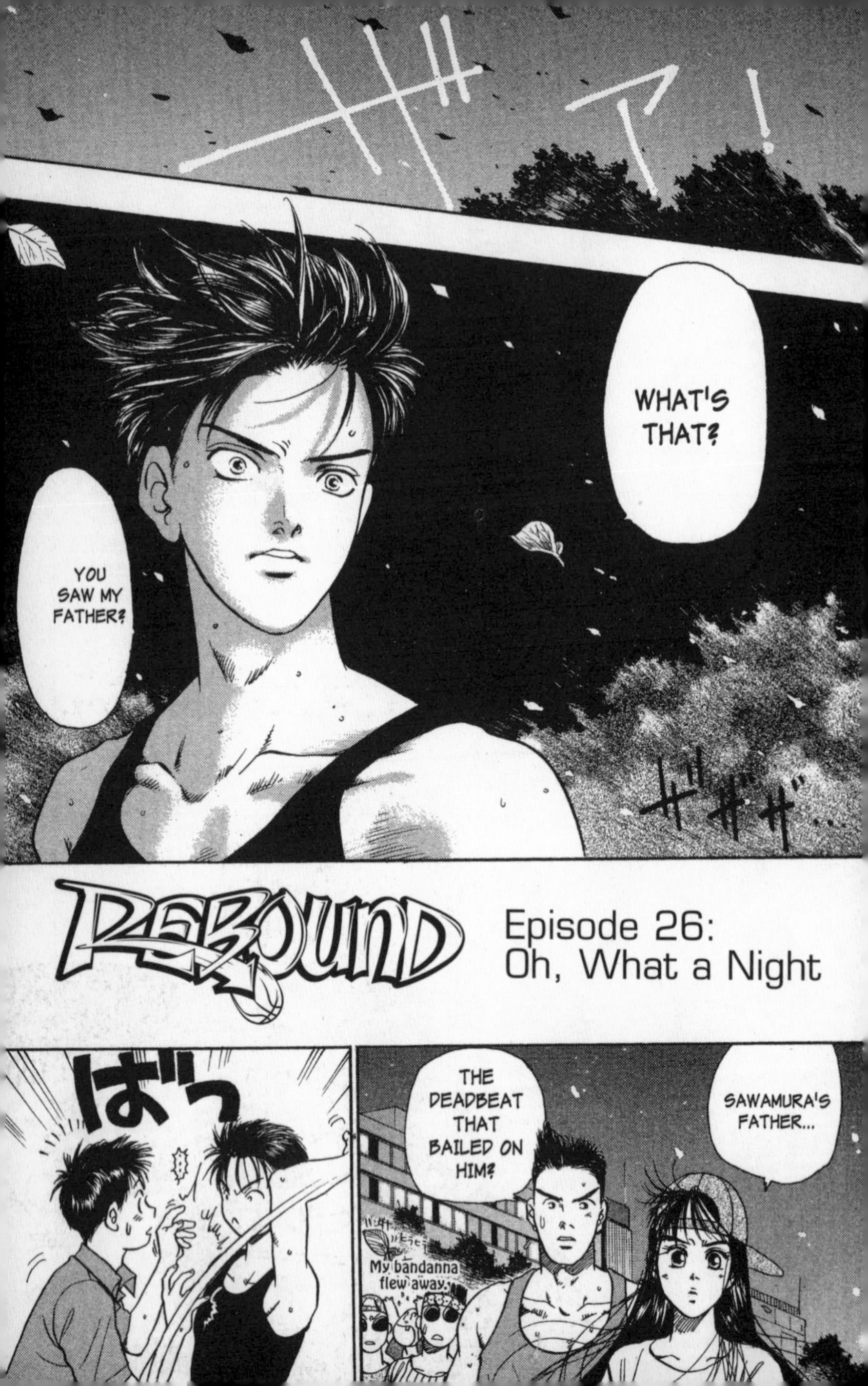
ザア！
WHAT'S THAT?
YOU SAW MY FATHER?
ザザザ…
REBOUND
Episode 26: Oh, What a Night
SAWAMURA'S FATHER...
THE DEADBEAT THAT BAILED ON HIM?
My bandanna flew away.
ばっ

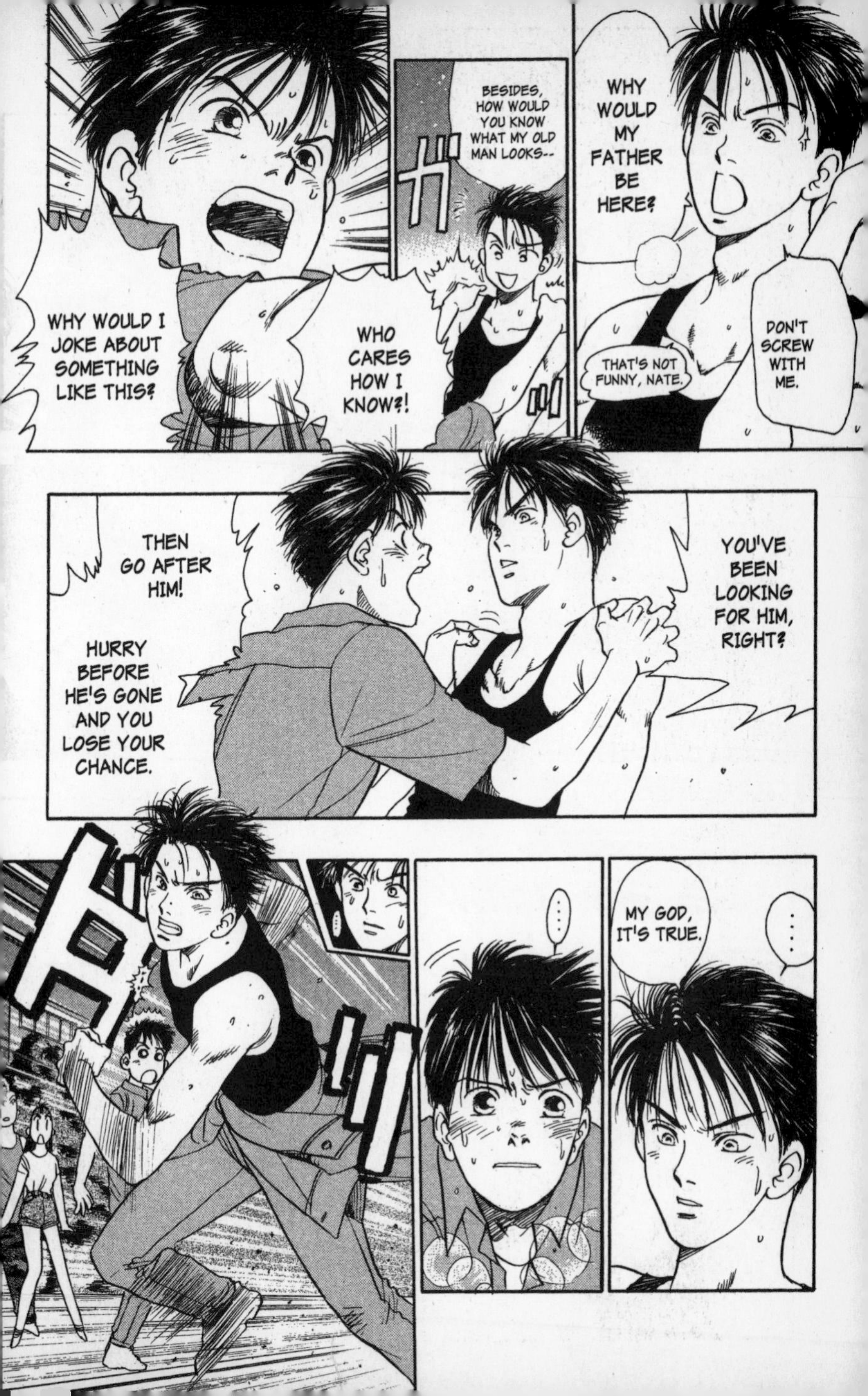

WHY WOULD MY FATHER BE HERE?
THAT'S NOT FUNNY, NATE.
DON'T SCREW WITH ME.
BESIDES, HOW WOULD YOU KNOW WHAT MY OLD MAN LOOKS--
ガ
WHO CARES HOW I KNOW?!
WHY WOULD I JOKE ABOUT SOMETHING LIKE THIS?
YOU'VE BEEN LOOKING FOR HIM, RIGHT?
THEN GO AFTER HIM!
HURRY BEFORE HE'S GONE AND YOU LOSE YOUR CHANCE.
....
MY GOD, IT'S TRUE.
...
...
ド

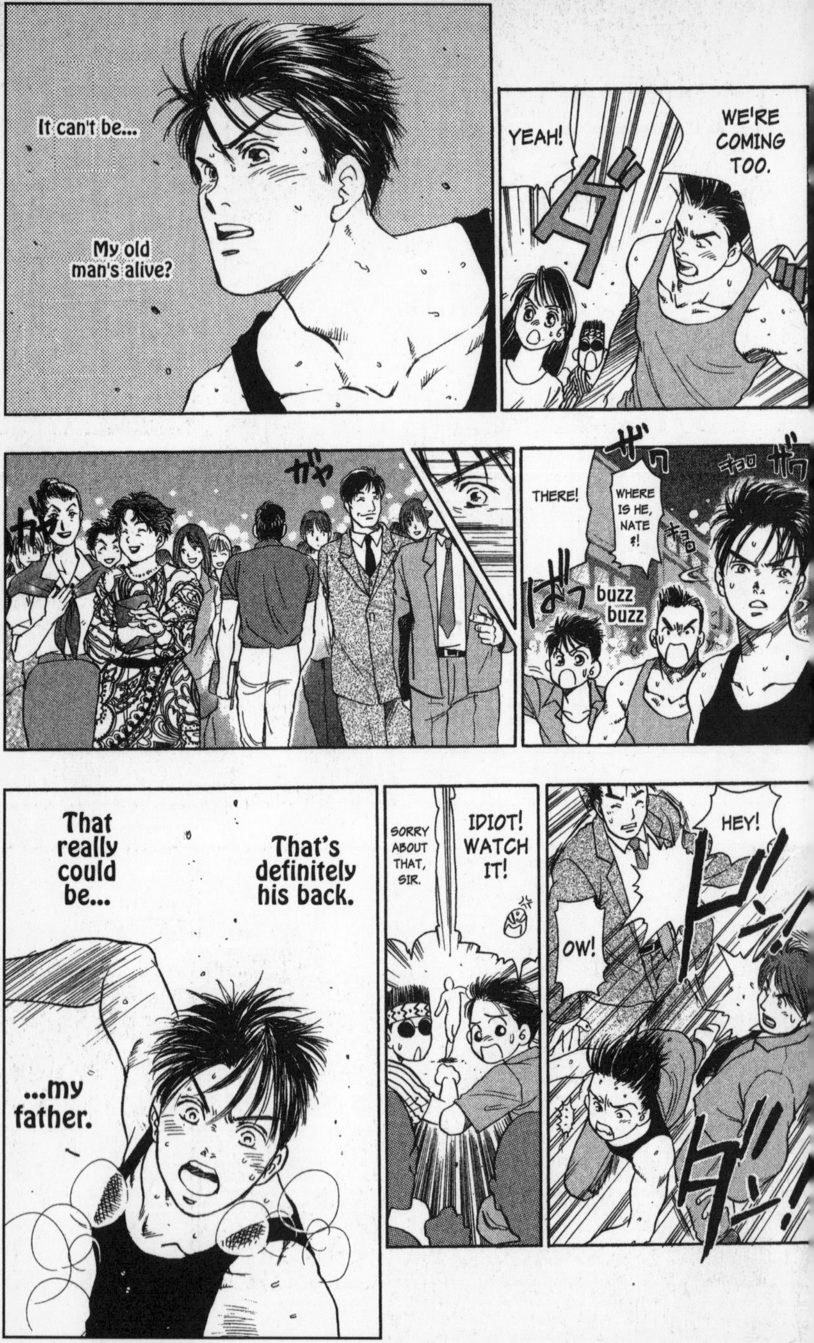
WE'RE COMING TOO.
YEAH!
It can't be...
My old man's alive?
WHERE IS HE, NATE?!
THERE!
buzz buzz
HEY!
OW!
IDIOT! WATCH IT!
SORRY ABOUT THAT, SIR.
That's definitely his back.
That really could be...
...my father.

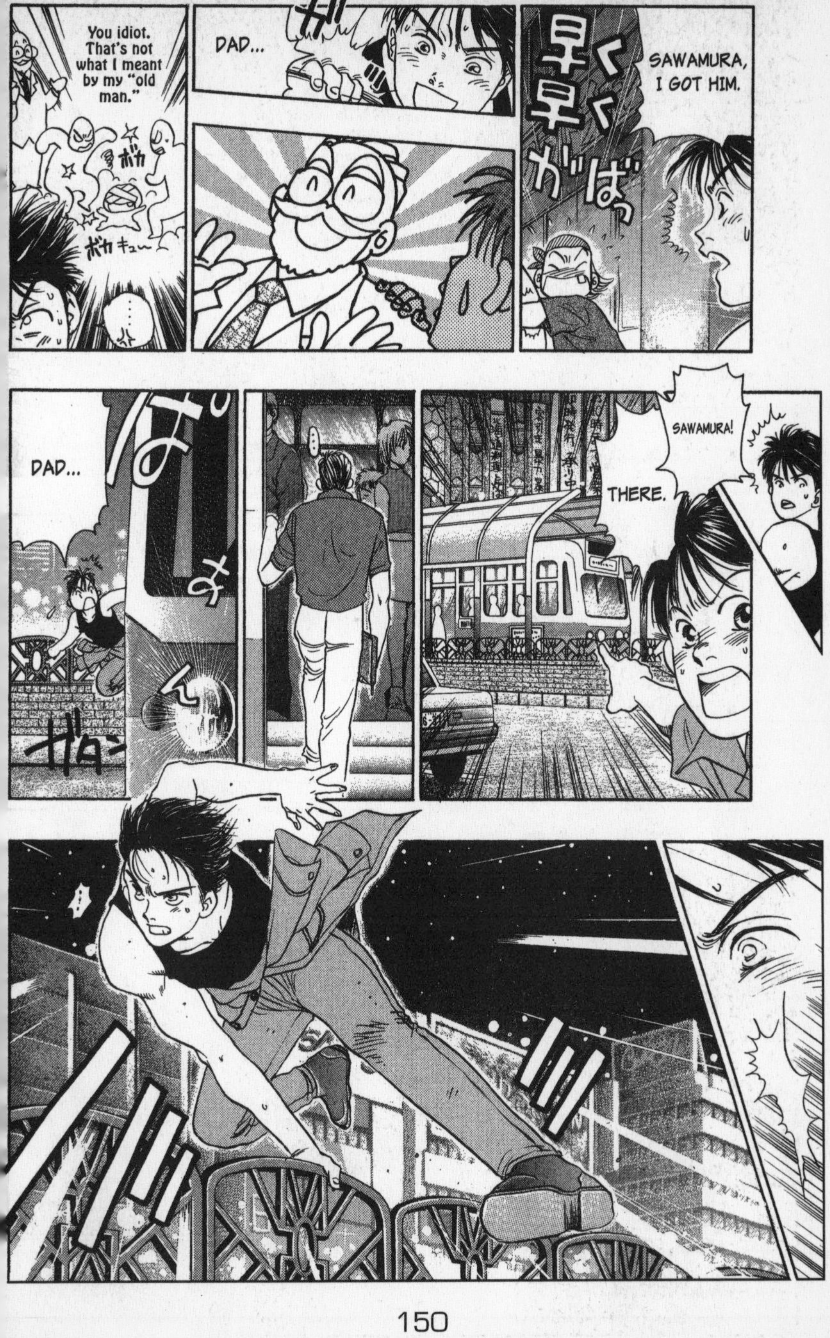
早く早く
がばっ
SAWAMURA, I GOT HIM.
DAD...
You idiot. That's not what I meant by my "old man."
SAWAMURA!
THERE.
DAD...

IDIOT! WATCH WHERE YOU'RE GOING!
MORON!
YOU'RE GONNA GET KILLED!
GET OUT OF THE ROAD.
WHOA!
HE'S A MANIAC.
THAT'S HIM.
MY DAD IS GETTING ON THAT TRAIN!
D...
DAAAD!
!!
AHH!
GOT YOUR BACK.
!!
HERE WE COME.
OH YEAH!

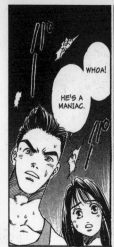

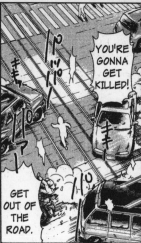

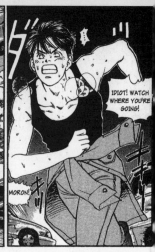

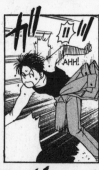

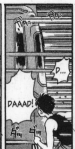

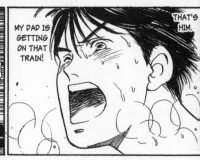

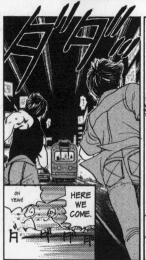

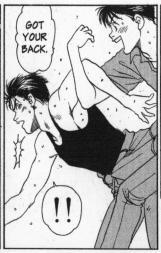

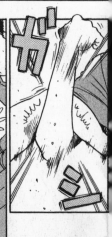

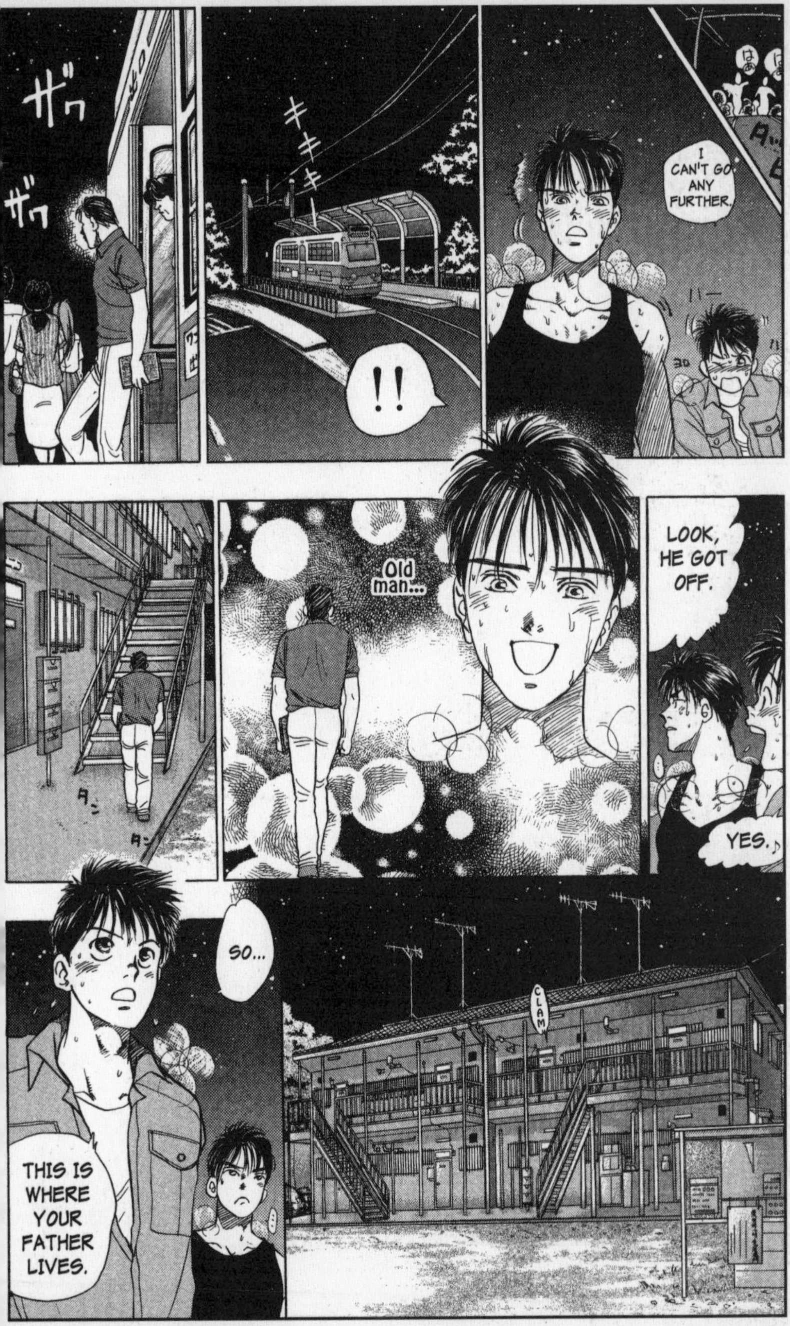
I CAN'T GO ANY FURTHER.
!!
キキキ
ザワ
ザワ
LOOK, HE GOT OFF.
...
YES.♪
Old man...
CLAM
SO...
THIS IS WHERE YOUR FATHER LIVES.
...

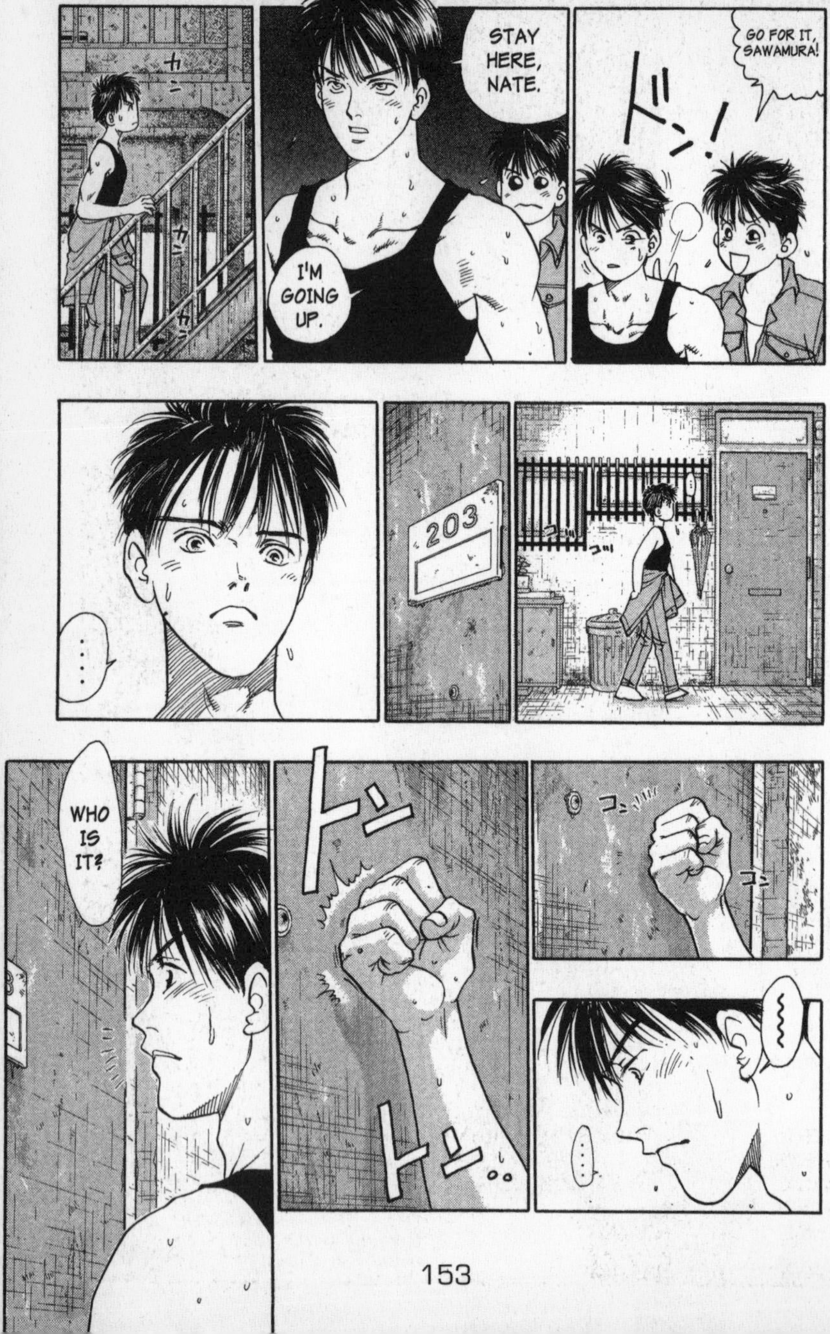
GO FOR IT, SAWAMURA!
ドン！
STAY HERE, NATE.
I'M GOING UP.
カン
カン
カン
...
203
.....
コン
コン
.....
...
トン
トン
WHO IS IT?

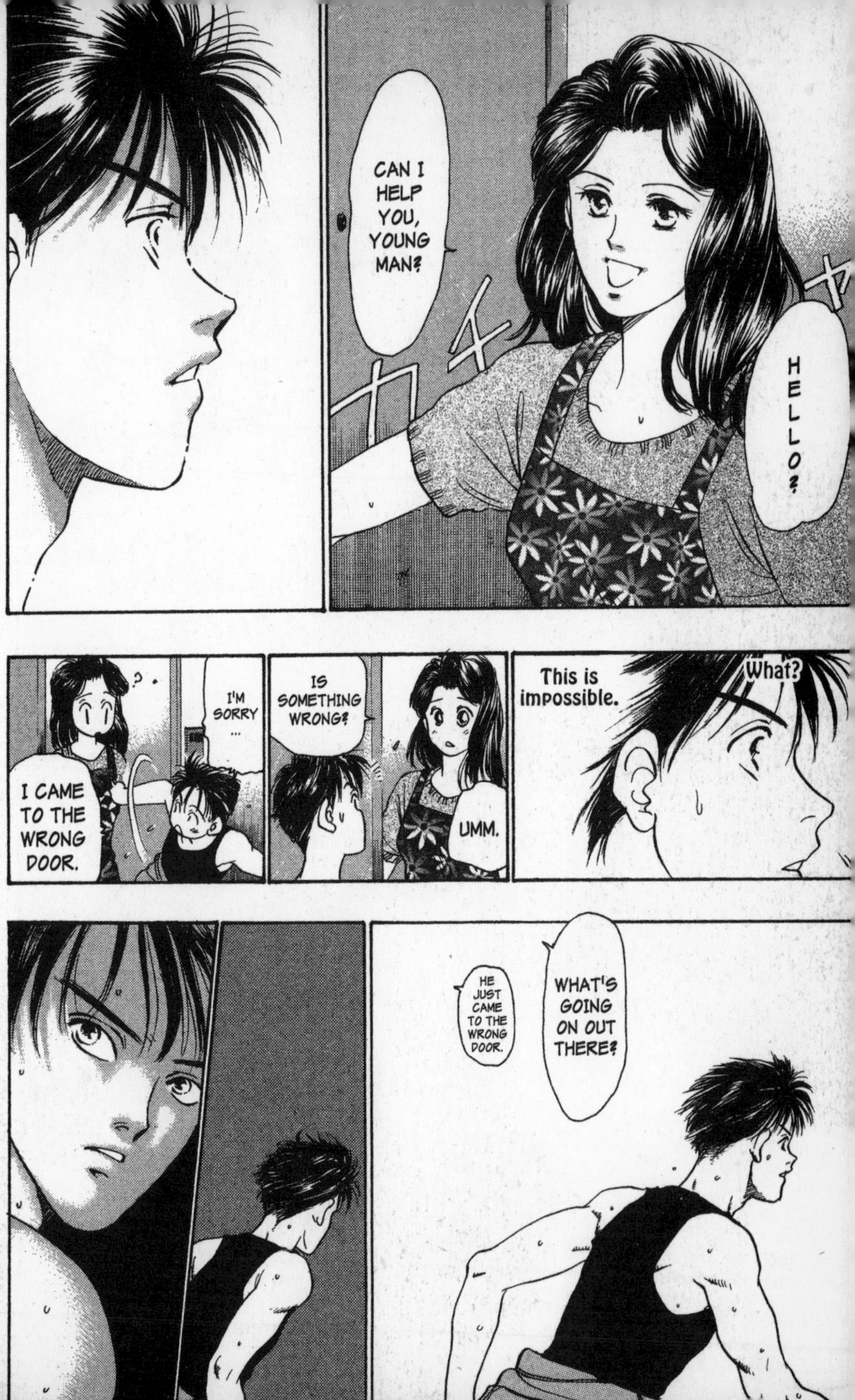
HELLO?
CAN I HELP YOU, YOUNG MAN?
What?
This is impossible.
IS SOMETHING WRONG?
UMM.
I'M SORRY ...
I CAME TO THE WRONG DOOR.
WHAT'S GOING ON OUT THERE?
HE JUST CAME TO THE WRONG DOOR.

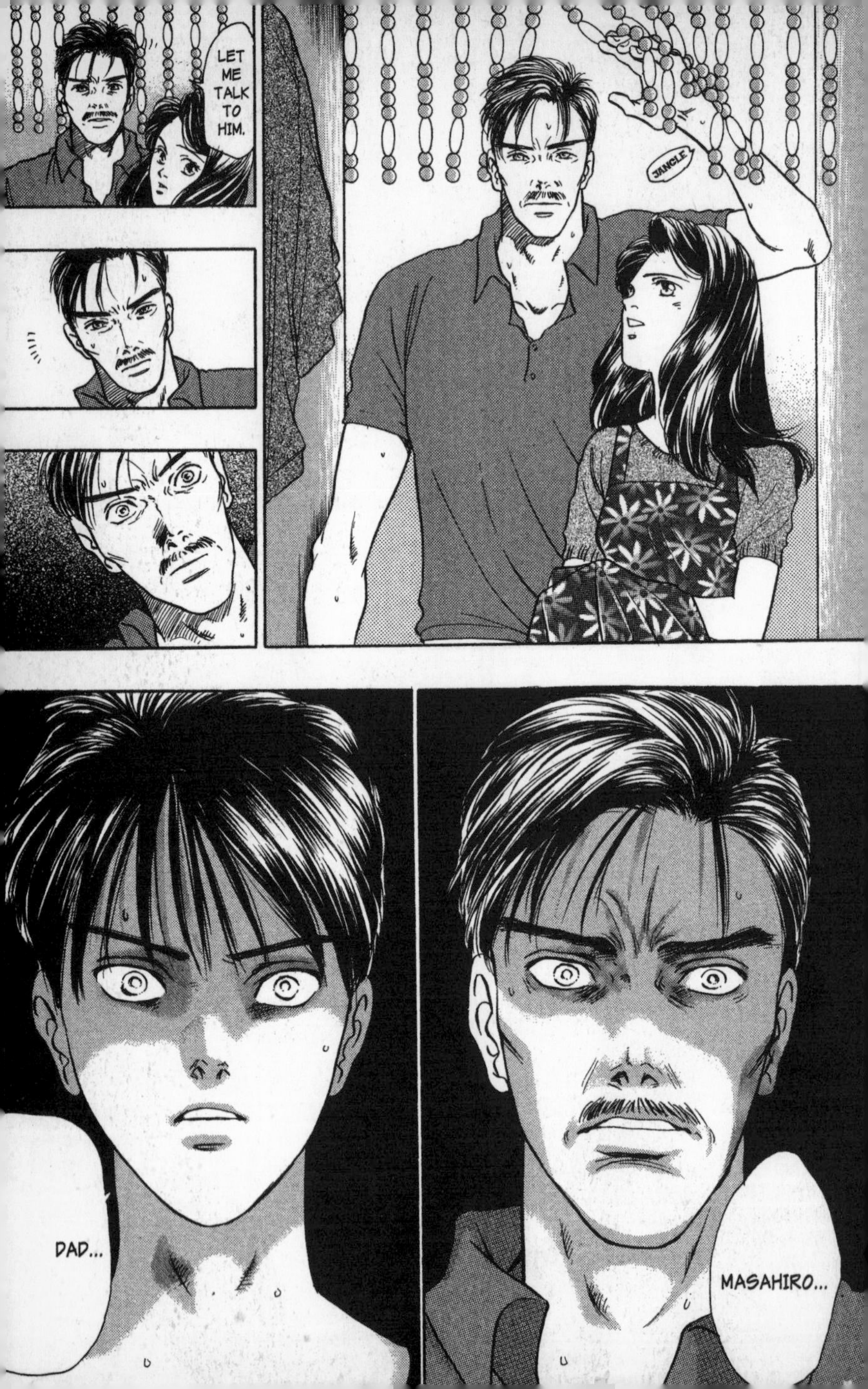
JANGLE
LET ME TALK TO HIM.
MASAHIRO...
DAD...

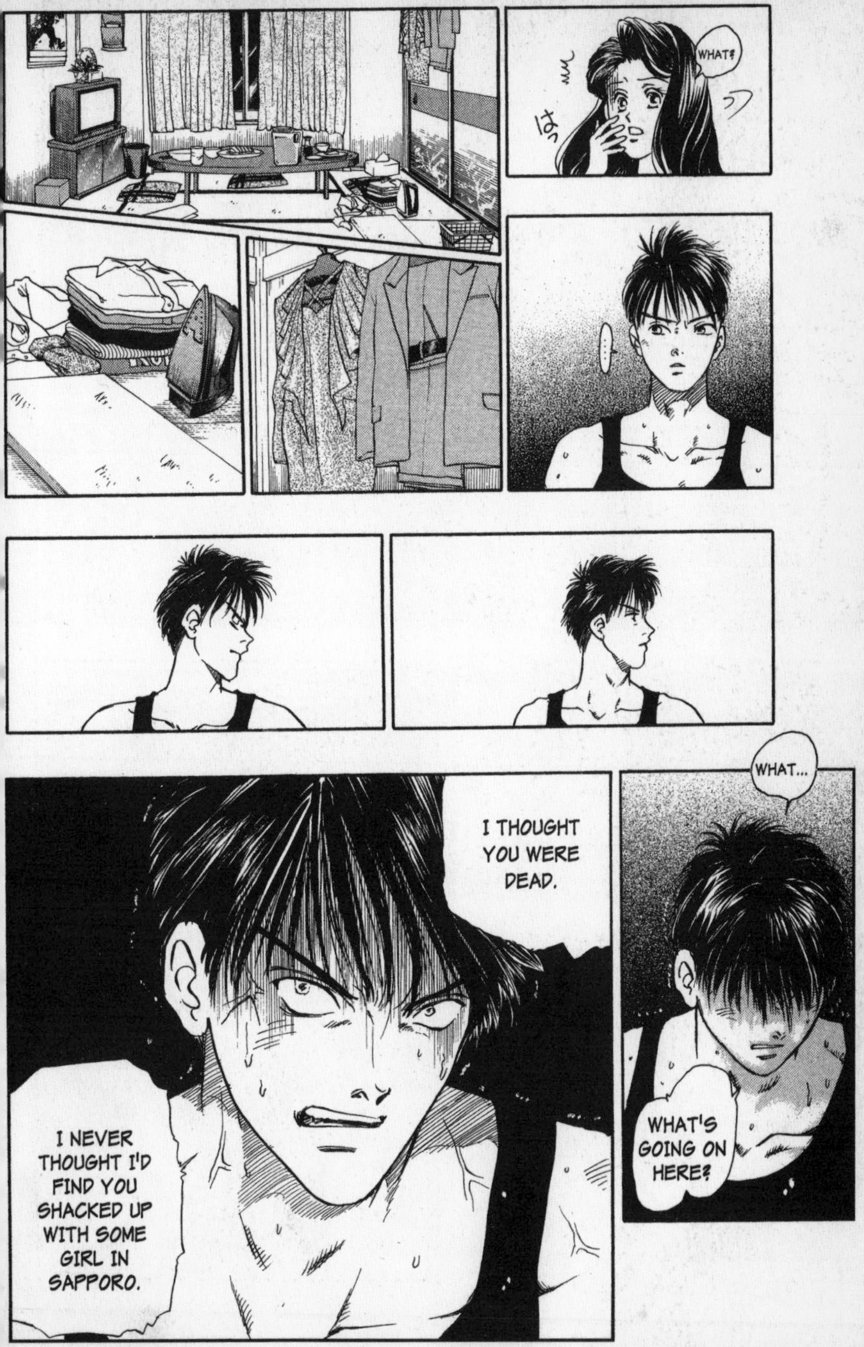

はっ
WHAT?
...
WHAT...
WHAT'S GOING ON HERE?
I THOUGHT YOU WERE DEAD.
I NEVER THOUGHT I'D FIND YOU SHACKED UP WITH SOME GIRL IN SAPPORO.

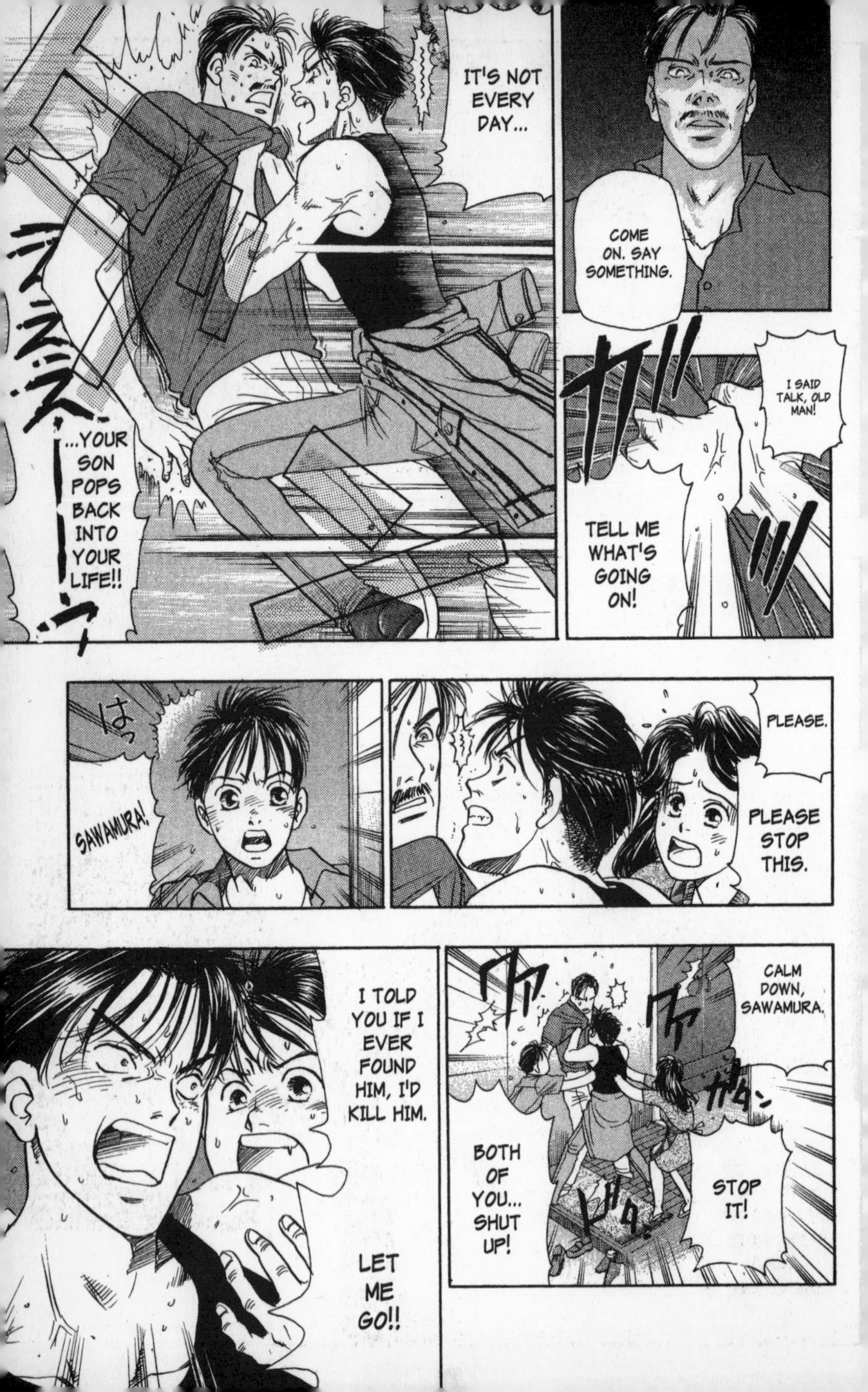
COME ON. SAY SOMETHING.
I SAID TALK, OLD MAN!
TELL ME WHAT'S GOING ON!
IT'S NOT EVERY DAY...
...YOUR SON POPS BACK INTO YOUR LIFE!!
PLEASE.
PLEASE STOP THIS.
はっ
SAWAMURA!
CALM DOWN, SAWAMURA.
STOP IT!
BOTH OF YOU... SHUT UP!
I TOLD YOU IF I EVER FOUND HIM, I'D KILL HIM.
LET ME GO!!

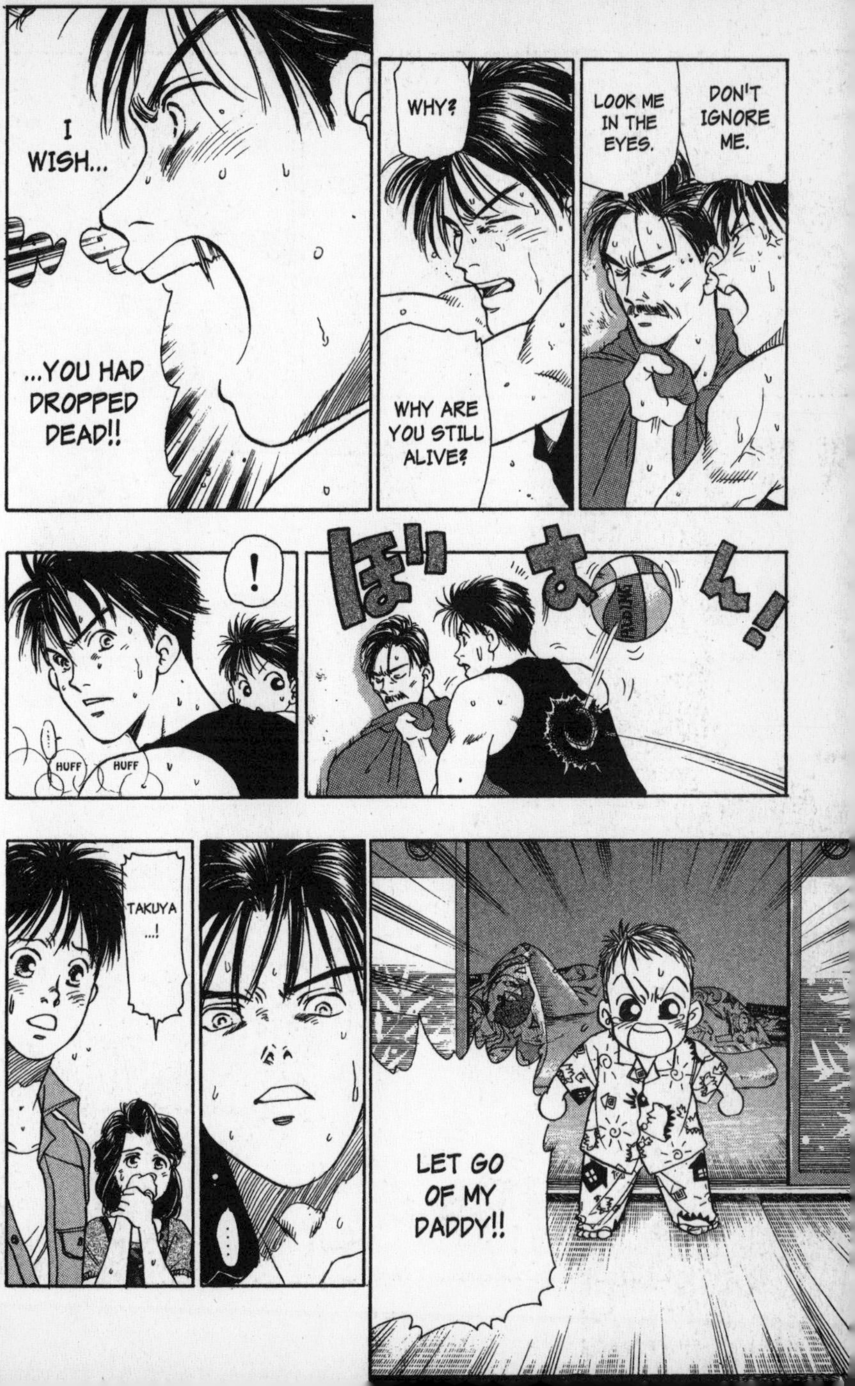
DON'T IGNORE ME.
LOOK ME IN THE EYES.
WHY?
WHY ARE YOU STILL ALIVE?
I WISH...
...YOU HAD DROPPED DEAD!!
!
...!
HUFF
HUFF
LET GO OF MY DADDY!!
...
TAKUYA ...!

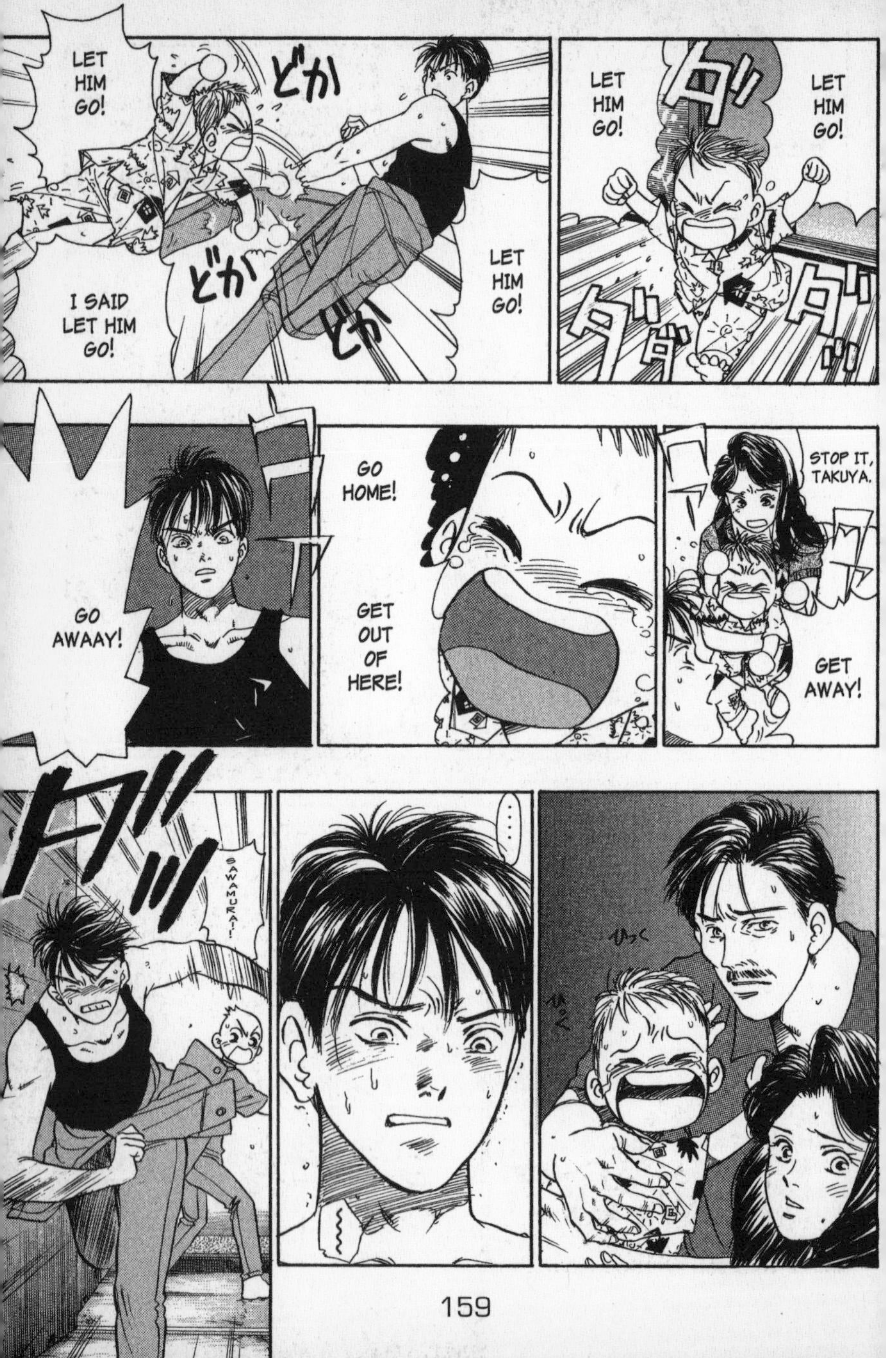
LET HIM GO!
LET HIM GO!
どか
LET HIM GO!
LET HIM GO!
どか
どか
I SAID LET HIM GO!
STOP IT, TAKUYA.
GET AWAY!
GO HOME!
GET OUT OF HERE!
GO AWAAY!
....
SAWAMURA!

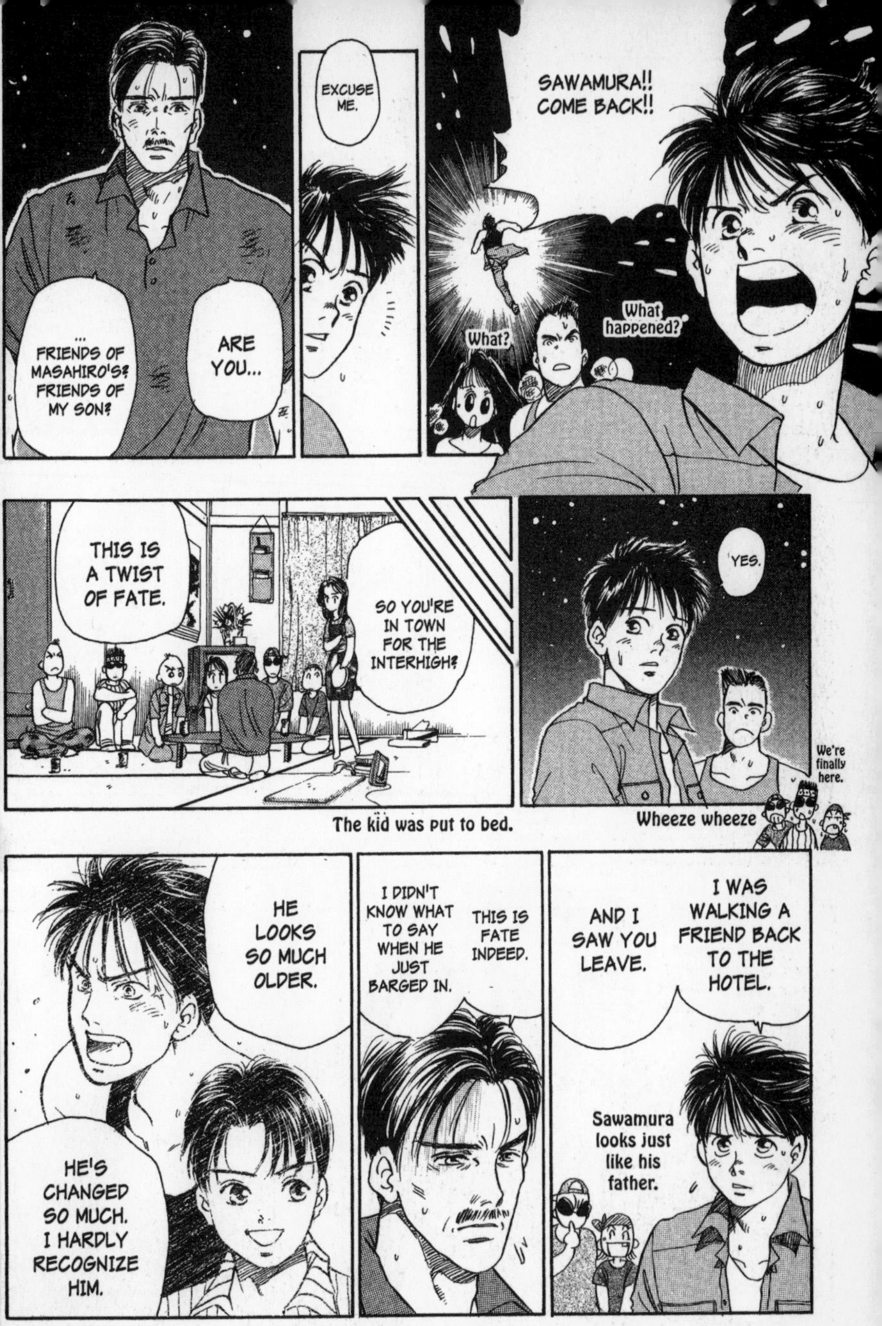
SAWAMURA!! COME BACK!!
What happened?
What?
EXCUSE ME.
ARE YOU...
... FRIENDS OF MASAHIRO'S? FRIENDS OF MY SON?
YES.
We're finally here.
Wheeze wheeze
SO YOU'RE IN TOWN FOR THE INTERHIGH?
THIS IS A TWIST OF FATE.
The kid was put to bed.
I WAS WALKING A FRIEND BACK TO THE HOTEL.
AND I SAW YOU LEAVE.
Sawamura looks just like his father.
THIS IS FATE INDEED.
I DIDN'T KNOW WHAT TO SAY WHEN HE JUST BARGED IN.
HE LOOKS SO MUCH OLDER.
HE'S CHANGED SO MUCH. I HARDLY RECOGNIZE HIM.

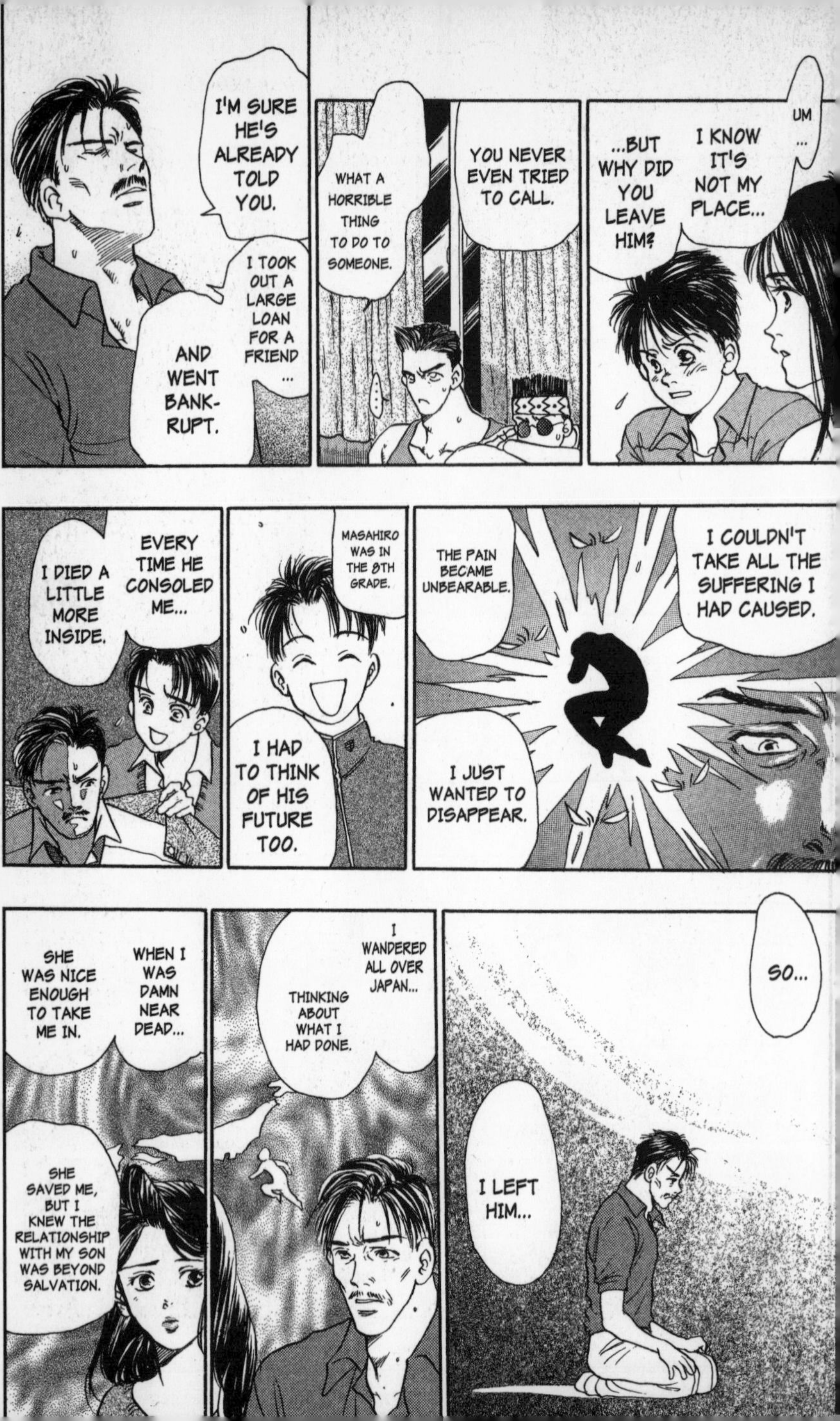
UM ...
I KNOW IT'S NOT MY PLACE...
...BUT WHY DID YOU LEAVE HIM?
YOU NEVER EVEN TRIED TO CALL.
WHAT A HORRIBLE THING TO DO TO SOMEONE.
I'M SURE HE'S ALREADY TOLD YOU.
I TOOK OUT A LARGE LOAN FOR A FRIEND ...
AND WENT BANKRUPT.
I COULDN'T TAKE ALL THE SUFFERING I HAD CAUSED.
THE PAIN BECAME UNBEARABLE.
I JUST WANTED TO DISAPPEAR.
MASAHIRO WAS IN THE 8TH GRADE.
I HAD TO THINK OF HIS FUTURE TOO.
EVERY TIME HE CONSOLED ME...
I DIED A LITTLE MORE INSIDE.
SO...
I LEFT HIM...
I WANDERED ALL OVER JAPAN...
THINKING ABOUT WHAT I HAD DONE.
WHEN I WAS DAMN NEAR DEAD...
SHE WAS NICE ENOUGH TO TAKE ME IN.
SHE SAVED ME, BUT I KNEW THE RELATIONSHIP WITH MY SON WAS BEYOND SALVATION.

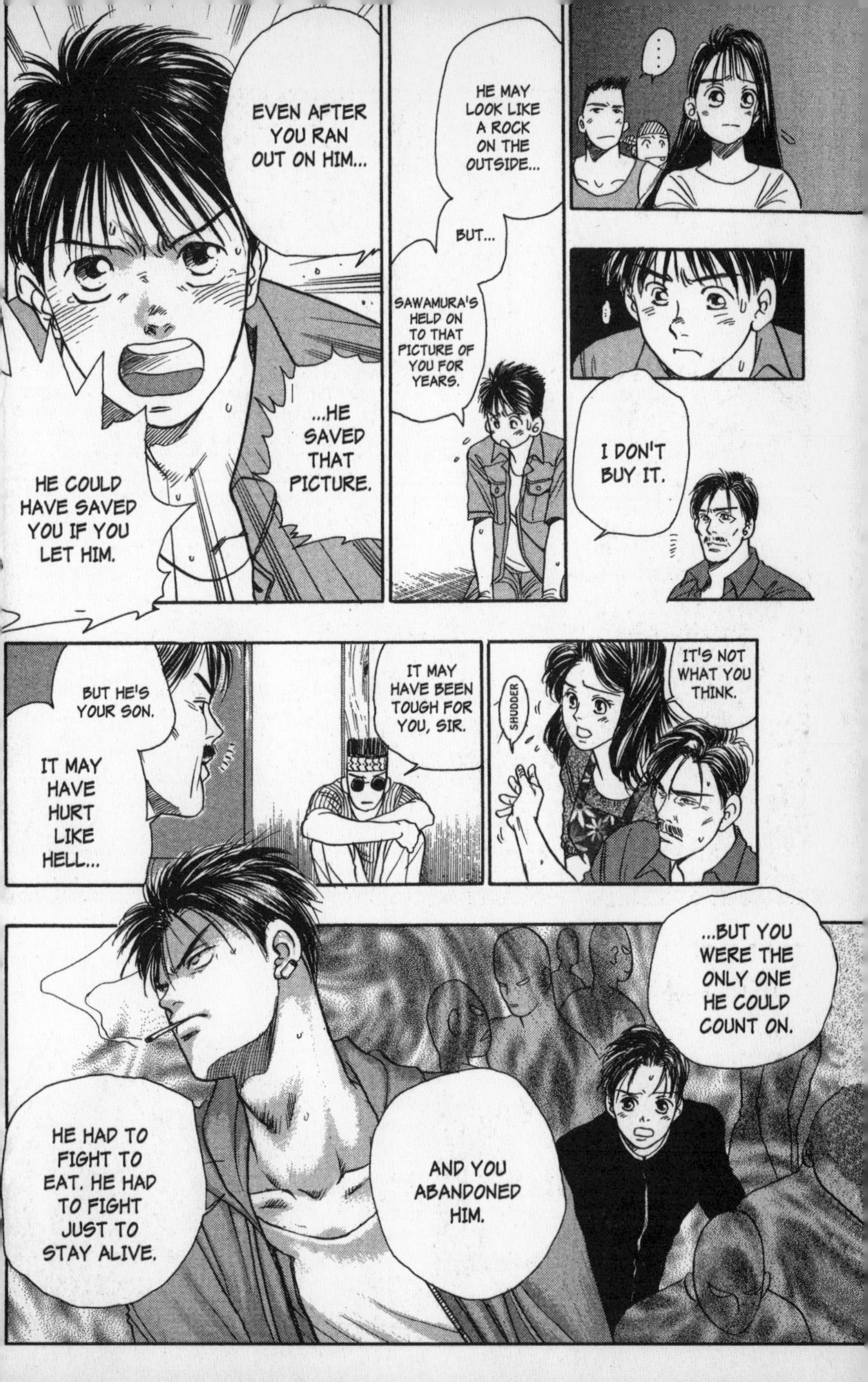
...
I DON'T BUY IT.
HE MAY LOOK LIKE A ROCK ON THE OUTSIDE...
BUT...
SAWAMURA'S HELD ON TO THAT PICTURE OF YOU FOR YEARS.
EVEN AFTER YOU RAN OUT ON HIM...
...HE SAVED THAT PICTURE.
HE COULD HAVE SAVED YOU IF YOU LET HIM.
IT'S NOT WHAT YOU THINK.
SHUDDER
IT MAY HAVE BEEN TOUGH FOR YOU, SIR.
BUT HE'S YOUR SON.
IT MAY HAVE HURT LIKE HELL...
...BUT YOU WERE THE ONLY ONE HE COULD COUNT ON.
AND YOU ABANDONED HIM.
HE HAD TO FIGHT TO EAT. HE HAD TO FIGHT JUST TO STAY ALIVE.

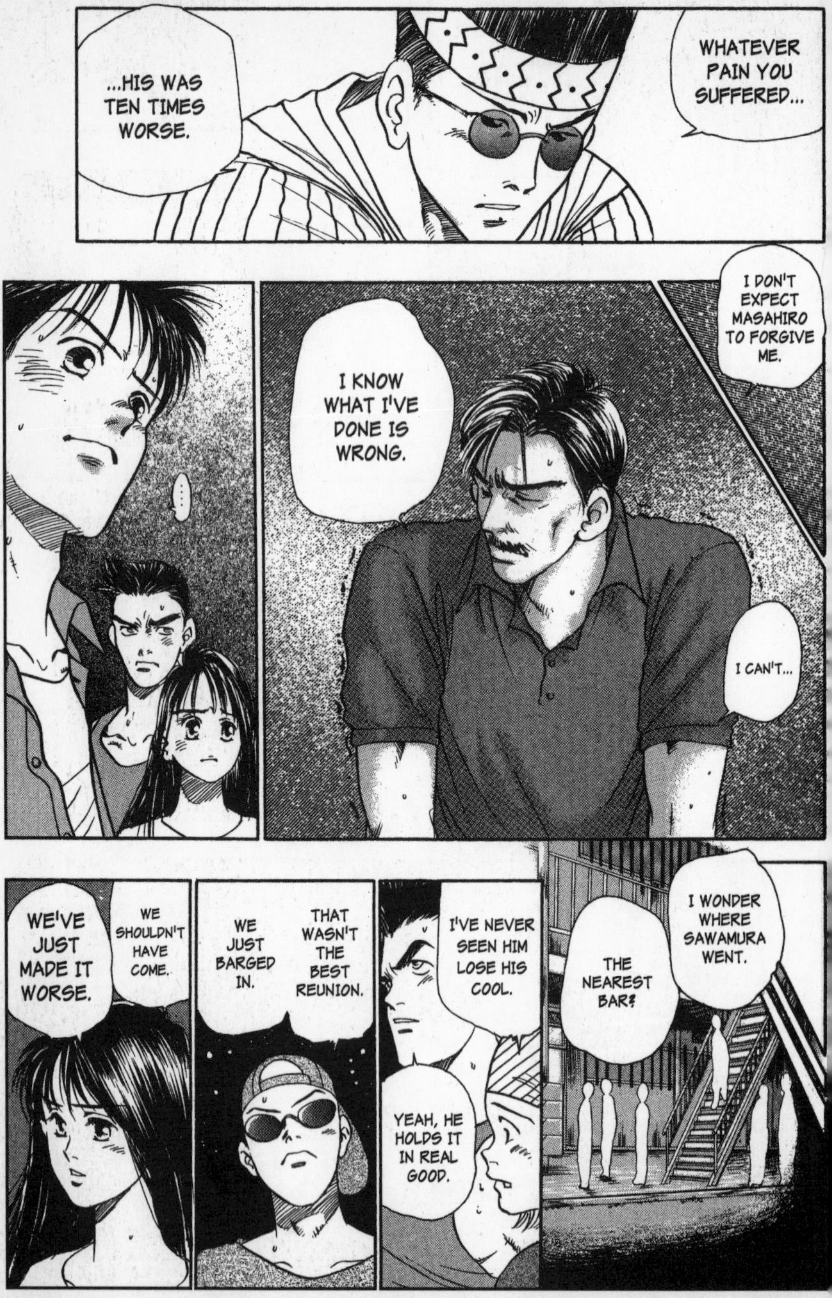
WHATEVER PAIN YOU SUFFERED...
...HIS WAS TEN TIMES WORSE.
I DON'T EXPECT MASAHIRO TO FORGIVE ME.
I KNOW WHAT I'VE DONE IS WRONG.
I CAN'T...
...
I WONDER WHERE SAWAMURA WENT.
THE NEAREST BAR?
I'VE NEVER SEEN HIM LOSE HIS COOL.
YEAH, HE HOLDS IT IN REAL GOOD.
THAT WASN'T THE BEST REUNION.
WE JUST BARGED IN.
WE SHOULDN'T HAVE COME.
WE'VE JUST MADE IT WORSE.

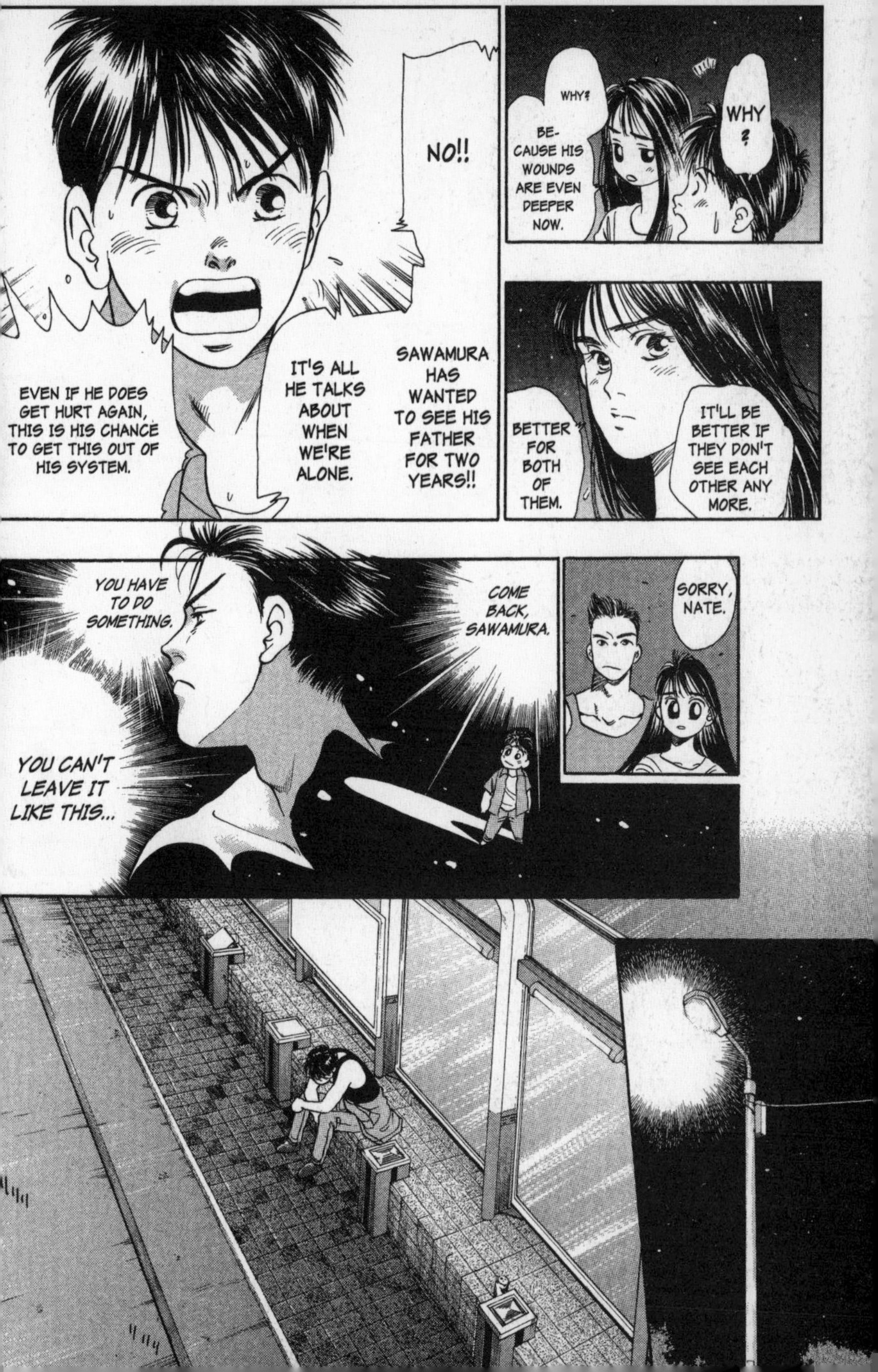
WHY?
WHY?
BE-CAUSE HIS WOUNDS ARE EVEN DEEPER NOW.
IT'LL BE BETTER IF THEY DON'T SEE EACH OTHER ANY MORE.
BETTER FOR BOTH OF THEM.
NO!!
SAWAMURA HAS WANTED TO SEE HIS FATHER FOR TWO YEARS!!
IT'S ALL HE TALKS ABOUT WHEN WE'RE ALONE.
EVEN IF HE DOES GET HURT AGAIN, THIS IS HIS CHANCE TO GET THIS OUT OF HIS SYSTEM.
SORRY, NATE.
COME BACK, SAWAMURA.
YOU HAVE TO DO SOMETHING.
YOU CAN'T LEAVE IT LIKE THIS...

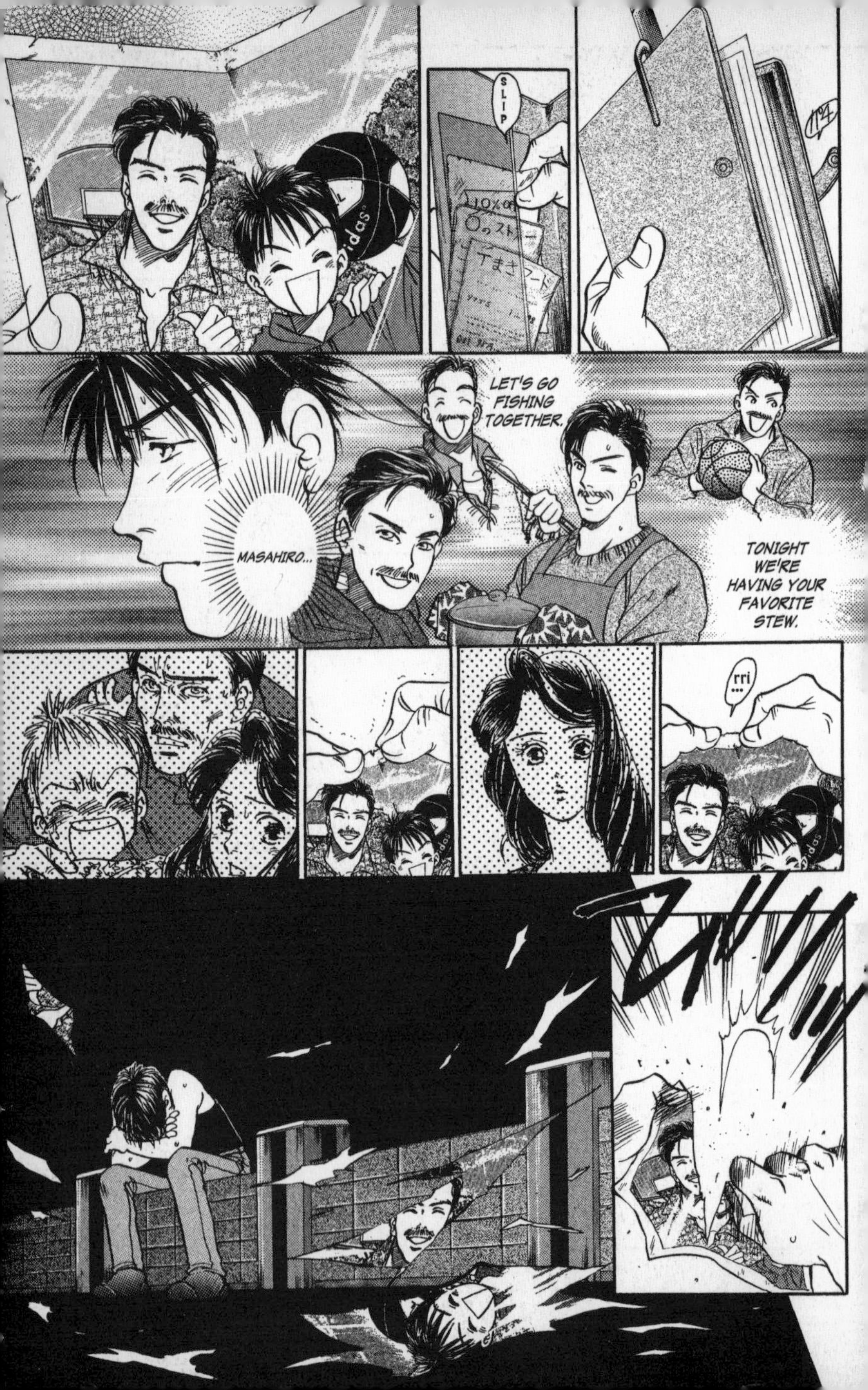
SLIP
TONIGHT WE'RE HAVING YOUR FAVORITE STEW.
LET'S GO FISHING TOGETHER.
MASAHIRO...
rri...

澤村博之（ひろゆき）

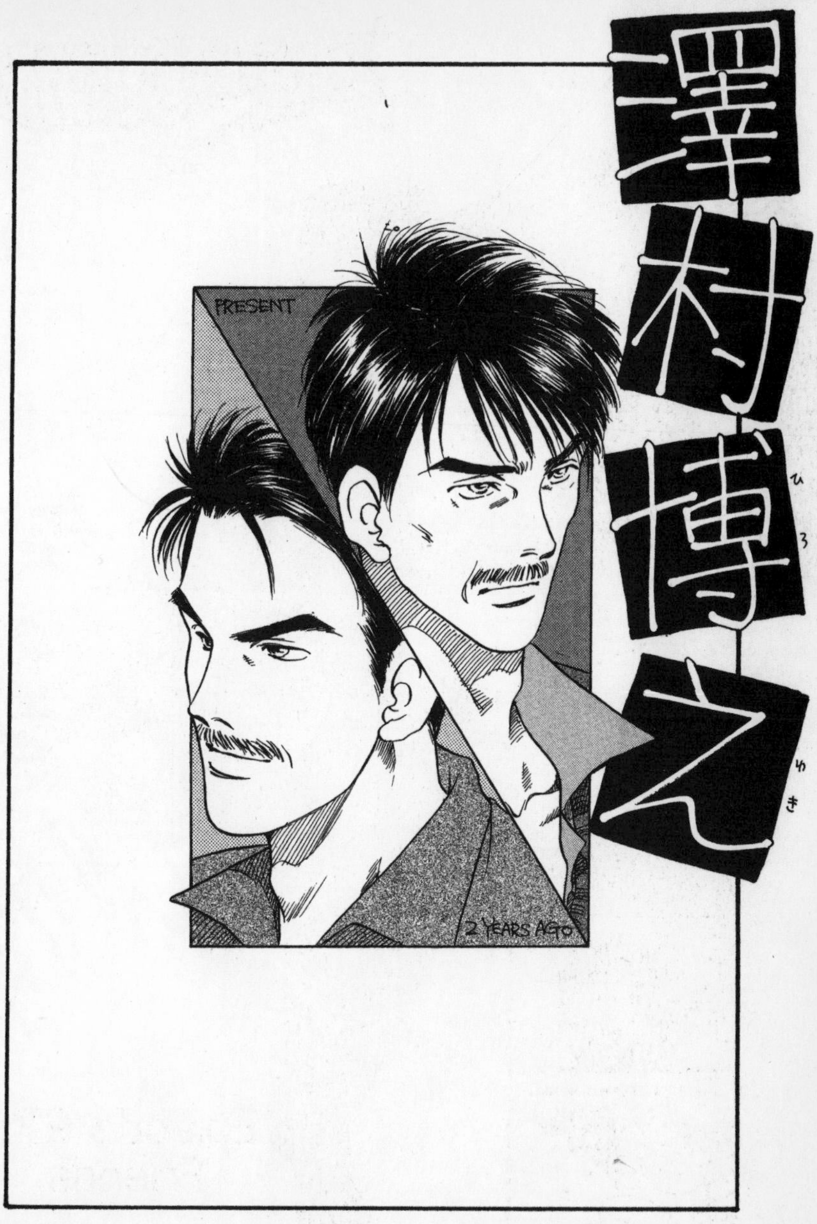
PRESENT
2 YEARS AGO

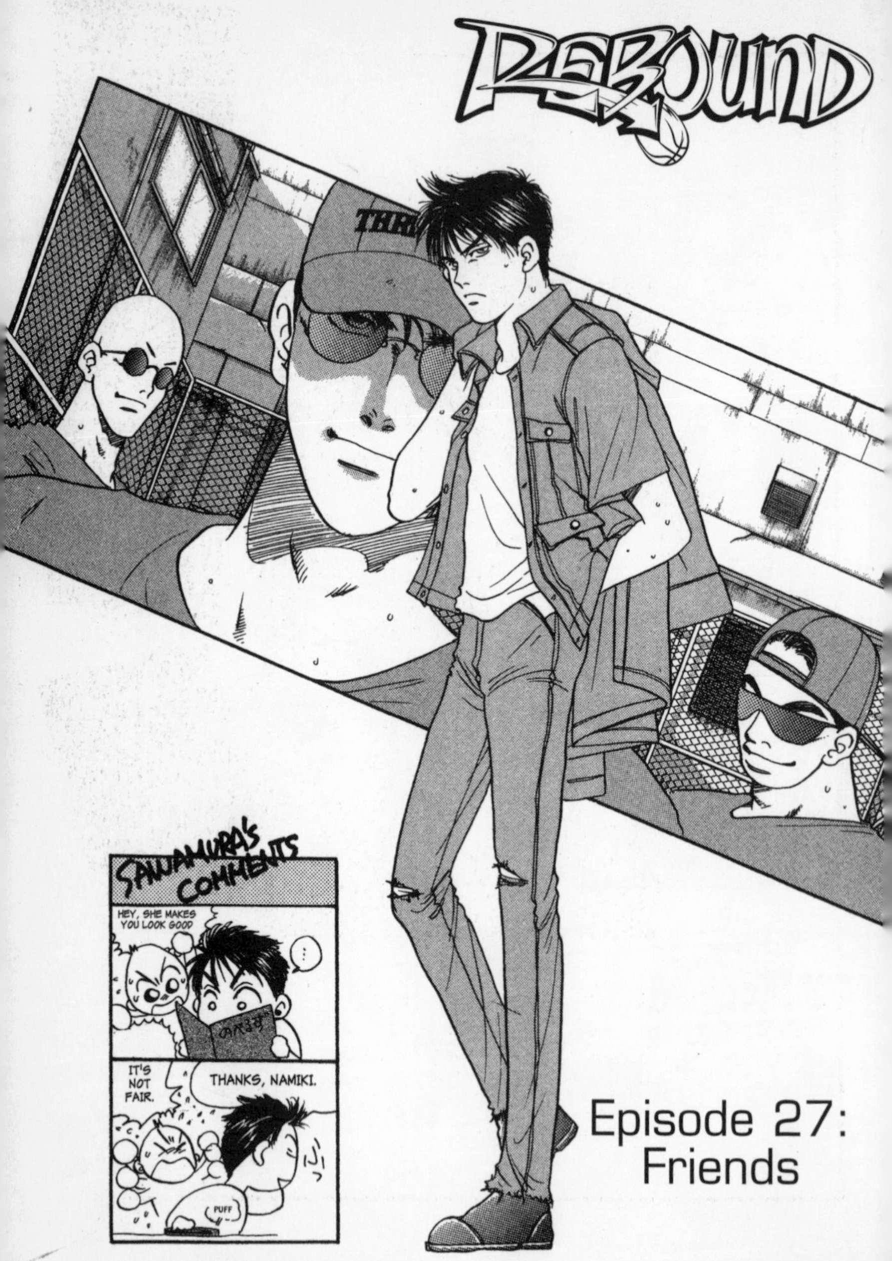
SAWAMURA'S COMMENTS
HEY, SHE MAKES YOU LOOK GOOD
...
THANKS, NAMIKI.
IT'S NOT FAIR.
PUFF

Episode 27: Friends

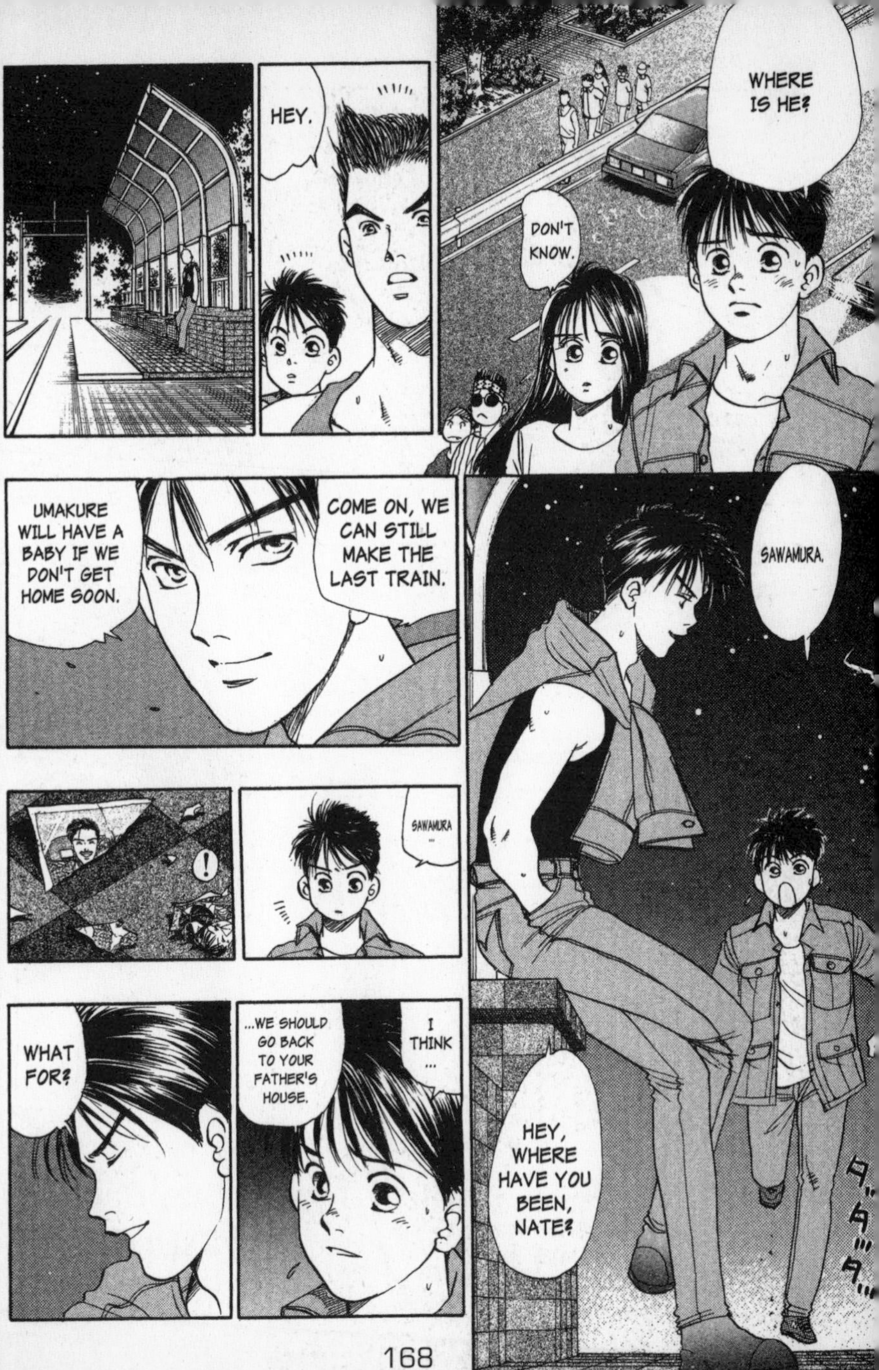
WHERE IS HE?
DON'T KNOW.
HEY.
SAWAMURA.
HEY, WHERE HAVE YOU BEEN, NATE?
COME ON, WE CAN STILL MAKE THE LAST TRAIN.
UMAKURE WILL HAVE A BABY IF WE DON'T GET HOME SOON.
SAWAMURA ...
!
I THINK ...
...WE SHOULD GO BACK TO YOUR FATHER'S HOUSE.
WHAT FOR?

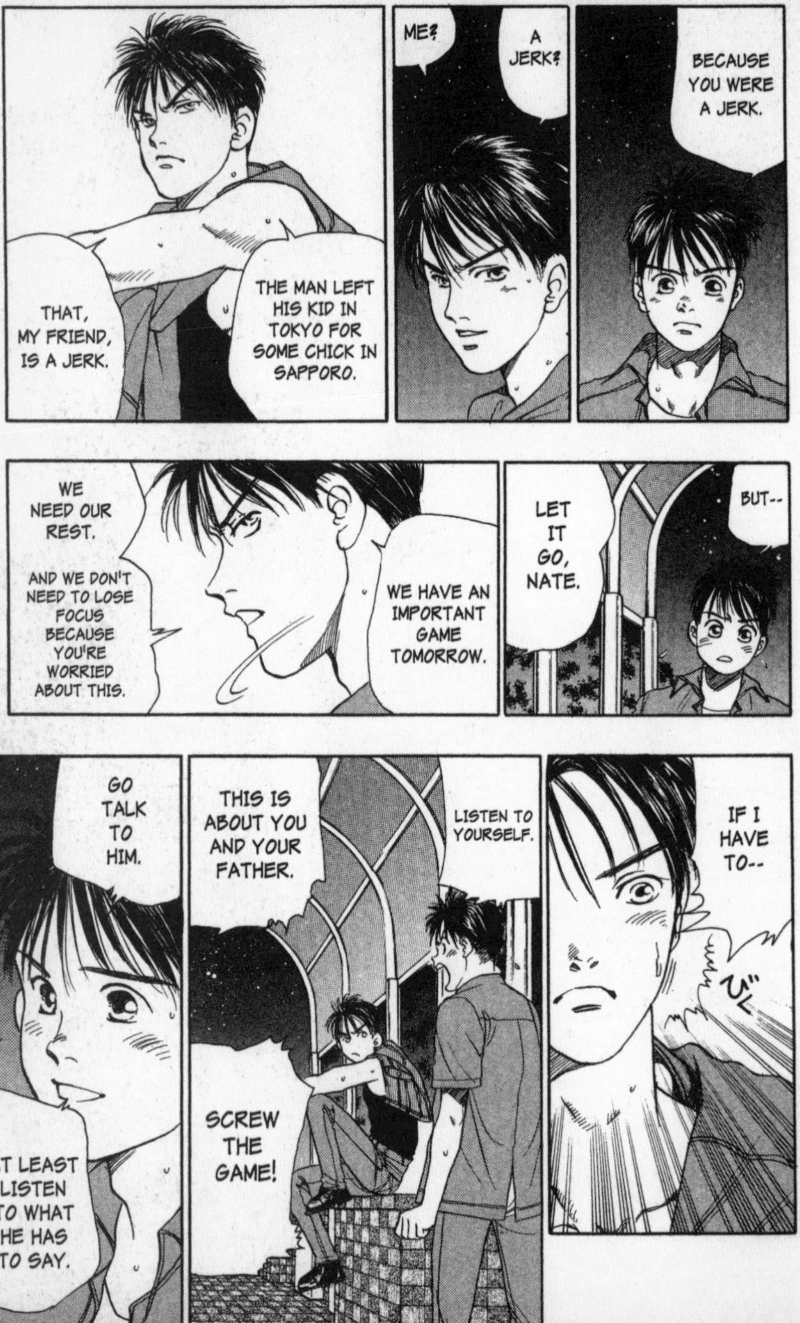
BECAUSE YOU WERE A JERK.
ME?
A JERK?
THE MAN LEFT HIS KID IN TOKYO FOR SOME CHICK IN SAPPORO.
THAT, MY FRIEND, IS A JERK.
BUT--
LET IT GO, NATE.
WE HAVE AN IMPORTANT GAME TOMORROW.
WE NEED OUR REST.
AND WE DON'T NEED TO LOSE FOCUS BECAUSE YOU'RE WORRIED ABOUT THIS.
IF I HAVE TO--
LISTEN TO YOURSELF.
THIS IS ABOUT YOU AND YOUR FATHER.
SCREW THE GAME!
GO TALK TO HIM.
AT LEAST LISTEN TO WHAT HE HAS TO SAY.

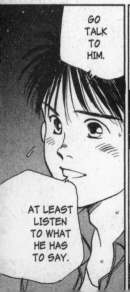

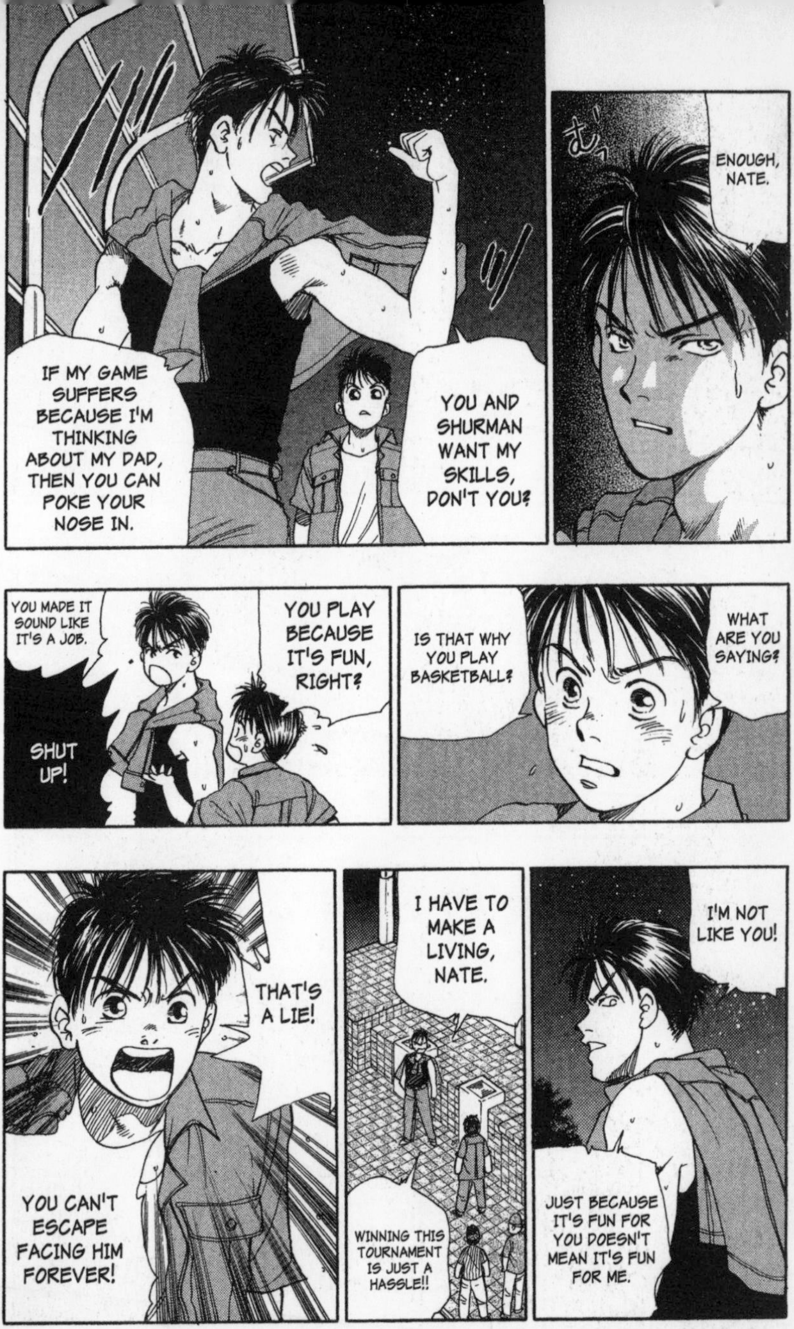
ENOUGH, NATE.
IF MY GAME SUFFERS BECAUSE I'M THINKING ABOUT MY DAD, THEN YOU CAN POKE YOUR NOSE IN.
YOU AND SHURMAN WANT MY SKILLS, DON'T YOU?
WHAT ARE YOU SAYING?
IS THAT WHY YOU PLAY BASKETBALL?
YOU PLAY BECAUSE IT'S FUN, RIGHT?
YOU MADE IT SOUND LIKE IT'S A JOB.
SHUT UP!
I'M NOT LIKE YOU!
JUST BECAUSE IT'S FUN FOR YOU DOESN'T MEAN IT'S FUN FOR ME.
I HAVE TO MAKE A LIVING, NATE.
WINNING THIS TOURNAMENT IS JUST A HASSLE!!
THAT'S A LIE!
YOU CAN'T ESCAPE FACING HIM FOREVER!

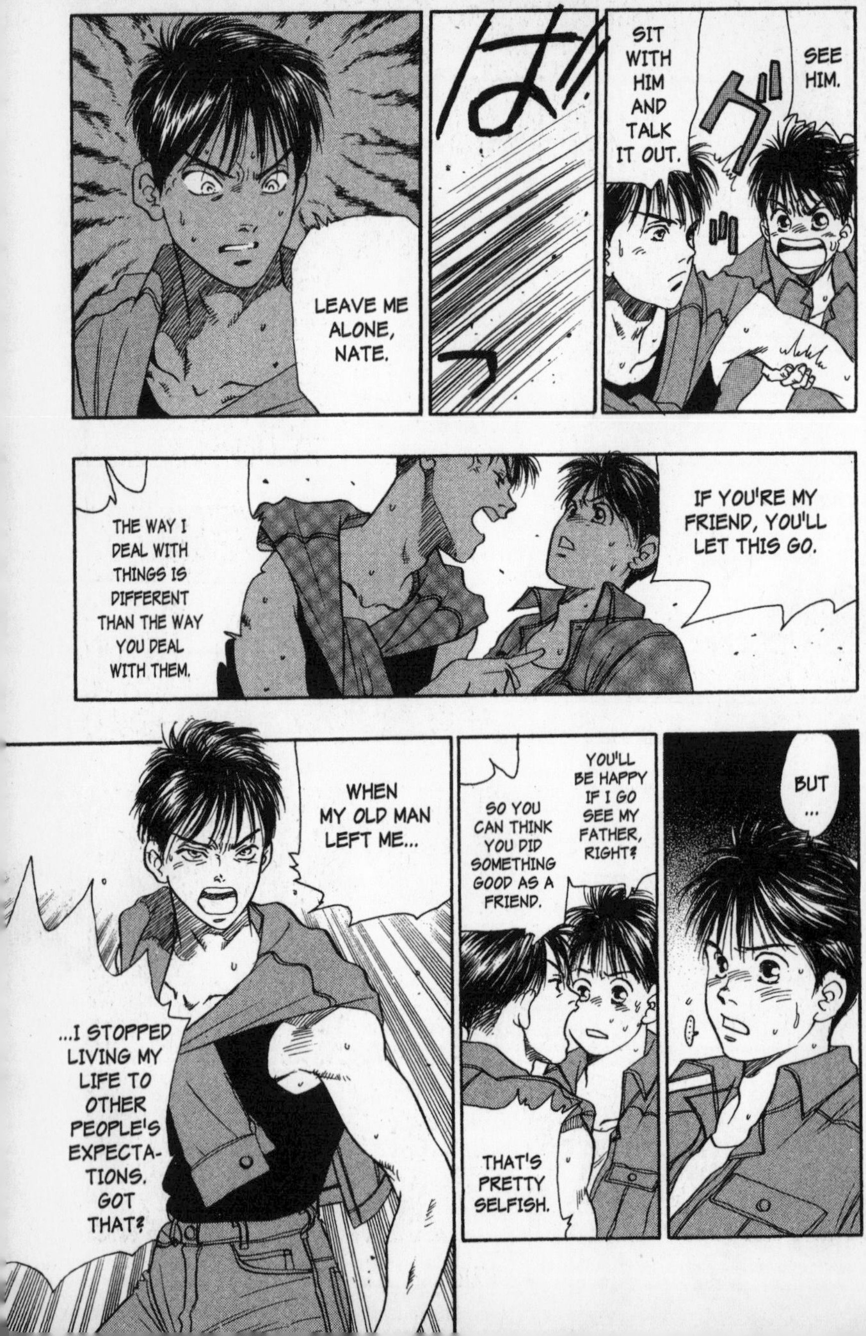
SEE HIM.
SIT WITH HIM AND TALK IT OUT.
LEAVE ME ALONE, NATE.
IF YOU'RE MY FRIEND, YOU'LL LET THIS GO.
THE WAY I DEAL WITH THINGS IS DIFFERENT THAN THE WAY YOU DEAL WITH THEM.
BUT ...
YOU'LL BE HAPPY IF I GO SEE MY FATHER, RIGHT?
SO YOU CAN THINK YOU DID SOMETHING GOOD AS A FRIEND.
THAT'S PRETTY SELFISH.
WHEN MY OLD MAN LEFT ME...
...I STOPPED LIVING MY LIFE TO OTHER PEOPLE'S EXPECTATIONS. GOT THAT?

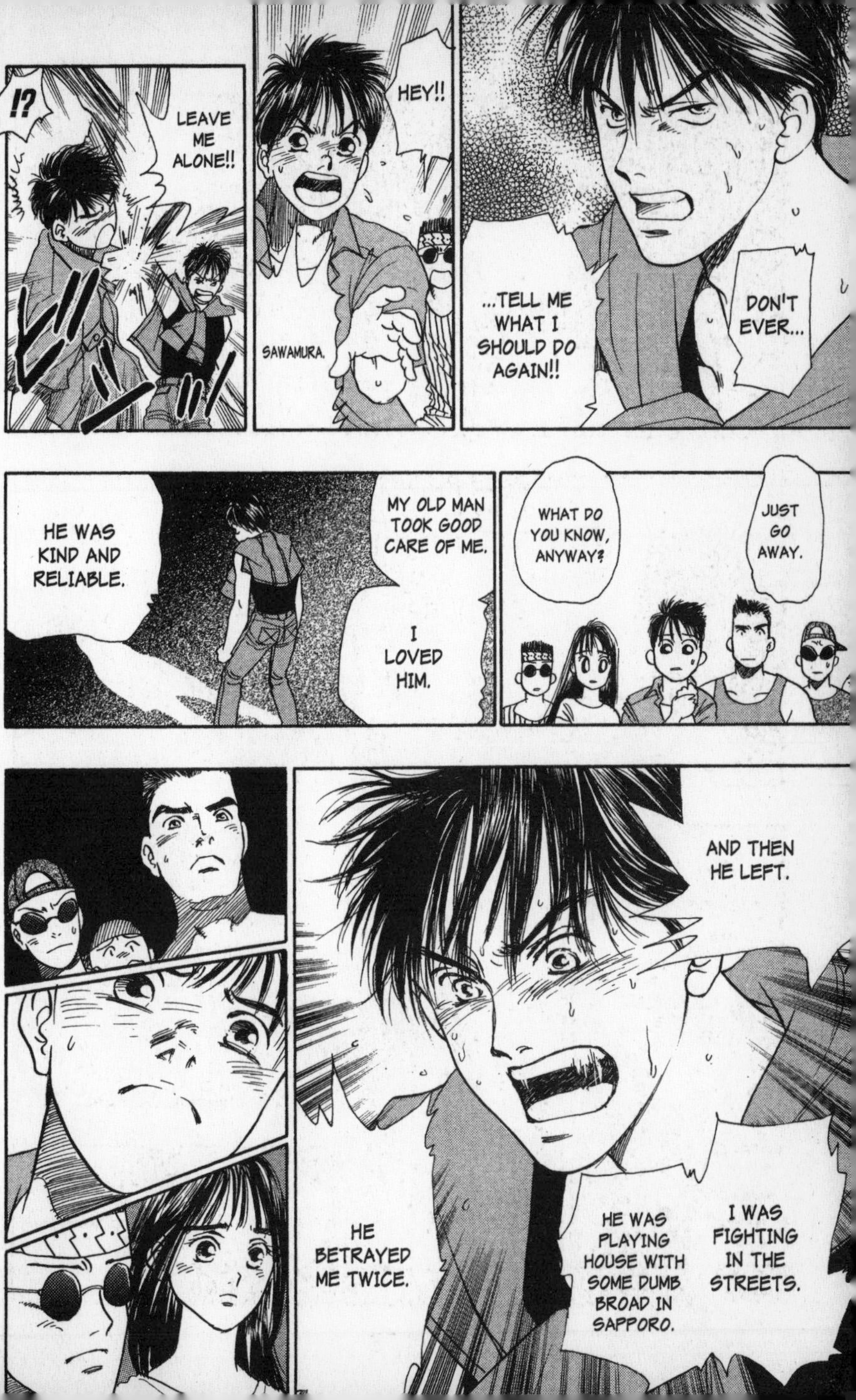
DON'T EVER...
...TELL ME WHAT I SHOULD DO AGAIN!!
HEY!!
SAWAMURA.
LEAVE ME ALONE!!
!?
JUST GO AWAY.
WHAT DO YOU KNOW, ANYWAY?
MY OLD MAN TOOK GOOD CARE OF ME.
I LOVED HIM.
HE WAS KIND AND RELIABLE.
AND THEN HE LEFT.
I WAS FIGHTING IN THE STREETS.
HE WAS PLAYING HOUSE WITH SOME DUMB BROAD IN SAPPORO.
HE BETRAYED ME TWICE.

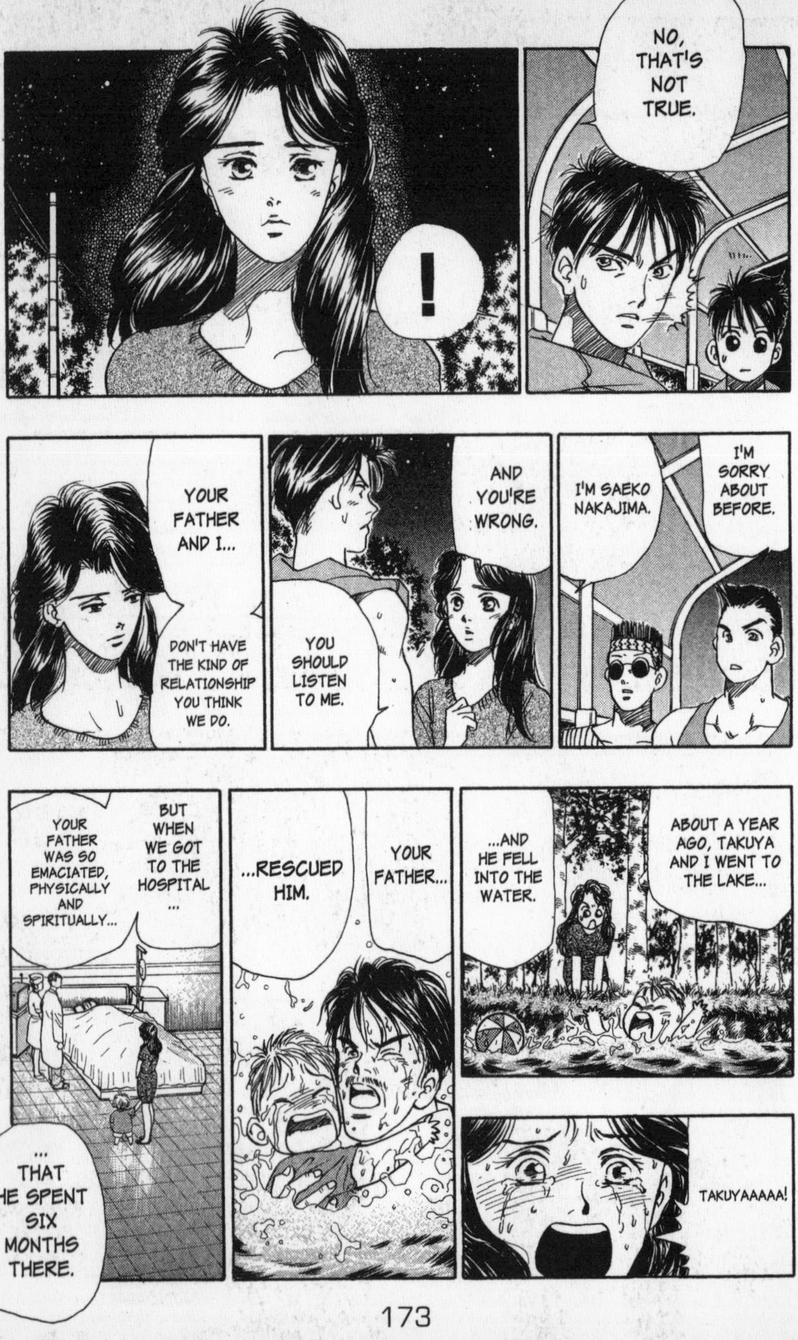
NO, THAT'S NOT TRUE.
!
I'M SORRY ABOUT BEFORE.
I'M SAEKO NAKAJIMA.
AND YOU'RE WRONG.
YOU SHOULD LISTEN TO ME.
YOUR FATHER AND I...
DON'T HAVE THE KIND OF RELATIONSHIP YOU THINK WE DO.
ABOUT A YEAR AGO, TAKUYA AND I WENT TO THE LAKE...
...AND HE FELL INTO THE WATER.
TAKUYAAAAA!
YOUR FATHER...
...RESCUED HIM.
BUT WHEN WE GOT TO THE HOSPITAL ...
YOUR FATHER WAS SO EMACIATED, PHYSICALLY AND SPIRITUALLY...
... THAT HE SPENT SIX MONTHS THERE.

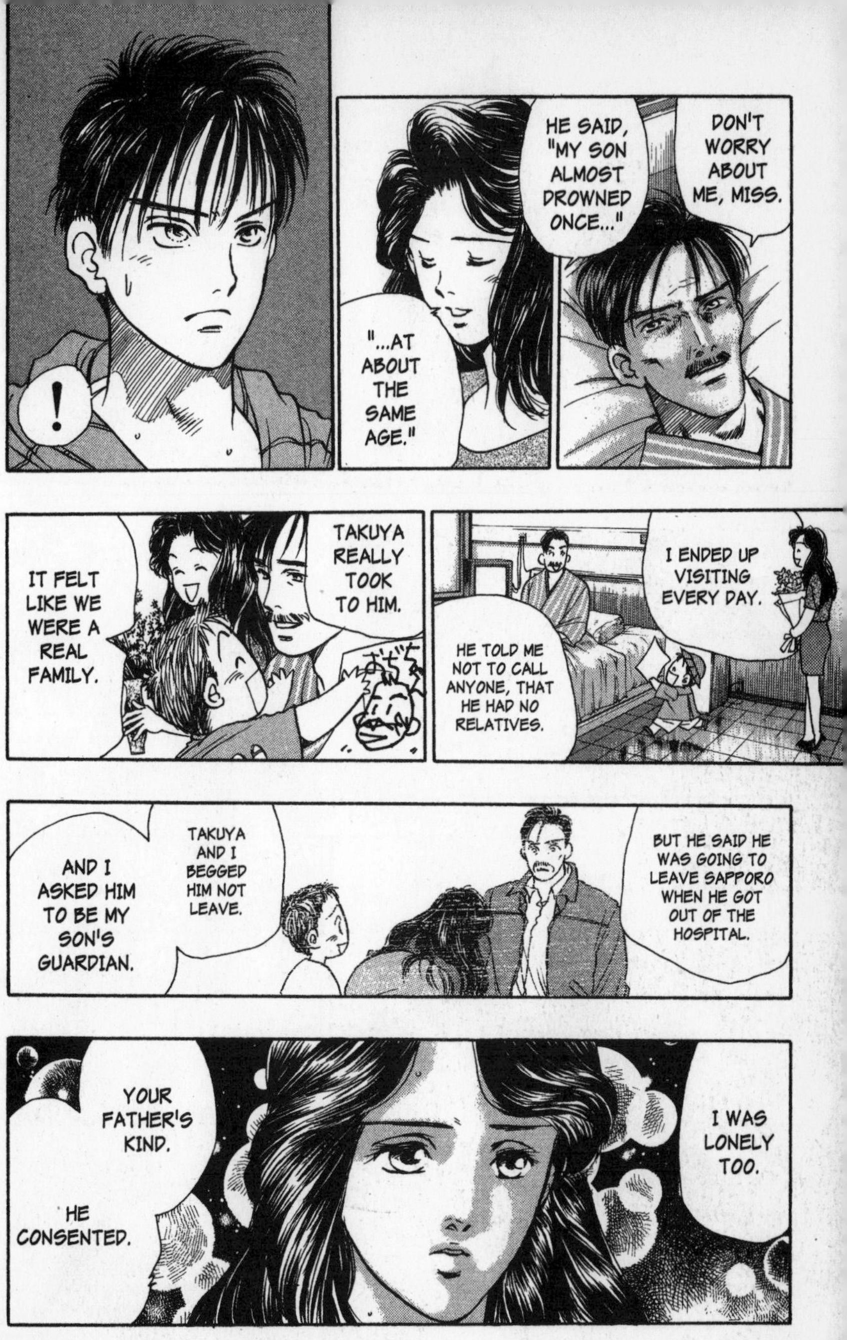
DON'T WORRY ABOUT ME, MISS.
HE SAID, "MY SON ALMOST DROWNED ONCE..."
"...AT ABOUT THE SAME AGE."
!
I ENDED UP VISITING EVERY DAY.
HE TOLD ME NOT TO CALL ANYONE, THAT HE HAD NO RELATIVES.
TAKUYA REALLY TOOK TO HIM.
IT FELT LIKE WE WERE A REAL FAMILY.
BUT HE SAID HE WAS GOING TO LEAVE SAPPORO WHEN HE GOT OUT OF THE HOSPITAL.
TAKUYA AND I BEGGED HIM NOT LEAVE.
AND I ASKED HIM TO BE MY SON'S GUARDIAN.
I WAS LONELY TOO.
YOUR FATHER'S KIND.
HE CONSENTED.

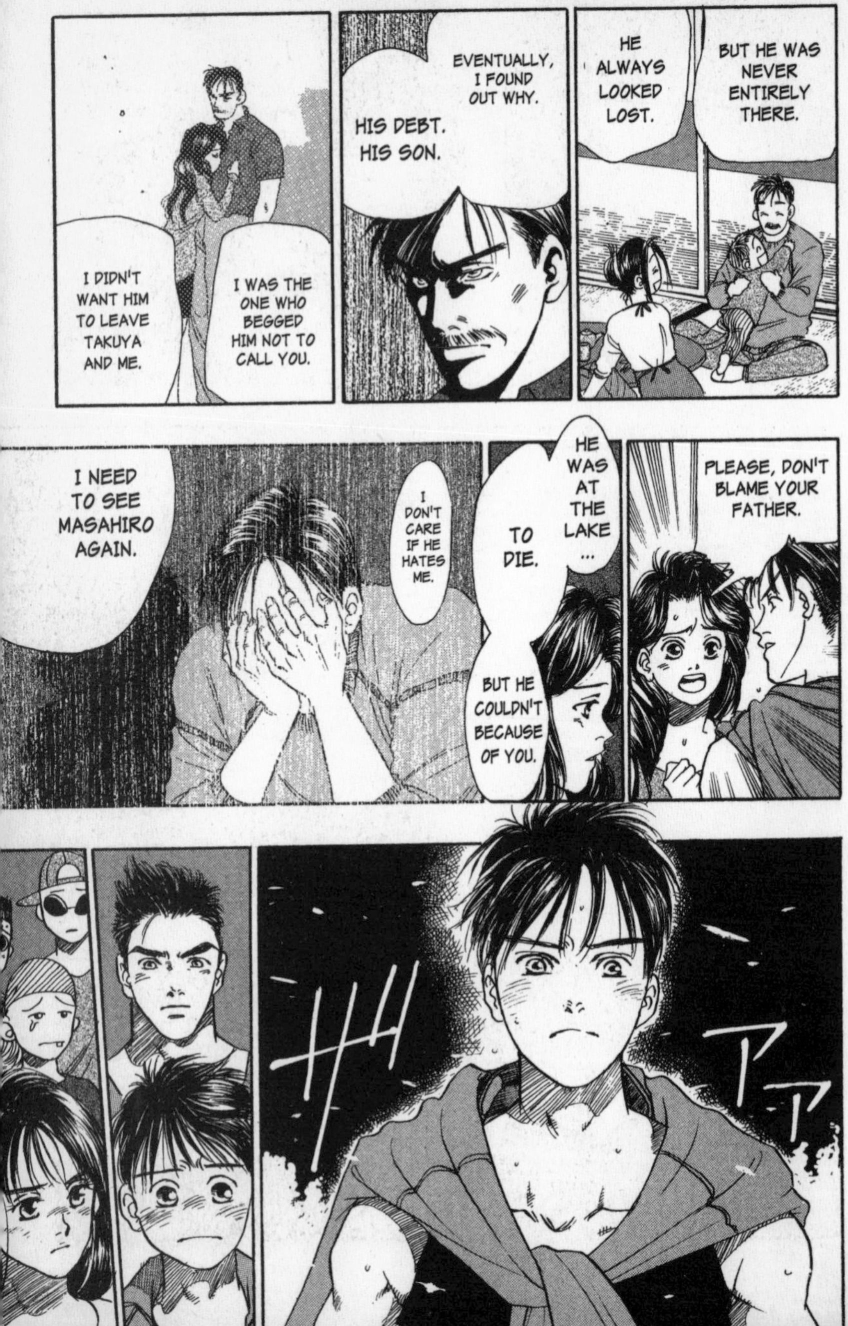
BUT HE WAS NEVER ENTIRELY THERE.
HE ALWAYS LOOKED LOST.
EVENTUALLY, I FOUND OUT WHY.
HIS DEBT. HIS SON.
I WAS THE ONE WHO BEGGED HIM NOT TO CALL YOU.
I DIDN'T WANT HIM TO LEAVE TAKUYA AND ME.
PLEASE, DON'T BLAME YOUR FATHER.
HE WAS AT THE LAKE ...
TO DIE.
BUT HE COULDN'T BECAUSE OF YOU.
I DON'T CARE IF HE HATES ME.
I NEED TO SEE MASAHIRO AGAIN.

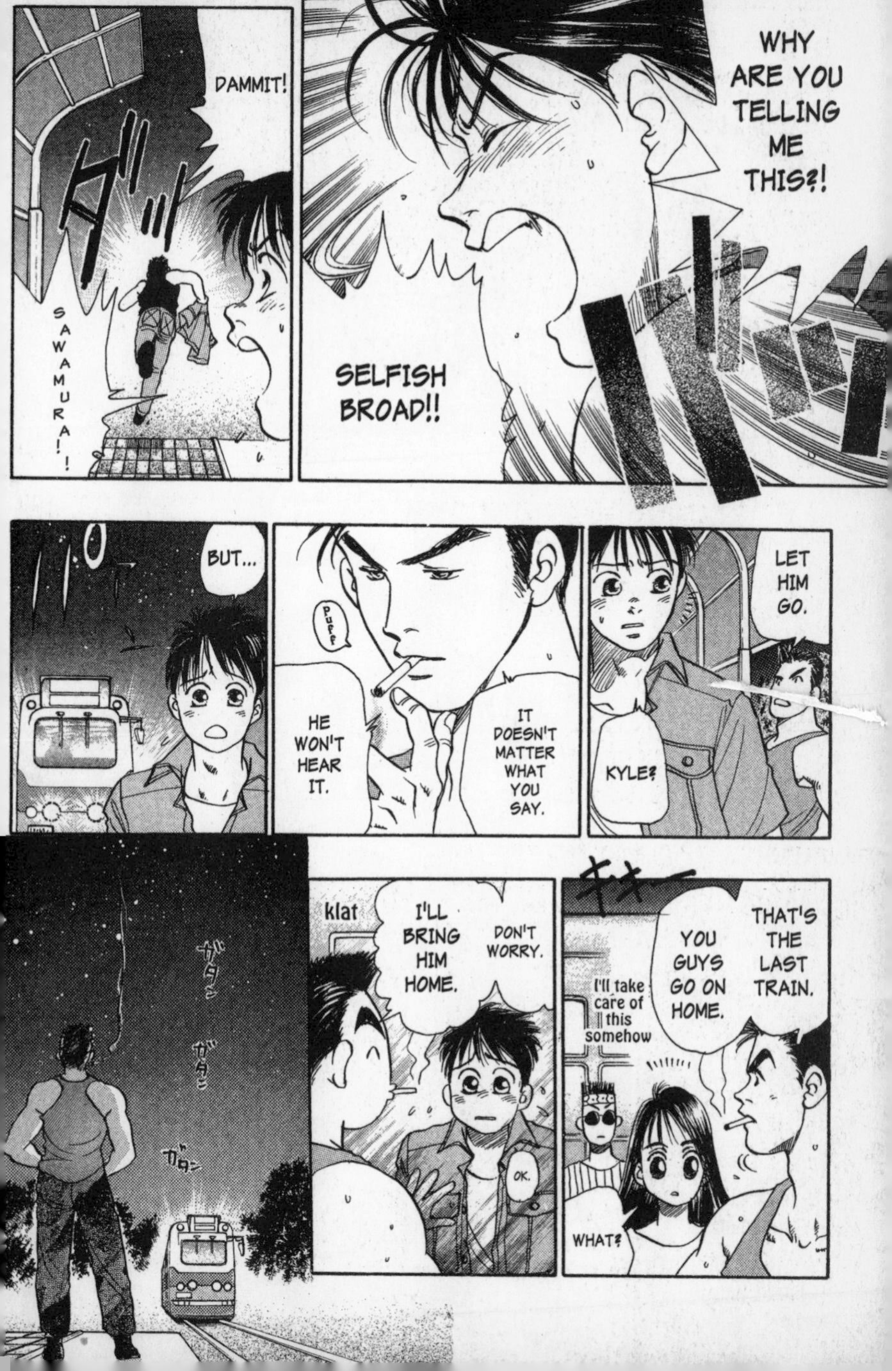
WHY ARE YOU TELLING ME THIS?!
SELFISH BROAD!!
DAMMIT!
ガッ
SAWAMURA!!
LET HIM GO.
KYLE?
puff
IT DOESN'T MATTER WHAT YOU SAY.
HE WON'T HEAR IT.
BUT...
キキー
THAT'S THE LAST TRAIN.
YOU GUYS GO ON HOME.
I'll take care of this somehow
WHAT?
klat
DON'T WORRY.
I'LL BRING HIM HOME.
OK.
ガタン
ガタン
ガタン

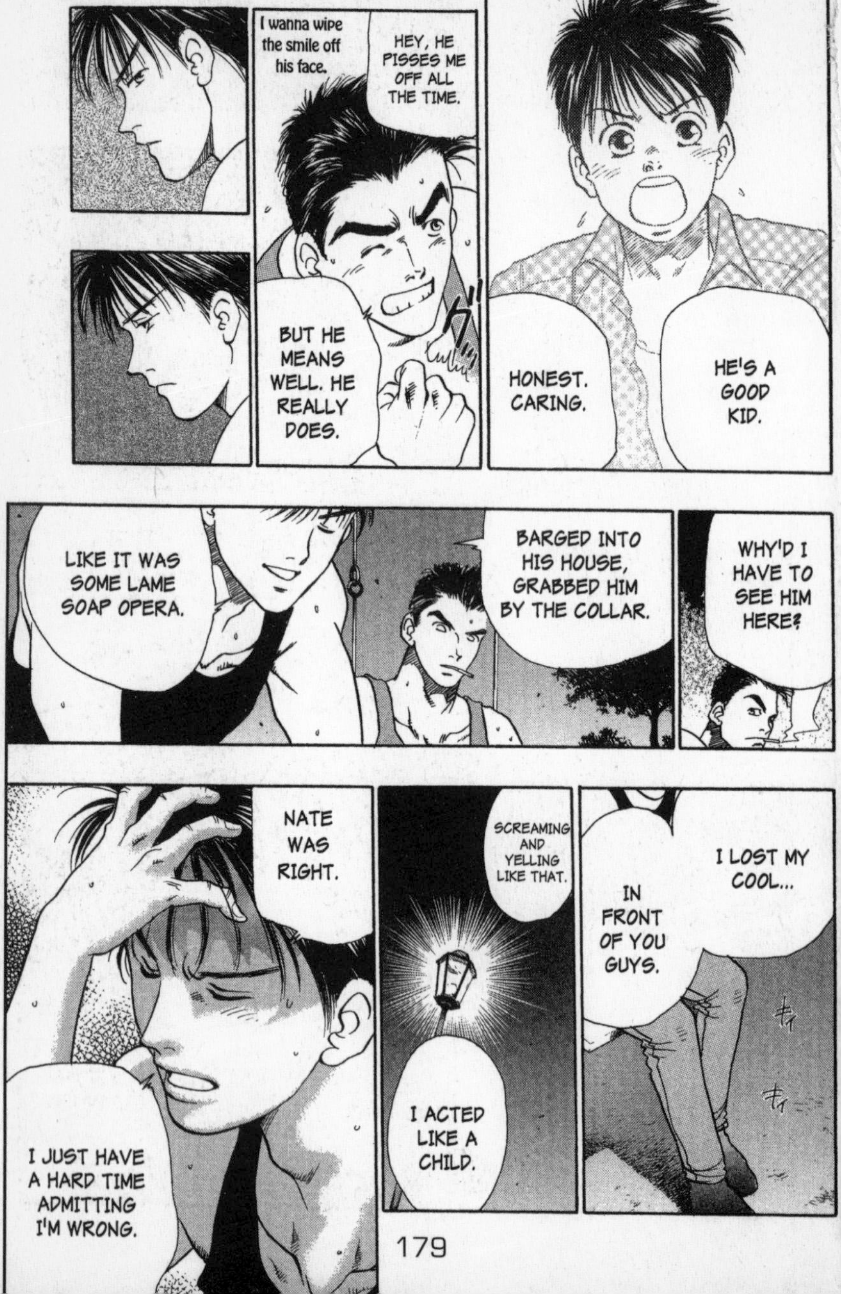
HE'S A GOOD KID.
HONEST. CARING.
HEY, HE PISSES ME OFF ALL THE TIME.
I wanna wipe the smile off his face.
BUT HE MEANS WELL. HE REALLY DOES.
WHY'D I HAVE TO SEE HIM HERE?
BARGED INTO HIS HOUSE, GRABBED HIM BY THE COLLAR.
LIKE IT WAS SOME LAME SOAP OPERA.
I LOST MY COOL...
IN FRONT OF YOU GUYS.
SCREAMING AND YELLING LIKE THAT.
I ACTED LIKE A CHILD.
NATE WAS RIGHT.
I JUST HAVE A HARD TIME ADMITTING I'M WRONG.

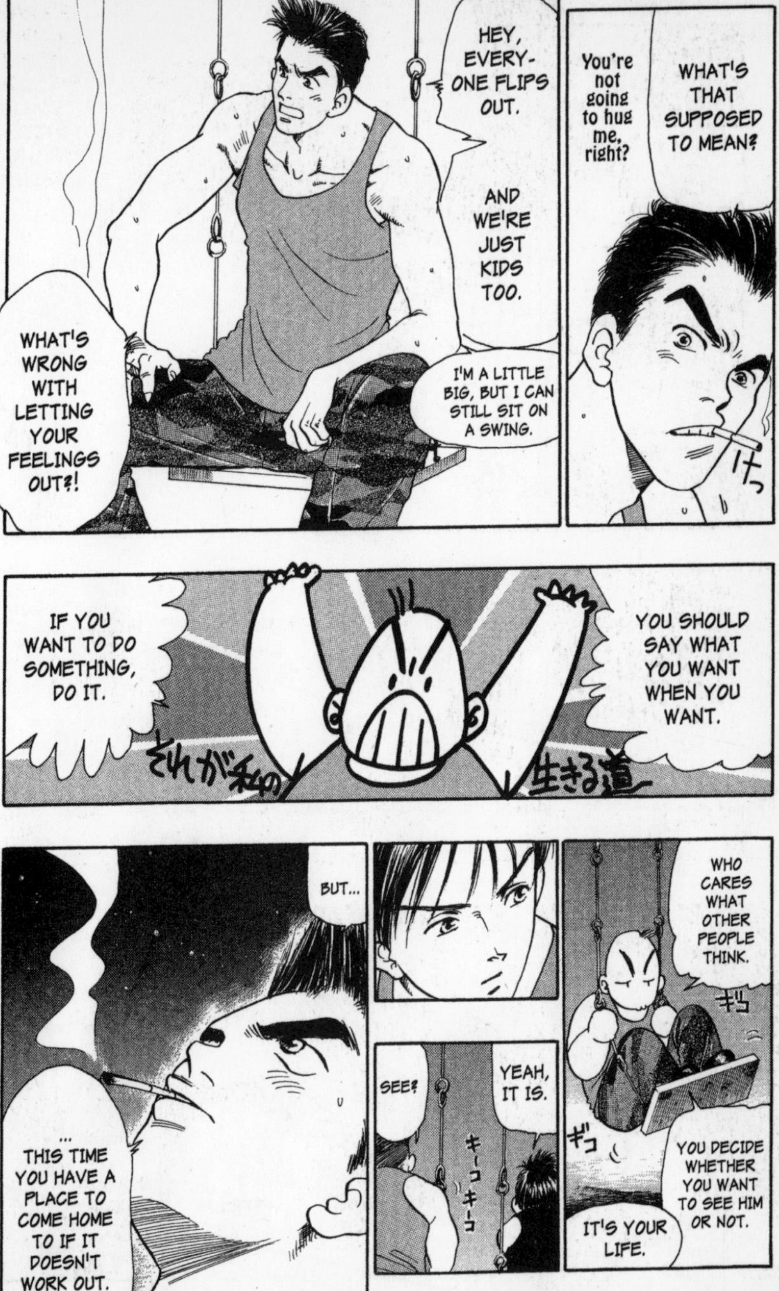
WHAT'S THAT SUPPOSED TO MEAN?
You're not going to hug me, right?
けっ
HEY, EVERY-ONE FLIPS OUT.
AND WE'RE JUST KIDS TOO.
I'M A LITTLE BIG, BUT I CAN STILL SIT ON A SWING.
WHAT'S WRONG WITH LETTING YOUR FEELINGS OUT?!
YOU SHOULD SAY WHAT YOU WANT WHEN YOU WANT.
IF YOU WANT TO DO SOMETHING, DO IT.
それが私の
生きる道
WHO CARES WHAT OTHER PEOPLE THINK.
ギコ
ギコ
YOU DECIDE WHETHER YOU WANT TO SEE HIM OR NOT.
IT'S YOUR LIFE.
YEAH, IT IS.
SEE?
キーコキーコ
BUT...
... THIS TIME YOU HAVE A PLACE TO COME HOME TO IF IT DOESN'T WORK OUT.

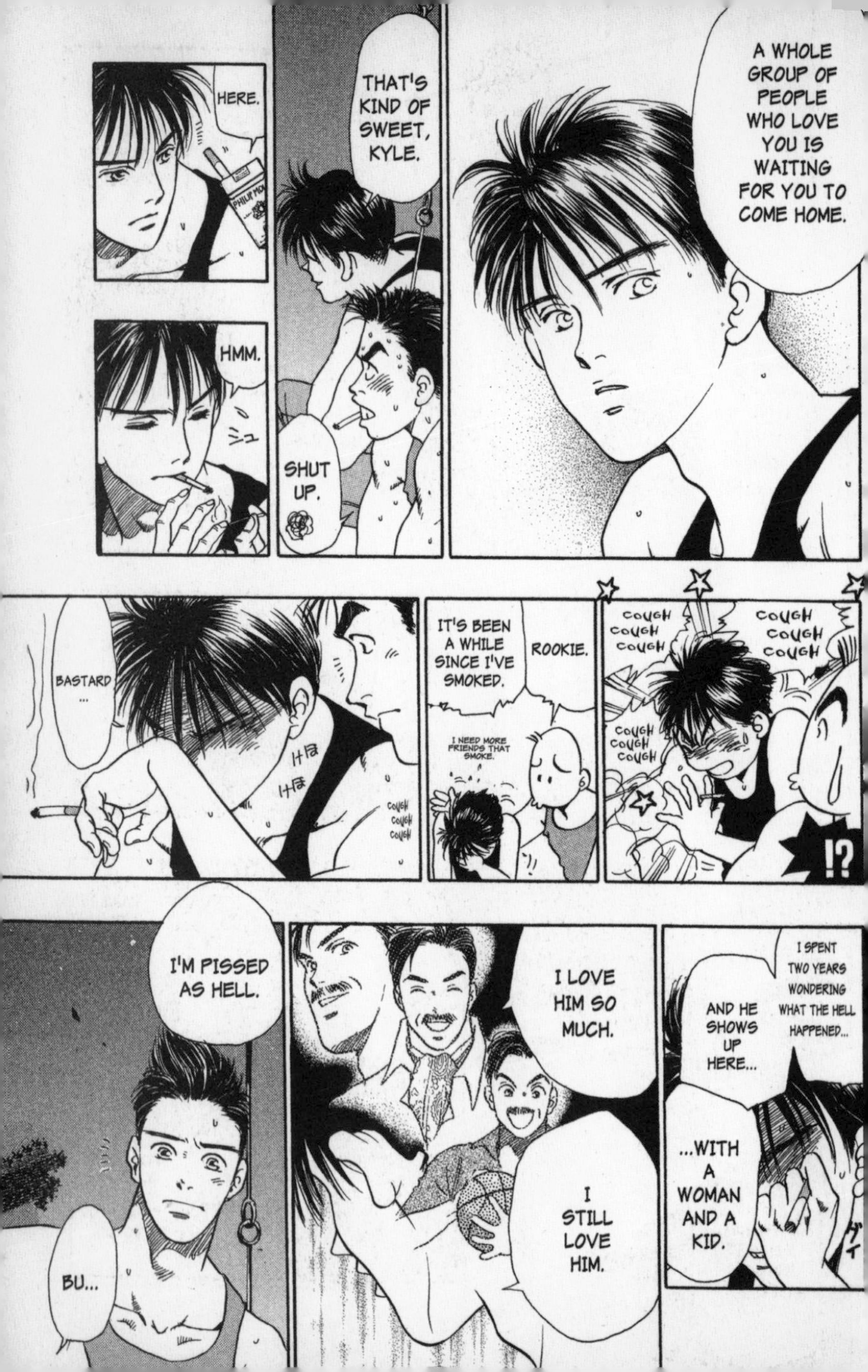
A WHOLE GROUP OF PEOPLE WHO LOVE YOU IS WAITING FOR YOU TO COME HOME.
THAT'S KIND OF SWEET, KYLE.
SHUT UP.
HERE.
HMM.
COUGH COUGH COUGH
COUGH COUGH COUGH
COUGH COUGH COUGH
!?
IT'S BEEN A WHILE SINCE I'VE SMOKED.
ROOKIE.
I NEED MORE FRIENDS THAT SMOKE.
BASTARD ...
けほ けほ
COUGH COUGH COUGH
I SPENT TWO YEARS WONDERING WHAT THE HELL HAPPENED...
AND HE SHOWS UP HERE...
...WITH A WOMAN AND A KID.
I LOVE HIM SO MUCH.
I STILL LOVE HIM.
I'M PISSED AS HELL.
BU...

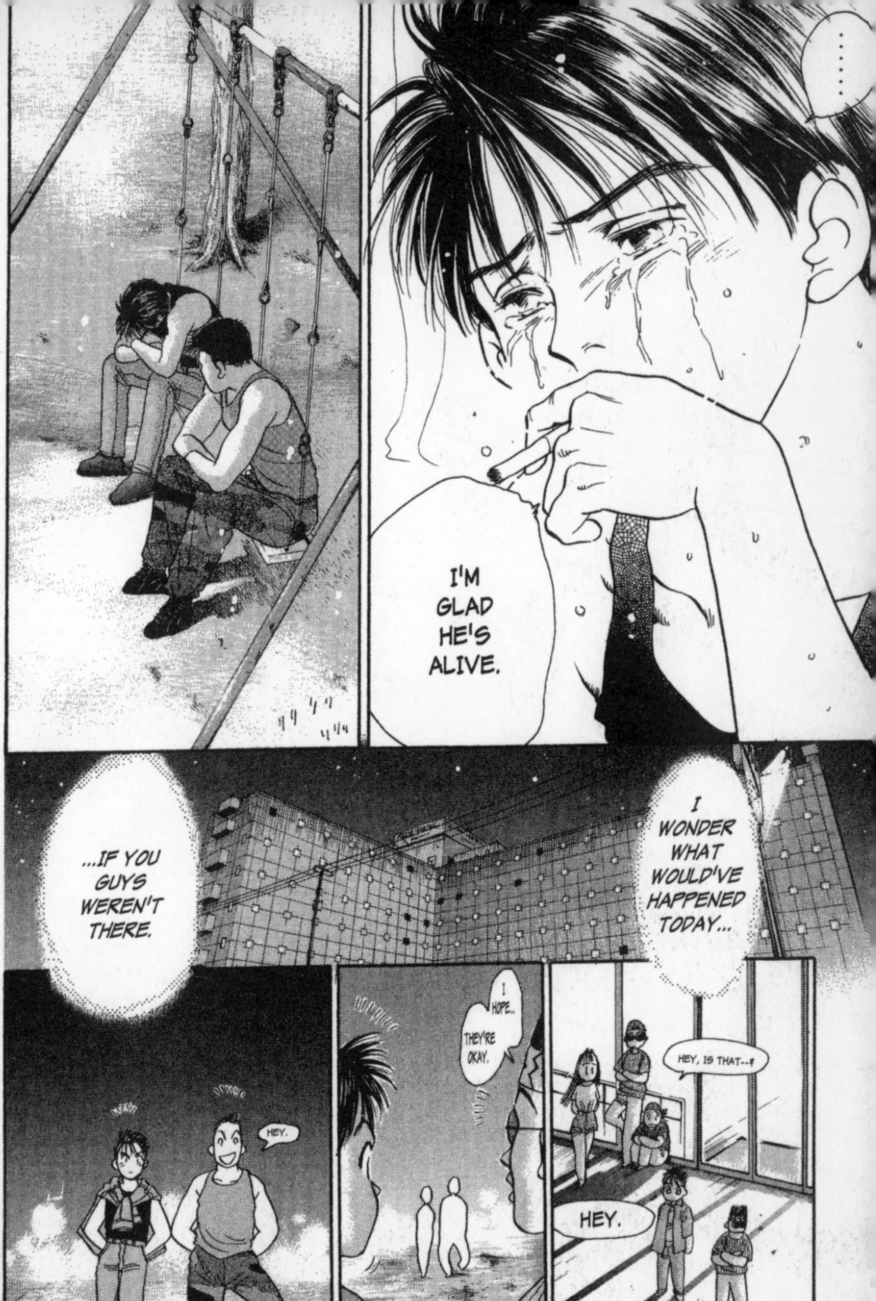
......
I'M GLAD HE'S ALIVE.
I WONDER WHAT WOULD'VE HAPPENED TODAY...
...IF YOU GUYS WEREN'T THERE.
HEY, IS THAT--?!
HEY.
I HOPE...
THEY'RE OKAY.
HEY.

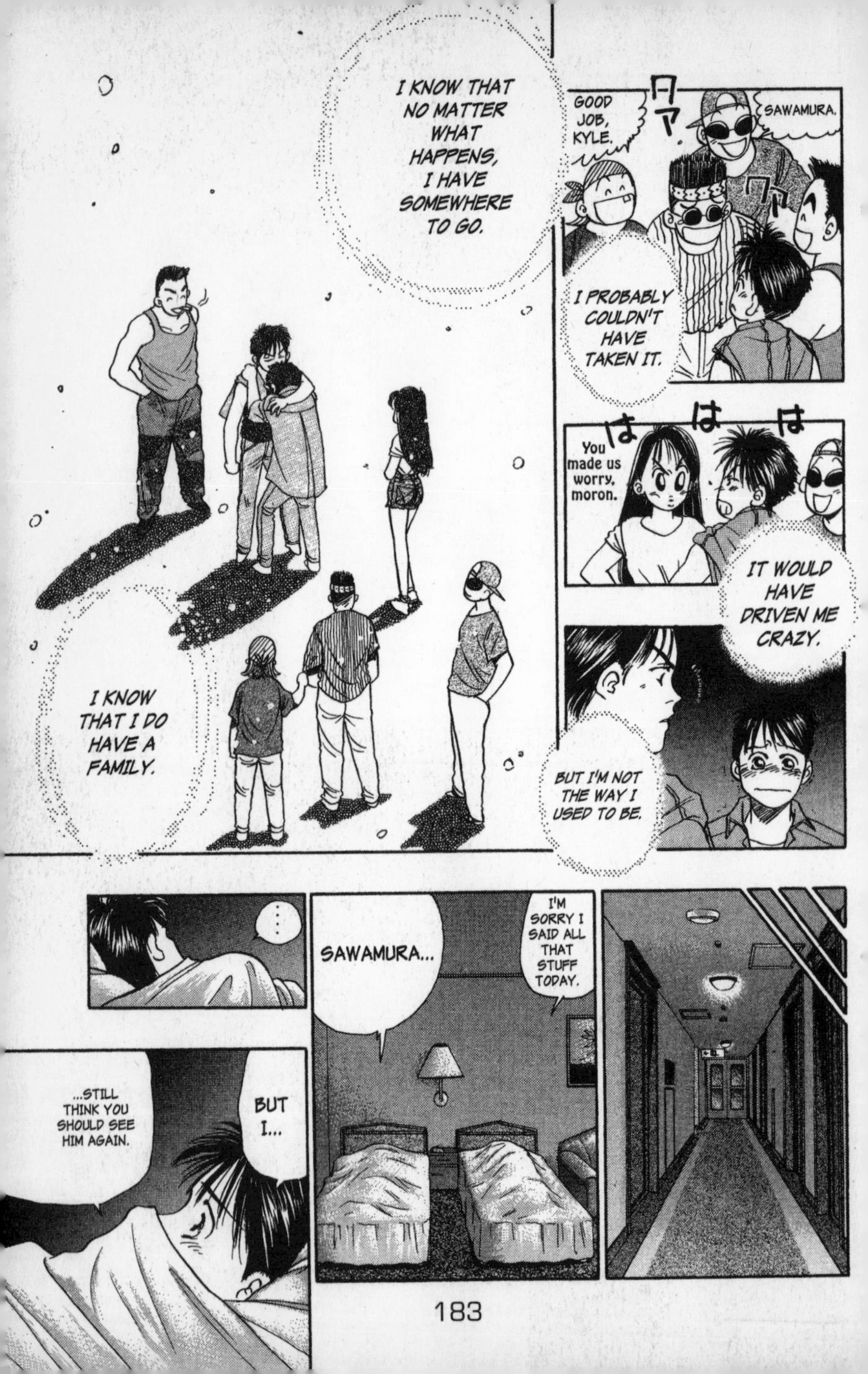
SAWAMURA.
ワァ
GOOD JOB, KYLE.
I PROBABLY COULDN'T HAVE TAKEN IT.
ははは
You made us worry, moron.
IT WOULD HAVE DRIVEN ME CRAZY.
BUT I'M NOT THE WAY I USED TO BE.
I KNOW THAT NO MATTER WHAT HAPPENS, I HAVE SOMEWHERE TO GO.
I KNOW THAT I DO HAVE A FAMILY.
I'M SORRY I SAID ALL THAT STUFF TODAY.
SAWAMURA...
...
BUT I...
...STILL THINK YOU SHOULD SEE HIM AGAIN.

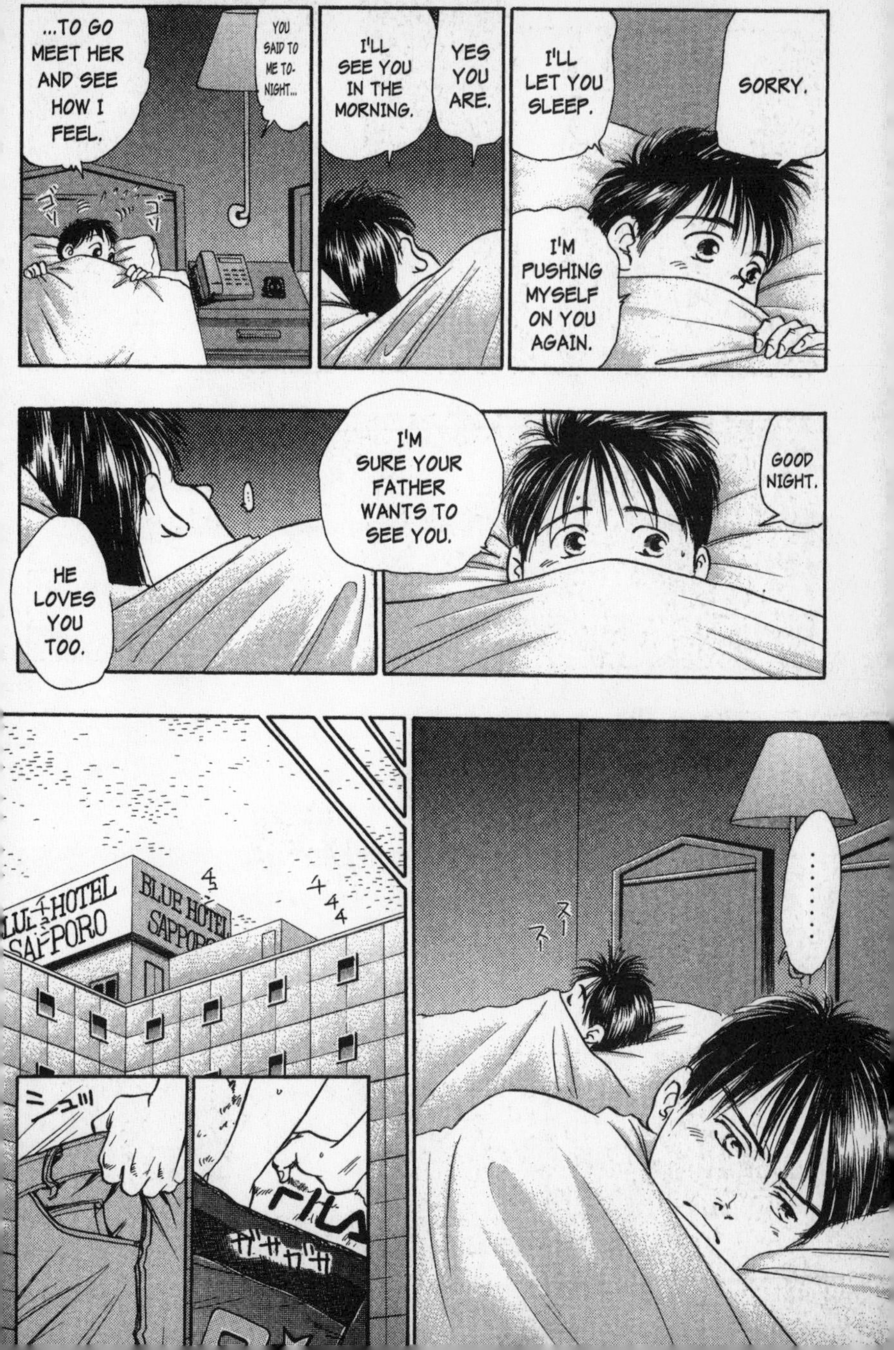
SORRY.
I'LL LET YOU SLEEP.
I'M PUSHING MYSELF ON YOU AGAIN.
YES YOU ARE.
I'LL SEE YOU IN THE MORNING.
YOU SAID TO ME TO-NIGHT...
...TO GO MEET HER AND SEE HOW I FEEL.
GOOD NIGHT.
I'M SURE YOUR FATHER WANTS TO SEE YOU.
HE LOVES YOU TOO.
......
BLUE HOTEL SAPPORO

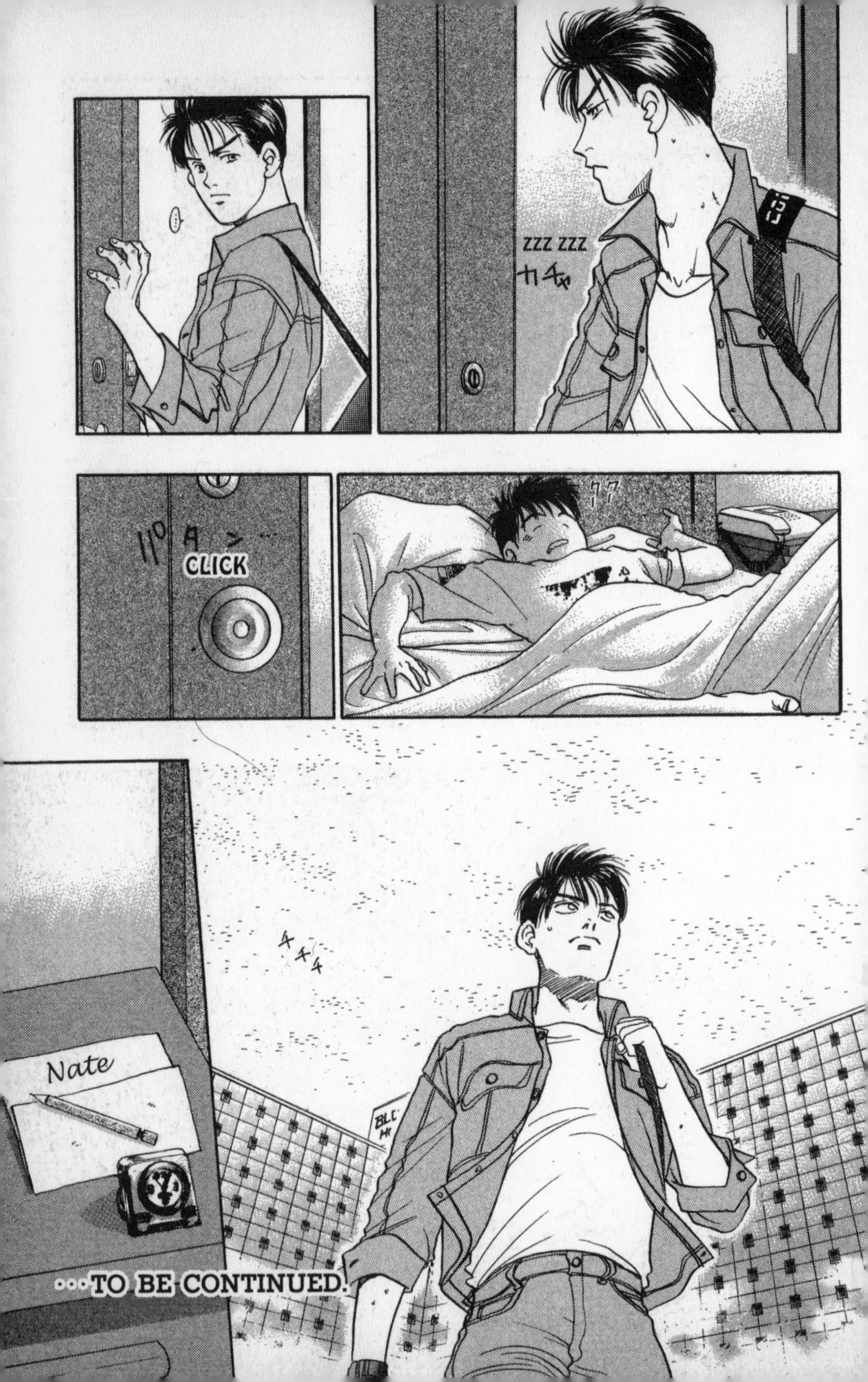
ZZZ ZZZ
カチャ
...
パタン…
CLICK
Nate
...TO BE CONTINUED.

STAY TUNED!!!

We hope you enjoyed your selected manga, *Rebound* Volume 3. Tune in two months from now when the tale continues and Johnan's basketball crew might be in for the basketball blues...

Preview for 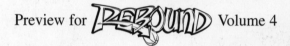 Volume 4

How will Sawamura's filial reunion affect his game? How will a night on the town affect Johnan's game as a whole? How will the team stand up to their archrivals when they finally meet them face to face? All questions to be answered in the next exciting volume of Rebound when the boys roll in from the streets and back on the court. It's going to take all they have to beat Tsukuba High School, but with one win already under their belt and a whole new reputation in Sapporo, Johnan's going to play better than ever before...if everything doesn't go horribly wrong.

And now, a commercial break...

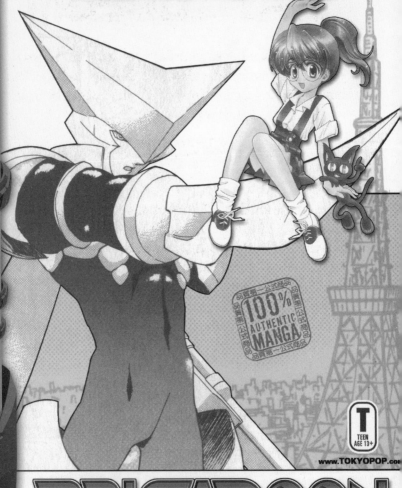

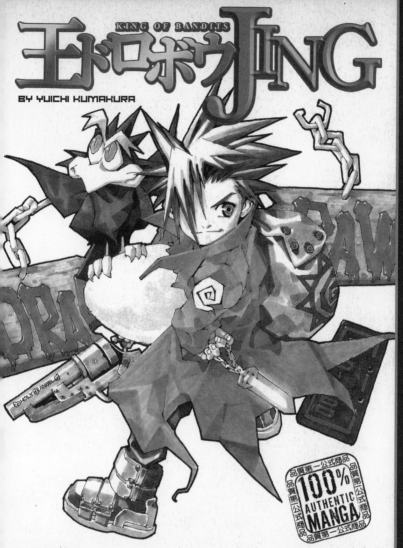

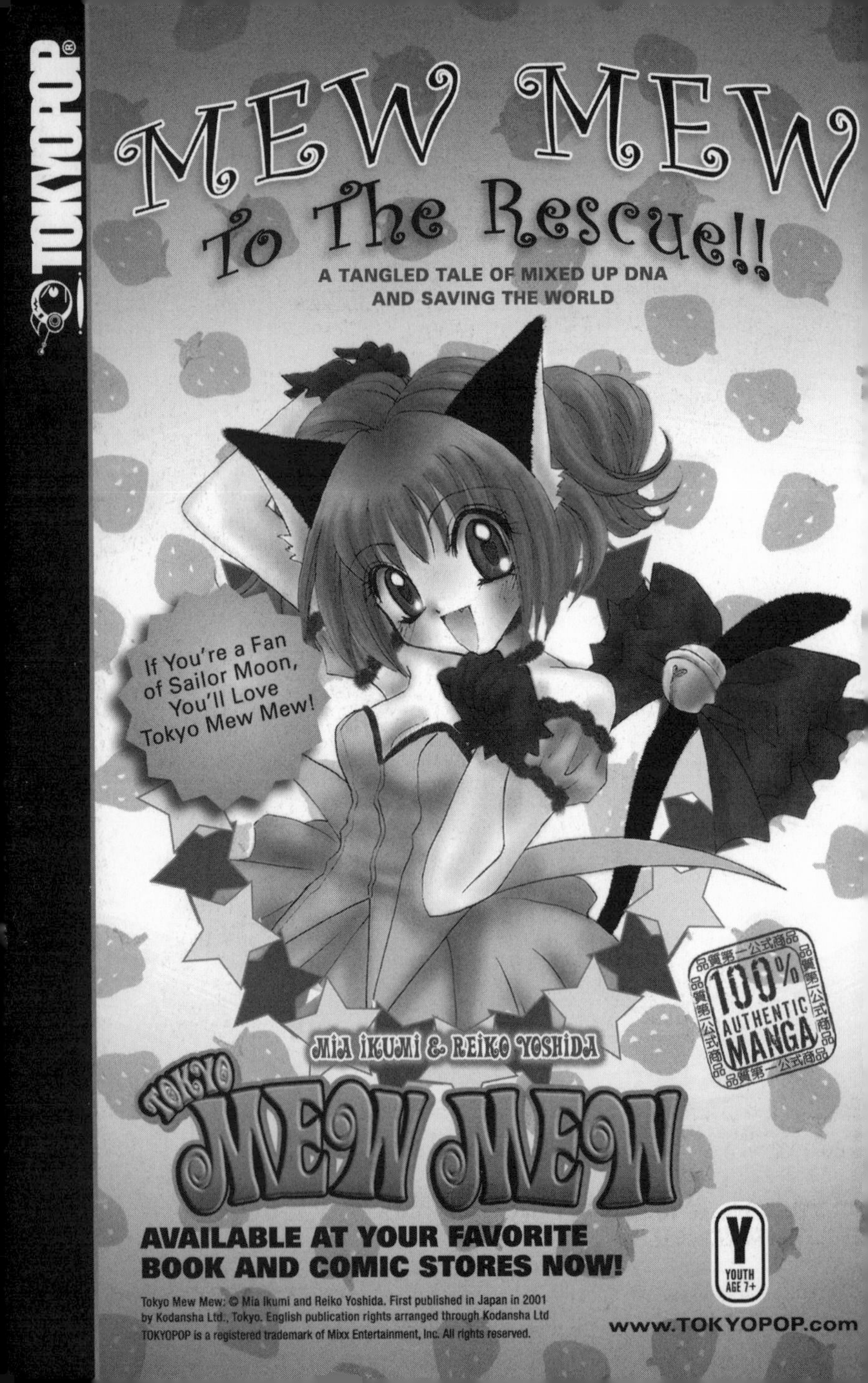
TOKYOPOP®
MEW MEW
To The Rescue!!
A TANGLED TALE OF MIXED UP DNA
AND SAVING THE WORLD
If You're a Fan of Sailor Moon, You'll Love Tokyo Mew Mew!
品質第一公式商品 100% AUTHENTIC MANGA
MIA IKUMI & REIKO YOSHIDA
TOKYO MEW MEW
AVAILABLE AT YOUR FAVORITE
BOOK AND COMIC STORES NOW!
Y YOUTH AGE 7+
Tokyo Mew Mew: © Mia Ikumi and Reiko Yoshida. First published in Japan in 2001 by Kodansha Ltd., Tokyo. English publication rights arranged through Kodansha Ltd TOKYOPOP is a registered trademark of Mixx Entertainment, Inc. All rights reserved.
www.TOKYOPOP.com

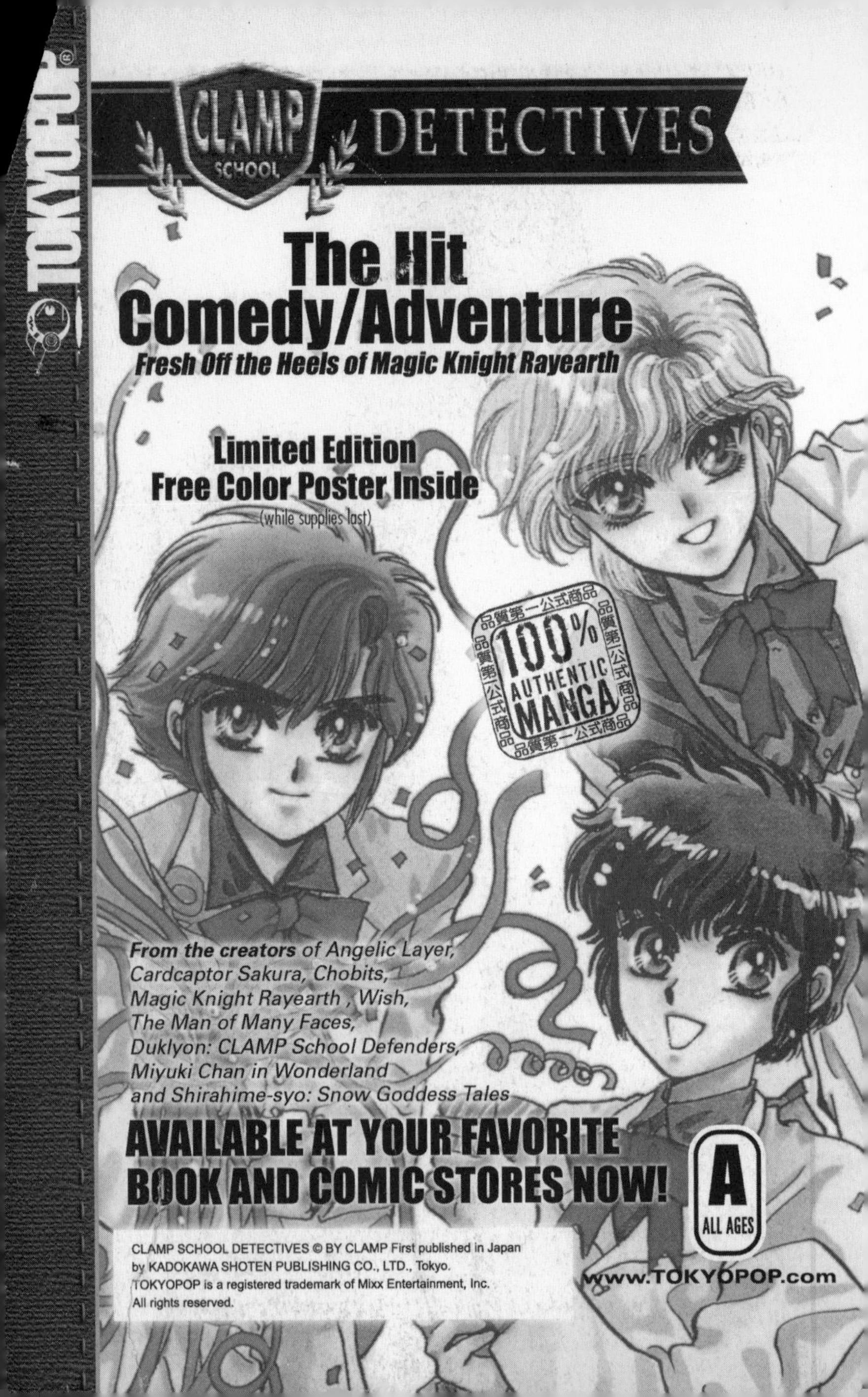
TOKYOPOP®
CLAMP SCHOOL DETECTIVES
The Hit Comedy/Adventure
Fresh Off the Heels of Magic Knight Rayearth
Limited Edition
Free Color Poster Inside
(while supplies last)
品質第一公式商品 100% AUTHENTIC MANGA
From the creators of Angelic Layer, Cardcaptor Sakura, Chobits, Magic Knight Rayearth , Wish, The Man of Many Faces, Duklyon: CLAMP School Defenders, Miyuki Chan in Wonderland and Shirahime-syo: Snow Goddess Tales
AVAILABLE AT YOUR FAVORITE BOOK AND COMIC STORES NOW!
A ALL AGES
CLAMP SCHOOL DETECTIVES © BY CLAMP First published in Japan by KADOKAWA SHOTEN PUBLISHING CO., LTD., Tokyo. TOKYOPOP is a registered trademark of Mixx Entertainment, Inc. All rights reserved.
www.TOKYOPOP.com

STOP!

This is the back of the book. You wouldn't want to spoil a great ending!

This book is printed "manga-style," in the authentic Japanese right-to-left format. Since none of the artwork has been flipped or altered, readers get to experience the story just as the creator intended. You've been asking for it, so TOKYOPOP® delivered: authentic, hot-off-the-press, and far more fun!

DIRECTIONS

1
2
3
4
5
6
7
8
9
10

If this is your first time reading manga-style, here's a quick guide to help you understand how it works.

It's easy... just start in the top right panel and follow the numbers. Have fun, and look for more 100% authentic manga from TOKYOPOP®!

100% AUTHENTIC MANGA

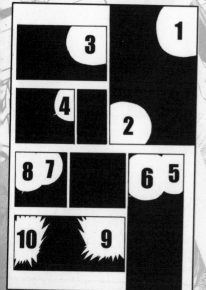

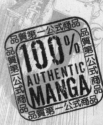